UNDERSTANDING FINANCIAL STATEMENTS

EIGHTH EDITION

Lyn M. Fraser

Aileen Ormiston

PEARSON

Prentice
Hall

Upper Saddle River, New Jersey 07458

Library of Congress Cataloging-in-Publication Data

Fraser, Lyn M.
   Understanding financial statements / Lyn M. Fraser, Aileen Ormiston.—8th ed.
     p. cm.
   Includes index.
   ISBN 0-13-187856-5
   1. Financial statements.   2. Corporation reports.   I. Ormiston, Aileen.   II. Title.
   HF5681.B2F764 2007
   657'.3—dc22

                                                 2006000729

Acquisitions Editor: Steve Sartori
VP/Editorial Director: Jeff Shelstad
Product Development Manager: Pamela Hersperger
Project Manager: Kerri Tomasso
Assistant Editor: Joanna Doxey
Executive Marketing Manager: John Wannemacher
Senior Managing Editor, Production: Cynthia Regan
Production Editor: Denise Culhane
Permissions Coordinator: Charles Morris
Production Manager: Arnold Vila
Manufacturing Buyer: Michelle Klein
Cover Design: Studio Indigo
Cover Illustration/Photo: Juan Silva/Iconica/Getty Images, Inc.
Composition: Integra Software Services
Full-Service Project Management: Thistle Hill Publishing Services, LLC
Printer/Binder: Courier—Stoughton
Typeface: 10/12 Times Ten Roman

Credits and acknowledgments borrowed from other sources and reproduced, with permission, in this textbook appear on appropriate page within text.

10 9 8 7 6 5
ISBN 0-13-187856-5

For Eleanor
—Lyn M. Fraser

For my father, Mike, Josh, and Jacqui
—Aileen Ormiston

Contents

Preface

The first edition of *Understanding Financial Statements,* published in 1984, included a cartoon showing a CEO addressing his board of directors. He says to the group assembled around the table, "Another successful year. . . . We broke even on operations and pulled a net profit on accounting procedures." Since then, the tremendous cost of corporate failures to employees, investors, and creditors by companies that have hidden behind slick annual reports, prepared by company officers and approved by their auditors, has shown us over and over again that this seemingly humorous statement is, in fact, no laughing matter. What I attempted to do in that first edition was to help readers get behind the numbers, dazzling presentations, and shiny covers to assess the actual financial condition and performance of the company. All of the editions since then, including this one, have the same objective. Enhanced regulations since the demise of companies such as Enron and WorldCom have buffed away some of the dazzle and shine of corporate annual reports, but the complexities and challenges remain.

Aileen Ormiston, who worked on the first edition of the book as my graduate assistant at Texas A&M University, became a co-author on the fifth. Many readers through the years—we are told—wait expectantly for subsequent editions not to find out the latest developments in the financial reporting environment but rather the latest developments in the lives of our children. Not to disappoint, my own daughter Eleanor, who was in grade school when I began this book, currently works for Universal Studios in London after completing an MBA at UCLA. She cooks better than her mother. Josh Ormiston, who was three when his mother was assisting me on the first edition, has followed in his mother's footsteps, earning his master's degree in finance at Texas A&M University. He now works in Arizona as a financial analyst for Stone & Youngberg, an investment banking firm. Jacqui Ormiston, age one for the first edition, wasted no time in completing her bachelor's degree in math at Michigan State University and master's degree in education at Arizona State University, and is teaching math at Gilbert High School in Arizona. Students at Mesa Community College now have the opportunity to experience two "Ormiston" professors since Jacqui also teaches at the college. And the final bit of news, Aileen and I had the great treat of getting together in person during 2005 for the first time in many years when we made a presentation to an investment club in Austin. I am pleased to report that the investors who followed our advice have been able to take early retirement; and that Aileen's hair is now almost as grey as mine.

Lyn M. Fraser

Organization of the Eighth Edition

Chapter 1 provides an overview of financial statements and presents approaches to overcoming some of the challenges, obstacles, and blind alleys that may confront the user of financial statements: (1) the volume of information, with examples of specific problems encountered in such areas as the auditor's report and the management discussion and analysis section as well as material that is sometimes provided by management but is not useful for the analyst; (2) the complexity of the accounting rules that underlie the preparation and presentation of financial statements; (3) the variations in quality of financial reporting, including management discretion in some important areas that affect analysis; and (4) the importance of financial information that is omitted or difficult to find in conventional financial statement presentations.

Chapters 2, 3, 4, and 6 describe and analyze financial statements for a mythical but potentially real company, Recreational Equipment and Clothing, Incorporated (R.E.C. Inc.), that sells recreational products through retail outlets in the southwestern United States. The specifics of this particular firm should be helpful in illustrating how financial statement analysis can provide insight into a firm's strengths and weaknesses. But the principles and concepts covered throughout the book apply to any set of published financial statements (other than for specialized industries, such as financial institutions and public utilities).

Because one company cannot provide every account and problem the user will encounter in financial statements, additional company examples are introduced throughout the text where needed to illustrate important accounting and analytical issues.

Chapters 2 through 4 discuss in detail a basic set of financial statements: the balance sheet in Chapter 2; the income (earnings) statement and statement of stockholders' equity in Chapter 3; and the statement of cash flows in Chapter 4. The emphasis in each of these chapters is on what the financial statements convey about the condition and performance of a business firm as well as how the numbers have been derived. Chapter 5 discusses and illustrates issues that relate to the quality, and thus the usefulness, of financial reporting. The chapter contains a step-by-step checklist of key items to help the analyst assess the quality of reporting, and real company examples of each step are provided.

With this material as background, Chapter 6 covers the interpretation and analysis of the financial statements discussed in Chapters 2 through 5. This process involves the calculation and interpretation of financial ratios, an examination of trends over time, a comparison of the firm's condition and performance with its competitors, and an assessment of the future potential of the company based on its historical record. Chapter 6 also reviews additional sources of information that can enhance the analytical process. The Appendix to Chapter 6 shows how to evaluate the segmental accounting data reported by diversified companies that operate in several unrelated lines of business.

Self-tests at the ends of Chapters 1 through 6 provide an opportunity for the reader to assess comprehension (or its absence) of major topics; solutions to the self-tests are given in Appendix B. For more extensive student assignments, study questions and problems are placed at the ends of the chapters. Cases drawn from actual company annual reports are used to highlight in a case-problem format many of the key issues discussed in the chapters.

Appendix A covers the computation and definition of the key financial ratios that are used in Chapter 6 to evaluate financial statements.

Appendix B contains solutions to self-tests for Chapters 1 through 6.

Appendix C presents a glossary of the key terms used throughout the book.

The ultimate goal of this book is to improve the reader's ability to translate financial statement numbers into a meaningful map for business decisions. It is hoped that the material covered in the chapters and the appendixes will enable each reader to approach financial statements with enhanced confidence and understanding of a firm's historical, current, and prospective financial condition and performance.

Uses for the Eighth Edition

Understanding Financial Statements is designed to serve a wide range of readers and purposes, which include:

1. Text or supplementary text for financial statement analysis courses.
2. Supplementary text for accounting, finance, and business management classes, which cover financial statement analysis.
3. Study material for short courses on financial statements in continuing education and executive development programs.
4. Self-study guide or course material for bank credit analysis training programs.
5. Reference book for investors and others who make decisions based on the analysis of financial statements.

Features of the Eighth Edition

In revising the text, we have paid close attention to the responses received from faculty who teach from the book, from students who take courses using the book as a primary or supplementary text, and from other readers of the book. Our primary objective remains to convey to readers the conceptual background and analytical tools necessary to understand and interpret business financial statements. Readers and reviewers of earlier editions have commented that the strengths of this book are its readability, concise coverage, and accessibility. We have attempted to retain these elements in the eighth edition.

The eighth edition incorporates the many new requirements and changes in accounting reporting and standards, as well as the following items:

- New examples are provided in all chapters to illustrate accounting concepts and the current accounting environment.
- Chapter 1 has been updated to include examples of accounting fraud that have occurred in recent years, as well as changes due to the Sarbanes–Oxley Act of 2002.
- A more extensive discussion of the analysis of accounts receivable has been added to Chapter 2.
- Chapter 3 now includes a discussion of how to analyze gross profit margin for firms with multiple revenue sources.
- Exhibits in Chapter 4 have been updated for better clarification of topics.
- Chapter 5 is new to this edition and covers the quality of financial reporting.
- Chapter 6 was Chapter 5 in prior editions and has been updated to be consistent with the reorganization of the entire text.
- Study questions and problems have been updated in each of the six chapters.
- The writing skills problems, Internet problems, and Intel problems (using the updated 2004 annual report) have been retained in this edition and a research problem has been added to each chapter. The Intel problems offer the student the opportunity to analyze a real company throughout the text and in this edition the highlighted company is Intel, a high-technology firm. Information for the Intel problems, as well as some of the Internet problems, is available on the Prentice Hall Web site: *www.prenhall.com/fraser.*
- A comprehensive problem has been added to the textbook to illustrate how to complete a financial statement analysis using the template available on the

Prentice Hall Web site: *www.prenhall.com/fraser.* The company used is Eastman Kodak and each chapter contains a problem to help students apply the content of the chapter as well as learn to use the financial statement analysis template.

- All cases at the end of the chapters have been replaced with more relevant, up-to-date cases based on real-world companies.
- The footnotes provided throughout the text contain resources that may be used by instructors to form the basis of a reading list for students.
- The eighth edition includes other features of earlier editions that readers have found useful: appendix on the analysis of segmental data; self-tests at the ends of chapters, with solutions provided; chapter-end study questions and problems; and a glossary of key terms used in the text.
- The Instructor's Manual, which is available at *www.prenhall.com/fraser*, contains solutions to study questions, problems, and cases; a sample course project with assignment outline and a test bank for Chapters 1 through 6. Both objective and short-answer test questions are included.
- The Web site for the text has been updated and includes templates to use for financial calculations, PowerPoint slides that can be downloaded for use in class, and Internet exercises.

We hope that readers will continue to find material in *Understanding Financial Statements* accessible, relevant, and useful.

Acknowledgments

We would like to acknowledge with considerable appreciation those who have contributed to the publication of this book.

Several individuals have made critical comments and suggestions on the manuscript. In particular, we would like to thank: Robert Roller, LeTourneau University; Corolyn Clark, Saint Joseph's University; Dr. Elisa Muresan, School of Business, Long Island University; Dane Sheldon, University of Miami; Dan Dowdy, Mary Baldwin College; H. Francis Bush, Virginia Military Institute; Bob Gregory, Bellevue University; Patricia Doherty, Boston University School of Management; Wei He, University of Texas of the Permian Basin; Kenton Walker, University of Wyoming; Sean Salter, University of Southern Mississippi; Paul Fisher, Rogue Community College; Ray Whitmire, Texas A&M University–Corpus Christi; Micah Frankel, California State University, Hayward; Seok-Young Lee, The University of Texas at Dallas; Sadhana Alangar, Cleary University; Scott Pardee, Middlebury College; Jill Whitley, University of Sioux Falls; John Baber; Maurice Johnson, Fashion Institute of Technology/SUNY; Melanie Mogg, University of Minnesota, Carlson School of Management; Richard Fendler, Georgia State University; William Seltz, Harvard University; Robert Ewalt, Bergen Community College; Richard Frederics, Lasell College; Tom Geurts, Marist College; Jen Adkins, North Central State College; Irvin Morgan, Bentley College; Jack Cathey, University of North Carolina–Charlotte; and Glenda Levendowski, Arizona State University.

We would also like to thank the editorial, production, and marketing departments of Prentice Hall for their assistance at each stage of the writing and production process. Special thanks go to Angela Williams Urquhart at Thistle Hill Publishing Services for her assistance throughout the production process.

The list would be incomplete without mentioning the pets in our households who helped keep us in good humor throughout the revision of this edition: R.T., Picadilly Circus, Toot, AddieMae, Dieter, Teddy, Tucker, Toby, and Torin.

Lyn M. Fraser

Aileen Ormiston

About the Authors

Lyn M. Fraser has taught undergraduate and graduate classes in financial statement analysis at Texas A&M University and has conducted numerous seminars on the subject for executive development and continuing education courses. A Certified Public Accountant, she is the co-author with Aileen Ormiston of *Understanding the Corporate Annual Report: Nuts, Bolts, and a Few Loose Screws* (Prentice Hall, 2003) and has published articles in the *Journal of Accountancy*, the *Journal of Commercial Bank Lending,* the *Magazine of Bank Administration,* and the *Journal of Business Strategies.* She has been recognized for Distinguished Achievement in Teaching by the Former Students Association at Texas A&M University and is a member of Phi Beta Kappa.

Aileen Ormiston teaches accounting in the Business Department of Mesa Community College in Mesa, Arizona and has taught in the MBA program at Arizona State University. She received her bachelor's degree in accounting from Michigan State University and a master's degree in finance from Texas A&M University. Aileen, prior to embarking on her teaching career, worked in cost accounting and also as an auditor in public accounting. Mesa Community College was one of 13 universities and colleges that received a grant from the Accounting Education Change Commission, and Aileen was actively involved in developing the new accounting curriculum. As a result of her pioneering work in changing accounting education, she was the recipient of the "Innovator of the Year" award from the League for Innovation in the Community College.

CHAPTER

Financial Statements

An Overview

maze (māz), n. 1. An intricate, usually confusing network of passages, some blind and some leading to a goal. 2. Anything made up of many confused or conflicting elements. 3. A mental state of confusion or perplexity.

Map or Maze

One of the major purposes of a *map* is to help its user reach a desired destination through clarity of representation. A *maze,* on the other hand, attempts to confuse its user by purposefully introducing conflicting elements and complexities that prevent reaching the desired goal. Business financial statements have the potential for being both map and maze (see Figure 1.1.).

As a map, financial statements form the basis for understanding the financial position of a business firm and for assessing its historical and prospective financial performance. Financial statements have the capability of presenting clear representations of a firm's financial health, leading to informed business decisions.

Unfortunately, there are mazelike interferences in financial statement data that hinder understanding the valuable information they contain. The sheer quantity of information contained in financial statements can be overwhelming and intimidating. Independent auditors attest to the fairness of financial statement presentation, but many lawsuits have been filed and won against accounting firms for issuing "clean" auditors' reports on companies that subsequently failed. The complexity of accounting policies underlying the preparation of financial statements can lead to confusion and variations in the quality of information presented. In addition, these rules are constantly evolving and changing. Management discretion in a number of areas influences financial statement content and presentation in ways that affect and even impede evaluation. Some key information needed to evaluate a company is not available in the financial statements, some is difficult to find, and much is impossible to measure.

FIGURE 1.1 A Maze of Information

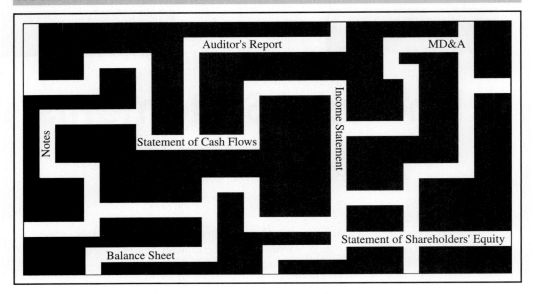

One of the main objectives of this book is to ensure that financial statements serve as a map, not a maze—that they lead to a determination of the financial health of a business enterprise that is as clear as possible for purposes of making sound business decisions about the firm.

The material in this book will convey information about how to read and evaluate business financial statements, and the authors will attempt to present the material in a straightforward manner that will be readily accessible to any reader, regardless of background or perspective. The book is designed for use by those who would like to learn more about the content and interpretation of financial statements for such purposes as making investment or credit decisions about a company, evaluating a firm for current or prospective employment, advancing professionally in the current business environment, or even passing an examination or course.

The reader can expect more than a dull exposition of financial data and accounting rules. Throughout these pages we will attempt with examples, illustrations, and explanations to get behind the numbers, accounting policies, and tax laws to assess how well companies are actually performing. The chapters and appendixes in the book show how to approach financial statements in order to obtain practical, useful information from their content. Although the examples in the book are based on corporate financial statements, the discussion also applies to the financial statements of small business firms that use generally accepted accounting principles.

The emphasis throughout the book is on analysis. In the first four chapters of the book, we will look at the contents of an annual report and break the financial statements into parts for individual study to better understand the whole of their content as a map to intelligent decision making. In order to fully analyze a firm, it is important to assess the value of the information supplied by management. This material will be covered in the fifth chapter on the quality of financial reporting. The final chapter of the book combines all parts learned in prior chapters with analytical tools and techniques to illustrate a comprehensive financial statement analysis.

Usefulness

Financial statements and their accompanying notes contain a wealth of useful information regarding the financial position of a company, the success of its operations, the policies and strategies of management, and insight into its future performance. The objective of the financial statement user is to find and interpret this information to answer questions about the company, such as the following:

- Would an investment generate attractive returns?
- What is the degree of risk inherent in the investment?
- Should existing investment holdings be liquidated?
- Will cash flows be sufficient to service interest and principal payments to support the firm's borrowing needs?
- Does the company provide a good opportunity for employment, future advancement, and employee benefits?
- How well does this company compete in its operating environment?
- Is this firm a good prospect as a customer?

The financial statements and other data generated by corporate financial reporting can help the user develop answers to these questions as well as many others. The remainder of this chapter will provide an approach to using effectively the information contained in a corporate annual report. Annual reports in this book will refer to the information package published primarily for shareholders and the general public. The Securities and Exchange Commission (SEC) requires large, publicly held companies to file annually a 10-K report, which is generally a more detailed document and is used by regulators, analysts, and researchers. The basic set of financial statements and supplementary data is the same for both documents, and it is this basic set of information—financial statements, notes, and required supplementary data—that is explained and interpreted throughout this book.

Volume of Information

The user of a firm's annual report can expect to encounter a great quantity of information that encompasses the required information—financial statements, notes to the financial statements, the auditor's report, a five-year summary of key financial data, high and low stock prices, management's discussion and analysis of operations—as well as material that is included in the report at the imagination and discretion of management. To understand how to navigate the vast amount of information available to financial statement users, background on the accounting rule-making environment is necessary. Financial statements are prepared according to generally accepted accounting principles (GAAP) that have been adopted in order to achieve a presentation of financial information that is understandable by users as well as relevant and reliable for decision making. The accounting rules that have been issued in order to achieve these objectives can be complicated and sometimes confusing. The two authorities primarily responsible for establishing GAAP in the United States are the SEC, a public-sector organization, and the Financial Accounting Standards Board (FASB), a private-sector organization.

The SEC regulates U.S. companies that issue securities to the public and requires the issuance of a prospectus for any new security offering. The SEC also requires regular filing of

- Annual reports (10-K)
- Quarterly reports (10-Q)
- Other reports dependent upon particular circumstances, such as a change in auditor, bankruptcy, financial restatements, or other important events (all filed as 8-K reports)

The SEC has congressional authority to set accounting policies and has issued rulings called Accounting Series Releases (ASRs) and Financial Reporting Rulings (FRRs). For the most part, however, accounting rule making has been delegated to the FASB.

The FASB is comprised of seven full-time, paid members. The board issues Statements of Financial Accounting Standards (SFASs) and interpretations, usually after a lengthy process of deliberation that includes the following steps:

1. Introduction of topic or project on the FASB agenda
2. Research and analysis of the problem
3. Issuance of a discussion memorandum
4. Public hearings
5. Board analysis and evaluation
6. Issuance of an exposure draft
7. Period for public comment
8. Review of public response, revision
9. Issuance of SFAS
10. Amendments and interpretations, as needed

The SEC and FASB have worked closely together in the development of accounting policy, with the SEC playing largely a supportive role. But at times the SEC has pressured the FASB to move on the issuance of accounting standards or to change its policies (inflation accounting, oil and gas accounting). Pressures on the FASB stem from the private sector and have been highly controversial in recent years. Figure 1.2 illustrates the relationship between the SEC and the FASB. An example of a measure that was vehemently opposed by the business sector was the FASB's proposal to require companies to deduct from profits compensation to executives in the form of stock options. The FASB first began exploring this issue in 1984, but it was not resolved until 1995 due to business and ultimately political intervention. Business lobbyists gained congressional support that effectively forced the FASB to compromise its stance on this issue.[1] As a result of the opposition, FASB Statement No. 123, "Accounting for Stock-Based Compensation," only required that companies disclose in the notes to the financial statements the effects on profits of new employee stock

---

[1]To learn more about this controversy see Stephen Barr, "FASB Under Siege," *CFO*, September 1994.

FIGURE 1.2   **FASB/SEC Relationship**

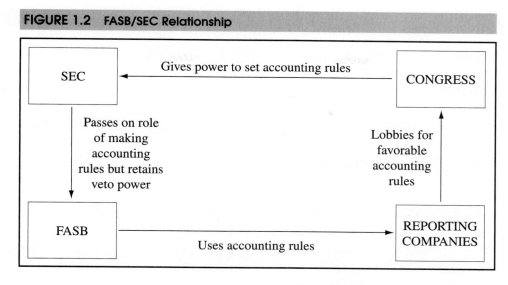

options based on the fair value at the date of grant. The controversy that arose with regard to stock-based compensation caused the SEC to take a closer look at the FASB's standard-setting process. In 1996, the SEC made public its concern that the standard-setting process is too slow; however, the SEC rejected suggestions from business executives that the private sector should have more influence in the process. The SEC vowed to maintain the FASB's effectiveness and independence.[2]

Recent corporate scandals such as Enron and WorldCom have brought to the forefront the challenges and pressures the FASB faces when creating accounting rules. The issue of stock-based compensation was reopened by the FASB in 2002. A new FASB proposal adopted in December 2002 to force the expensing of all employee stock compensation from profits once again resulted in congressional interference, delaying the new rule from taking effect until after June 15, 2005. The SEC and the FASB continue to examine potential rule changes or new rules in a variety of areas such as off-balance sheet financing, overhauling the income statement, and acquisition disclosures.

Where to Find a Company's Financial Statements

Corporate financial statements are available from several sources. First, all publicly held companies must file a Form 10-K annually with the SEC. The information in this document is mandated by the SEC and contains uniform content, presented in the same order for all filing companies. Figure 1.3 shows a sample of required 10-K items. Documents filed with the SEC can usually be accessed through the Electronic Data Gathering, Analysis, and Retrieval (EDGAR) database at the SEC's Web site, www.sec.gov. Some companies mail the firm's 10-K report to shareholders, rather than producing a separate annual report. Other firms send a slickly prepared annual

---

[2]"SEC Calls for More Efficient FASB but Rejects Stronger Outside Influence," *Journal of Accountancy*, May 1996.

FIGURE 1.3   Form 10-K Components

Item #	Item Title
Item 1.	Business
Item 2.	Properties
Item 3.	Legal Proceedings
Item 4.	Submission of Matters to a Vote of Security Holders
Item 5.	Market for Registrant's Common Equity and Related Stockholder Matters
Item 6.	Selected Financial Data
Item 7.	Management's Discussion and Analysis of Financial Condition and Results of Operations
Item 7A.	Quantitative and Qualitative Disclosures about Market Risk
Item 8.	Financial Statements and Supplementary Data
Item 9.	Changes in and Disagreements with Accountants on Accounting and Financial Disclosure
Item 9A.	Controls and Procedures
Item 9B.	Other Information
Item 10.	Directors and Executive Officers of the Registrant
Item 11.	Executive Compensation
Item 12.	Security Ownership of Certain Beneficial Owners and Management and Related Stockholder Matters
Item 13.	Certain Relationships and Related Transactions
Item 14.	Principal Accountant Fees and Services
Item 15.	Exhibits, Financial Statement Schedules, and Reports on Form 8-K

report that includes the financial statements as well as other public relations material to shareholders and prospective investors. Finally, most corporations now post their annual report (or provide a link to the EDGAR database) on their corporate Web site.

The Financial Statements

A corporate annual report contains four basic financial statements, illustrated in Exhibit 1.1 for R.E.C. Inc.

1. The *balance sheet* shows the financial position—assets, liabilities, and stockholders' equity—of the firm on a particular date, such as the end of a quarter or a year.
2. The *income or earnings statement* presents the results of operations—revenues, expenses, net profit or loss, and net profit or loss per share—for the accounting period.
3. The *statement of stockholders' equity* reconciles the beginning and ending balances of all accounts that appear in the stockholders' equity section of the balance sheet.

EXHIBIT 1.1 R.E.C. Inc. Consolidated Balance Sheets at December 31, 2007 and 2006 (in Thousands)

	2007	2006
Assets		
Current Assets		
Cash	$ 4,061	$ 2,382
Marketable securities (Note A)	5,272	8,004
Accounts receivable, less allowance for doubtful accounts of $448 in 2007 and $417 in 2006	8,960	8,350
Inventories (Note A)	47,041	36,769
Prepaid expenses	512	759
Total current assets	65,846	56,264
Property, Plant, and Equipment (Notes A, C, and E)		
Land	811	811
Buildings and leasehold improvements	18,273	11,928
Equipment	21,523	13,768
	40,607	26,507
Less accumulated depreciation and amortization	11,528	7,530
Net property, plant, and equipment	29,079	18,977
Other Assets (Note A)	373	668
Total Assets	$95,298	$75,909
Liabilities and Stockholders' Equity		
Current Liabilities		
Accounts payable	$14,294	$ 7,591
Notes payable—banks (Note B)	5,614	6,012
Current maturities of long-term debt (Note C)	1,884	1,516
Accrued liabilities	5,669	5,313
Total current liabilities	27,461	20,432
Deferred Federal Income Taxes (Notes A and D)	843	635
Long-Term Debt (Note C)	21,059	16,975
Commitments (Note E)		
Total liabilities	49,363	38,042
Stockholders' Equity		
Common stock, par value $1, authorized, 10,000,000 shares; issued, 4,803,000 shares in 2007 and 4,594,000 shares in 2006 (Note F)	4,803	4,594
Additional paid-in capital	957	910
Retained Earnings	40,175	32,363
Total stockholders' equity	45,935	37,867
Total Liabilities and Stockholders' Equity	$95,298	$75,909

The accompanying notes are an integral part of these statements.

EXHIBIT 1.1 (Continued) **R.E.C. Inc. Consolidated Statements of Earnings for the Years Ended December 31, 2007, 2006, and 2005 (in Thousands Except Per Share Amounts)**

	2007	2006	2005
Net sales	$215,600	$153,000	$140,700
Cost of goods sold (Note A)	129,364	91,879	81,606
Gross profit	86,236	61,121	59,094
Selling and administrative expenses (Notes A and E)	45,722	33,493	32,765
Advertising	14,258	10,792	9,541
Depreciation and amortization (Note A)	3,998	2,984	2,501
Repairs and maintenance	3,015	2,046	3,031
Operating profit	19,243	11,806	11,256
Other income (expense)			
Interest income	422	838	738
Interest expense	(2,585)	(2,277)	(1,274)
Earnings before income taxes	17,080	10,367	10,720
Income taxes (Notes A and D)	7,686	4,457	4,824
Net earnings	$ 9,394	$ 5,910	$ 5,896
Basic earnings per common share (Note G)	$ 1.96	$ 1.29	$ 1.33
Diluted earnings per common share (Note G)	$ 1.93	$ 1.26	$ 1.31

The accompanying notes are an integral part of these statements.

Some firms prepare a statement of retained earnings, frequently combined with the income statement, which reconciles the beginning and ending balances of the retained earnings account. Companies choosing the latter format will generally present the statement of stockholders' equity in a footnote disclosure.

4. The *statement of cash flows* provides information about the cash inflows and outflows from operating, financing, and investing activities during an accounting period.

Each of these statements will be illustrated, described, and discussed in detail in later chapters of the book.

Notes to the Financial Statements

Immediately following the four financial statements is the section entitled Notes to the Financial Statements (Exhibit 1.2). The notes are, in fact, an integral part of the statements and must be read in order to understand the presentation on the face of each financial statement.

The first note to the financial statements provides a summary of the firm's accounting policies. If there have been changes in any accounting policies during the reporting period, these changes will be explained and the impact quantified in a financial

EXHIBIT 1.1 (Continued) R.E.C. Inc. Consolidated Statements of Cash Flows
for the Years Ended December 31, 2007, 2006, and 2005 (in Thousands)

	2007	2006	2005
Cash Flows from Operating Activities—Indirect Method			
Net income	$ 9,394	$ 5,910	$ 5,896
Adjustments to reconcile net income to cash provided (used) by operating activities			
Depreciation and amortization	3,998	2,984	2,501
Deferred income taxes	208	136	118
Cash provided (used) by current assets and liabilities			
Accounts receivable	(610)	(3,339)	(448)
Inventories	(10,272)	(7,006)	(2,331)
Prepaid expenses	247	295	(82)
Accounts payable	6,703	(1,051)	902
Accrued liabilities	356	(1,696)	(927)
Net cash provided (used) by operating activities	$ 10,024	($ 3,767)	$ 5,629
Cash Flows from Investing Activities			
Additions to property, plant, and equipment	(14,100)	(4,773)	(3,982)
Other investing activities	295	0	0
Net cash provided (used) by investing activities	($ 13,805)	($ 4,773)	($ 3,982)
Cash Flows from Financing Activities			
Sales of common stock	256	183	124
Increase (decrease) in short-term borrowings (includes current maturities of long-term debt)	(30)	1,854	1,326
Additions to long-term borrowings	5,600	7,882	629
Reductions of long-term borrowings	(1,516)	(1,593)	(127)
Dividends paid	(1,582)	(1,862)	(1,841)
Net cash provided (used) by financing activities	$ 2,728	$ 6,464	$ 111
Increase (decrease) in cash and marketable securities	($ 1,053)	($ 2,076)	$ 1,758
Cash and marketable securities, beginning of year	10,386	12,462	10,704
Cash and marketable securities, end of year	9,333	10,386	12,462
Supplemental cash flow information:			
Cash paid for interest	$ 2,585	$ 2,277	$ 1,274
Cash paid for taxes	7,478	4,321	4,706

The accompanying notes are an integral part of these statements.

statement note. Other notes to the financial statements present details about particular accounts, such as

> Inventory
> Property, plant, and equipment
> Investments
> Long-term debt
> The equity accounts

EXHIBIT 1.1 (Continued) R.E.C. Inc. Consolidated Statements of Stockholders' Equity for the Years Ended December 31, 2007, 2006, and 2005 (in Thousands)

	COMMON STOCK		ADDITIONAL PAID-IN CAPITAL	RETAINED EARNINGS	TOTAL
	SHARES	AMOUNT			
Balance at December 31, 2004	4,340	$4,340	$857	$24,260	$29,457
Net earnings				5,896	5,896
Proceeds from sale of shares from exercise of stock options	103	103	21		124
Cash dividends				(1,841)	(1,841)
Balance at December 31, 2005	4,443	$4,443	$878	$28,315	$33,636
Net earnings				5,910	5,910
Proceeds from sale of shares from exercise of stock options	151	151	32		183
Cash dividends				(1,862)	(1,862)
Balance at December 31, 2006	4,594	$4,594	$910	$32,363	$37,867
Net earnings				9,394	9,394
Proceeds from sale of shares from exercise of stock options	209	209	47		256
Cash dividends				(1,582)	(1,582)
Balance at December 31, 2007	4,803	$4,803	$957	$40,175	$45,935

The notes also include information about

- Any major acquisitions or divestitures that have occurred during the accounting period
- Officer and employee retirement, pension, and stock option plans
- Leasing arrangements
- The term, cost, and maturity of debt
- Pending legal proceedings
- Income taxes
- Contingencies and commitments
- Quarterly results of operations
- Operating segments

Certain supplementary information is also required by the governmental and accounting authorities—primarily the SEC and the FASB—that establish accounting policies. There are, for instance, supplementary disclosure requirements relating to reserves for companies operating in the oil, gas, or other areas of the extractive industries. Firms operating in foreign countries show the effect of foreign currency translations. If a firm has several lines of business, the notes will contain a section showing financial information for each reportable segment. (The analysis of segmental data is discussed in the appendix to Chapter 6.)

EXHIBIT 1.2   R.E.C. Inc. Notes to Consolidated Financial Statements December 31, 2007, December 31, 2006, and December 31, 2005

Note A—Summary of Significant Accounting Policies

R.E.C. Inc. is a retailer of recreational equipment and clothing.

Consolidation: The consolidated financial statements include the accounts and transactions of the company and its wholly owned subsidiaries. The company accounts for its investment in its subsidiaries using the equity method of accounting. All significant intercompany transactions have been eliminated in consolidation.

Marketable Securities: Marketable securities consist of short-term, interest-bearing securities.

Inventories: Inventories are stated at the lower of cost—last in, first out (LIFO)—or market. If the first-in, first-out (FIFO) method of inventory accounting had been used, inventories would have been approximately $2,681,000 and $2,096,000 higher than reported at December 31, 2007 and 2006.

Depreciation and Amortization: Property, plant, and equipment is stated at cost. Depreciation expense is calculated principally by the straight-line method based on estimated useful lives of 3 to 10 years for equipment, 3 to 30 years for leasehold improvements, and 40 years for buildings. Estimated useful lives of leasehold improvements represent the remaining term of the lease in effect at the time the improvements are made.

Expenses of New Stores: Expenses associated with the opening of new stores are charged to expense as incurred.

Other Assets: Other assets are investments in properties not used in business operations.

Note B—Short-Term Debt

The company has a $10,000,000 bank line of credit. Interest is calculated at the prime rate plus 1% on any outstanding balance. Any balance on March 31, 2009, converts to a term note payable in quarterly installments over 5 years.

Note C—Long-Term Debt

Long-term debt consists of the following at the end of each year:

	2007	2006
Mortgage notes collateralized by land and buildings (approximate cost of $7,854,000) payable in aggregate monthly installments of $30,500 plus interest at 8 3/4–10 1/2% maturing in 15 to 25 years	$ 3,808,000	$ 4,174,000
Unsecured promissory note due December 2013, payable in quarterly installments of $100,000 plus interest at 8 1/2%	4,800,000	5,200,000
Promissory notes secured by equipment (approximate cost of $9,453,000) payable in semiannual installments of $375,000 plus interest at 13%, due in January 2015	6,000,000	6,750,000
Unsecured promissory note payable in three installments of $789,000 in 2009, 2010, and 2011, plus interest at 9 1/4% payable annually	2,367,000	2,367,000
Promissory notes secured by equipment (approximate cost of $8,546,000) payable in annual installments of $373,000 plus interest at 12 1/2% due in June 2017	5,968,000	—
	22,943,000	18,491,000
Less current maturities	1,884,000	1,516,000
	$21,059,000	$16,975,000

EXHIBIT 1.2 (Continued)

Current maturities for each of the following 5 years are:

December 31, 2008	$ 2,678,000
2009	2,678,000
2010	2,678,000
2011	1,884,000
2012	1,884,000

Note D — Income Taxes

A reconciliation of income tax expense computed by using the federal statutory tax rate to the Company's effective tax rate is as follows:

	2007		2006		2005	
Federal income tax at statutory rate	$7,859,000	46%	$4,769,000	46%	$4,931,000	46%
Increases (decreases)						
State income taxes	489,000	3	381,000	4	344,000	3
Tax credits	(465,000)	(3)	(429,000)	(4)	(228,000)	(2)
Other items, net	(197,000)	(1)	(264,000)	(3)	(223,000)	(2)
Income tax expense reported	$7,686,000	45%	$4,457,000	43%	$4,824,000	45%

Deferred income taxes reflect the net tax effects of temporary differences between the carrying amount of assets and liabilities for financial reporting purposes and the amounts used for income tax purposes.

Significant components of the Company's deferred tax assets and liabilities at fiscal year-ends were as follows:

	2007	2006	2005
Excess of tax depreciation over book depreciation	$628,000	$430,000	$306,000
Temporary differences applicable to installment sales	215,000	205,000	112,000
Total	$843,000	$635,000	$418,000

Note E — Commitments

The company conducts some of its operations in facilities leased under noncancellable operating leases. Certain agreements include options to purchase the property and certain agreements include renewal options with provisions for increased rental during the renewal term. Rental expense was $13,058,000 in 2007, $7,111,000 in 2006, and $7,267,000 in 2005.

Minimum annual rental commitments as of December 31, 2007, are as follows:

2008	$ 14,561,000
2009	14,082,000
2010	13,673,000
2011	13,450,000
2012	13,003,000
Thereafter	107,250,000
	$176,019,000

Note F — Common Stock

The company has a stock option plan providing that options may be granted to key employees at an option price of not less than 100% of the market value of the shares at the time the options are granted. As of December 31, 2007, the company has under option 75,640 shares (2006 — 96,450 shares). All options expire 5 years from date of grant.

EXHIBIT 1.2 (Continued)

Note G—Earnings Per Share

Basic earnings per share are computed by dividing net income by the weighted average of common shares outstanding during each period. Earnings per share assuming dilution are computed by dividing net income by the weighted average number of common shares outstanding during the period after giving effect to dilutive stock options. A reconciliation of the basic and diluted per share computations for fiscal 2007, 2006, and 2005 is as follows:

FISCAL YEAR ENDED

	DECEMBER 31, 2007			DECEMBER 31, 2006			DECEMBER 31, 2005		
	NET INCOME	WEIGHTED AVERAGE SHARES	PER SHARE AMOUNT	NET INCOME	WEIGHTED AVERAGE SHARES	PER SHARE AMOUNT	NET INCOME	WEIGHTED AVERAGE SHARES	PER SHARE AMOUNT
Earnings per common share— basic	$9,394	4,793	$1.96	$5,910	4,581	$1.29	$5,896	4,433	$1.33
Effect of dilutive securities: options		76			96			82	
Earnings per common share— assuming dilution	$9,394	4,869	$1.93	$5,910	4,677	$1.26	$5,896	4,515	$1.31

Auditor's Report

Related to the financial statements and notes is the report of an independent auditor (Exhibit 1.3). Management has responsibility for the preparation of financial statements, including the notes, and the auditor's report attests to the fairness of the presentation. In addition, beginning in 2005, the Sarbanes-Oxley Act of 2002, Section 404, requires corporate executives and auditors to document and certify to investors that their internal financial controls work properly.

An *unqualified* report, illustrated for R.E.C. Inc. in Exhibit 1.3, states that the financial statements present fairly, in all material respects, the financial position, the results of operations, and the cash flows for the accounting period, in conformity with GAAP. Some circumstances warrant reports other than an unqualified opinion and are called *qualified* reports. A departure from GAAP will result in a qualified opinion and the use of the following language in the opinion sentence: "In our opinion, *except* for the (nature of the departure explained), the financial statements present fairly . . . " If the departure from GAAP affects numerous accounts and financial statement relationships, then an *adverse* opinion is rendered, which states that the financial statements have not been presented fairly in accordance with GAAP. A scope limitation means that the extent of the audit work has been limited. This will result in a qualified opinion unless the limitation is so material as to require a *disclaimer of opinion*, which

EXHIBIT 1.3 Auditor's Report

Board of Directors and Stockholders
R.E.C. Inc.

We have audited the accompanying consolidated balance sheets of R.E.C. Inc., and subsidiaries as of December 31, 2007 and 2006, and the related consolidated statements of earnings, shareholders' equity, and cash flows for each of the three years in the period ended December 31, 2007. These financial statements are the responsibility of the Company's management. Our responsibility is to express an opinion on these financial statements based on our audits.

We conducted our audits in accordance with the standards of the Public Company Accounting Oversight Board (United States). Those standards require that we plan and perform the audits to obtain reasonable assurance about whether the financial statements are free of material misstatement. An audit includes examining, on a test basis, evidence supporting the amounts and disclosures in the financial statements. An audit also includes assessing the accounting principles used and significant estimates made by management, as well as evaluating the overall financial statement presentation. We believe that our audits provide a reasonable basis for our opinion.

In our opinion, the consolidated financial statements referred to above present fairly, in all material respects, the consolidated financial position of R.E.C. Inc. and subsidiaries at December 31, 2007 and 2006, and the consolidated results of their operations and their cash flows for each of the three years in the period ended December 31, 2007, in conformity with accounting principles generally accepted in the United States of America.

We also have audited, in accordance with the standards of the Public Company Accounting Oversight Board (United States), the effectiveness of R.E.C. Inc.'s internal control over financial reporting as of December 31, 2007, based on criteria established in Internal Control-Integrated Framework issued by the Committee of Sponsoring Organizations of the Treadway Commission, and our report dated February 15, 2008, expressed an unqualified opinion thereon.

J. J. Michaels and Company
Dime Box, TX
February 15, 2008

---

means the auditor cannot evaluate the fairness of the statements and therefore expresses no opinion on them. Lack of independence by the auditor will also result in a disclaimer of opinion.

Many circumstances warrant an *unqualified opinion with explanatory language* such as: a consistency departure due to a change in accounting principle, uncertainty caused by future events such as contract disputes and lawsuits, or events that the auditor wishes to describe because they may present business risk and going-concern problems. Unqualified reports with explanatory language result in additional paragraphs to the standard report.

In theory, the auditing firm performing the audit and issuing the report is "independent" of the firm being audited. The annual report reader should be aware, however, that the auditor is hired by the firm whose financial statements are under review. Over time, a lack of independence and conflicts of interest between companies and their hired auditors led to a series of accounting scandals that eroded investors' confidence in the capital markets. The collapse of Enron and WorldCom was a catalyst for some of the most sweeping corporate reforms since the Securities Act of 1934 was passed. Congress was quick to pass the Sarbanes-Oxley Act of 2002 in hopes of ending future accounting scandals and renewing investor confidence in the marketplace. This act established the Public Company Accounting Oversight Board (PCAOB), a private, nonprofit organization, which has been given the authority to register, inspect, and discipline auditors of all publicly owned companies. In addition, the act also prohibits audit firms from providing certain nonaudit services when conducting an external audit of a firm and requires that the chief executive officer and the chief financial officer of a publicly owned company certify the accuracy of the financial statements. An officer who certifies a report that is later found to be inaccurate could face up to $1 million in fines and/or a jail sentence of up to 10 years.

The Enron case highlighted the relationship many firms had established with their audit firms—consultant first, auditor second. In 2000, Enron paid Arthur Andersen (one of the five largest public accounting firms) fees of $52 million—$25 million for the audit and the remainder for other work, including consulting fees.[3] Drowned by greed and corporate scandal, Arthur Andersen was ordered to stop auditing publicly traded companies in 2002 after the firm was convicted of obstructing justice during the federal investigation of Enron. (The Supreme Court overturned the conviction on May 31, 2005.) Arthur Andersen, once the employer of more than 85,000 employees, will most likely go down in history not for once being the largest accounting firm known for its integrity, but for being the auditor of scandal-plagued and bankrupt companies Enron, WorldCom, Global Crossing, and SunBeam.[4]

The Big Four accounting firms remaining after the demise of Arthur Andersen have also been involved in the audits of firms accused of accounting and other violations: Ernst & Young clients Cendant, HealthSouth, and Computer Associates; Price WaterhouseCoopers clients BCCI, Tyco, and AIG; KPMG clients RiteAid, Xerox, and Lernout & Hauspie Speech Products NV; and Deloitte & Touche clients Adelphia Communications and Parmalat. Besides paying millions of dollars in settlements as a result of shareholder lawsuits, many of these firms have been fined by the SEC. While Arthur Andersen's fine of $7 million in 2001 for the failed audit of Waste Management was the largest fine to date, the SEC has since levied fines to the tune of $25 million against Lucent Technologies for its failure to cooperate with an SEC investigation, $250 million against Qwest Communications for pervasive fraud, and a record $750 million against MCI Inc. (formerly WorldCom) for the company's $11 billion accounting fraud.[5]

Given the legislation passed and the penalties levied since 2001, can investors now be confident that they can once again rely on auditors' assessments of publicly traded firms? Before deciding, consider the following:

- The first audit firm inspection reports (released in 2004) conducted by the PCAOB revealed that the four largest accounting firms misapplied standards and failed to properly maintain records of some audits.[6]

---

[3]Jonathan Weil, "What Enron's Financial Reports Did—and Didn't—Reveal," *Wall Street Journal*, November 5, 2001.
[4]Jeffrey Zaslow, "How the Former Staff of Arthur Andersen Is Faring Two Years After Its Collapse," *Wall Street Journal*, April 8, 2004.
[5]Tim Reason, "The Limits of Mercy," *CFO*, April 2005.
[6]Robert Schmidt and Mark Jaffe, "Accounting Firms Fail to Maintain Audit Info," *The Arizona Republic*, August 27, 2004.

- In 1998, KPMG chose not to register a new tax-sheltering strategy after a KPMG partner sent a memo indicating the potential penalties were vastly lower than the potential registration fees.[7]
- The SEC imposed a six-month suspension on Ernst & Young in April 2004, barring the firm from taking on new audit clients as a result of inadequate internal controls at the audit firm. Best Buy fired Ernst & Young as its auditor as of February 2005 after learning of a business relationship between a Best Buy director and Ernst & Young.[8]
- All of the Big Four accounting firms have been sued for billing clients for the full face amount of travel expenses while pocketing rebates and discounts received for possibly a period of 10 years.[9]
- Barry Melancon, chief executive officer of the American Institute of Certified Public Accountants (AICPA), the organization once responsible for monitoring audit firms, pursued a for-profit venture in late 1999 deemed a conflict of interest by some AICPA members, while at the same time neglecting his duties to monitor and punish audit firms not abiding by the rules.[10]

It will take time to determine whether the new laws and enforcement procedures will replace corruption and unethical behavior with integrity and professionalism in the auditing process. Regardless of the outcome, this history of problems underscores the need for users of financial statements to gain a basic understanding of financial statement content and analysis for decision-making purposes.

Management Discussion and Analysis

The *Management Discussion and Analysis* (MD&A) section, sometimes labeled "Financial Review," is of potential interest to the analyst because it contains information that cannot be found in the financial data. The content of this section includes coverage of any favorable or unfavorable trends and significant events or uncertainties in the areas of liquidity, capital resources, and results of operations. In particular, the analyst can expect to find a discussion of the following:

1. The internal and external sources of liquidity
2. Any material deficiencies in liquidity and how they will be remedied
3. Commitments for capital expenditures, the purpose of such commitments, and expected sources of funding
4. Anticipated changes in the mix and cost of financing resources
5. Unusual or infrequent transactions that affect income from continuing operations
6. Events that cause material changes in the relationship between costs and revenues (such as future labor or materials price increases or inventory adjustments)
7. A breakdown of sales increases into price and volume components

---

[7]Cassell Bryan-Low, "KPMG Didn't Register Strategy," *Wall Street Journal*, November 17, 2003.
[8]Jonathan Weil, "Best Buy to Dismiss Auditor Ernst, Citing Conflict of Interest," *Wall Street Journal*, December 31, 2004.
[9]Jonathan Weil, "Court Files Offer Inside Look at PriceWaterhouse Billing Clash," *Wall Street Journal*, January 5, 2004.
[10]David Henry and Mike McNamee, "Bloodied and Bowed," *Business Week*, January 20, 2003.

FIGURE 1.4   MD&A Discussion Items: What Do They Mean?

Item	Translation
1. Internal and external sources of liquidity.	From where does the company obtain cash—sales of products or services (internal source) or through borrowing and sales of stock (external sources)?
2. Material deficiencies in liquidity and how they will be remedied.	If the firm does not have enough cash to continue to operate in the long term, what are they doing to obtain cash and prevent bankruptcy?
3. Commitments for capital expenditures, the purpose of such commitments, and expected sources of funding.	How much is the company planning to spend next year for investments in property, plant, and equipment or acquisitions? Why? How will they pay for these items?
4. Anticipated changes in the mix and cost of financing resources.	Will the percentage of debt and equity change in the future relative to prior years—i.e., will the company borrow more or less, sell more stock, or generate significant profits or losses?
5. Unusual or infrequent transactions that affect income from continuing operations.	Will revenues or expenses be affected in the future by events not expected in the normal course of business operations?
6. Events that cause material changes in the relationship between costs and revenues.	Will significant changes occur that cause revenues (or expenses) to increase or decrease without a corresponding change in expenses (or revenues)?
7. Breakdown of sales increases into price and volume components.	Did the company's sales increase because they sold more products or services, or was the increase the result of price increases (with even a possible decrease in volume)?

See Figure 1.4 for a more detailed explanation of these items.

Alas, there are problems as well with the usefulness of the MD&A section. One of the SEC goals in mandating this section was to make publicly available information about future events and trends that might affect future business operations. One study to determine whether the data in the MD&A section provides useful clues to future financial performance revealed that companies did a good job of describing historical events, but very few provided accurate forecasts. Many companies provided essentially no forward-looking information at all.[11]

---

[11]Moses L. Parva and Marc J. Epstein, "How Good Is MD&A as an Investment Tool?" *Journal of Accountancy*, March 1993.

The events of 2001, including the economic downturn, September 11, and the collapse of Enron, appear to have had an impact on the quantity of precautionary and explanatory information companies have added to their MD&A sections of annual reports since 2001. Some firms include a plethora of statements covering every possible negative event that could possibly occur, such as:

> We may not be able to expand, causing sales to decrease.
> We may be unable to successfully develop new products.
> We may not be successful in our marketing efforts.
> Our operating results may fluctuate, causing our stock price to decline.
> Our suppliers may not meet our demand for materials.
> Our products may have significant defects.

And on and on! While these statements may be true, an assessment of the probability that these events may occur would be more useful to the reader of this information.

More helpful has been the addition to the MD&A of explanations about why changes have occurred in profitability and liquidity. For example, General Electric Company (GE) responded to criticisms of not disclosing enough information by delivering a 116-page 2004 annual report that included 24 pages of MD&A alone. The discussion of liquidity and capital resources in the MD&A is often less than a page in length for many companies; however, GE's 2004 discussion included more than seven pages comprised of explanations of why certain accounts had increased or decreased. This change is welcome, but GE and other companies still have not offered much in the way of forward-looking information in the MD&A.

Five-Year Summary of Selected Financial Data and Market Data

A five-year summary of selected financial data required by the SEC includes net sales or operating revenues, income or loss from continuing operations, income or loss from continuing operations per common share, total assets, long-term obligations and redeemable preferred stock, and cash dividends per common share. Companies often choose to include more than five years of data and/or additional items. The summary offers the user of financial statements a quick look at some overall trends; however, the discussion in this book will focus on the financial statements themselves, not the summary data.

The market data required by the SEC contains two years of high and low common stock prices by quarter. Since the financial statements do not include market values of common stock, this item is useful when analyzing how well the firm does in the marketplace.

Pandora (A.K.A. "PR Fluff")

In addition to the material required for presentation, many companies add to the annual report an array of colored photographs, charts, a shareholders' letter from the CEO, and other items to make the report and the company attractive to current and prospective investors. Some of these creations also appear on corporate Web sites. Getting to what is needed through the "PR Fluff" can be a challenge. Prior to the Enron collapse some companies cleverly moved key financial information out of the annual report and put it in a separate black-and-white and unappealing document or in the *proxy statement* (discussed later). One has to wonder if these firms actually hoped that investors would keep the pretty report and throw out the important financial information needed to thoroughly analyze the company.

For example, in 2001, Motorola and Texas Instruments put most of the important information needed by investors and creditors in their proxy statements. Interestingly, Motorola's stock price went from a high in 2000 of $61.42 per share to a low of $10.45 per share in 2001, and Texas Instruments' stock price ranged from a high of $99.78 in 2000 to a low of $20.10 in 2001. Fast forward to the 2004 annual reports of Motorola and Texas Instruments. Both companies have now put all of the basic financial information in the annual report instead of the proxy statement. Motorola has eliminated all fluff and put a plain white paper cover around its Form 10-K. The stock prices have begun to rise at both firms, with Motorola's stock price hitting a high of $20.89 and Texas Instruments' stock rebounding to a high of $33.65 in 2004.

The SEC has probably had much to do with these changes. Beginning in fall 2004, the SEC began publishing its comments on companies' filings, as well as the correspondence between the SEC and firms as they resolve disputes over financial reporting.[12]

Public relations material, including the shareholders' letter, is often informative but can also be misleading. The chairman and CEO of TimeWarner explains in the 2003 letter to shareholders how well the company has performed. Nowhere in the letter, however, does he mention the ongoing SEC and Department of Justice investigations regarding the possibly incorrect reporting of certain transactions by its wholly-owned subsidiary AOL. The 2004 TimeWarner letter to shareholders is even more upbeat than the 2003 letter, despite the fact that the company reached a settlement with the Department of Justice and proposed a settlement with the SEC to pay significant penalties. Stock prices of TimeWarner have tumbled. The high price in 2002 of $32.92 per share fell to a low of $8.70 and never made it back to even $20.00 per share in either 2003 or 2004.

Proxy Statement

The SEC requires companies to solicit shareholder votes in a document called the *proxy statement*, since many shareholders do not attend shareholder meetings. The proxy statement contains voting procedures and information, background information about the company's nominated directors, director compensation, executive compensation and any proposed changes in compensation plans, the audit committee report, and a breakdown of audit and nonaudit fees paid to the auditing firm. This information is important in assessing who manages the firm and how management is paid and potential conflict-of-interest issues.

Investors and creditors should try to learn as much about top management as possible regarding issues such as longevity of management and excessive management compensation, not only from the proxy statement, but also by researching newspapers and periodicals. The proxy statement should also be scrutinized to learn about important items such as corporate governance, audit-related matters, director and executive compensation including option grants, and related party transactions. Reading the 2005 proxy

---

[12]Mike McNamee, "The SEC Opens the Door—Wide," *Business Week*, July 12, 2004.

statement of Action Performance Companies, Inc. revealed that the son of the chairman of the board, president and CEO of the firm, ". . . serves as an independent commissioned representative of our company." The son received $137,468 for fiscal 2004. In 2002, investors were shocked to learn that on top of high executive compensation, some CEOs had significant loans from companies at abnormally low interest rates. Adding to the outrage were CEOs who defaulted on the loans and had the loans forgiven by the company. One of the most egregious cases was the loan to WorldCom's CEO, Bernie Ebbers, in an amount well over $300 million at an interest rate of 2.1 percent. Ebbers was replaced as CEO as the SEC began its investigation into WorldCom's accounting practices.[13] The Sarbanes-Oxley Act of 2002 has put restrictions on firms' extending personal loans to company executives.

Since the Enron scandal the SEC has increased the number of investigations of and enforcements against firms that are potentially violating securities laws. In a recent case, on December 20, 2004 (SEC Administrative Proceeding File No. 3-11777) the SEC imposed a cease-and-desist order against the Walt Disney Company for not revealing related party transactions from 1999 through 2001. Disney failed to disclose information about the employment by Disney of three adult children of Disney board members, the employment of a wife of a board member by a company in which Disney had a 50% interest, and payments for travel and other services for two other board members. The SEC became aware of the violations when Disney first disclosed these items in SEC filings in 2002.

Missing and Hard-to-Find Information

Some of the facts needed to evaluate a company are not available in the financial statements. These include such intangibles as employee relations with management, the morale and efficiency of employees, the reputation of the firm with its customers, its prestige in the community, the effectiveness of management, provisions for management succession, and potential exposure to changes in regulations—such as environmental or food and drug enforcement. These qualities impact the firm's operating success both directly and indirectly but are difficult to quantify.

Publicity in the media, which affects public perception of a firm, can also impact its financial performance. The Reputation Institute, a New York research group, worked with Harris Interactive Inc. in 2004 to develop corporate reputation rankings. At the number one spot for the sixth year in a row was Johnson & Johnson, with Enron in last place.[14] Johnson & Johnson delivered a stock return of 25.2% from 2003 to 2004. Most likely, the way in which each of these two companies handled crisis situations has affected the perception of the public. Johnson & Johnson is well known for its ethical decision to put consumer safety above financial profits; the company recalled all Tylenol capsules after seven people died taking cyanide-laced Tylenol. On the other hand, Enron executives are known for denying their involvement in any wrongdoing.

---

[13]Dawn Gilbertson, "Executive Privilege," *The Arizona Republic*, May 12, 2002.
[14]Ronald Alsop, "In Business Ranking, Some Icons Lose Luster," *Wall Street Journal*, November 15, 2004.

How companies handle social issues also impacts public perception. Global philanthropy is one way companies can increase sales and profit and generate new business opportunities, while also creating great social dividends. Pfizer, for example, has created a program in which it sends skilled professionals to developing countries. These professionals help Third World countries address public health issues and even help inspire and educate local people to become entrepreneurs. In one case a Pfizer pharmacist trained 18 students who went on to become pharmacists in Uganda.[15]

Some relevant facts are available in the financial statements but may be difficult for an average user to find. For example, the amount of long-term debt a firm has outstanding is disclosed on the face of the balance sheet in the noncurrent liability section. However, "long-term" could apply to debt due in 12.5 months or 2 years or 15 years. To determine when cash resources will be required to meet debt principal payments, the user must find and analyze the note to the financial statements on long-term debt with its listing of principal, interest, and maturity of a firm's long-term debt instruments.

Another important form of supplementary information is that reported by diversified companies operating in several unrelated lines of business. These conglomerates report financial information for the consolidated entity on the face of its financial statements. For a breakdown of financial data by individual operating segments, the analyst must use information in notes to the financial statement. Since 1998, companies have had to comply with FASB Statement No. 131, "Disclosures about Segments of an Enterprise and Related Information." (The analysis of segmental data is discussed in the appendix to Chapter 6.)

The Enron collapse highlighted that some companies use complicated financing schemes that may or may not be completely revealed in the notes to the financial statements. Even with notes available, most average users may find these items beyond their comprehension unless they acquire a Ph.D. in accounting or finance or read the authors' discussion of Enron in their other book, *Understanding the Corporate Annual Report—Nuts, Bolts, and a Few Loose Screws*.

Complexities

A Global Marketplace

The globalization of business activity has resulted in the need for a set of accounting rules that would be uniform in all countries. Investors and creditors in international markets would benefit from financial statements that are consistent and comparable regardless of the firm's location.

To address this need, the International Accounting Standards Board (IASB), formerly the International Accounting Standards Committee, was formed in 1973. The goal of the IASB is to eventually have worldwide acceptance of a set of international generally accepted accounting principles. This would allow companies to list securities in any market without having to prepare more than one set of financial statements. The United States is currently one of several countries that have not

---

[15]Jessi Hempel and Lauren Gard, "The Corporate Givers," *Business Week*, November 29, 2004.

accepted the current international accounting standards; however, that could change in the next decade. Corporate scandals globally have caused all parties involved in creating international accounting standards to understand the need for one accepted set of rules. While Enron was the catalyst for rethinking accounting standards in the United States, Europe also had a comparable scandal when Italian dairy food giant Parmalat filed for bankruptcy after committing financial fraud. Today the FASB and the IASB are working on a convergence of standards. Beginning in 2005 the European Union required publicly traded companies to use the international accounting rules, and it appears the United States could soon follow. The focus throughout this textbook will be on U.S. standards; however, investors interested in foreign investments should take the time to research the accounting standards used in other countries.

Mythical Mountain

GAAP—as established by the FASB and the SEC—provide a measure of uniformity, but they also allow considerable discretion in the preparation of financial statements. In order to illustrate the implications of these issues for financial statement users, the following comprehensive example is provided for the depreciation of *fixed assets* (also called *tangible fixed assets, long-lived assets*, and *capital assets*). Fixed assets are those assets, such as machinery and equipment, that benefit the firm for several years and are generally shown on the balance sheet as property, plant, and equipment. When such an asset is acquired, the cost of the asset is allocated or spread over its useful life rather than expensed in the year of purchase. This allocation process is depreciation. (The exception is land, which is not depreciated because land has a theoretically unlimited useful life.)

Assume that R.E.C. Inc. purchases an artificial ski mountain for its Houston flagship store in order to demonstrate skis and allow prospective customers to test-run skis on a simulated black diamond course. The cost of the mountain is $50,000. Several choices and estimates must be made in order to determine the annual depreciation expense associated with the mountain. For example, R.E.C. Inc. management must estimate how long the mountain will last and the amount, if any, of salvage value at the end of its useful life.

Furthermore, management must choose a method of depreciation: The straight-line method allocates an equal amount of expense to each year of the depreciation period, whereas the accelerated method apportions larger amounts of expense to the earlier years of the asset's depreciable life and lesser amounts to the later years.

If the $50,000 mountain is estimated to have a five-year useful life and $0 salvage value at the end of that period, annual depreciation expense would be calculated as follows for the first year.

Straight line

$$\frac{\text{Depreciable base (cost less salvage value)}}{\text{Depreciation period}} = \text{Depreciation expense}$$

$$\frac{\$50,000 - \$0}{5 \text{ years}} = \$10,000$$

Accelerated[16]

Cost less accumulated depreciation × twice the straight line rate = Depreciation expense

$$\$50,000 \times (2 \times .2) = \$20,000$$

The choices and estimates relating to the depreciation of equipment affect the amounts shown on the financial statements relating to the asset. The fixed asset account on the balance sheet is shown at historical cost less accumulated depreciation, and the annual depreciation expense is deducted on the income statement to determine net income. At the end of year 1, the accounts would be different according to the method chosen:

Straight line

Balance Sheet		*Income Statement*	
Fixed assets	$50,000	Depreciation expense	$10,000
Less accumulated depreciation	(10,000)		
Net fixed assets	$40,000		

Accelerated

Balance Sheet		*Income Statement*	
Fixed assets	$50,000	Depreciation expense	$20,000
Less accumulated depreciation	(20,000)		
Net fixed assets	$30,000		

The amounts would also vary if the estimates were different regarding useful life or salvage value. For example, if R.E.C. Inc. management concludes the mountain could be sold to Denver Mountaineering Co. at the end of five years for use in testing snowshoes, the mountain would then have an expected salvage value that would enter into the calculations. This example is compounded by all of the firm's depreciable assets and by the other accounts that are affected by accounting methods, such as the inventory account (discussed in detail in Chapter 2).

Other Discretionary Issues

Not only are financial statements encumbered by accounting choices and estimates, such as those regarding depreciation, but they also reflect an attempt to "match" expenses with revenues in appropriate accounting periods. If a firm sells goods on credit, there is a delay between the time the product is sold and the time the cash is collected. GAAP-based financial statements are prepared according to the "accrual" rather than the "cash" basis of accounting. The accrual method means that the revenue is recognized in the accounting period when the sale is made rather than when the cash is received. The same principle applies to expense recognition; the expense associated

---

[16] The example uses the double-declining balance method of figuring accelerated depreciation, which is twice the straight-line rate times the net book value (cost less accumulated depreciation) of the asset. Depreciation for year 2 would be:

Straight line $50,000/5 = $10,000   Accelerated $30,000 × .4 = $12,000

with the product may occur before the cash is paid out. The process of matching expense and revenue to accounting periods involves considerable estimation and judgment and, like the depreciation example, affects the outcome of the financial statement numbers.

If, for instance, the mythical $50,000 mountain needed expensive repairs because one enthusiastic customer tried snowboarding, thereby creating a heretofore nonexistent back bowl in the mountain, management would have to determine whether to recognize the cost of repair in year 2 or to spread it over years 2 through 5.

Furthermore, financial statements are prepared on certain dates at the end of accounting periods, such as a year or a quarter. Whereas the firm's life is continuous, financial data must be appropriated to particular time periods.

More Complications

Because the accounting principles that underlie the preparation of financial statements are complicated, the presentation of data based on the accounting rules can be perplexing. The issuance of FASB Statement No. 142, "Goodwill and Other Intangible Assets," effective as of January 1, 2002, most likely caused confusion as the rule was initially implemented. This rule resulted in some firms recording large losses as a result of removing assets that have lost value, while other firms had an increased earnings number (on paper) as a result of no longer recording amortization on goodwill—a topic discussed in later chapters.

The goodwill and intangible asset rules are just one of a vast number of financial statement puzzles. Sorting out the consolidation of a parent and subsidiaries, the accounting for leases and pensions, or the translation of foreign operations of a U.S. company can cause nightmares for the financial analyst. Off-balance-sheet financing, a technique used to enable firms to borrow money without recording the debt as a liability on the balance sheet, continues to concern the FASB. As a result, the board issued FASB Statement No. 133, "Accounting for Derivative Instruments and Hedging Activities," which has added to the complexity. Obligations from derivatives, financial instruments that derive their value from an underlying asset or index, such as futures and option contracts,[17] now must be recorded on the balance sheet. Statement No. 133 also requires a company to disclose information about the types of instruments it holds, its objectives in holding the instruments, and its strategies for achieving these objectives.[18]

Another significant change occurred in 1998 when FASB Statement No. 130, "Reporting Comprehensive Income," became effective. Companies must now report an additional income number, comprehensive income, which includes items that previously bypassed the income statement and were reported as a component of stockholders' equity.[19] (This important change is discussed more fully in Chapter 3.)

---

[17]A futures contract is a contract to buy or sell a commodity or a financial claim at a specified price at a specified future time. An option contract is a contract to buy or sell a fixed number of shares at a specified price over a specified period of time.

[18]"Accounting for Derivative Instruments and Hedging Activities," FASB Statement of Financial Accounting Standards No. 133, 1998.

[19]"Reporting Comprehensive Income," FASB Statement of Financial Accounting Standards No. 130, 1997.

Also complicating matters are two sets of accounting rules used by management—one for reporting purposes (preparation of financial statements for the public) and one for tax purposes (calculations of taxes for the Internal Revenue Service [IRS]). In the previous section, there was an example of the choices associated with the depreciation of an asset. Firms typically select one depreciation method for reporting purposes and use the method for tax purposes that is specified by the tax laws (currently the most frequently used tax method is the Modified Accelerated Cost Recovery System [MACRS]). The objective for tax purposes is to pay the smallest amount of tax possible, whereas the objective for reporting purposes is to report the highest possible income but also a smooth earnings stream. Thus, for reporting purposes, the firm might choose the straight-line method because it spreads the expense evenly and results in higher reported income than an accelerated method in the earlier years of an asset's life. Referring to the previous example, the following results were obtained according to the two depreciation methods for year 1:

Straight line	Accelerated
Depreciation expense $10,000	Depreciation expense $20,000

Use of the straight-line method produces an expense deduction that is $10,000 less than the accelerated method; net income, therefore, would be $10,000 higher in year 1 under the straight-line method. Assume for purposes of illustration that the accelerated method allowed by the IRS also yields a depreciation expense in year 1 of $20,000. By using the straight-line method, the tax paid to the IRS under the allowed accelerated method would be less than the income tax expense reported in the published income statement because taxable income would be less than reported income.[20] (Eventually this difference would reverse, because in the later years of the asset's useful life, accelerated depreciation would be less than straight line; the total amount of depreciation taken is the same under both methods.) To reconcile the difference between the amounts of tax expense, there is an account on the balance sheet called *deferred taxes.* This account and its interpretation, discussed in Chapter 2, introduce still another challenge to the financial statement user.

Quality of Financial Reporting

It has already been pointed out that management has considerable discretion within the overall framework of GAAP. As a result, the potential exists for management to "manipulate" the bottom line (profit or loss) and other accounts in financial statements. Ideally, financial statements should reflect an accurate picture of a company's financial condition and performance. The information should be useful both to assess the past and predict the future. The sharper and clearer the picture presented through the financial data and the closer that picture is to financial reality, the higher is the quality of the financial statements and reported earnings.

---

[20]For a firm with a 34% marginal tax rate, the difference would be $3,400. [Accelerated depreciation expense less straight-line depreciation expense times the marginal tax rate: ($20,000 − $10,000) × .34 = $3,400.]

Many opportunities exist for management to affect the quality of financial statements; some illustrations follow.

Accounting Policies, Estimates—Choices and Changes

In preparing financial statements, management makes choices with respect to accounting policies and makes estimations in the applications of those policies. One such choice (others will be discussed in subsequent chapters) was covered in the preceding section related to the depreciation of fixed assets. To continue the depreciation example, in choosing a depreciation method, management decides how to allocate the depreciation expense associated with a fixed asset acquisition.

Assume that the $50,000 ski mountain is more productive in the early years of its operating life, before would-be skiers dig ruts in the simulated runs. Financial reality would argue for the selection of an accelerated depreciation method, which would recognize higher depreciation expense in the early years of its useful life. An environment of rising prices would also support accelerated depreciation because inflation increases the replacement cost of most assets, resulting in an understatement of depreciation based on historical cost. If, however, management wanted to show higher earnings in the early years, the straight-line method would be selected. Note the difference in depreciation expense recognized for year 1:

Straight line	Accelerated
Income Statement	*Income Statement*
Depreciation expense $10,000	Depreciation expense $20,000

Remember that the lower the expense, the higher the reported net income. Therefore, under the straight-line method, net income would be $10,000 higher than with the accelerated method. The choice of depreciation method clearly affects the earnings stream associated with the asset, and it also affects the *quality* of the earnings figure reported. Use of accelerated depreciation would produce earnings of higher quality in this particular situation.

Management can also elect to change an accounting policy or estimate if the change can be justified as preferable to what was previously used. In the depreciation example, it was estimated that the mountain had a useful life of five years. It could be argued that competitive sporting goods stores depreciate their mountains over a ten-year rather than a five-year period. If the firm had chosen to use the straight-line method and made this accounting change (called a "change in accounting estimate"), depreciation expense would be decreased from $10,000 to $5,000 per year, and net income would increase by $5,000.

Before change in estimate	After change in estimate
Income Statement	*Income Statement*
Depreciation expense $10,000	Depreciation expense $5,000

When a company makes such a change, the quantitative effect of the change must be disclosed in notes to the financial statement.

Timing of Revenue and Expense Recognition

One of the generally accepted accounting principles that provides the foundation for preparing financial statements is the matching principle: Expenses are matched with the generation of revenues in order to determine net income for an accounting period. Reference was made earlier to the fact that published financial statements are based on the accrual rather than the cash basis of accounting, which means that revenues are recognized when earned and expenses are recognized when incurred, regardless of when the cash inflows and outflows occur. This matching process involves judgments by management regarding the timing of expense and revenue recognition. Although accounting rules provide guidelines helpful in making the necessary and appropriate allocations, these rules are not always precise.

For example, suppose that a company learns near the end of an accounting period that a material accounts receivable is probably uncollectible. When will the account be written off as a loss—currently, or in the next accounting period when a final determination is made? Pose the same question for obsolete inventory sitting on the warehouse shelves gathering dust. These are areas involving sometimes arbitrary managerial decisions. Generally speaking, the more conservative management is in making such judgments (conservatism usually implies the choice that is least favorable to the firm), the higher the quality of earnings resulting from the matching of revenues and expenses in a given accounting period.

In recent years, the accounting practices of many companies have been questioned, and in some cases, shareholders have filed lawsuits as a result of abuses in financial reporting. Xerox Corporation was accused of violating accounting principles by creating a variety of schemes to inflate profits and revenues from 1997 to 2000. Former finance manager and whistle-blower James Bingham claims that executives at Xerox assigned accountants the task of producing profits through accounting actions. Bingham explained to the SEC how he was involved in packaging short-term rental agreements for copiers in Brazil as if they were long-term deals. By doing this, Xerox was able to record revenues immediately. The deals were done to meet analysts' expectations, but investors and creditors had no way of determining that these actions had been taken.[21]

In 2004, Bristol-Myers Squibb Company agreed to pay the SEC $150 million in penalties related to charges of an accounting fraud used to inflate revenues. The company used incentives to encourage wholesalers to purchase unneeded drugs for the sole purpose of increasing revenues and profits.[22] In March 2003, Bristol-Myers announced that it had overstated revenue from 1999 to 2001 by $2.5 billion. Prior to the SEC settlement Bristol-Myers settled a shareholder lawsuit related to the inflated revenue scheme for $300 million despite the fact that a judge had dismissed the case.[23]

Discretionary Items

Many of the expenditures made by a business firm are discretionary in nature. Management exercises control over the budget level and timing of expenditures for

---

[21]James Bandler and Mark Maremont, "How Ex-Accountant Added Up to Trouble for Humbled Xerox," *Wall Street Journal*, June 28, 2001.
[22]Barbara Martinez, "Bristol-Mayers Settles SEC Fraud Case," *Wall Street Journal*, August 5, 2004.
[23]Deborah Solomon, "SEC Settlement by Bristol-Myers to Top $75 Million," *Wall Street Journal*, August 4, 2004.

the repair and maintenance of machinery and equipment, marketing and advertising, research and development, and capital expansion. Policies are also flexible with respect to the replacement of plant assets, the development of new product lines, and the disposal of an operating division. Each choice regarding these discretionary items has both an immediate and a long-term impact on profitability, perhaps not in the same direction. A company might elect to defer plant maintenance in order to boost current period earnings; ultimately, the effect of such a policy could be detrimental.

The nature of a business dictates to a certain extent how discretionary dollars should be spent. For some industries, there is a direct relationship between dollars spent for advertising and market share. Through investment in advertising, Coca-Cola and Pepsi have become the two key players in the soft drink market. As early as 1909, Coca-Cola was winning the advertising war with Pepsi, spending more than $750,000. Although Pepsi struggled in the beginning, the company became a formidable competitor by creating the first-ever 15-second radio jingle in 1939. These two companies have used not only radio but television, celebrities, slogans, and online advertising to promote their products.[24] In 2001, Coca-Cola controlled 43.7% of the soft drink market, and Pepsi followed with a 31.6% share; however, these numbers reflect a 0.4% slip in market share for Coca-Cola and a 0.2% increase in market share for Pepsi.[25] A possible explanation for this change could be that in 2001 Coca-Cola chose to postpone advertising spending, and this in turn increased income by 21% for the second quarter of the year.[26] Coca-Cola responded with aggressive and possibly questionable marketing tactics to promote its Frozen Coke drink at Burger King. The company spent millions of dollars to offer incentives to clubs and nonprofit groups, including payment for children's meals at Burger King. This could help explain why market share for Coca-Cola rose to 44.3% while Pepsi's share dropped to 31.4%.[27]

While advertising expenditures generally produce higher sales, such spending can also backfire in other ways. The pharmaceutical industry has discovered that direct-to-consumer ads for prescription drugs have increased sales. It has been estimated that a dollar spent on drug ads generates an additional $4.20 in sales. Consumers demanding that their doctors prescribe drugs as seen on television can ultimately lead to problems, however, in the form of lawsuits due to negative side effects of the drug. The high cost of health care has also angered many people, causing both the public and government to scrutinize the pharmaceutical industry.[28] In 2004, Pfizer, Inc. mailed a separate, glossy, public relations brochure to its shareholders in which it tried to explain away all the issues that have negatively impacted the entire industry. Despite a 17.4% increase in sales, a 190.6% increase in net income, and a 51.5% increase in cash generated by operating activities from 2003 to 2004, Pfizer's stock price dropped from a first-quarter high of $38.89 per share to a fourth-quarter low of $21.99 per share, a 43.5% decline.[29]

[24]Lawrence Dietz., *Soda Pop*. New York: Simon and Schuster, 1973.
[25]Betsy McKay, "Pepsico Inc. Gains in Soda Market as Coca-Cola's Share and Sales Slip," *Wall Street Journal*, March 1, 2002.
[26]Betsy McKay, "Coke Net Rises 21%, as Spending Is Put Off," *Wall Street Journal*, July 19, 2001.
[27]Chad Terhune, "How Coke Officials Beefed Up Results of Marketing Test," *Wall Street Jounral*, August 20, 2003.
[28]Deb Price, "Drug Ads Making Big Impact on Health Care," *The Arizona Republic*, August 17, 2003.
[29]Pfizer, Inc. 2004 Annual Report, 2004.

Research and development expenditures are of critical importance to some industries, such as high technology and the medical and pharmaceutical industries. Intense competition in these areas often results in higher research and development costs while at the same time reducing prices to gain market share. *BusinessWeek*, in its annual "Information Technology" report, examined 2,000 public technology companies and how they fared through two economic downturns in 1985 and 1990. Certain characteristics were common to those firms that were successful after the downturns. One common trait was to boost research and development despite the downturn. Veritas Software, for example, increased its research and development spending by 36% in 2001 and ended up with 2% more of the market share in their industry. Microsoft and Intel decided to use this tactic in 2001 and 2002 and were able to grow both sales and profits through fiscal 2004.[30]

The financial analyst should carefully scrutinize management's policies with respect to these discretionary items through an examination of expenditure trends (absolute and relative amounts) and comparison with industry competitors. Such an analysis can provide insight into a company's existing strengths and weaknesses and contribute to an assessment of its ability to perform successfully in the future.

Nonrecurring and Nonoperating Items

Business firms may execute financial transactions that are nonrecurring and/or nonoperating in nature. If the analyst is seeking an earnings figure that reflects the *future* operating potential of the firm, such transactions—which are not part of normal ongoing business—should be reviewed and possibly eliminated from earnings. Examples of transactions that should be considered as nonrecurring and/or nonoperating include gains and losses on the sale of an asset or business segment, write-downs for the impairment of assets, accounting changes, and extraordinary items. The user of financial statements must read the notes to the financial statements and the MD&A carefully to find items that are one-time in nature. Reader's Digest took a one-time charge of $27 million in 2004 due to a change in how the company planned to record its magazine promotion costs. This amount was not shown as a one-time charge on the income statement, but was buried in the promotion, marketing, and administrative expense account. Since Reader's Digest generated only $66.1 million of income before taxes in 2004, the $27 million charge represents a significant deduction. Such an item is both nonrecurring and nonoperating in nature and should be ignored in measuring the enterprise's ability to generate future operating profits.

In the past, restructuring charges or costs to reorganize a company were considered to be one-time, nonrecurring expenses. However, in the 1980s and 1990s companies have used restructuring charges as a way to manipulate their operating earnings numbers. If a company records restructuring charges on a regular basis, the analyst begins to question whether these charges are in fact a recurring operating expense of the company. One company for which restructuring charges are certainly not a one-time event is Eastman Kodak Company. The company has recorded restructuring charges every year since 1992 and claims that these charges will end in 2007. The first

---

[30]Steve Hamm, Faith Keenan, and Andy Reinhardt, "Making the Tech Slump Pay Off," *BusinessWeek*, June 24, 2002.

12 years of restructuring charges served to wipe out approximately half of the company's operating earnings.[31]

Many other examples of items affecting the quality of financial reporting exist and are discussed in more detail in Chapter 5.

The Journey Through The Maze Continues

Numerous other examples exist to illustrate the difficulty in finding and interpreting financial statement information. Many such examples are discussed in the chapters that follow. Annual reports provide a wealth of useful information, but finding what is relevant to financial decision-making may involve overcoming mazelike challenges. The remaining chapters in this book are intended to help readers find and effectively use the information in financial statements and supplementary data.

SELF-TEST

Solutions are provided in Appendix B.

_____ 1. Why should an individual learn to read and interpret financial statements?
  (a) Understanding financial statements will guarantee at least a 20% return on investments.
  (b) An individual need not learn to read and interpet financial statements since auditors offer a report indicating whether the company is financially sound or not.
  (c) Learning to read and interpret financial statements will enable individuals to gain employment.
  (d) Individuals cannot necessarily rely on auditors and management of firms to offer honest information about the financial well-being of firms.

_____ 2. What are the basic financial statements provided in an annual report?
  (a) Balance sheet and income statement.
  (b) Statement of financial earnings and statement of stockholders' equity.
  (c) Balance sheet, income statement, and statement of cash flows.
  (d) Balance sheet, income statement, statement of cash flows, and statement of stockholders' equity.

_____ 3. What items are included in the notes to the financial statements?
  (a) Summary of accounting policies.
  (b) Changes in accounting policies, if any.
  (c) Detail about particular accounts.
  (d) All of the above.

_____ 4. What does an unqualified auditor's report indicate?
  (a) The financial statements unfairly and inaccurately present the company's financial position for the accounting period.
  (b) The financial statements present fairly the financial position, the results of operations, and the changes in cash flows for the company.

---

[31]Faith Arner, "Kodak's Fuzzy Numbers," *Business Week*, February 9, 2004.

(c) There are certain factors that might impair the firm's ability to continue as a going concern.

(d) Certain managers within the firm are unqualified and, as such, are not fairly or adequately representing the interests of the shareholders.

_____ 5. Which of the following statements is false?

(a) The Sarbanes-Oxley Act of 2002 was the cause of the demise of Arthur Andersen.

(b) The FASB and the IASB are working closely to develop a set of accounting rules that would ultimately be used by all publicly traded companies worldwide.

(c) The Public Company Accounting Oversight Board is responsible for monitoring auditors of all publicly owned companies.

(d) The Sarbanes-Oxley Act of 2002 requires the chief executive officer and the chief financial officer of a publicly traded company to certify the accuracy of the financial statements.

_____ 6. What subject(s) should the management discussion and analysis section discuss?

(a) Liquidity.

(b) Commitments for capital expenditures.

(c) A breakdown of sales increases into price and volume components.

(d) All of the above.

_____ 7. Which of the following statements is true?

(a) Annual reports only contain glossy pictures.

(b) Public relations material should be used cautiously.

(c) Market data refers to the advertising budget of a firm.

(d) The shareholders' letter should be ignored.

_____ 8. What information can be found in a proxy statement?

(a) Information on voting procedures.

(b) Information on executive compensation.

(c) Information on the breakdown of audit and non-audit fees paid to the audit firm.

(d) All of the above.

_____ 9. What is the allocation of the cost of fixed assets called?

(a) Fixed cost allocation.

(b) Salvage value.

(c) Depreciation.

(d) Matching revenues and expenses.

_____ 10. Why could depreciation expense be considered a discretionary item?

(a) Management must estimate the useful life of the asset.

(b) A salvage value must be estimated.

(c) Management must select a method of depreciation.

(d) All of the above.

_____ 11. What do the choices and estimates relating to depreciation affect?

(a) Gross fixed assets on the balance sheet and depreciation expense on the income statement.

(b) Accumulated depreciation on the income statement and depreciation expense on the balance sheet.

(c) Net fixed assets on the balance sheet and depreciation expense on the income statement.

(d) Only net fixed assets on the balance sheet.

_____ 12. Which of the following statements is true?

(a) GAAP-based financial statements are prepared according to the cash basis of accounting.

(b) GAAP-based financial statements are prepared according to the accrual basis of accounting.

(c) GAAP-based financial statements may be prepared according to either the accrual or cash basis of accounting.

(d) GAAP-based financial statements must be prepared according to both the accrual and cash basis of accounting.

_____ 13. Why was the implementation of FASB Statement No. 142, "Goodwill and Other Intangible Assets," confusing?

(a) The rule allowed companies to borrow money without recording the debt.

(b) The rule required that certain revenues and expenses bypass the income statement.

(c) The rule causes some firms to record large losses, while other firms report increased earnings.

(d) The rule requires companies to keep two sets of books.

_____ 14. Which of the following is not generally considered to be a one-time, non-recurring, or nonoperating item?

(a) A gain on the sale of a business.

(b) An accounting change.

(c) An extraordinary item.

(d) The costs of operating a business.

_____ 15. Why might the use of accelerated depreciation rather than straight-line depreciation produce earnings of higher quality?

(a) Accelerated depreciation more accurately reflects financial reality because higher depreciation expense would be taken in the early years of its productive period.

(b) During inflationary periods, rising prices increase replacement costs of most assets, resulting in an understatement of depreciation based on historical cost.

(c) Both (a) and (b).

(d) None of the above.

_____ 16. Which of the following are methods by which management can manipulate earnings and possibly lower the quality of reported earnings?

(a) Changing an accounting policy to increase earnings.

(b) Refusing to take a loss on inventory in an accounting period when the inventory is known to be obsolete.

(c) Decreasing discretionary expenses.

(d) All of the above.

_____ 17. Where would you find the following information?

_____ (1) An attestation to the fairness of financial statements.

_____ (2) Summary of significant accounting policies.

_____ (3) Cash flow from operating, financing, and investing activities.
_____ (4) A qualified opinion.
_____ (5) Information about principal, interest, and maturity of long-term debt.
_____ (6) Financial position on a particular date.
_____ (7) Discussion of the company's results of operations.
_____ (8) Description of pension plans.
_____ (9) Anticipated commitments for capital expenditures.
_____(10) Reconciliation of beginning and ending balances of equity accounts.
    (a) Financial statements.
    (b) Notes to the financial statements.
    (c) Auditor's report.
    (d) Management discussion and analysis.

STUDY QUESTIONS AND PROBLEMS

1.1. What is the difference between an annual report and a 10-K report?

1.2. What are the particular items an analyst should review and study in an annual report, and what material should be read with caution?

1.3. What causes an auditor's report to be qualified? adverse? a disclaimer of opinion? unqualified with explanatory language?

1.4. What is a proxy statement, and why is it important to the analyst?

1.5. What are the intangible factors that are important in evaluating a company's financial position and performance but are not available in the annual report?

1.6. Why is depreciation expense not a precise measure of the annual outflow associated with capital assets?

1.7. What is meant by keeping "two sets of books," and what is the significance to the financial statement analyst?

1.8. Timber Products recently purchased new machinery at a cost of $450,000. Management estimates that the equipment will have a useful life of 15 years and no salvage value at the end of the period. If the straight-line depreciation method is used for financial reporting, calculate:

(a) Annual depreciation expense.

(b) Accumulated depreciation at the end of year 1 and year 2.

(c) The balance sheet account: fixed assets (net), at the end of years 1 and 2.

Use the following information to answer parts (d) and (e): Assume depreciation expense for tax purposes in year 1 is $45,000 and that the firm's tax rate is 30%.

(d) How much depreciation expense reported for tax purposes in year 1 will exceed depreciation expense reported in the financial statements in year 1.

(e) The difference between taxes actually paid in year 1 and tax expense reported in the financial statements in year 1.

1.9. R-M Corp.—An earnings quality problem.

C. Stern, chief financial officer of R-M Corp., has just reviewed the current year's third-quarter financial results with company president R. Macon. R-M Corp. sets an annual target for earnings growth of 12%. It now appears likely that the company will fall short of that goal and achieve only a 9% increase in earnings. This would have a potentially detrimental impact on the firm's stock price. Macon has directed Stern to develop alternative plans to stimulate earnings during the last quarter in order to reach the 12% target. Stern has approached you, a recent finance graduate of a well-known southwestern business school, to make recommendations for meeting the firm's earnings growth objective during the current year. Discuss techniques that could be used to increase earnings. Differentiate between those that would

(a) Increase earnings but lower quality of reported earnings.

(b) Increase earnings and also have a positive "real" impact on the firm's financial position.

1.10. Writing Skills Problem

Staff members from the marketing department of your firm are doing a splendid job selling products to customers. Many of the customers are so pleased, in fact, they are also buying shares in the company's stock, which means that they receive a copy of the firm's annual report. Unfortunately, questions sometimes arise that the marketing staff members are woefully inadequate at answering. Technical questions about the firm's financial condition and performance are referred to the chief financial officer, but the director of marketing has asked you to write a memo in which you explain the key elements in an annual report so that marketing representatives are better prepared to respond to questions of a more general nature.

Required: Write a memo no longer than one page (single-spaced, double-spaced between paragraphs) in which you describe the contents of an annual report so that marketing personnel can understand the basic requirements. The memo should be dated and addressed to B. R. Neal, Director of Marketing, from you; the subject is "Contents of an Annual Report."

To the Student: In business writing, the primary elements are *clarity* and *conciseness*. You must keep in mind the audience you are addressing and the objective of the communication.

1.11. Research Problem

Locate the Sarbanes-Oxley Act of 2002. In a concise essay (no more than one to two pages, single-spaced, double-spaced between paragraphs) outline the key components of the act.

1.12. Internet Problem

Arthur Levitt, chairman of the SEC, gave a speech entitled "The Numbers Game" on September 28, 1998, at the New York University Center for Law and Business. The complete text of the Levitt speech is available at www.prenhall.com/fraser. Read the speech and then answer the following questions:

(a) What is earnings management?

(b) Why do companies employ earnings management techniques?

(c) Describe five popular techniques used by companies that Levitt believes are illusions. Do you know of companies that have used these techniques?

(d) What recommendations does Levitt propose to address the problems created by earnings management?

(e) What concerns does Levitt have with regard to the auditing process? What remedies to this problem does he suggest? Do you believe these remedies will be effective? Why or why not?

1.13. Intel Problem

The 2004 Intel Annual Report can be found at the following Web site: www.prenhall.com/
fraser. Using the annual report, answer the following questions:

(a) Describe the type of business in which Intel operates.

(b) Read the "Letter to our stockholders" and discuss any information learned from this
letter that might be useful to an analyst.

(c) What type of audit opinion was given for the financial statements and the
internal financial controls of Intel? Explain the key items discussed in the audit
report.

(d) Read the Management Discussion and Analysis (MD&A). Discuss whether the
items that should be discussed in the MD&A are included. Support your answer
with examples from the Intel MD&A.

(e) After reading the MD&A, discuss the future prospects of Intel. Do you have any
concerns? If so, describe those concerns.

**1.14. Eastman Kodak Comprehensive Analysis Problem Using the Financial Statement
Analysis Template**

Each chapter in the textbook contains a continuation of this problem. The objective is to
learn how to do a comprehensive financial statement analysis in steps as you learn the
content of each chapter.

(a) The financial statement analysis template can be found at the following Web site:
www.prenhall.com/fraser. Once you have linked to the template you should see a
window that asks if you want to enable the macros. You must click on "Enable
Macros" to use the template. (You may have to change the security setting on your
computer in order to use this feature.) Familiarize yourself with the instructions.
The tab for the instructions is at the bottom of your screen and is labeled
"ReadMe." Print out a copy of the instructions to be used for all Eastman
Kodak problems in each chapter of the text. Click on the link at the bottom of
the screen labeled "Cover." Enter all of the required data in the template for
Eastman Kodak. Use the instructions to help you locate the necessary information.
When filling in the cash flow data use the cash flow numbers for continuing
operations only. Print the cover sheet when it is completed. Save the template
on your computer or a disk in order to use it with subsequent problems in
later chapters.

(b) Access newspaper and periodical articles about Eastman Kodak to learn of any
information that would be helpful in understanding the company's financial condition as well as future plans. Summarize what you learn in a short paper.

(c) Access the 2004 Eastman Kodak Annual Report and Form 10-K at
www.prenhall.com/fraser and use these two reports to do the following:

Review the letter to the shareholders titled "Management's Letter," the
Management's Report on Internal Control over Financial Reporting, and the Report
of Independent Registered Public Accounting Firm located in the 2004 Annual
Report. Write a concise summary of the important items learned from reading these
three items.

Review Items 1, 3, and 4 of the Form 10-K. Write a concise summary of the
important items learned from reading these three items.

Note: Keep all information from this problem in a notebook or folder to be used with the
Eastman Kodak problems in later chapters.

C A S E S

Case 1.1   The Walt Disney Company

The Walt Disney Company is an internationally renowned entertainment company. The corporation consists of four segments: Parks and Resorts, Media Networks, Studio Entertainment, and Consumer Products. Excerpts from the Walt Disney Company Proxy Statements, January 6, 2005 and January, 28, 2003 are on pages 36–39.

Required

1. Estimate the total compensation of Michael Eisner, Chief Executive Officer (CEO), for 2001, 2002, 2003, and 2004. Explain your rationale in determining this amount.
2. The CEO of a company usually works more than the normal 40 hour work week (or 2080 hours per year). Assuming Michael Eisner averages 4000 working hours per year, what is his hourly salary in each of the four

years from 2001 to 2004 based on your answer to part 1?
3. What was the percentage pay increase Eisner received in 2002, 2003, and 2004?
4. What are the possible reasons for the pay rate that the CEO receives?
5. Using the information from the "Comparison of Cumulative Total Returns" calculate the rate of return an individual shareholder would have earned for 2002, 2003, and 2004 assuming the shareholder held Walt Disney stock throughout these three years. Also calculate the average return the shareholder received over the three-year period.
6. Present arguments both for and against the pay increases Michael Eisner received.
7. Do you believe the compensation of Michael Eisner is appropriate? Why or why not?

SUMMARY COMPENSATION TABLE

| Name and Principal Position | Fiscal Year | Annual Compensation | | | Other Annual Compensation(2) | All Other Compensation(6) |
| | | Salary | Annual Bonus | | | |
			Cash	Stock Units(1)		
Michael D. Eisner	2004	$1,000,000	$7,250,000	—	$57,473	$4,900
Chief Executive	2003	1,000,000	—	$6,250,000	63,656	4,775
Officer	2002	1,000,000	—	5,000,000	88,176	4,718
	2001	1,000,000	0	0	—	4,020

(1) Stock units awarded for fiscal 2003 were made in the amounts indicated effective January 22, 2004, based upon the $24.635 fair market value of the Company's common stock on that date. Accordingly, Mr. Eisner received a total of 253,704 units. Fractional shares were disregarded with respect to the foregoing awards. Stock unit awards for fiscal 2002 were made in the amounts indicated effective January 27, 2003, based upon the $16.735 fair market value of the Company's common stock on that date. Accordingly, Mr. Eisner received a total of 298,775.02 units.

The stock units awarded for fiscal 2003 and 2002 are scheduled to vest in two tranches: 50% of each grant vests on the second anniversary of the date of grant, and the other 50% two years thereafter, except that in the case of Messrs. Eisner and Iger, 50% of the stock units awarded for fiscal 2002 and 100% of the stock units awarded for fiscal 2003 vest at the end of the terms of their employment under their respective employment agreements. In addition, all such units will vest upon the recipient's death or disability, an involuntary termination of the recipient's employment by the Company without cause or by the recipient for good reason. Dividends payable prior to vesting of restricted stock units are paid on the restricted stock units in the form of additional restricted stock units. At September 30, 2004, the restricted stock units previously awarded had a value, based upon the fair market value of the Company's common stock on September 30, 2004, of $12,472,214

for Mr. Eisner, $2,265,334 for Mr. Iger, and $985,667 for each of Messrs. Murphy and Staggs.

(2) In accordance with SEC rules, disclosure is omitted where total Other Annual Compensation is less than $50,000. Of the amount shown for Mr. Eisner for 2004, $17,873 represents the cost of a leased automobile provided to Mr. Eisner. The Company maintains an overall security program for Messrs. Eisner and Iger, due to business-related security concerns. Under this program, the Company requires Mr. Eisner to use Company aircraft for non-business as well as business travel for the Company's benefit rather than as a personal benefit or perquisite. The incremental cost to the Company associated with the non-business use by Mr. Eisner of Company-provided aircraft is included in the table and totaled $39,600 in fiscal 2004, $48,316 in fiscal 2003 and $72,926 in fiscal 2002. In additon, Mr. Eisner and Mr. Iger are provided with security systems and equipment for their residences and/or automobiles and with security advice and personal protection services at their residences and on other appropriate occasions. The cost of these systems and services are incurred as a result of business-related concerns and are not maintained as perquisites or otherwise for the personal benefit of Messrs. Eisner and Iger. As a result, the Company has not included such costs in the column on Other Annual Compensation, but notes the following costs to the Company of providing these systems and services:

	Fiscal Year	Security Systems and Equipment	Security Advice and Personal Protection Services
Michael D. Eisner	2004	$18,663	$716,335
	2003	28,483	808,965
	2002	16,422	480,591
Robert A. Iger	2004	$ 2,470	$471,646
	2003	1,910	414,933
	2002	2,448	228,087

As Chief Executive Officer of the Company, Mr. Eisner devotes significant efforts to Company matters in New York in addition to his California-based responsibilities. In lieu of reimbursing Mr. Eisner for hotel business expenses while in New York on Company business, the Company has paid Mr. Eisner, during the last three years, an allowance of $10,000 per month toward the expense of maintaining an apartment in New York for which he bears all expenses (which exceed the amount of the monthly allowance). This cost is incurred for the benefit of the Company and, for each of the last three years, the estimated expenses the Company would have incurred for hotel business expenses would have exceeded the amount of the allowance. Accordingly, these amounts are not included in the column on Other Annual Compensation. Of the amount shown for Mr. Iger for fiscal 2002, $120,000 represents a portion of payments in the net amount of $267,000 made to him during the year in connection with his maintenance of an apartment in New York during the period from his relocation to Los Angeles in 2000 through fiscal 2002. During this period, as Chairman of the ABC Group and President of Walt Disney International, and later as President and Chief Operating Officer of the Company, Mr. Iger devoted significant efforts to the operations of ABC and other Company matters in New York in addition to his California-based responsibilities. The table reflects the amount by which the net payment to Mr. Iger exceeded the cost that the Company estimates it would otherwise have incurred if it had provided local hotel accommodations to him.

(6) The Company provides the named executive officers with certain group life, health, medical and other noncash benefits generally available to all salaried employees, which are not included in this column pursuant to SEC rules. The amounts shown in this column include the following:

- Matching contributions by the Company under the Disney Salaried Savings and Investment Plan (and, in the case of Mr. Braverman, the ABC, Inc. Savings & Investment Plan), all of which were initially invested in common stock of the Company. During fiscal 2004, 2003 and 2002, the Company's matching contributions were $4,100, 4,000, and $4,000, respectively, for each of the named executive officers.
- Insurance premiums under personal liability insurance plans that the Company provides for certain key employees with coverage up to $5,000,000. Benefits under the plan supplement each employee's personal homeowner's and automobile liability insurance coverage. The Company paid $800, $775 and $718 in premiums on behalf of each of Messrs. Eisner, Iger, Murphy, Staggs and Braverman during fiscal 2004, 2003 and 2002, respectively, except the premiums paid on behalf of Mr. Braverman were $320 in fiscal 2002.

Comparison of Cumulative Total Returns

The following graph compares the performance of the Company's common stock with the performance of the Standard & Poor's 500 Composite Stock Price Index and a peer group index over the five-year period extending through the end of fiscal 2004. The graph assumes that $100 was invested on September 30, 1999 in the Company's common stock, the S&P 500 Index and the peer group index and that all dividends were reinvested.

The peer group index consists of the companies that were formerly included in the Standard & Poor's Entertainment and Leisure Index. Although Standard & Poor's discontinued this index in January 2002, the Company believes the companies included in the index continue to provide a representative sample of enterprises in the primary lines of business in which the Company engages. These companies are, in addition to The Walt Disney Company, media enterprises Time Warner Inc.

and Viacom Inc.; resort and leisure-oriented companies Carnival Corporation, Harrah's Entertainment, Inc., Hilton Hotels Corporation, Marriott International, Inc. and Starwood Hotels and Resorts Worldwide, Inc.; and consumer-oriented businesses Brunswick Corporation, Darden Restaurants, Inc., McDonald's Corporation, Starbucks Corporation, Yum! Brands, Inc. and Wendy's International Inc.

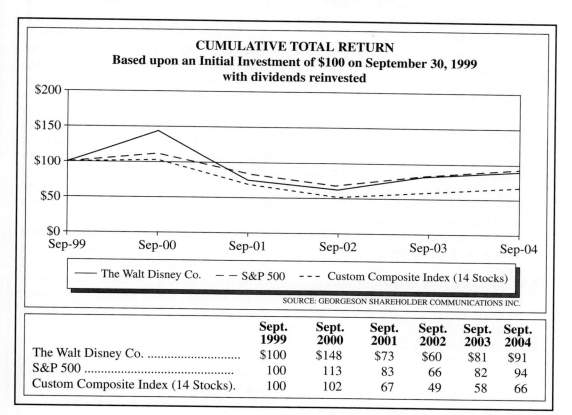

CUMULATIVE TOTAL RETURN
Based upon an Initial Investment of $100 on September 30, 1999 with dividends reinvested

Legend: —— The Walt Disney Co.   — — S&P 500   - - - Custom Composite Index (14 Stocks)

SOURCE: GEORGESON SHAREHOLDER COMMUNICATIONS INC.

	Sept. 1999	Sept. 2000	Sept. 2001	Sept. 2002	Sept. 2003	Sept. 2004
The Walt Disney Co.	$100	$148	$73	$60	$81	$91
S&P 500	100	113	83	66	82	94
Custom Composite Index (14 Stocks).	100	102	67	49	58	66

Case 1.2　　Ultimate Electronics, Inc.

Excerpts from the Management Discussion and Analysis of Financial Condition and Results of Operations (MD&A) of Ultimate Electronics' 2004 annual report are found on pages 40–43.

Required

1. Why is the MD&A section of the annual report useful to the financial analyst? What types of information can be found in this section?
2. Using the excerpts from the MD&A of Ultimate Electronics, Inc. 2004 annual report, discuss whether each of the items that should be discussed in an MD&A are, in fact, presented in this section. Give examples to support your answer.
3. Evaluate the overall quality of the information presented by Ultimate Electronics, Inc. in the MD&A.
4. Based on this section only, what is your assessment of the prospects for this company?

Excerpts From Management's Discussion and Analysis of Financial Condition and Results of Operations

Overview

Ultimate Electronics is a leading specialty retailer of consumer electronics and home entertainment products in the Rocky Mountain, Midwest and Southwest regions of the United States. We focus on mid- to high-end audio, video, television and mobile electronics products sold by a highly trained, knowledgeable, commissioned sales force. We offer approximately 4,000 SKU's at a wide range of price points representing approxi-

mately 130 brands, including a broad presentation of the most popular names and a large selection of limited-distribution, upscale brands and lines. We emphasize products with the latest technology by dedicating significant resources to their promotion, advertising, merchandising and related product training.

We embarked on an aggressive expansion strategy in fiscal 2001, adding five new stores to our store base of 31 stores in that year, followed by 10 stores in fiscal 2002, 12 stores in fiscal 2003 and seven stores in fiscal 2004. New markets opened during this period include Phoenix, Oklahoma City, St. Louis, Dallas/Ft. Worth, Kansas City, Wichita, and Austin. We believe we have a solid and competitive store base in the markets we serve. We believe our store base will provide a strategic advantage in capitalizing on new technologies. We currently operate 65 stores, including 54 stores in Arizona, Idaho, Illinois, Iowa, Kansas, Minnesota, Missouri, Nevada, New Mexico, Oklahoma, South Dakota, Texas, and Utah under the trade name Ultimate Electronics® and 11 stores in Colorado under the trade name SoundTrack®. In addition, we operate Fast Trak Inc., an independent electronics repair company and a wholly owned subsidiary of Ultimate Electronics.

Retail Industry We operate in a highly competitive and price sensitive industry. We face strong sales competition from large national chains, numerous smaller specialty stores and consumer electronics departments of many department, discount and home improvement stores. Additionally, we compete with a number of retailers for prime retail site locations and for attracting and retaining quality employees. We, like other retail companies, are influenced by a number of factors, including but not limited to: cost of goods, discretionary consumer spending, economic conditions, customer preferences, unemployment rate, and weather patterns.

Key Items in Fiscal 2004 Significant financial items during fiscal 2004 were:

- Although we added seven new stores during fiscal 2004, our total sales increased by only 1% from fiscal 2003 to $712.9 million. Comparable stores sales decreased by 9%.
- We experienced an operating loss of $25.2 million.
- Total assets increased 14% to $336 million at January 31, 2004.

We struggled during fiscal 2004 with the ineffectiveness of our television advertising campaign, price compression in key products categories, slowing demand in established categories, low consumer confidence, competitive pressures and a dilution of skilled personnel resulting from our recent expansion. In the third and fourth quarters, these issues were compounded by the unexpected problems we experienced following our September conversion to a new management information system.

Problems Experienced with New Management Information System. Following the September conversion to our new management information system, we experienced problems with inventory visibility and tracking, product distribution, commission calculations, general reporting and processing of receivables and service repairs. These problems negatively impacted our sales and operating results in our third and fourth quarters.

Failure of Our Marketing Campaign to Generate an Increase in Store Traffic. We shifted a considerable percentage of our marketing budget toward a mass market television campaign designed to increase the name awareness of our company, with less emphasis on direct mail, radio and print advertising products. This shift in marketing did not produce the intended results, as we do not believe our store traffic improved.

Weakened Execution at the Store Level. As a result of the rapid expansion, we had less experienced sales associates and other store personnel, resulting in lower individual sales performance and reduced levels of customer service. In addition, integration issues associated with our new management information system compounded our deficiencies in execution in the second half of fiscal 2004.

Company Performance Measures

- *Comparable Store Sales.* Comparable store sales, also referred to as "same store sales" or "comps" by others within the retail industry, is a measure that indicates whether our existing stores are performing better year over year. We consider comparable store sales to be sales for stores open at least 13 months and exclude (i) sales for stores recently relocated and expanded until 13 months after completion and (ii) sales for stores in new markets until 13 months after 75% of the initial number of stores planned for the market have opened. Our comparable store sales also include sales from our specialty markets division, builder division and main distribution center. As of January 31, 2004, 57 of our 65 stores were included as comparable stores. We experienced a decrease in our comparable store sales of 9%. The negative comparable store sales growth is reflective of, among other things, a weak economy, an ineffective marketing campaign, problems with our new management information system and dilution of skilled personnel resulting from our recent expansion.
- *Gross Profit Margins.* For many retailers, gross profit margins equal revenues minus the cost of goods sold and occupancy costs. We calculate gross profit margins as revenues less cost of goods sold. Write-downs associated with our exit from certain categories

and higher shrink associated with integration issues experienced with our new system accounted for the decrease in our gross profit margins to 32.2% in fiscal 2004 from 32.7% in fiscal 2003.

- *Inventory Levels and Inventory Turns.* Generally, inventory levels should not increase at a rate higher than sales. Inventory levels increasing at a rate faster than sales could be a warning that merchandise is not selling and write-downs of merchandise may be needed. Our sales increased 1% in fiscal 2004, but our inventory increased by 7%. Our inventory levels increased during fiscal 2004 due to the addition of 12% more stores than the previous year. Our inventory turns (a measure of how quickly inventory is sold) were 4.2 during fiscal 2004, down from 4.5 in fiscal 2003 (based on average monthly inventories), and suffered during fiscal 2004 due to only a 1% increase in sales despite the addition of seven additional stores. In addition, we recognized write-downs in our inventory during fiscal 2004 associated with our exit from the computer category, video gaming hardware and software and PDA devices.

- *Selling, General and Administrative Expenses.* Selling, general and administrative expense includes much of the corporate and "overhead" costs of our business. Selling, general and administrative expenses increased as a percentage of sales to 35.7% from 31.2%, primarily due to increased advertising costs and higher occupancy and labor costs. Advertising costs increased due to lower advertising credits earned from vendors and increased advertising expenditures during the fourth quarter designed to increase sales during the holiday selling season. General and administrative labor costs, including salaries and wages at the store and corporate level, increased due to the

opening of seven new stores and competitive pressures in the industry for store management.

- *Cash Flows/EBITDA.* We need to generate enough cash flow to service our debt. Our cash flow from operations was a negative $17.2 million during fiscal 2004, primarily as a result of the increase in our accounts receivable and inventory levels and our net loss for the year. In addition, our revolving line of credit requires that we maintain minimum EBITDA (earnings before interest, taxes, depreciation and amortization) over a rolling 12-month period beginning with April of 2004.

- *Debt-to-Equity Ratio.* Our debt-to-equity ratio, a measure of the amount of debt in the capitalization of our company and a monitor of our borrowing, increased to 32% at January 31, 2004 from 5% at January 31, 2003. We increased our borrowings under our revolving line of credit to $63.2 million at January 31, 2004, from $8.3 million at January 31, 2003. Borrowings increased due to the shortfall in our sales, the increase in our inventory levels and capital expenditures for the seven new stores we opened and the conversion to our new management information system during fiscal 2004. Through a focused strategy of cost control, inventory management, and limiting capital expenditures to approximately $12 million, we plan to increase liquidity and reduce outstanding borrowing levels as a percentage of our borrowing capacity by our fiscal 2005 year end.

Liquidity and Capital Resources

Historically, our primary sources of liquidity have been net cash from operations, revolving credit lines, term debt and issuances of common stock. Our primary cash requirements have historically been expenditures for new store openings and the relocation and/or remodeling of existing store locations and inventory build-up prior to the holiday selling season. Expenditures for new store openings include leasehold improvements, fixtures and equipment, additional inventory requirements, preopening expenses and selling, general and administrative expenses.

Net cash used in operating activities was $17.2 million for fiscal 2004 compared to net cash used in operating activities of $12.3 million for fiscal 2003, primarily due to higher receivables in the current year. At January 31, 2004, we had an $8.0 million income tax receivable.

Net cash used in investing activities was $37.1 million for fiscal 2004 compared to $47.8 million in fiscal 2003, primarily for capital expenditures on new store openings and enhancements of our new management information system. We opened seven new stores in fiscal 2004 compared to 12 new stores in fiscal 2003.

We expect total capital expenditures to be approximately $12 million in fiscal 2005. We intend to focus our capital expenditures on the resolution of issues with, and enhancements of, our management information system; in-store projects tied to merchandising initiatives; the relocation of our St. Cloud, Minnesota store in March 2004; one new store in the Kansas City metropolitan area, anticipated to open in early 2005; and minor remodels of some existing stores.

Net cash provided by financing activities totaled $56.1 million during fiscal 2004, compared to net cash provided by financing activities of $60.1 million during fiscal 2003. Net cash provided by financing activities for fiscal 2004 was primarily due to borrowings under our revolving line of credit. Net cash provided by financing activities for fiscal 2003 was primarily the result of the net proceeds we received from our May 6, 2002 offering, partially offset by net repayments of our revolving line of credit.

At January 31, 2004 we had an $80 million credit agreement with Wells Fargo Retail Finance, LLC, of which $63.2 million was outstanding. On April 2, 2004, we amended and restated our revolving line of credit. We now have a $100 million credit agreement with Wells Fargo Finance, LLC, which expires in April 2008. As of April 2, 2004, we had an outstanding balance under our revolving line of credit of approximately $76 million, and a borrowing capacity of approximately $90 million. If our sales continue to decline or our inventories continue to rise, we will have less amounts available for borrowing. We believe that our cash flow from operations (including our income tax refund expected to be received by the end of the second quarter of fiscal 2005) and borrowings under our revolving line of credit will be sufficient to fund our operations, debt repayment and anticipated expansion through fiscal 2005.

CHAPTER

The Balance Sheet

Old accountants never die; they just lose their balance.
— ANONYMOUS

A balance sheet, also called the *statement of condition* or *statement of financial position*, provides a wealth of valuable information about a business firm, particularly when examined over a period of several years and evaluated in relation to the other financial statements. A prerequisite to learning what the balance sheet can teach us, however, is a fundamental understanding of the accounts in the statement and the relationship of each account to the financial statements as a whole.

Consider, for example, the balance sheet *inventory* account. Inventory is an important component of liquidity analysis, which considers the ability of a firm to meet cash needs as they arise. (Liquidity analysis will be discussed in Chapter 6.) Any measure of liquidity that includes inventory as a component would be meaningless without a general understanding of how the balance sheet inventory amount is derived. This chapter will thus cover such issues as what inventories are, how the inventory balance is affected by accounting policies, why companies choose and sometimes change methods of inventory valuation, where to find disclosures regarding inventory accounting, and how this one account contributes to the overall measurement of a company's financial condition and operating performance. This step-by-step descriptive treatment of inventories and other balance sheet accounts will provide the background necessary to analyze and interpret balance sheet information.

Financial Condition

The balance sheet shows the financial condition or financial position of a company *on a particular date*. The statement is a summary of what the firm *owns* (assets) and what the firm *owes* to outsiders (liabilities) and to internal owners (stockholders' equity). By definition, the account balances on a balance sheet must balance; that is, the total of all assets must equal the sum of liabilities and stockholders' equity. The balancing equation is expressed as:

$$\text{Assets} = \text{Liabilities} + \text{Stockholders' equity}$$

This chapter will cover account by account the consolidated balance sheet of Recreational Equipment and Clothing, inc. (R.E.C. Inc.) (Exhibit 2.1). This particular firm sells recreational products through retail outlets, some owned and some leased, in cities located throughout the southwestern United States. Although the accounts on a balance sheet will vary somewhat by firm and by industry, those described in this chapter will be common to most companies.

Consolidation

Note first that the statements are "consolidated" for R.E.C. Inc. and subsidiaries. When a parent owns more than 50% of the voting stock of a subsidiary, the financial statements are combined for the companies in spite of the fact that they are separate legal entities. The statements are consolidated because the companies are *in substance* one company, given the proportion of control by the parent. In the case of R.E.C. Inc., the subsidiaries are wholly owned, which means that the parent controls 100% of the voting shares of the subsidiaries. Where less than 100% ownership exists, there are accounts in the consolidated balance sheet and income statement to reflect the minority interest in net assets and income.

Balance Sheet Date

The balance sheet is prepared at a point in time at the end of an accounting period, a year, or a quarter. Most companies, like R.E.C. Inc., use the calendar year with the accounting period ending on December 31. Interim statements would be prepared for each quarter, ending March 31, June 30, and September 30. Some companies adopt a fiscal year ending on a date other than December 31.

The fact that the balance sheet is prepared on a particular date is significant. For example, cash is the first account listed on the balance sheet and represents the amount of cash on December 31; the amount could be materially different on December 30 or January 2.

Comparative Data

Financial statements for only one accounting period would be of limited value because there would be no reference point for determining changes in a company's financial record over time. As part of an integrated disclosure system required by the SEC, the information presented in annual reports to shareholders includes two-year audited balance sheets and three-year audited statements of income and cash flows. The balance sheet for R.E.C. Inc. thus shows the condition of the company at December 31, 2007 and 2006.

Common-Size Balance Sheet

A useful tool for analyzing the balance sheet is a common-size balance sheet. Common-size financial statements are a form of vertical ratio analysis that allows for comparison of firms with different levels of sales or total assets by introducing a common denominator. Common-size statements are also useful to evaluate trends within a firm and to make industry comparisons. The common-size balance sheet for R.E.C. Inc. is presented in Exhibit 2.2. Information from the common-size balance sheet will be used throughout this chapter and also in Chapter 6. A common-size balance sheet

EXHIBIT 2.1 R.E.C. Inc. Consolidated Balance Sheets at December 31, 2007 and 2006 (in Thousands)

	2007	2006
Assets		
Current Assets		
Cash	$ 4,061	$ 2,382
Marketable securities (Note A)	5,272	8,004
Accounts receivable, less allowance for doubtful accounts of $448 in 2007 and $417 in 2006	8,960	8,350
Inventories (Note A)	47,041	36,769
Prepaid expenses	512	759
Total current assets	65,846	56,264
Property, Plant, and Equipment (Notes A, C, and E)		
Land	811	811
Buildings and leasehold improvements	18,273	11,928
Equipment	21,523	13,768
	40,607	26,507
Less accumulated depreciation and amortization	11,528	7,530
Net property, plant, and equipment	29,079	18,977
Other Assets (Note A)	373	668
Total Assets	$95,298	$75,909
Liabilities and Stockholders' Equity		
Current Liabilities		
Accounts payable	$14,294	$ 7,591
Notes payable—banks (Note B)	5,614	6,012
Current maturities of long-term debt (Note C)	1,884	1,516
Accrued liabilities	5,669	5,313
Total current liabilities	27,461	20,432
Deferred Federal Income Taxes (Notes A and D)	843	635
Long-Term Debt (Note C)	21,059	16,975
Commitments (Note E)		
Total liabilities	49,363	38,042
Stockholder's Equity		
Common stock, par value $1, authorized, 10,000,000 shares; issued, 4,803,000 shares in 2007 and 4,594,000 shares in 2006 (Note F)	4,803	4,594
Additional paid-in capital	957	910
Retained earnings	40,175	32,363
Total stockholders' equity	45,935	37,867
Total Liabilities and Stockholders' Equity	$95,298	$75,909

The accompanying notes are an integral part of these statements.

EXHIBIT 2.2   R.E.C. Inc. Common-Size Balance Sheets (Percent)

	2007	2006	2005	2004	2003
Assets					
Current Assets					
Cash	4.3	3.1	3.9	5.1	4.9
Marketable securities	5.5	10.6	14.9	15.3	15.1
Accounts receivable, less allowance for doubtful accounts	9.4	11.0	7.6	6.6	6.8
Inventories	49.4	48.4	45.0	40.1	39.7
Prepaid expenses	.5	1.0	1.6	2.4	2.6
Total current assets	69.1	74.1	73.0	69.5	69.1
Property, Plant, and Equipment					
Land	.8	1.1	1.2	1.4	1.4
Buildings and leasehold improvements	19.2	15.7	14.4	14.1	14.5
Equipment	22.6	18.1	17.3	15.9	16.5
Less accumulated depreciation and amortization	(12.1)	(9.9)	(6.9)	(3.1)	(3.0)
Net property, plant, and equipment	30.5	25.0	26.0	28.3	29.4
Other Assets	.4	.9	1.0	2.2	1.5
Total Assets	100.0	100.0	100.0	100.0	100.0
Liabilities and Stockholders' Equity					
Current Liabilities					
Accounts payable	15.0	10.0	13.1	11.4	11.8
Notes payable—banks	5.9	7.9	6.2	4.4	4.3
Current maturities of long-term debt	2.0	2.0	2.4	2.4	2.6
Accrued liabilities	5.9	7.0	10.6	7.7	5.7
Total current liabilities	28.8	26.9	32.3	25.9	24.4
Deferred Federal Income Taxes	.9	.8	.7	.5	.4
Long-Term Debt	22.1	22.4	16.2	14.4	14.9
Total liabilities	51.8	50.1	49.2	40.8	39.7
Stockholders' Equity					
Common stock	5.0	6.1	6.7	7.3	7.5
Additional paid-in capital	1.0	1.2	1.3	1.6	1.8
Retained earnings	42.2	42.6	42.8	50.3	51.0
Total stockholders' equity	48.2	49.9	50.8	59.2	60.3
Total Liabilities and Stockholders' Equity	100.0	100.0	100.0	100.0	100.0

expresses each item on the balance sheet as a percentage of total assets. Common-size statements facilitate the internal or structural analysis of a firm. The common-size balance sheet reveals the composition of assets within major categories, for example, cash and cash equivalents relative to other current assets, the distribution of assets in which funds are invested (current, long-lived, intangible), the capital structure of the firm (debt relative to equity), and the debt structure (long-term relative to short-term).

Assets

Current Assets

Assets are segregated on a balance sheet according to how they are utilized (Exhibit 2.3). Current assets include cash or those assets expected to be converted into cash within one year or one operating cycle, whichever is longer. The *operating cycle* is the time required to purchase or manufacture inventory, sell the product, and collect the cash. For most companies, the operating cycle is less than one year, but in some industries—such as tobacco and wine—it is longer. The designation "current" refers essentially to those assets that are continually used up and replenished in the ongoing operations of the business. The term *working capital* or *net working capital* is used to designate the amount by which current assets exceed current liabilities (current assets less current liabilities).

Cash and Marketable Securities

These two accounts, shown separately for R.E.C. Inc. in Exhibit 2.3, are often combined as "cash and cash equivalents." The cash account is exactly that, cash in any form—cash awaiting deposit or in a bank account. Marketable securities (also referred to as short-term investments) are cash substitutes, cash that is not needed immediately in the business and is temporarily invested to earn a return. These investments are in instruments with short-term maturities (less than one year) to minimize the risk of interest rate fluctuations. They must be relatively riskless securities and highly liquid so

EXHIBIT 2.3   R.E.C. Inc. Consolidated Balance Sheets at December 31, 2007 and 2006 (in Thousands)

	2007	2006
Assets		
Current Assets		
Cash	$ 4,061	$ 2,382
Marketable securities (Note A)	5,272	8,004
Accounts receivable, less allowance for doubtful accounts of $448 in 2007		
and $417 in 2006	8,960	8,350
Inventories (Note A)	47,041	36,769
Prepaid expenses	512	759
Total current assets	65,846	56,264
Property, Plant, and Equipment (Notes A, C, and E)		
Land	811	811
Buildings and leasehold improvements	18,273	11,928
Equipment	21,523	13,768
	40,607	26,507
Less accumulated depreciation and amortization	11,528	7,530
Net property, plant, and equipment	29,079	18,977
Other Assets (Note A)	373	668
Total Assets	$95,298	$75,909

that funds can be readily withdrawn as needed. Instruments used for such purposes include U.S. Treasury bills, certificates, notes, and bonds; negotiable certificates of deposit at financial institutions; and commercial paper (unsecured promissory notes of large business firms). As can be seen on the common-size balance sheet, there has been a change in the amount of cash and marketable securities held by R.E.C. Inc. from 20% in 2003 to less than 10% in 2007. This has resulted in increases to other asset accounts.

Under an accounting rule issued in 1993, the valuation of marketable securities on the balance sheet as well as other investments in debt and equity securities depends on the intent of the investment. Statement of Financial Accounting Standards No. 115, "Accounting for Certain Investments in Debt and Equity Securities,"[1] effective for fiscal years beginning after December 15, 1993, requires the separation of investment securities into three categories:

1. *Held to maturity* applies to those debt securities that the firm has the positive intent and ability to hold to maturity; these securities are reported at amortized cost.
2. *Trading securities* are debt and equity securities that are held for resale in the short term, as opposed to being held to realize longer-term gains from capital appreciation. These securities are reported at *fair value* with unrealized gains and losses included in earnings.
3. *Securities available for sale* are debt and equity securities that are not classified as one of the other two categories, either held to maturity or trading securities. Securities available for sale are reported at fair value with unrealized gains and losses included in comprehensive income. The cumulative net unrealized gains or losses are reported in the accumulated other comprehensive income section of stockholders' equity.

Financial Accounting Standards Board (FASB) Statement No. 115 does not apply to investments in consolidated subsidiaries nor to investments in equity securities accounted for under the equity method (discussed in Chapter 3).

This accounting requirement most significantly affects financial institutions and insurance companies, which trade heavily in securities as part of their operating activities. The kinds of securities held by companies such as R.E.C. Inc. under the category "marketable securities" or "cash equivalents" are selected for ready conversion into cash, and they have market values that are equal to or very close to cost, as reported in Note A (see Exhibit 1.2) to the R.E.C. Inc. financial statements. ("Marketable securities consist of short-term, interest-bearing securities stated at cost, which approximates

---

[1]Some terms that may be helpful to the reader are the following: Debt securities are securities representing a creditor relationship, including U.S. Treasury securities, municipal securities, corporate bonds, convertible debt, and commercial paper. Equity securities represent an ownership interest in an entity, including common and preferred stock. Fair value is the amount at which a financial instrument could be exchanged in a current transaction between willing parties; if a quoted market price is available, the fair value is the number of trading units multiplied by the market price. Amortized cost refers to the fact that bonds (a debt security) may sell at a premium or discount because the stated rate of interest on the bonds is different from the market rate of interest; the premium or discount is "amortized" over the life of the bonds so that at maturity the cost equals the face amount.

For more reading about FASB Statement No. 115, see J. T. Parks, "FASB 115: It's Back to the Future for Market Value Accounting," *Journal of Accountancy*, September 1993.

market.") Should values be different from cost, however, then the company would have to determine which category of investment applies. For example, if these kinds of securities were considered to be "available for sale," they would be marked to current value, and cumulative unrealized gains and losses would be carried as a component of stockholders' equity in the balance sheet.

Accounts Receivable

Accounts receivable are customer balances outstanding on credit sales and are reported on the balance sheet at their net realizable value, that is, the actual amount of the account less an *allowance for doubtful accounts*. Management must estimate — based on such factors as past experience, knowledge of customer quality, the state of the economy, the firm's collection policies — the dollar amount of accounts they expect will be uncollectible during an accounting period. Actual losses are written off against the allowance account, which is adjusted at the end of each accounting period.

The allowance for doubtful accounts can be important in assessing earnings quality. If, for instance, a company expands sales by lowering its credit standards, there should be a corresponding percentage increase in the allowance account. The estimation of this account will affect both the valuation of accounts receivable on the balance sheet and the recognition of bad debt expense on the income statement. The analyst should be alert to changes in the allowance account — both relative to the level of sales and the amount of accounts receivable outstanding — and to the justification for any variations from past practices.

The allowance account for R.E.C. Inc. represents approximately 5% of total customer accounts receivable. To obtain the exact percentage figure, the amount of the allowance account must be added to the net accounts receivable balance shown on the face of the statement:

	2007		2006	
Allowance for doubtful accounts	448	$= 4.8\%$	417	$= 4.8\%$
Accounts receivable (net) + Allowance	$8{,}960 + 448$		$8{,}350 + 417$	

The allowance account, which is deducted from the balance sheet accounts receivable account, should reflect the volume of credit sales, the firm's past experience with customers, the customer base, the firm's credit policies, the firm's collection practices, economic conditions, and changes in any of these. There should be a consistent relationship between the rate of change or growth rates in sales, accounts receivable, and the allowance for doubtful accounts. If the amounts are changing at significantly different rates or in different directions, for example, if sales and accounts receivable are increasing, but the allowance account is decreasing or is increasing at a much smaller rate, the analyst should be alert to the potential for manipulation using the allowance account. Of course, there could be a plausible reason for such a change.

The relevant items needed to relate sales growth with accounts receivable and the allowance for doubtful accounts are found on the income statement (sales) and balance sheet (accounts receivable and allowance for doubtful accounts). The following information is from the income statement and balance sheet of R.E.C. Inc.

(In Thousands)	2007	2006	Growth Rate* (% Change)
Net sales	$215,600	$153,000	40.9
Accounts receivable (total)	9,408	8,767	7.3
Allowance for doubtful accounts	448	417	7.4

*Growth rates are calculated using the following formula: $\dfrac{\text{Current amount} - \text{Prior Amount}}{\text{Prior Amount}}$

To analyze the preceding information consider the following:

- The relationship among changes in sales, accounts receivable, and the allowance for doubtful accounts—are all three accounts changing in the same directions and at consistent rates of change?
- If the direction and rates of change are not consistent, what are possible explanations for these differences?
- If there is not a normal relationship between the growth rates, what are possible reasons for the abnormal pattern?

For R.E.C. Inc., sales, accounts receivable, and the allowance for doubtful accounts have all increased, but sales have grown at a much greater rate. The percentage increase in accounts receivable and the allowance account seems lower than expected relative to the change in sales. This relationship is probably a positive one for R.E.C. because it means that the company has collected more sales in cash and thus will have potentially fewer defaults. The allowance account has increased appropriately in relation to accounts receivable, 7.4% and 7.3% respectively; the allowance account, relative to accounts receivable, is constant at 4.8% in both years. Had the allowance account decreased there would be concern that management may be manipulating the numbers in order to increase the earnings number.

Additional information helpful to the analysis of accounts receivable and the allowance account is provided in the schedule of "Valuation and Qualifying Accounts" required by the SEC in the Form 10-K. Companies sometimes include this schedule in the notes to the financial statements, but usually it is found under Item 15 of the Form 10-K. R.E.C. Inc.'s schedule from the Form 10-K is shown here:

R.E.C. Inc.
Schedule II—Valuation and Qualifying Accounts
December 31, 2007, 2006, and 2005
(in Thousands)

	Balance at Beginning of Year	Additions Charged to Costs and Expenses	Deductions	Balance at End of Year
Allowance for doubtful accounts				
2007	$417	$271	$240	$448
2006	$400	$217	$200	$417
2005	$391	$259	$250	$400

The column labeled "Additions Charged to Costs and Expenses" is the amount R.E.C. Inc. has estimated and recorded as bad debt expense each year on the income statement. The "Deductions" column represents the actual amount that the firm has written off as accounts receivable they no longer expect to recover from customers. Since the expense is estimated each year this amount also includes corrections of prior years' over- or under-estimations. The analyst should use this schedule to assess the probability that the firm is intentionally over- or under-estimating the allowance account in order to manipulate the net earnings number on the income statement. R.E.C. Inc. appears to estimate an expense fairly close to the actual amount written off each year, although the firm has estimated slightly more expense than has actually been incurred. Further analysis of accounts receivable and its quality is covered in Chapters 5 and 6.

Inventories

Inventories are items held for sale or used in the manufacture of products that will be sold. A retail company, such as R.E.C. Inc., lists only one type of inventory on the balance sheet: merchandise inventories purchased for resale to the public. A manufacturing firm, in contrast, would carry three different types of inventories: raw materials or supplies, work-in-process, and finished goods. For most firms, inventories are the firm's major revenue producer. Exceptions would be service-oriented companies that carry little or no inventory. Exhibit 2.4 illustrates the proportion of inventories at the manufacturing, wholesale, and retail levels. For these industries—drugs, household furniture, and sporting goods—the percentage of inventories to total assets ranges from 21.2% to 38.8% at the manufacturing stage to 37.4% to 60.0% for retail firms. The common-size balance sheet (Exhibit 2.2) for R.E.C. Inc. reveals that inventories comprise 49.4% and 48.4% of total assets, respectively, in 2007 and 2006. As mentioned previously, from 2003 to 2007, cash and marketable securities have decreased by approximately 10%. Inventories have increased by almost 10% in this same time frame, indicating a shift in asset structure. Most likely, R.E.C. Inc. has chosen to spend cash to expand. As new stores are opened, they must be stocked with inventory.

EXHIBIT 2.4

Inventories as a Percentage of Total Assets	%
Manufacturing	
Pharmaceutical preparations	21.2
Household furniture	37.4
Sporting and athletic goods	38.8
Wholesale	
Drugs	32.5
Furniture	30.2
Sporting and recreational goods	44.4
Retail	
Drug stores	37.4
Furniture stores	50.4
Sporting goods stores	60.0

Source: The Risk Management Association, *Annual Statement Studies*, Philadelphia, PA, 2004.

Given the relative magnitude of inventory, the accounting method chosen to value inventory and the associated measurement of cost of goods sold have a considerable impact on a company's financial position and operating results. Understanding the fundamentals of inventory accounting and the effect various methods have on a company's financial statements is essential to the user of financial statement information.

Inventory Accounting Methods

The method chosen by a company to account for inventory determines the value of inventory on the balance sheet and the amount of expense recognized for cost of goods sold on the income statement. The significance of inventory accounting is underlined by the presence of inflation and by the implications for tax payments and cash flow. Inventory valuation is based on an *assumption* regarding the flow of goods and has nothing whatever to do with the *actual* order in which products are sold. The cost flow assumption is made in order to *match* the cost of products sold during an accounting period to the revenue generated from the sales and to assign a dollar value to the inventory remaining for sale at the end of the accounting period.

The three cost flow assumptions most frequently used by U.S. companies are *FIFO* (first in, first out), *LIFO* (last in, first out), and *average cost*. As the terms imply, the FIFO method assumes the first units purchased are the first units sold during an accounting period; LIFO assumes that the items bought last are sold first; and the average cost method uses an average purchase price to determine the cost of products sold. A simple example should highlight the differences in the three methods. A new company in its first year of operations purchases five products for sale in the order and at the prices shown:

Item	Purchase Price
#1	$ 5
#2	$ 7
#3	$ 8
#4	$ 9
#5	$11

The company sells three of these items, all at the end of the year. The cost flow assumptions would be:

Accounting Method	Goods Sold	Goods Remaining in Inventory
FIFO	#1, #2, #3	#4, #5
LIFO	#5, #4, #3	#2, #1
Average cost	[Total cost/5] × 3	[Total cost/5] × 2

The resulting effect on the income statement and balance sheet would be:

Accounting Method	Cost of Goods Sold (Income Statement)	Inventory Valuation (Balance Sheet)
FIFO	$20	$20
LIFO	$28	$12
Average cost	$24	$16

It can be clearly seen that during a period of inflation, with product prices increasing, the LIFO method produces the highest cost of goods sold expense ($28) and the lowest ending valuation of inventory ($12). Further, cost of goods sold under the LIFO method most closely approximates the current cost of inventory items since they are the most recent purchases. On the other hand, inventories on the balance sheet are undervalued with respect to replacement cost because they reflect the older costs when prices were lower. If a firm uses LIFO to value inventory, no restatement is required to adjust cost of goods sold for inflation because LIFO matches current costs to current sales. Inventory on the balance sheet, however, would have to be revalued upward to account for inflation. FIFO has the opposite effect; during a period of rising prices, balance sheet inventory is valued at current cost, but cost of goods sold on the income statement is understated.

In an annual survey of accounting practices followed by 600 industrial and merchandising corporations in the United States in the early 1970s, 146 companies surveyed reported using LIFO to account for all or part of inventory. By the 1990s, this number had increased to 326 but then fell to 251 by 2003.[2] Why did so many companies switch to LIFO in the 1990s? The answer is taxes.

Referring back to the example, note that when prices are rising (inflation), LIFO produces the largest cost of goods sold expense. The greater the expense deduction, the lower is taxable income. Use of LIFO thus reduces a company's tax bill during inflation. Unlike the case for some accounting rules—where a firm is allowed to use one method for tax and another method for reporting purposes—a company that elects LIFO to figure taxable income must also use LIFO for reported income. The many companies that have switched to LIFO from other methods are apparently willing to trade lower reported earnings for the positive cash benefits resulting from LIFO's beneficial tax effect. The evidence, however, is that the trend toward LIFO is reversing and that the number of firms electing FIFO is gradually increasing. Reasons could include both a lower inflation rate and the desire to report higher accounting earnings.

In the earlier example, LIFO produced lower earnings than FIFO or average cost, but there can be exceptions. Obviously, in a *period of falling prices* (deflation) the results would reverse. Also, some firms experience price movements that are counter to the general trend—the high-technology industry, where prices on many products have declined, is a case in point.[3]

Because the inventory cost flow assumption has a significant impact on financial statements—the amount of inventory reported on the balance sheet and the cost of goods sold expense in the income statement—it is important to know where to find its disclosure (see Figure 2.1). The method used to value inventory will generally be shown in the note to the financial statements relating to inventory. R.E.C. Inc. has the following explanation in Note A: Inventories are carried at the lower of cost (LIFO) or market. This statement indicates that the LIFO method is used to determine cost. The fact that inventories are valued at the lower of cost or market reflects the accounting convention of conservatism. If the actual market value of inventory falls below cost, as determined by the cost flow assumption (LIFO for R.E.C. Inc.), then inventory will be

---

[2]*Accounting Trends and Techniques*, American Institute of Certified Public Accountants, 1971, 1998, 2004.
[3]Another exception that causes higher earnings when using LIFO during inflationary periods is a base LIFO layer liquidation. This occurs when a firm sells more goods than purchased or manufactured during an accounting period, resulting in the least expensive items being charged to cost of goods sold. To avoid the LIFO liquidation problem, some firms use the dollar-value LIFO method, which is applied to goods in designated pools and measures inventory changes in cost dollars—using a price index—rather than physical units.

FIGURE 2.1   Inventory Methods

Accounting Method	Cost of Goods Sold (Income Statement)	Inventory Valuation (Balance Sheet)
FIFO	First purchases	Last purchases (close to current cost)
LIFO	Last purchases (close to current cost)	First purchases
Average Cost	Average of all purchases	Average of all purchases

written down to market price. Notice that the phrase is "lower" of cost or market. The carrying value of inventory would never be written up to market value—only down.

The inventory note for R.E.C. Inc. also provides information regarding the value of inventory had FIFO been used, since the FIFO valuation would be higher than that recorded on the balance sheet and more closely approximates current value: "If the first in, first out (FIFO) method of inventory accounting had been used, inventories would have been approximately $2,681,000 and $2,096,000 higher than reported at December 31, 2007 and 2006."

Prepaid Expenses

Certain expenses, such as insurance, rent, property taxes, and utilities, are sometimes paid in advance. They are included in current assets if they will expire within one year or one operating cycle, whichever is longer. Generally, prepayments are not material to the balance sheet as a whole. For R.E.C. Inc., prepaid expenses represent less than 1% of total current assets in 2007.

Property, Plant, and Equipment

This category encompasses a company's fixed assets (also called *tangible, long-lived*, and *capital* assets)—those assets not used up in the ebb and flow of annual business operations. These assets produce economic benefits for more than one year, and they are considered "tangible" because they have a physical substance. Fixed assets other than land (which has a theoretically unlimited life span) are "depreciated" over the period of time they benefit the firm. The process of depreciation is a method of allocating the cost of long-lived assets. The original cost, less any estimated residual value at the end of the asset's life, is spread over the expected life of the asset. Cost is also considered to encompass any expenditures made to ready the asset for operating use. On any balance sheet date, property, plant, and equipment is shown at book value, which is the difference between original cost and any accumulated depreciation to date.

Management has considerable discretion with respect to fixed assets, as was explained in Chapter 1. Depreciation involves estimates of the economic life of the asset and any salvage value expected to be recoverable at the end of this life. Further, the amount of depreciation expense recognized each period is determined by the depreciation method chosen. Although the total amount of depreciation over the asset's life is the same regardless of method, the rate of depreciation varies. The straight-line method spreads the expense evenly by periods, and the accelerated methods yield higher depreciation expense in the early years of an asset's useful life, and lower depreciation expense in the later years. Another depreciation choice is the units-of-production method, which bases depreciation expense for a given period on actual use. According to *Accounting Trends and Techniques*, the vast majority of companies use the straight-line method for financial reporting:[4]

Straight line	580
Accelerated	68
Units of production	30

Refer now to the property, plant, and equipment section of the R.E.C. Inc. balance sheet. First note that there are three categories listed separately: land, buildings and leasehold improvements, and equipment. *Land*, as designated in the fixed asset section, refers to property used in the business; this would be land on which there are corporate offices and retail stores. Any land held for investment purposes would be segregated from property used in the business. (For R.E.C. Inc., see the "Other Assets" section.)

R.E.C. Inc. owns some of its retail outlets, and others are leased. *Buildings* would include those stores owned by the company as well as its corporate offices. *Leasehold improvements* are additions or improvements made to leased structures. Because leasehold improvements revert to the property owner when the lease term expires, they are amortized by the lessee over the economic life of the improvement or the life of the lease, whichever is shorter.[5]

Some companies may also have an account called *construction in progress*. These are the costs of constructing new buildings that are not yet complete. R.E.C. Inc. does not include this account on their balance sheet.

Equipment represents the original cost, including delivery and installation charges, of the machinery and equipment used in business operations. Included are a variety of items such as the centralized computer system; equipment and furnishings for offices, stores, and warehouses; and delivery trucks. The final two lines under the property, plant, and equipment section for R.E.C. Inc. show the amount of accumulated depreciation and amortization (for all items except land) and the amount of net property, plant, and equipment after the deduction of accumulated depreciation and amortization.

The relative proportion of fixed assets in a company's asset structure will largely be determined by the nature of the business. A firm that manufactures products would likely be more heavily invested in capital equipment than a retailer or wholesaler. Exhibit 2.5 shows the relative percentage of net fixed assets to total assets for the same three industries identified in Exhibit 2.4. Realize, however, that firms with newly purchased fixed assets will have a higher percentage than firms with older, and hence, lower net fixed asset numbers.

---

[4]*Accounting Trends and Techniques*, American Institute of Certified Public Accountants, 2004.
[5]*Amortization* is the term used to designate the cost allocation process for assets other than buildings, machinery, and equipment—such as leasehold improvements and intangible assets, discussed later in the chapter.

EXHIBIT 2.5

Net Fixed Assets as a Percent of Total Assets	%
Manufacturing	
Pharmaceutical preparations	22.8
Household furniture	20.5
Sporting and athletic goods	15.5
Wholesale	
Drugs	10.6
Furniture	13.1
Sporting and recreational goods	10.5
Retail	
Drug stores	13.8
Furniture stores	18.4
Sporting goods stores	15.8

Source: The Risk Management Association, *Annual Statement Studies*, Philadelphia, PA, 2004.

Fixed assets are most prominent at the manufacturing level; retailers are next, probably because retailers require stores and buildings in which to sell products; and the wholesale segment requires the least investment in fixed assets.

For R.E.C. Inc., net fixed assets have increased in proportion to total assets between 2006 and 2007 from 25.0% to 30.5% as can be seen on the common-size balance sheet (Exhibit 2.2). Chapter 6 covers the financial ratios used to measure the efficiency of managing these assets.

Other Assets

Other assets on a firm's balance sheet can include a multitude of other noncurrent items such as property held for sale, start-up costs in connection with a new business, the cash surrender value of life insurance policies, and long-term advance payments. For R.E.C. Inc., other assets represent minor holdings of property not used in business operations (as explained in Note A to the financial statements).

Additional categories of noncurrent assets frequently encountered (but not present for R.E.C. Inc.) are long-term investments[6] and intangible assets, such as goodwill recognized in business combinations, patents, trademarks, copyrights, brand names, and franchises. Of the intangible assets, *goodwill* is the most important for analytical purposes because of its potential materiality on the balance sheet of firms heavily involved in acquisitions activity. Goodwill arises when one company acquires another company (in a business combination accounted for as a purchase) for a price in excess of the fair market value of the net identifiable assets (identifiable assets less liabilities assumed) acquired.

---

[6]Reporting requirements for investments in debt and equity securities must follow the provisions of FASB Statement No. 115, presented earlier in the chapter. A more extensive discussion of investments in unconsolidated subsidiaries is provided in Chapter 3. As noted earlier in the chapter, FASB Statement No. 115 does not apply to investments in consolidated subsidiaries nor to investments in equity securities accounted for by the equity method.

This excess price is recorded on the books of the acquiring company as goodwill. Prior to the issuance of FASB Statement No. 142, "Goodwill and Other Intangible Assets," there were two methods of accounting for acquisitions: pooling (financial statements combined and no goodwill recognized) and purchase (creation of goodwill for amount in excess of net identifiable assets). As of January 1, 2002, the FASB eliminated the pooling method entirely, and goodwill under the purchase method will no longer be amortized. Beginning in 2002, companies evaluated goodwill and determined whether it had lost value. If it had, the amount of impairment was expensed in the year the determination was made. No write-up is recorded for gains. What that means is that some corporations will take enormous write-offs when companies they have acquired have lost value. As implementation of this new rule takes place, earnings may increase for some firms relative to prior years because amortization expense will no longer be recorded—the increased earnings reflect a "paper" increase due to the FASB rule change. Companies will also have some discretion in deciding when and how much write-off to take as a result of goodwill impairment.

In a study of the 1,000 largest U.S. companies conducted by *BusinessWeek* and Standard & Poor's in 2001, it was estimated that dozens of companies would have multimillion-dollar goodwill write-offs.[7] Qwest, for example, announced that its 2002 write-off would be $30 to $40 billion, arising largely from the acquisition of U.S. West. On the plus side, firms will not have to deduct amortization expense each year, which will increase earnings for many companies. Kodak estimated that in 2002, the year the rule becomes effective, not having to deduct amortization expense will boost earnings by 45 cents per share.

Liabilities

Current Liabilities

Liabilities represent claims against assets, and current liabilities are those that must be satisfied in one year or one operating cycle, whichever is longer. Current liabilities include accounts and notes payable, the current portion of long-term debt, accrued liabilities, unearned revenue, and deferred taxes.

Accounts Payable

Accounts payable are short-term obligations that arise from credit extended by suppliers for the purchase of goods and services. For example, when R.E.C. Inc. buys inventory on credit from a wholesaler for eventual sale to its own customers, the transaction creates an account payable.

This account is eliminated when the bill is satisfied. The ongoing process of operating a business results in the spontaneous generation of accounts payable, which increase and decrease depending on the credit policies available to the firm from its suppliers, economic conditions, and the cyclical nature of the firm's own business operations. Note that R.E.C. Inc. has almost doubled the amount of accounts payable between 2006 and 2007 (Exhibit 2.6). Part of the balance sheet analysis should include an exploration of

---

[7]Peter Elstrom, David Henry, David Welsh, and Stephanie Anderson, "Today, Nortel. Tomorrow . . . ," *BusinessWeek*, July 2, 2001, pp. 32–35.

EXHIBIT 2.6   R.E.C. Inc. Consolidated Balance Sheets at December 31, 2007 and 2006 (in Thousands)

	2007	2006
Liabilities and Stockholders' Equity		
Current Liabilities		
Accounts payable	$14,294	$ 7,591
Notes payable — banks (Note B)	5,614	6,012
Current maturities of long-term debt (Note C)	1,884	1,516
Accrued liabilities	5,669	5,313
Total current liabilities	27,461	20,432
Deferred Federal Income Taxes (Notes A and D)	843	635
Long-term debt (Note C)	21,059	16,975
Commitments (Note E)		
Total liabilities	49,363	38,042
Stockholders' Equity		
Common stock, par value $1, authorized, 10,000,000 shares; issued, 4,803,000 shares in 2007 and 4,594,000 shares in 2006 (Note F)	4,803	4,594
Additional paid-in capital	957	910
Retained earnings	40,175	32,363
Total stockholders' equity	45,935	37,867
Total Liabilities and Stockholders' Equity	$95,298	$75,909

The accompanying notes are an integral part of these statements.

the causes for this increase. To jump briefly ahead, the reader might also note that the income statement reveals a significant sales increase in 2007. Perhaps the increase in accounts payable is at least partially explained by this sales growth.

Notes Payable

Notes payable are short-term obligations in the form of promissory notes to suppliers or financial institutions. For R.E.C. Inc. these notes (explained in Note B to the financial statements) are payable to a bank and reflect the amount extended under a line of credit. A line of credit permits borrowing from a financial institution up to a maximum amount. The total amount that can be borrowed under R.E.C. Inc.'s line of credit is $10 million, of which about half ($5,614,000) was outstanding debt at the end of 2007.

Current Maturities of Long-Term Debt

When a firm has bonds, mortgages, or other forms of long-term debt outstanding, the portion of the principal that will be repaid during the upcoming year is classified as a current liability. The currently maturing debt for R.E.C. Inc. occurs as the result of several long-term obligations, described in Note C to the financial statements. The note lists the amount of long-term debt outstanding, less the portion due currently, and also provides the schedule of current maturities for the next five years.

Accrued Liabilities

Like most large corporations, R.E.C. Inc. uses the accrual rather than the cash basis of accounting: Revenue is recognized when it is earned, and expenses are recorded when they are incurred, regardless of when the cash is received or paid. Accrued liabilities result from the recognition of an expense in the accounting records prior to the actual payment of cash. Thus, they are liabilities because there will be an eventual cash outflow to satisfy the obligations.

Assume that a company has a $100,000 note outstanding, with 12% annual interest due in semiannual installments on March 31 and September 30. For a balance sheet prepared on December 31, interest will be accrued for three months (October, November, and December):

$$\$100,000 \times .12 = \$12,000 \text{ annual interest}$$
$$\$12,000/12 = \$1,000 \text{ monthly interest}$$
$$\$1,000 \times 3 = \$3,000 \text{ accrued interest for three months}$$

The December 31 balance sheet would include an accrued liability of $3,000. Accruals also arise from salaries, rent, insurance, taxes, and other expenses.

Reserve accounts are often set up for the purpose of estimating obligations for items such as warranty costs, sales returns, or restructuring charges, and are recorded as accrued liabilities. Generally, the only way to determine if a company has set up a reserve account is to read the notes to the financial statements carefully. Prior to 2003, many firms appeared to be abusing the use of reserve accounts for restructuring charges. By overestimating the reserve and recording all potential restructuring costs in the period when the decision to restructure was made, companies could later reverse the charge, thus giving a boost to the net earnings number. The SEC's concern regarding this possible abuse resulted in the FASB requiring firms to implement Statement of Financial Accounting Standard No. 146, "Accounting for Costs Associated with Exit or Disposal Activities" effective January 1, 2003. This standard prohibits companies from recognizing a liability for a cost associated with an exit or disposal activity unless and until a liability has actually been incurred. Reserve accounts are also set up to record declines in asset values and the allowance for doubtful accounts explained earlier in the chapter is an example.

Unearned Revenue or Deferred Credits

Companies that are paid in advance for services or products record a liability upon the receipt of cash. The liability account is referred to as *unearned revenue* or *deferred credits*. The amounts in this account will be transferred to a revenue account when the service is performed or the product delivered as required by the matching concept of accounting. R.E.C. Inc. does not have unearned revenue because it is a retail company that does not generally receive payment in advance of selling its products. However, companies in high-technology, publishing, or manufacturing industries are apt to have unearned revenue accounts on their balance sheets. For example, Intel Corporation shows $592 million on its 2004 balance sheet for "Deferred income on shipments to distributors." In the footnotes to the financial statements, this account is explained as follows under the heading "Revenue recognition": "The company recognizes net revenues when the earnings process is complete, as evidenced by an agreement with the customer, transfer of title and acceptance if applicable, as well as fixed pricing and probable collectibility. Because of frequent sales price reductions and rapid technology obsolescence in the industry, sales made to distributors under agreements allowing price protection and/or right of return are deferred until the distributors sell the merchandise."[8]

Deferred Federal Income Taxes

Deferred taxes are the result of temporary differences in the recognition of revenue and expense for taxable income relative to reported income. The accounting principles for recording and reporting deferred taxes are specified in Statement of Financial Accounting Standards No. 109, "Accounting for Income Taxes," which superseded Statement of Financial Accounting Standards No. 96 and is effective for fiscal years beginning after December 15, 1992. Most large companies use one set of rules for calculating income tax expense, paid to the IRS, and another set for figuring income reported in the financial statements. The objective is to take advantage of all available tax deferrals in order to reduce actual tax payments, while showing the highest possible amount of reported net income. There are many areas in which firms are permitted to use different procedures for tax and reporting purposes. One such example, based on depreciation methods, was discussed in Chapter 1. Most firms use an accelerated method (the Modified Accelerated Cost Recovery System) to figure taxable income and the straight-line method for reporting purposes. The effect is to recognize more depreciation expense in the early years of an asset's useful life for tax calculations.

Although depreciation methods are the most common source, other temporary differences arise from the methods used to account for installment sales, long-term contracts, leases, warranties and service contracts, pensions and other employee benefits, and subsidiary investment earnings. They are called *temporary differences* (or timing differences) because, in theory, the total amount of expense and revenue recognized will eventually be the same for tax and reporting purposes. There are also *permanent differences* in income tax accounting. Municipal bond revenue, for example, is recognized as income for reporting purposes but not for tax purposes; life insurance premiums on officers are recognized as expense for financial reporting purposes but are not deductible for income tax purposes. These permanent differences do not affect deferred taxes because a tax will never be paid on the income or the expense will never be deducted on the tax return.

The deferred tax account reconciles the temporary differences in expense and revenue recognition for any accounting period. Under FASB Statement No. 109,[9] business firms recognize deferred tax liabilities for all temporary differences when the item causes financial income to exceed taxable income with an expectation that the

---

[8]Intel, 2004 Annual Report, p. 54.
[9]For more reading about FASB Statement No. 109, its application and implementation, see W. J. Read and A. J. Bartsch, "Accounting for Deferred Taxes Under FASB 109"; and G. J. Gregory, T. R. Petree, and R. J. Vitray, "FASB 109: Planning for Implementation and Beyond," *Journal of Accountancy,* December 1992.

difference will be offset in future accounting periods. Deferred tax assets are reported for deductible temporary differences and operating loss and tax credit carryforwards. A deductible temporary difference is one that causes taxable income to exceed financial income, with the expectation that the difference will be offset in the future. Measurement of tax liabilities and assets is based on provisions of the enacted tax law; effects of future anticipated changes in tax law are not considered. A *valuation allowance* is used to reduce deferred tax assets to expected realizable amounts when it is determined that it is more likely than not that some of the deferred tax assets will not be realized.

To illustrate the accounting for deferred taxes, assume that a company has a total annual revenue of $500,000; expenses other than depreciation are $250,000; and depreciation expense is $100,000 for tax accounting and $50,000 for financial reporting (eventually this difference would reverse and the reported depreciation expense in later years would be greater than the tax depreciation expense). The income for tax and reporting purposes would be computed two ways, assuming a 34% tax rate:

	Tax	Reporting
Revenue	$500,000	$500,000
Expenses	(350,000)	(300,000)
Earnings before tax	$150,000	$200,000
Tax expense ($\times$ .34)	(51,000)	(68,000)
Net income	$ 99,000	$132,000

Taxes actually paid ($51,000) are less than the tax expense ($68,000) reported in the financial statements. To reconcile the $17,000 difference between the expense recorded and the cash outflow, there is a deferred tax liability of $17,000:

Reported tax expense	$68,000
Cash paid for taxes	51,000
Deferred tax liability	$17,000

For an additional example of deferred taxes, including the ultimate reversal of the temporary difference, see Figure 2.2.

Deferred taxes are classified as current or noncurrent on the balance sheet, corresponding to the classification of related assets and liabilities underlying the temporary difference. For example, a deferred tax asset arising from accounting for 90-day warranties would be considered current. On the other hand, a temporary difference based on five-year warranties would be noncurrent; depreciation accounting would also result in a noncurrent deferred tax because of the noncurrent classification of the underlying plant and equipment account. A deferred tax asset or liability that is not related to an asset or liability for financial reporting, including deferred tax assets related to carryforwards, is classified according to anticipated reversal or benefit. At the end of the accounting period, the firm will report one net current amount and one net noncurrent amount unless the liabilities and assets are attributable to different tax-paying components of the enterprise or to different tax jurisdictions. Thus, the deferred tax account can conceivably appear on the balance sheet as a current asset, current liability, noncurrent asset, or noncurrent liability.

FIGURE 2.2   Deferred Taxes—An Example

A company purchases a piece of equipment for $30,000. The equipment is expected to last three years and have no salvage value at the end of the three-year period. Straight-line depreciation is used for financial reporting purposes and an accelerated method is used for tax purposes. The following table shows the amounts of depreciation that would be recorded for both sets of books over the three-year life of the equipment:

Year	Depreciation expense (Financial reporting)	Depreciation expense (Tax reporting)
1	$10,000	$20,000
2	$10,000	$ 6,667
3	$10,000	$ 3,333

Assume that revenues are $90,000 and all expenses other than depreciation are $20,000 each year, the tax rate is 30%, and depreciation is the only temporary difference that creates the deferred tax account. Calculations to determine tax expense for reporting purposes and tax paid are below:

Year 1	Income Statement		Tax Return
Revenues	$90,000		$90,000
Expenses:			
Depreciation	(10,000)		(20,000)
Other	(20,000)		(20,000)
Earnings before taxes	$60,000	Taxable income	$50,000
Tax rate	× 0.30		× 0.30
Tax expense	$18,000		$15,000

The recording of taxes at the end of year 1 will involve a decrease in the cash account of $15,000, an increase in tax expense of $18,000, and an increase in the deferred tax liability account of the difference, $3,000.

Year 2	Income Statement		Tax Return
Revenues	$90,000		$90,000
Expenses:			
Depreciation	(10,000)		(6,667)
Other	(20,000)		(20,000)
Earnings before taxes	$60,000	Taxable income	$63,333
Tax rate	× 0.30		× 0.30
Tax expense	$18,000		$19,000

The recording of taxes at the end of year 2 will involve a decrease in the cash account of $19,000, an increase in tax expense of $18,000, and a decrease in the deferred tax liability account of the difference, $1,000. The deferred tax liability account will now have a balance of $2,000 at the end of year 2.

Year 3	Income Statement		Tax Return
Revenues	$90,000		$90,000
Expenses:			
Depreciation	(10,000)		(3,333)
Other	(20,000)		(20,000)
Earnings before taxes	$60,000	Taxable income	$66,667
Tax rate	× 0.30		× 0.30
Tax expense	$18,000		$20,000

The recording of taxes at the end of year 3 will involve a decrease in the cash account of $20,000, an increase in tax expense of $18,000, and a decrease in the deferred tax liability account of the difference, $2,000. The deferred tax liability account will now have a balance of $0 at the end of year 3, as the temporary difference has completely reversed.

Notice that the total amount of income tax expense ($54,000) recorded for reporting purposes is exactly equal to the tax paid ($54,000) over the three-year period.

R.E.C. Inc. reports deferred federal income taxes as a noncurrent liability. The temporary differences are based on depreciation methods and long-term installment sales.

An illustration of the disclosures related to deferred income taxes follows. Exhibit 2.7 shows an excerpt from Reader's Digest, 2004 footnote on income taxes. The seven temporary differences that have created the net deferred tax asset are listed at the top of the exhibit. Five items have resulted in deferred tax liabilities. This means that Reader's Digest has taken greater deductions on their tax return for these items than was recorded on their income statement. The deferred tax assets indicate the company has deducted more items on the income statement compared to the deductions taken on the tax return. The overall net deferred tax asset of $55.5 indicates that in the future, Reader's Digest should pay $55.5 less in taxes when these temporary differences reverse. The main reason for the net deferred tax asset is the "Accounts receivable and other allowances". The company has recorded expenses such as bad debt estimates, but is not allowed to deduct these expenses for tax purposes until the amounts are actually written off. The valuation allowance of $12.2 is the amount that Reader's Digest projects will not be realized in the future. Notice that Reader's Digest recognizes deferred tax items in four classifications on the balance sheet: current assets, noncurrent assets, current liabilities, and noncurrent liabilities.

EXHIBIT 2.7 Income Taxes—Reader's Digest

Components of deferred tax assets and liabilities are as follows:

In Millions	2004	2003
Deferred compensation and other employee benefits	$ 9.0	$ 21.9
Accounts receivable and other allowances	42.8	42.0
Net operating loss carryforwards	22.2	15.2
Other operating items, net	8.2	12.3
Tax credit carryforwards	29.8	27.3
Other accrued items	15.4	15.9
Other, net	4.3	5.0
Gross Deferred Tax Assets	131.7	139.6
Valuation allowance	(12.2)	(6.9)
Total Net Assets	119.5	132.7
Deferred compensation and other employee benefits	8.5	7.6
Deferred promotion	12.3	20.5
Depreciation and amortization	14.5	6.0
Deferred agency commissions	19.1	19.2
Other, net	9.6	12.8
Total Net Liabilities	64.0	66.1
Net Deferred Taxes	$ 55.5	$ 66.6

Balance sheet classifications of deferred tax assets and liabilities are as follows:

	2004	2003
Prepaid expenses and other current assets	$ 38.7	$ 44.4
Other noncurrent assets	38.7	64.4
Other current liabilities	(5.3)	(14.8)
Other noncurrent liabilities	(16.6)	(27.4)
Net Deferred Taxes	$ 55.5	$ 66.6

Long-Term Debt

Obligations with maturities beyond one year are designated on the balance sheet as noncurrent liabilities. This category can include bonded indebtedness, long-term notes payable, mortgages, obligations under leases, pension liabilities, and long-term warranties. In Note C to the financial statements, R.E.C. Inc. specifies the nature, maturity, and interest rate of each long-term obligation. Even though long-term debt increased by over $4,000 from 2006 to 2007, notice that on the common-size balance sheet (Exhibit 2.2), the percentage of long-term debt relative to total assets has declined. This has been caused by the much larger increase in accounts payable.

Capital Lease Obligations

A commonly used type of leasing arrangement is a capital lease. Capital leases are, in substance, a "purchase" rather than a "lease." If a lease contract meets any one of four criteria—transfers ownership to the lessee, contains a bargain purchase option, has a lease term of 75% or more of the leased property's economic life, or has minimum lease payments with a present value of 90% or more of the property's fair value—the lease must be capitalized by the lessee according to the requirements of FASB Statement No. 13, "Accounting for Leases." Leases not meeting one of the four criteria are treated as operating leases, discussed under commitments and contingencies later in the chapter. R.E.C. Inc. uses only operating leases.

   Both the balance sheet and the income statement are affected by a capital lease. An asset and a liability are recorded on the lessee's balance sheet equal to the present value of the lease payments to be made under the contract. The asset account reflects what is, in essence, the purchase of an asset; and the liability is the obligation incurred in financing the purchase. Each lease payment is apportioned partly to reduce the outstanding liability and partly to interest expense. The asset account is amortized with amortization expense recognized on the income statement, just as a purchased asset would be depreciated. Disclosures about capital leases can be found in the notes to the financial statements, often under both the property, plant, and equipment note and the commitments and contingencies note.

Postretirement Benefits Other Than Pensions

Other liability accounts (not present for R.E.C. Inc.), such as pension and postretirement benefit obligations, can appear under the liability section of the balance sheet.[10] Statement of Financial Accounting Standards No. 106, "Employers' Accounting for Postretirement Benefits Other Than Pensions," adopted by the FASB in 1990, has had a significant impact on many corporate balance sheets. This statement requires companies to disclose as a balance sheet liability the obligation for paying medical bills of retired employees and spouses—in accordance with the accrual method of accounting—by accruing promised future benefits as a form of deferred compensation. Most companies previously deducted medical expenses in the year paid. This accounting rule also impacts profitability for many firms by substantially increasing the recognition of annual postretirement benefit expense. Statement of Financial Accounting Standards

---

[10]The disclosures relating to pension obligations are discussed in Chapter 5.

No. 112, "Employers' Accounting for Postemployment Benefits," established accounting standards for benefits provided to former or inactive employees, their dependents, and beneficiaries and is effective for fiscal years beginning after December 15, 1993.

Commitments and Contingencies

Many companies will list an account titled "Commitments and Contingencies" on the balance sheet even though no dollar amount will appear. This disclosure is intended to draw attention to the fact that required disclosures can be found in the notes to the financial statements. *Commitments* refer to contractual agreements that will have a significant financial impact on the company in the future. R.E.C. Inc. reports commitments in Note E that describe the company's operating leases.

If the leasing contract does not meet one of the four criteria required to record the lease as a capital lease, the lessee will record "rent expense" on the income statement and a corresponding reduction to cash. Operating leases are a form of *off-balance-sheet financing*. In fact, the lessee is contractually obligated to make lease payments, but is not required by generally accepted accounting principles (GAAP) to record this obligation as a debt on the balance sheet. Companies could purposely negotiate a lease as an operating lease so that the long-term commitment does not have to be shown on the balance sheet; however, astute users of financial statements will know to look at the notes to the financial statements to determine any commitment the company may have with regard to operating leases. For R.E.C. Inc., Note E indicates that the company will be required to make lease payments in the amount of $176,019,000 in the future.

Many firms use complicated financing schemes—product financing arrangements, sales of receivables with recourse, limited partnerships, joint ventures—that do not have to be recorded on balance sheets. Disclosures about the extent, nature, and terms of off-balance sheet financing arrangements are in the notes to the financial statements, but they may be very complex and difficult to understand, and require putting pieces together from several different sections.

Contingencies refer to potential liabilities of the firm such as possible damage awards assessed in lawsuits. Generally, the firm cannot reasonably predict the outcome and/or the amount of the future liability; however, information about the contingency must be disclosed in the notes to the financial statements.

Hybrid Securities

Some companies have *mandatorily redeemable preferred stock* outstanding. R.E.C. Inc. does not issue these securities, but they are explained here because they have the characteristics of both debt and equity. The financial instrument is called *preferred stock* (see discussion in the stockholders' equity section), but the issuing company must retire the shares at a future date, so it is actually debt. Prior to the FASB issuing Statement of Financial Accounting Standard No. 150, "Accounting for Certain Financial Instruments with Characteristics of Both Liabilities and Equity" in May, 2003, companies unsure of where to classify this financial instrument disclosed it between debt and equity on the balance sheet. The FASB has cleared up this confusion by requiring mandatorily redeemable preferred stock to be reported as a liability unless redemption is required only upon liquidation or termination of the reporting entity.

Stockholders' Equity

The ownership interests in the company are represented in the final section of the balance sheet, stockholders' equity or shareholders' equity. Ownership equity is the residual interest in assets that remains after deducting liabilities. The owners bear the greatest risk because their claims are subordinate to creditors in the event of liquidation, but owners also benefit from the rewards of a successful enterprise. The relationship between the amount of debt and equity in a firm's capital structure and the concept of financial leverage, by which shareholder returns are magnified, is explored in Chapter 6.

Common Stock

R.E.C. Inc. has only common stock shares outstanding. Common shareholders do not ordinarily receive a fixed return but do have voting privileges in proportion to ownership interest. Dividends on common stock are declared at the discretion of a company's board of directors. Further, common shareholders can benefit from stock ownership through potential price appreciation (or the reverse can occur if the share price declines).

The amount listed under the common stock account is based on the par or stated value of the shares issued. The par or stated value usually bears no relationship to actual market price but rather is a floor price below which the stock cannot be sold initially. At year-end 2007, R.E.C. Inc. had 4,803,000 shares outstanding of $1 par value stock, rendering a total of $4,803,000 in the common stock account.

Additional Paid-In Capital

This account reflects the amount by which the original sales price of the stock shares exceeded par value. If, for example, a company sold 1,000 shares of $1 par value stock for $3 per share, the common stock account would be $1,000, and additional paid-in capital would total $2,000.

Reference to the additional paid-in capital account for R.E.C. Inc. reveals that the firm's common stock initially sold at a price slightly higher than the $1 par value. The additional paid-in capital account is not affected by the price changes resulting from stock trading subsequent to its original issue.[11]

Retained Earnings

The retained earnings account is the sum of every dollar a company has earned since its inception, less any payments made to shareholders in the form of cash or stock dividends. Retained earnings do not represent a pile of unused cash stashed away in corporate vaults; retained earnings are funds a company has elected to reinvest in the operations of the business rather than pay out to stockholders in dividends. Retained earnings should not be confused with cash or other financial resources currently or prospectively available to satisfy financial obligations. Rather, the retained earnings account is the measurement of all undistributed earnings. The retained earnings account is a key link between the income statement and the balance sheet. Unless

---

[11]The paid-in capital account can be affected by treasury stock transactions, preferred stock, retirement of stock, stock dividends, and warrants and by the conversion of debt into stock.

there are unusual transactions affecting the retained earnings account, the following equation illustrates this link:

Beginning retained earnings ± Net income (loss) − Dividends = Ending retained earnings

Other Equity Accounts

In addition to the stockholders' equity accounts shown on the R.E.C. Inc. balance sheet, there are other accounts that can appear in the equity section. These include preferred stock, accumulated other comprehensive income, and treasury stock. Exhibit 2.8 illustrates these additional items for Pfizer, Inc.

Preferred stock usually carries a fixed annual dividend payment but no voting rights. Pfizer, Inc. issued preferred stock in connection with an acquisition.

Beginning in 1998, companies must report comprehensive income or loss for the accounting period. Prior to the issuance of FASB Statement No. 130, "Reporting Comprehensive Income," several comprehensive income items bypassed the income statement and were reported as components of equity. Comprehensive income consists of two parts, net income and other comprehensive income. Other comprehensive income is reported in a separate equity account on the balance sheet generally referred to as *accumulated other comprehensive income/(expense)*. This account includes up to four items: (1) unrealized gains or losses in the market value of investments in available-for-sale securities, (2) any change in the excess of additional pension liability over unrecognized prior service cost, (3) certain gains and losses on derivative financial instruments, and (4) foreign currency translation adjustments resulting from converting financial statements from a foreign currency into U.S. dollars. (Comprehensive income and the four items noted above are discussed in Chapter 3.)

Firms often repurchase shares of their own stock for a variety of reasons that include meeting requirements for employee stock option and retirement plans, building shareholdings for potential merger needs, increasing earnings per share by reducing the number of shares outstanding in order to build investor confidence, preventing takeover attempts by reducing the number of shareholders, and as an investment use of excess cash holdings. If the repurchased shares are not retired, they are designated as

EXHIBIT 2.8 Pfizer, Inc. Shareholders' Equity at December 31 (in Millions)

	2004	2003
Shareholders' Equity		
Preferred stock, without par value, at stated value; 27 shares authorized; issued: 2004−4,791; 2003−5,445	193	219
Common stock, $.05 par value; 12,000 shares authorized; issued: 2004−8,754; 2003−8,702	438	435
Additional paid-in capital	67,098	66,396
Employee benefit trust	(1,229)	(1,898)
Treasury stock, shares at cost; 2004−1,281; 2003−1,073	(35,992)	(29,352)
Retained earnings	35,492	29,382
Accumulated other comprehensive income	2,278	195
Total shareholders' equity	68,278	65,377

treasury stock and are shown as an offsetting account in the stockholders' equity section of the balance sheet. Pfizer, Inc. held 1,281 million shares of treasury stock at the end of 2004. The cost of the shares is shown as a reduction of stockholders' equity.[12]

Employee benefit trust, an account shown in the Pfizer, Inc. shareholders' equity section, is explained as follows:

> The Pfizer, Inc. Employee Benefit Trust (EBT) was established in 1999 to fund our employee benefit plans through the use of its holdings of Pfizer, Inc. stock. The consolidated balance sheet reflects the fair value of the shares owned by the EBT as a reduction of Shareholders' Equity.[13]

Other Balance Sheet Items

Corporate balance sheets are not limited to the accounts described in this chapter for R.E.C. Inc. and other companies. The reader of annual reports will encounter additional accounts and will also find many of the same accounts listed under a variety of different titles. Those discussed in this chapter, however, should be generally sufficient for understanding the basics of most balance sheet presentations in a set of published financial statements. The balance sheet will recur through the remaining chapters of this book due to the interrelationship among the financial statements and because of its important role in the analysis of financial data.

SELF-TEST

Solutions are provided in Appendix B.

————— **1.** What does the balance sheet summarize for a business enterprise?
   (a) Operating results for a period.
   (b) Financial position at a point in time.
   (c) Financing and investment activities for a period.
   (d) Profit or loss at a point in time.

————— **2.** What is the balancing equation for the balance sheet?
   (a) Assets = Liabilities + Stockholders' equity.
   (b) Assets + Stockholders' equity = Liabilities.
   (c) Assets + Liabilities = Stockholders' equity.
   (d) Revenues − Expenses = Net income.

————— **3.** What is a common-size balance sheet?
   (a) A statement that expresses each account on the balance sheet as a percentage of net income.
   (b) A statement that is common to an industry.
   (c) A statement that expresses each account on the balance sheet as a percentage of total assets.
   (d) A statement that expresses each asset account on the balance sheet as a percentage of total assets and each liability account on the balance sheet as a percentage of total liabilities.

---

[12]The two methods used to account for treasury stock transactions are the cost method (deducting the cost of the purchased shares from equity) and the par value method (deducting the par or stated value of the shares from equity). Most companies use the cost method.
[13]Pfizer, Inc., 2004. Annual Report, p. 53.

_____ **4.** Which of the following securities would be classified as marketable securities in the current asset section of the balance sheet?
  (a) Commercial paper, U.S. Treasury bills, land held for investment.
  (b) Commercial paper, U.S. Treasury bills, negotiable certificates of deposit.
  (c) Commercial paper, land held for investment, bonds with maturities in 10 years.
  (d) U.S. Treasury bills, long-term stock investment, bonds with maturities in 10 years.

_____ **5.** What items should be calculated when analyzing the accounts receivable and allowance for doubtful accounts?
  (a) The growth rates of sales and inventories.
  (b) The growth rates of sales, accounts receivable, and the allowance for doubtful accounts, as well as the percentage of the allowance account relative to the total or gross accounts receivable.
  (c) The common-size balance sheet.
  (d) The growth rates of all assets and liabilities.

_____ **6.** What type of firm generally has the highest proportion of inventory to total assets?
  (a) Retailers.
  (b) Wholesalers.
  (c) Manufacturers.
  (d) Service-oriented firms.

_____ **7.** Why is the method of valuing inventory important?
  (a) Inventory valuation is based on the actual flow of goods.
  (b) Inventories always account for more than 50% of total assets and therefore have a considerable impact on a company's financial position.
  (c) Companies desire to use the inventory valuation method which minimizes the cost of goods sold expense.
  (d) The inventory valuation method chosen determines the value of inventory on the balance sheet and the cost of goods sold expense on the income statement, two items having considerable impact on the financial position of a company.

_____ **8.** What are three major cost flow assumptions used by U.S. companies in valuing inventory?
  (a) LIFO, FIFO, average market.
  (b) LIFO, FIFO, actual cost.
  (c) LIFO, FIFO, average cost.
  (d) LIFO, FIFO, double-declining balance.

_____ **9.** Assuming a period of inflation, which statement is true?
  (a) The FIFO method understates balance sheet inventory.
  (b) The FIFO method understates cost of goods sold on the income statement.
  (c) The LIFO method overstates balance sheet inventory.
  (d) The LIFO method understates cost of goods sold on the income statement.

_____ **10.** Why would a company switch to the LIFO method of inventory valuation?

(a) By switching to LIFO, reported earnings will be higher.

(b) A new tax law requires companies using LIFO for reporting purposes also to use LIFO for figuring taxable income.

(c) LIFO produces the largest cost of goods sold expense in a period of inflation and thereby lowers taxable income and taxes.

(d) A survey by *Accounting Trends and Techniques* revealed that the switch to LIFO is a current accounting "fad."

_____ **11.** Where can one most typically find the cost flow assumption used for inventory valuation for a specific company?

(a) In The Risk Management Association, *Annual Statement Studies.*

(b) In the statement of retained earnings.

(c) On the face of the balance sheet with the total current asset amount.

(d) In the notes to the financial statements.

_____ **12.** What type of firm generally has the highest proportion of fixed assets to total assets?

(a) Manufacturers.

(b) Retailers.

(c) Wholesalers.

(d) Retailers and wholesalers.

_____ **13.** As of January 1, 2002, how is goodwill evaluated?

(a) Goodwill must be amortized over a 40-year period.

(b) No goodwill is to be recognized after January 1, 2002.

(c) Companies should determine if goodwill has lost value, and if so, the loss in value should be written off.

(d) Goodwill is to be written off at the end of the tenth year.

_____ **14.** Which group of items would most likely be included in the other assets account on the balance sheet?

(a) Inventories, marketable securities, bonds.

(b) Land held for investment purposes and long-term prepayments.

(c) One-year prepaid insurance policy, stock investments, copyrights.

(d) Inventories, franchises, patents.

_____ **15.** What do current liabilities and current assets have in common?

(a) Current assets are claims against current liabilities.

(b) If current assets increase, then there will be a corresponding increase in current liabilities.

(c) Current liabilities and current assets are converted into cash.

(d) Current liabilities and current assets are those items that will be satisfied and converted into cash, respectively, in one year or one operating cycle, whichever is longer.

_____ **16.** How can a reserve account be abused by management?

(a) Management can intentionally overestimate the reserve account to decrease earnings or underestimate the reserve account to increase earnings.

(b) Management can charge the estimates of obligations to be paid in the future to a reserve account.

(c) There is no way for management to abuse this account.

(d) None of the above.

_____ 17. Which of the following items could cause the recognition of accrued liabilities?

(a) Sales, interest expense, rent.

(b) Sales, taxes, interest income.

(c) Salaries, rent, insurance.

(d) Salaries, interest expense, interest income.

_____ 18. Which statement is false?

(a) Deferred taxes are the product of temporary differences in the recognition of revenue and expense for taxable income relative to reported income.

(b) Deferred taxes arise from the use of the same method of depreciation for tax and reporting purposes.

(c) Deferred taxes arise when taxes actually paid are less than tax expense reported in the financial statements.

(d) Temporary differences causing the recognition of deferred taxes may arise from the methods used to account for items such as depreciation, installment sales, leases, and pensions.

_____ 19. Which of the following would be classified as long-term debt?

(a) Mortgages, current maturities of long-term debt, bonds.

(b) Mortgages, long-term notes payable, bonds due in 10 years.

(c) Accounts payable, bonds, obligations under leases.

(d) Accounts payable, long-term notes payable, long-term warranties.

_____ 20. What accounts are most likely to be found in the stockholders' equity section of the balance sheet?

(a) Common stock, long-term debt, preferred stock.

(b) Common stock, additional paid-in capital, liabilities.

(c) Common stock, retained earnings, dividends payable.

(d) Common stock, additional paid-in capital, retained earnings.

_____ 21. What does the additional paid-in capital account represent?

(a) The difference between the par and the stated value of common stock.

(b) The price changes that result for stock trading subsequent to its original issue.

(c) The market price of all common stock issued.

(d) The amount by which the original sales price of stock exceeds the par value.

_____ 22. What does the retained earnings account measure?

(a) Cash held by the company since its inception.

(b) Payments made to shareholders in the form of cash or stock dividends.

(c) All undistributed earnings.

(d) Financial resources currently available to satisfy financial obligations.

23. Listed below are balance sheet accounts for Elf's Gift Shop. Mark current accounts with "C" and noncurrent accounts with "NC."

_____ (a) Long-term debt.

_____ (b) Inventories.

_____ (c) Accounts payable.

_____ (d) Prepaid expenses.

_____ (e) Equipment.

_____ (f) Accrued liabilities.

_____ (g) Accounts receivable.

_____ (h) Cash.

_____ (i) Bonds payable.

_____ (j) Patents.

24. Dot's Delicious Donuts has the following accounts on its balance sheet:

(1) Current assets.

(2) Property, plant, and equipment.

(3) Intangible assets.

(4) Other assets.

(5) Current liabilities.

(6) Deferred federal income taxes.

(7) Long-term debt.

(8) Stockholders' equity.

How would each of the following items be classified?

_____ (a) Land held for speculation.

_____ (b) Current maturities on mortgage.

_____ (c) Common stock.

_____ (d) Mortgage payable.

_____ (e) Balances outstanding on credit sales to customers.

_____ (f) Accumulated depreciation.

_____ (g) Buildings used in business.

_____ (h) Accrued payroll.

_____ (i) Preferred stock.

_____ (j) Debt outstanding from credit extended by suppliers.

_____ (k) Patents.

_____ (l) Land on which warehouse is located.

_____ (m) Allowance for doubtful accounts.

_____ (n) Liability due to difference in taxes paid and taxes reported.

_____ (o) Additional paid-in capital.

25. Match the following terms to the correct definitions.

_____ (a) Consolidated financial statements.

_____ (b) Current assets.

_____ (c) Depreciation.

_____ (d) Deferred taxes.

_____ (e) Allowance for doubtful accounts.

_____ (f) Prepaid expenses.

_____ (g) Current maturities.

(1) Used up within one year or operating cycle, whichever is longer.

(2) Expenses incurred prior to cash outflow.

(3) An agreement to use assets that is in substance a purchase.

(4) Estimation of uncollectible accounts receivable.

_____ (h) Accrued expense.
_____ (i) Capital lease.
_____ (j) Market value of stock.

(5) Cost allocation of fixed assets other than land.
(6) Expenses paid in advance.
(7) Combined statements of parent company and controlled subsidiary companies.
(8) Price at which stock trades.
(9) Difference in taxes reported and taxes paid.
(10) Portion of debt to be repaid during the upcoming year.

Study Questions and Problems

2.1. How can the allowance for doubtful accounts be used to assess earnings quality?

2.2. Why is the valuation of inventories important in financial reporting?

2.3. Why would a company switch to the LIFO method of inventory valuation in an inflationary period?

2.4. Discuss the difference between the straight-line method of depreciation and the accelerated methods. Why do companies use different depreciation methods for tax reporting and financial reporting?

2.5. How is it possible for a company with positive retained earnings to be unable to pay a cash dividend?

2.6. The following data are available for three companies, A, B, and C:

	A	B	C
Inventories	$ 280,000	$ 280,000	$ 280,000
Net fixed assets	400,000	65,000	70,000
Total assets	1,000,000	430,000	650,000

Which company is most likely a retailer? A wholesaler? A manufacturer?

2.7. The F.L.A.C. Corporation sells a single product. The following is information on inventory, purchase, and sales for the current year:

		Number of units	Unit cost	Sale price
January 1	Inventory	10,000	$3.00	
January 10	Purchase	4,000	3.50	
January 1–March 31	Sales	8,000		$5.00
April 25	Purchase	10,000	4.00	
April 1–June 30	Sales	11,000		5.50
July 10	Purchase	6,000	4.50	
July 1–September 30	Sales	3,000		6.00
October 15	Purchase	8,000	5.00	
Ocotber 1–December 31	Sales	9,000		6.50

(a) Compute the inventory balance and the cost of goods sold expense reported at the end of the year using the following methods: FIFO, LIFO, and average cost.

(b) Discuss the effect of each method on the balance sheet and income statement during periods of inflation.

2.8. The IOU Corporation has a $150,000 note outstanding with 14% annual interest due in semiannual installments on January 31 and July 31. What amount will be shown as accrued interest on a December 31 balance sheet?

2.9. The King Corporation has total annual revenue of $800,000; expenses other than depreciation of $350,000; depreciation expense of $200,000 for tax purposes; and depreciation expense of $130,000 for reporting purposes. The tax rate is 34%. Calculate net income for reporting purposes and for tax purposes. What is the deferred tax liability?

2.10. Explain how treasury stock affects the stockholders' equity section of the balance sheet and the calculation of earnings per share.

2.11. Using the following amounts (in millions) reported in Texas Instruments' consolidated balance sheets and statements of income at December 31, 2004 and 2003, analyze the receivables and allowance account for all years.

	2004	2003	2002
Net Revenues	$12,580	$9,834	$8,383
Accounts receivable, net of allowances for customer adjustments and doubtful accounts of $41 in 2004, $47 in 2003, and $60 in 2002	1,696	1,451	1,217

2.12. The following information is available for Kennametal Inc's inventories as of June 30, 2004:

(in Thousands)	2004	2003
Finished goods	$264,134	$272,080
Work in process and powder blends	110,992	108,607
Raw materials and supplies	37,322	36,283
Inventories at current cost	412,448	416,970
Less LIFO valuation	(24,371)	(27,357)
Total inventories	$388,077	$389,613

We used the LIFO method of valuing our inventories for approximately 41% and 40% of total inventories at June 30, 2004 and 2003, respectively. We use the LIFO method in order to more closely match current costs with current revenues, thereby reducing the effects of inflation on earnings.

(a) What method of inventory is used for the other 59% and 60% of total inventories?

(b) Explain the meaning of each of the numbers listed in the table.

2.13. At fiscal year-end January 29, 2005, Target Corporation had the following assets and liabilities on its balance sheet (in millions):

Current liabilities	$ 8,220
Long-term debt	9,034
Other liabilities	2,010
Total assets	32,293

Target reported the following information on leases in the notes to the financial statements:

Total rent expense was $240 million in 2004, $150 million in 2003 and $150 million in 2002. Most of the long-term leases include options to renew, with terms varying from one to 50 years. Certain leases also include options to purchase the property.

Future minimum lease payments required under noncancelable lease agreements existing at January 29, 2005, were:

Future Minimum Lease Payments		
(millions)	Operating Leases	Capital Leases
2005	$146	$12
2006	142	12
2007	137	13
2008	117	13
2009	102	12
After 2009	2,405	127
Total future minimum lease payments	$3,049***	$189
Less: Interest*		(98)
Present value of minimum capital lease payments		$91**

*Calculated using the interest rate at inception for each lease.
**Includes current portion of $3 million.
***Total contractual lease payments include certain options to extend lease terms, in the amount of $1,415, that are expected to be exercised because the investment in leasehold improvement is significant.

(a) What information would be included on the financial statements of Target related to capital leases for the year ended January 29, 2005? Give dollar amounts where possible.

(b) What information would be included on the financial statements of Target related to the operating leases for the year ended January 29, 2005?

(c) Of what value is this information to the financial statement user?

2.14. From the following accounts, prepare a balance sheet for Chester Co. for the current calendar year.

Accrued interest payable	$ 1,400
Property, plant, and equipment	34,000
Inventory	12,400
Additional paid-in capital	7,000
Deferred taxes payable (noncurrent)	1,600
Cash	1,500
Accumulated depreciation	10,500
Bonds payable	14,500
Accounts payable	4,300
Common stock	2,500
Prepaid expenses	700
Land held for sale	9,200
Retained earnings	?
Current portion of long-term debt	1,700
Accounts receivable	6,200
Notes payable	8,700

2.15. Writing Skills Problem

You have read Chapter 2 of the text and have noticed that there are no drawings. The non-text material in Chapter 2 consists only of tables, which you find a bit dry. Visual modes of expression are an integral part of business writing and often convey ideas better than prose. Visuals are used both to supplement written communication and in some cases to carry the message entirely. Some of the more commonly used forms of visual in technical communication are drawings, diagrams, bar charts, pie charts, flow charts, line graphs, tables, and photographs. Technical communication can be greatly enhanced by visual forms of expression.

Required: Select some aspect of Chapter 2 and design a visual (other than a table) to accompany, supplement, or replace a section of the text.

2.16. Research Problem

Locate a library that carries "The Risk Management Association, Annual Statement Studies." Choose three industries from Annual Statement Studies (different from those illustrated in Exhibits 2.4 and 2.5 in Chapter 2) and create a table with the percentages for the following items: accounts receivable, inventories, fixed assets, accounts payable, and long-term debt as a percentage of total assets.

2.17. Internet Problem

Choose a publicly held corporation (unless your teacher assigns a particular corporation for this assignment) and find the balance sheet and notes to the financial statements in the most recent Form 10-K. The Form 10-K can be located by going to the homepage of the Securities and Exchange Commission and locating the SEC EDGAR Database. The address for the homepage is www.sec.gov/.

Using the information you find answer the following questions:

(a) What current assets are included on the balance sheet?

(b) If the company lists accounts receivable and an allowance account, analyze these accounts.

(c) What method does the company use to value inventory?

(d) What depreciation method does the company use?

(e) What assets other than current assets and property, plant, and equipment are included on the balance sheet?

(f) What current liabilities are included on the balance sheet?

(g) How many deferred tax accounts are included on the balance sheet? Under which classification(s) are deferred taxes found? What temporary differences caused the creation of the deferred tax account(s)?

(h) Does the company have long-term debt? How much?

(i) Does the company have commitments and contingencies? If so, what commitments does the company have and for what amount is the company committed? Explain any contingencies.

(j) What stockholders' equity accounts are included on the balance sheet?

2.18. Intel Problem

The 2004 Intel Annual Report can be found at the following Web site: www.prenhall.com/fraser. Using the annual report, answer the following questions:

(a) Prepare a common-size balance sheet for Intel for all years presented.

(b) Describe the types of assets Intel owns. Which assets are the most significant to the company? Using the notes to the financial statements, discuss the accounting methods used to value assets. What other information can be learned about the asset accounts from the notes? Have there been significant changes to the asset structure from 2003 to 2004?

(c) Analyze the accounts receivable and allowance accounts.

(d) Describe the types of liabilities Intel has incurred. Which liabilities are the most significant to the company? Have there been significant changes to the liability and equity structure from 2003 to 2004?

(e) Describe the commitments and contingencies of Intel.

(f) Under which classification(s) are deferred taxes listed? What item is the most significant component of deferred taxes?

(g) What equity accounts are included on the balance sheet of Intel?

2.19. Eastman Kodak Comprehensive Analysis Problem Using the Financial Statement Analysis Template

Each chapter in the textbook contains a continuation of this problem. The objective is to learn how to do a comprehensive financial statement analysis in steps as the content of each chapter is learned. Using the 2004 Eastman Kodak Annual Report or Form 10-K that can be found at www.prenhall.com/fraser complete the following requirements:

(a) Open the financial statement analysis template that you saved from the Chapter 1 Eastman Kodak problem and input the data from the Eastman Kodak balance sheet. Eastman Kodak has combined many of their asset and liability accounts into one comprehensive account on the balance sheet. Be sure to read the notes to determine the correct numbers to input on the template. For example, the company has combined many items in the account "Other long-term assets" that should be separated into appropriate accounts. When you have finished inputting the data, review the balance sheet to make sure there are no red blocks indicating that your numbers do not match the cover sheet information you input from the Chapter 1 problem. Make any necessary corrections before printing out both your input and the common-size balance sheet that the template automatically creates for you.

(b) Analyze the balance sheet. Write a summary that includes important points that an analyst would use in assessing the financial condition of Eastman Kodak.

C A S E S

Case 2.1   Lucent Technologies

The following is an excerpt from Lucent Technologies' Management's Discussion and Analysis of Financial Condition and Results of Operations:

Executive Summary

We design and deliver the systems, software and services that drive next-generation communications networks. Backed by Bell Labs research and development, we use our strengths in mobility, optical, access, data and voice networking technologies, as well as services, to create new revenue-generating opportunities for our customers, while enabling them to quickly deploy and better manage their networks. Our customer base includes communications service providers, governments and enterprises worldwide.

We have three segments organized around the products and services we sell. The reportable segments are Integrated Network Solutions ("INS"), Mobility Solutions ("Mobility") and Lucent Worldwide Services ("Services"). INS provides a broad range of software and wireline equipment related to voice networking (primarily consisting of switching products, which we sometimes refer to as convergence solutions, and voice messaging products), data and network management (primarily consisting of access and related data networking equipment and operating support software) and optical networking. Mobility provides software and wireless equipment to support radio access and core networks. Services provides deployment, maintenance, professional and managed services in support of both our product offerings as well as multi-vendor networks.

Beginning in fiscal 2001, the global telecommunications market deteriorated, resulting from a decrease in the competitive local exchange carrier market and a significant reduction in capital spending by established service providers. This trend intensified during fiscal 2002 and continued into fiscal 2003. Reasons for the market deterioration included general economic slowdown, network overcapacity, customer bankruptcies, network build-out delays and limited availability of capital.

We believe that the market for telecommunications equipment has stabilized and is starting to grow in certain areas. The growing demands of enterprises and consumers for additional services tailored to their needs is creating the need for a new convergence of networks, technologies and applications.

Required

1. Using the Consolidated Balance Sheets for Lucent Technologies for September 30, 2004 and 2003, prepare a common-size balance sheet.
2. Evaluate the asset, debt, and equity structure of Lucent Technologies, as well as trends and changes found on the common-size balance sheet.
3. What concerns would investors and creditors have based on only this information?
4. What additional financial and non-financial information would investors and creditors need to make investing and lending decisions for Lucent Technologies?

LUCENT TECHNOLOGIES INC. AND SUBSIDIARIES
CONSOLIDATED BALANCE SHEETS
(in Millions, Except per Share Amounts)

	September 30, 2004	September 30, 2003
Assets		
Cash and cash equivalents	$ 3,379	$ 3,821
Marketable securities	858	686
Receivables	1,359	1,511
Inventories	822	632
Other current assets	1,813	1,213
Total current assets	8,231	7,863
Marketable securities	636	—
Property, plant, and equipment, net	1,376	1,593
Prepaid pension costs	5,358	4,659
Goodwill and other acquired intangibles, net	434	188
Other assets	928	1,608
Total assets	$ 16,963	$ 15,911
Liabilities		
Accounts payable	$ 872	$ 1,072
Payroll and benefit-related liabilities	1,232	1,080
Debt maturing within one year	1	389
Other current liabilities	2,361	2,393
Total current liabilities	4,466	4,934
Postretirement and postemployment benefit liabilities	4,881	4,669
Pension liabilities	1,874	2,494
Long-term debt	4,837	4,439
Liability to subsidiary trust issuing preferred securities	1,152	1,152
Other liabilities	1,132	1,594
Total liabilities	18,342	19,282
Commitments and contingencies		
8.00% redeemable convertible preferred stock	—	868
Shareowners' Deficit		
Preferred stock—par value $1.00 per share; authorized shares: 250; issued and outstanding: none	—	—
Common stock—par value $.01 per share; Authorized shares: 10,000; 4,396 issued and 4,395 outstanding shares as of September 30, 2004, and 4,170 issued and 4,169 outstanding shares as of September 30, 2003	44	42
Additional paid-in capital	23,005	22,252
Accumulated deficit	(20,793)	(22,795)
Accumulated other comprehensive loss	(3,635)	(3,738)
Total shareowners' deficit	(1,379)	(4,239)
Total liabilities, redeemable convertible preferred stock and shareowners' deficit	$ 16,963	$ 15,911

See notes to consolidated financial statements.

Case 2.2   1-800 Contacts, Inc.

1-800 Contacts, Inc. was formed in 1995 as a direct marketer of replacement contact lenses. Since 2002, the firm has made acquisitions of firms that manufacture, develop and distribute contact lenses in Singapore and the United Kingdom. Anticompetitive barriers in the industry created by eye care practitioners and contact lens manufacturers resulted in 1-800 Contacts, Inc. investing heavily in lobbying efforts that ultimately resulted in Congress passing the Fairness to Contact Lens Consumers Act, effective February 4, 2004. Selected information from 1-800 Contacts, Inc.'s Form 10-K is given on pages 81–86.

Required

1. Using the Consolidated Balance Sheets for 1-800 Contacts, Inc. for the years ended January 3, 2004 and January 1, 2005, prepare a common-size balance sheet.
2. Which current asset is the most significant?
3. To the extent possible analyze the allowance for doubtful accounts relative to accounts receivable and net sales.
4. What types of inventories does 1-800 Contacts carry? Why? What inventory method is used to account for the inventories? Does this method reflect current cost at year-end?
5. Based on the inventory valuation method used, would you expect 1-800 Contacts to have tax savings or pay more in taxes? Explain your answer. (You do not need to do any calculations.)
6. Which noncurrent asset categories are the most significant? Are the relative proportions of current and noncurrent assets what you would expect for a contact lens distributor? Explain.
7. Which two current liabilities are the most significant? Which two noncurrent liabilities are the most significant? Are the relative proportions of current and non-current liabilities what you would expect for a contact lens distributor? Explain.
8. Discuss any significant changes in the asset, liability, and equity structure of 1-800 Contacts.
9. Does 1-800 Contacts have commitments and contingencies? If so, what is the significance of these items?
10. Explain what has caused the change in the retained earnings account from January 3, 2004 to January 1, 2005.

OPERATING INFORMATION (in thousands)			
Fiscal Year 2004	**U.S. Retail**	**International**	**Total**
Net sales	$204,406	$ 7,272	$211,678
Fiscal Year 2003	**U.S. Retail**	**International**	**Total**
Net sales	$181,331	$ 5,972	$187,303
Fiscal Year 2002	**U.S. Retail**	**International**	**Total**
Net sales	$166,511	$ 2,069	$168,580
	2002	**2003**	**2004**
Net loss	$ (4,004)	$(1,438)	$ (616)

1-800 CONTACTS, INC. AND SUBSIDIARIES
CONSOLIDATED BALANCE SHEETS
ASSETS
(in Thousands)

	January 3, 2004	January 1, 2005
Current Assets		
Cash	$ 1,075	$ 3,105
Accounts receivable, net	944	3,178
Other receivables	659	2,398
Inventories, net	24,127	22,206
Prepaid income taxes	797	—
Deferred income taxes	548	1,328
Other current assets	1,093	1,546
Total current assets	29,243	33,761
Property, Plant, and Equipment		
Office, computer and other equipment	7,591	7,997
Manufacturing equipment	3,219	11,680
Manufacturing facility	7,045	7,329
Leasehold improvements	2,179	4,217
	20,034	31,223
Less—accumulated depreciation and amortization	(6,851)	(10,605)
Net property, plant and equipment	13,183	20,618
Other Assets		
Deferred income taxes	710	720
Goodwill	33,853	34,320
Definite-lived intangibles, net	9,207	17,897
Other	735	1,669
Total other assets	44,505	54,606
Total assets	$86,931	$108,985

LIABILITIES AND STOCKHOLDERS' EQUITY
(in Thousands, Except per Share Amount)

	January 3, 2004	January 1, 2005
Current Liabilities		
Current portion of long-term debt	$ 3,381	$ 1,632
Current portion of capital lease obligations	191	47
Acquisition payable	150	—
Income taxes payable	—	1,560
Accounts payable	8,558	9,762
Accrued liabilities	4,474	7,303
Unearned revenue	223	3,500
Total current liabilities	16,977	23,804
Long-Term Liabilities		
Line of credit	—	14,404
Long-term debt, net of current portion	14,683	8,170

	January 3, 2004	January 1, 2005
Capital lease obligations, net of current portion	64	98
Deferred income tax liabilities	—	1,458
Unearned revenue, net of current portion	—	1,667
Other long-term liabilities	—	880
Total long-term liabilities	14,747	26,677
Commitments and Contingencies (Notes 1, 3, 4 and 5)		
Stockholders' Equity		
Common stock, $.01 par value, 20,000 shares authorized, 13,113 and 13,299 shares issued, respectively	131	133
Additional paid-in capital	42,346	45,958
Retained earnings.	12,834	12,218
Accumulated other comprehensive income (loss)	(104)	195
Total stockholders' equity	55,207	58,504
Total liabilities and stockholders' equity	$ 86,931	$108,985

See accompanying notes to consolidated financial statements.

Notes to Consolidated Financial Statements

Note 1. Nature of Operations and Organization of Business

ClearLab is the Company's international contact lens development, manufacutring and distribution business, focusing on the marketing and selling of contact lens products to major retailers and distributors, as well as providing contract manufacturing capacity for other contact lens manufacturers. ClearLab recently began to sell frequent replacement lenses in the U.S. through the Company's retail optical partnership.

ClearLab has operation facilities in Singapore and the United Kingdom. The Singapore facility was acquired on July 24, 2002, when the Company completed the acquisition of certain net assets and the majority of the business operations of IGEL (subsequently renamed ClearLab International), a developer and manufacturer of contact lenses based in Singapore. ClearLab expanded it manufacturing capabilities on February 24, 2004 when the Company acquired VisionTec (subsequently renamed ClearLab UK), a developer and manufacturer of daily contact lenses based in the United Kingdom that has developed a method for low cost, high quality production of daily disposable contact lenses.

The Company has two operating segments. The Company's domestic segment is represented by operations within the United States and is referred to as "U.S. Retail" by the Company, whereas the Company's international segment is represented by operations in both Singapore and the United Kingdom and is referred to as "ClearLab" by the Company.

Note 2. Summary of Significant Accounting Policies

Revenue Recognition

Revenues are generally recognized when products are shipped, the customer takes ownership and assumes risk of loss, collection of the related receivable is probable, persuasive evidence of an arrangement exists, and the sales price is fixed or determinable. Payments for the U.S. Retail product are typically received prior to shipment. Unearned revenue represents amounts received for which shipment or services have not occurred. U.S. Retail net sales consist of product sales less a provision for sales returns and allowances and estimated customer rebates. The Company accrues an estimated amount for unclaimed customer rebates and sales returns and allowances based on historical information, adjusted for economic trends. Shipping and handling fees charged to customers are included as part of net sales. The related freight costs and supplies expense directly associated with shipping products to customers are included as a component of cost of goods sold. Other indirect shipping and handling costs, consisting mainly of labor and facilities costs, are included as a component of other operating expenses.

ClearLab net sales consist of product sales less a provision for sales returns and allowances. The Company provides its customers with standard industry payment terms and performs ongoing credit evaluations of its customers and provides for doubtful accounts to the extent determined necessary based on historical data and current economic trends. As of January 1, 2005, there is an allowance for doubtful accounts of approximately $27,000.

Inventories

Inventories are recorded at the lower of cost (using the first-in, first-out method) or market value. Elements of cost in the Company's manufactured inventories generally include raw materials, direct labor, manufacturing overhead, and freight in. Inventories consisted of the following (in thousands):

	January 3, 2004	January 1, 2005
Purchased contact lenses	$20,943	$16,216
Manufactured contact lenses:		
Raw materials	429	930
Work in process	2,681	1,796
Finished goods	74	3,264
Total	$24,127	$22,206

Provision is made to reduce excess and obsolete inventories to their estimated net realizable values. The Company's inventory provisions are summarized in the table below (in thousands):

	December 28, 2002	January 3, 2004	January 1, 2005
Beginning of year	$1,091	$ 731	$ 623
Provision for losses	130	231	720
Write-offs	(490)	(339)	(141)
End of year	$ 731	$ 623	$1,202

Definite-Lived Intangible Assets

Intangible assets mainly consist of amounts paid to secure the rights to the Company's telephone numbers and Internet addresses; acquired technology relating to the development and manufacturing of contact lenses; non-compete agreements; and customer databases. The costs relating to the definite-lived intangible assets are amortized over the estimated lives using straight-line and accelerated methods. As of January 1, 2005, the weighted average amortization period for all intangible assets was 8 years. The weighted average amortization periods for telephone numbers and Internet addresses is 4 years, acquired customer databases is 5 years, core and completed technologies is 12 years and non-compete agreements is 5 years.

Note 5. Commitments and Contingencies

Operating Leases

The Company leases land, office and warehouse facilities and certain equipment under noncancelable operating leases. Lease expense for fiscal 2002, 2003, and 2004 totaled approximately $1,556,000, $1,594,000 and $2,029,000, respectively.

Future minimum lease payments under noncancelable operating leases are as follows (in thousands):

Fiscal Year	Amount
2005	$ 1,776
2006	1,386
2007	1,344
2008	1,224
2009	1,135
Thereafter	3,475
	$10,340

Advertising Commitments

As of January 1, 2005, the Company had entered into certain noncancelable commitments with various advertising companies that will require the Company to pay approximately $14.6 million for advertising during 2005.

Purchase Commitments

As of January 1, 2005, the Company had entered into certain noncancelable commitments with a certain supplier that will require the Company to purchase approximately $322,000 of inventory during fiscal 2005.

As of January 1, 2005, the Company had entered into certain noncancelable commitments with a certain production vendor that will require the Company to purchase approximately $1.6 million in production and manufacturing equipment during fiscal 2005.

Other Commitments

As of January 1, 2005, the Company had a remaining minimum service commitment with a telecommunications provider of approximately $665,000 through fiscal 2006.

The Company entered into an agreement in December 2004 with a regional optical chain in Utah. Under the terms of the agreement, the Company agreed to pay a fee based on a percentage of the partnerships earnings, as defined in the agreement. The fee arrangement has a minimum guarantee of $500,000 during fiscal 2005.

Income Statement and Statement of Stockholders' Equity

Learning about earnings, the bottom line,
Is very important most of the time.
A phony number
Just may encumber
Those folks trying to make more than a dime.[1]

—A. ORMISTON

The operating performance of a business firm has traditionally been measured by its success in generating earnings—the "bottom line." Investors, creditors, and analysts eagerly await companies' earnings reports. One objective of this book is to broaden the reader's perspective of operating success to consider such yardsticks as "cash flow from operations" as well as net income. In this chapter, however, the focus will be on the income statement and how a company arrives at its "bottom line." Chapter 5 presents examples of some of the ways companies manipulate their "bottom line" and what readers can look for to detect and adjust for these strategies.

The *income statement*, also called the *statement of earnings*, presents revenues, expenses, net income, and earnings per share for an accounting period, generally a year or a quarter. (The terms *income, earnings*, and *profit* are used interchangeably throughout the book.) The statement of stockholders' equity is an important link between the balance sheet and the income statement. This statement documents the changes in the balance sheet equity accounts from one accounting period to the next. Companies may choose to report the information on the statement of stockholders' equity in a supplementary schedule or in a note to the financial statements rather than

---

[1]According to the *New Book of Knowledge* (1985) by Grolier Incorporated, limericks are difficult to write. Limericks, a form of nonsense-verse, consist of five lines, of which lines one, two, and five rhyme and have from eight to eleven syllables each; lines three and four rhyme, with five to seven syllables each. Although thousands exist in literature, it is estimated that only 200 are probably genuine, flawless examples. Readers may submit limericks for possible inclusion in future editions!

preparing a formal financial statement. Annual reports include three years of income statements and stockholders' equity information.

R.E.C. Inc. prepares a formal statement of stockholders' equity. Both the income statement and statement of stockholders' equity will be discussed in this chapter using the R.E.C. Inc. statements as the basis for a description of each statement and the accounts that typically appear in the statements.

The Income Statement

Regardless of the perspective of the financial statement user—investor, creditor, employee, competitor, supplier, regulator—it is essential to understand and analyze the earnings statement. But it is also important that the analyst realize that a company's report of earnings and other information presented on the income statement are not complete and sufficient barometers of financial performance. The income statement is one of many pieces of a financial statement package, and, like the other pieces, the income statement is partially the product of a wide range of accounting choices, estimates, and judgments that affect reported results, just as business policies, economic conditions, and many other variables affect results. How these issues, introduced in Chapter 1, affect reported results will continue to be considered throughout this chapter.

It has previously been explained that earnings are measured on an accrual rather than a cash basis, which means that income reported on the income statement is not the same as cash generated during the accounting period. Cash flow from operations and its importance to analysis are covered in Chapter 4. The purpose of this chapter is not to minimize the importance of the income statement, however, but to provide a clear context for its interpretation.

The income statement comes in two basic formats and with considerable variation in the degree of detail presented. The earnings statement for R.E.C. Inc. is presented in a *multiple-step* format, which provides several intermediate profit measures—gross profit, operating profit, and earnings before income tax—prior to the amount of net earnings for the period. (See Exhibit 3.1.) The *single-step* version of the income statement groups all items of revenue together, then deducts all categories of expense to arrive at a figure for net income. Exhibit 3.2 illustrates the single-step approach if R.E.C. Inc. used that method to report earnings. For purposes of analysis, the multiple-step format should be used. If a company presents income statement information in single-step or a modified multiple-step format, the user of the financial statements should redo the income statement in multiple-step format before beginning an analysis.

Certain special items, if they occur during an accounting period, must be disclosed separately on an income statement, regardless of format. These include *discontinued operations, extraordinary transactions*, and prior to 2006 the *cumulative effect of changes in accounting principles*, discussed later in this chapter.

As noted in Chapter 2, the Financial Accounting Standards Board (FASB) passed a new rule, effective in 1998, requiring companies to report *comprehensive income*. According to FASB Statement of Financial Accounting Concepts No. 6, "Elements of Financial Statements," comprehensive income is the change in equity of a company during a period from transactions, other events, and circumstances relating to nonowner sources. It includes all changes in equity during a period except

EXHIBIT 3.1   R.E.C., Inc. Consolidated Statements of Earnings for the Years Ended December 31, 2007, 2006, and 2005 (in Thousands Except per Share Amounts)

	2007	2006	2005
Net Sales	$215,600	$153,000	$140,700
Cost of goods sold (Note A)	129,364	91,879	81,606
Gross profit	86,236	61,121	59,094
Selling and administrative expenses (Notes A and E)	45,722	33,493	32,765
Advertising	14,258	10,792	9,541
Depreciation and amortization (Note A)	3,998	2,984	2,501
Repairs and maintenance	3,015	2,046	3,031
Operating profit	19,243	11,806	11,256
Other income (expense)			
Interest income	422	838	738
Interest expense	(2,585)	(2,277)	(1,274)
Earnings before income taxes	17,080	10,367	10,720
Income taxes (Notes A and D)	7,686	4,457	4,824
Net Earnings	$ 9,394	$ 5,910	$ 5,896
Basic earnings per common share (Note G)	$ 1.96	$ 1.29	$ 1.33
Diluted earnings per common share (Note G)	$ 1.93	$ 1.26	$ 1.31

The accompanying notes are an integral part of these statements.

EXHIBIT 3.2   R.E.C., Inc. Consolidated Statements of Earnings for Years Ended December 31, 2007, 2006, 2005 (in Thousands Except per Share Amounts)

	2007	2006	2005
Income			
Net sales	$215,600	$153,000	$140,700
Interest income	422	838	738
	216,022	153,838	141,438
Costs and Expenses			
Cost of goods sold	129,364	91,879	81,606
Marketing, administrative, and other expenses	66,993	49,315	47,838
Interest expense	2,585	2,277	1,274
Income taxes	7,686	4,457	4,824
Net Earnings	$ 9,394	$ 5,910	$ 5,896
Basic earnings per Common Share	$ 1.96	$ 1.29	$ 1.33
Diluted earnings per Common Share	$ 1.93	$ 1.26	$ 1.31

those resulting from investments by owners and distributions to owners. Companies are required to report total comprehensive income in one of three ways:

- on the face of its income statement,
- in a separate statement of comprehensive income, or
- in its statement of stockholders' equity.

Data are presented in corporate income statements for three years to facilitate comparison and to provide evidence regarding trends of revenues, expenses, and net earnings. Because R.E.C. Inc. has only net earnings and no other comprehensive income, the company does not have a statement of comprehensive income. The statements for R.E.C. Inc. are consolidated, which means that the information presented is a combination of the results for R.E.C. Inc. and its wholly owned subsidiaries. The disclosure of comprehensive income and the accounting methods used for subsidiary investments will be discussed later in the chapter under the headings "Comprehensive Income" and "Equity Earnings."

Common-Size Income Statement

As discussed in Chapter 2, common-size financial statements are a useful analytical tool to compare firms with different levels of sales or total assets, facilitate internal or structural analysis of a firm, evaluate trends, and make industry comparisons. The common-size income statement expresses each income statement item as a percentage of net sales. The common-size income statement shows the relative magnitude of various expenses relative to sales, the profit percentages (gross profit, operating profit, and net profit margins), and the relative importance of "other" revenues and expenses. Exhibit 3.3

EXHIBIT 3.3   R.E.C. Inc. Common-Size Income Statements (Percent)

	2007	2006	2005	2004	2003
Net Sales	100.0	100.0	100.0	100.0	100.0
Cost of Goods Sold	60.0	60.1	58.0	58.2	58.2
Gross Profit	40.0	39.9	42.0	41.8	41.8
Operating Expenses					
Selling and administrative expenses	21.2	21.8	23.2	20.3	20.0
Advertising	6.6	7.1	6.8	6.4	6.3
Depreciation and amortization	1.9	2.0	1.8	1.4	1.2
Repairs and maintenance	1.4	1.3	2.2	2.7	2.7
Operating Profit	8.9	7.7	8.0	11.0	11.6
Other Income (Expense)					
Interest income	.2	.5	.5	.3	.3
Interest expense	(1.2)	(1.5)	(.9)	(.9)	(1.0)
Earnings before income taxes	7.9	6.7	7.6	10.4	10.9
Income Taxes	3.6	2.9	3.4	5.4	5.7
Net Earnings	4.3	3.8	4.2	5.0	5.2

presents the common-size income statement for R.E.C. Inc. that will be used in this chapter and Chapter 6 to analyze the firm's profitability.

Net Sales

Total sales revenue for each year of the three-year period is shown net of returns and allowances. A *sales return* is a cancellation of a sale, and a *sales allowance* is a deduction from the original sales invoice price. Since sales are the major revenue source for most companies, the trend of this figure is a key element in performance measurement. Although most of the analysis of R.E.C. Inc.'s financial statements will be conducted in Chapter 6, the reader can look for clues on the income statement.

It would appear, for instance, that R.E.C. Inc. had a much better sales year in 2007 than 2006: sales increased 40.9% ($62.6 million) between 2006 and 2007, compared with an 8.7% ($12.3 million) growth between 2005 and 2006. If a company's sales are increasing (or decreasing), it is important to determine whether the change is a result of price, volume, or a combination of both. Are sales growing because the firm is increasing prices or because more units are being sold, or both? It would seem that, in general, higher-quality earnings would be the product of both volume and price increases (during inflation). The firm would want to sell more units and keep prices increasing at least in line with the rate of inflation. The reasons for sales growth (or decline) are covered in a firm's Management Discussion and Analysis section of the annual or 10-K report (see Chapter 1).

A related issue is whether sales are growing in "real" (inflation-adjusted) as well as "nominal" (as reported) terms. The change in sales in nominal terms can be readily calculated from the figures reported on the income statement. An adjustment of the reported sales figure with the Consumer Price Index (CPI) (or some other measure of general inflation) will enable the analyst to make a comparison of the changes in real and nominal terms. To make the calculation to compare real with nominal sales, begin with the sales figures reported in the income statement, and adjust years prior to the current year with the CPI or some other price index. For R.E.C. Inc., the nominal growth rate was already calculated to be 40.9%. Assuming the CPIs for 2007 and 2006 are 322.2 and 311.1, respectively, the adjusted or real sales figure for 2006 is $158,459, (322.2/311.1) × $153,000. Sales when adjusted for inflation still increased 36.1% from 2006 to 2007, but at a smaller rate. Note A (see Exhibit 1.2) to the R.E.C. Inc. financial statements indicates that new store openings have occurred that could explain the large sales growth in the past year.

The remainder of the income statement reveals management's ability to translate sales dollars into profits. The sales or revenue number is the common denominator in the common-size income statement (Exhibit 3.3) and is, therefore, 100% for all companies when preparing this statement. The calculations are shown for other important items on the common-size income statement as they are discussed in this chapter.

Cost of Goods Sold

The first expense deduction from sales is the cost to the seller of products or services sold to customers. This expense is called *cost of goods sold* or *cost of sales*. The amount of cost of goods sold for any accounting period, as explained in Chapter 2, will be affected by the cost flow assumption used to value inventory. R.E.C. Inc. uses the last-in, first-out (LIFO) method, which means that the last purchases made during the year have been charged to expense. The LIFO method generally results in the matching of current costs with current revenues and therefore produces higher-quality earnings than either first-in, first-out (FIFO) or average cost.

The relationship between cost of goods sold and net sales—called the *cost of goods sold percentage*—is an important one for profit determination because cost of goods sold is the largest expense item for many firms.

	2007	2006	2005
$\dfrac{\text{Cost of goods sold}}{\text{Net sales}}$	$\dfrac{129{,}364}{215{,}600} = 60.0\%$	$\dfrac{91{,}879}{153{,}000} = 60.1\%$	$\dfrac{81{,}606}{140{,}700} = 58.0\%$

The cost of goods sold percentage for R.E.C. Inc. increased between 2005 and 2006. This is a result of the firm lowering prices or increasing costs. See Figure 3.1 for a more detailed explanation. Since then, the firm either has controlled costs more effectively and/or has been able to pass along price increases to customers. The cost of goods sold percentage will vary significantly by industry, according to markup policies and other factors. For example, the cost of goods sold percentage for jewelry retailers averages 55.5%, compared with 76.0% for retailers of groceries.[2]

Gross Profit

The difference between net sales and cost of goods sold is called *gross profit* or *gross margin*. Gross profit is the first step of profit measurement on the multiple-step income

FIGURE 3.1   Understand the Math!

If the cost of goods sold (COGS) percentage increases or decreases, this does not necessarily mean that costs have increased or decreased. The change in the percentage may be caused by decreases or increases in the selling price. Here's an example:

Assume it costs a company $4 to make a toy that sells for $10 in year 1. In year 2, competition is fierce, and the company must drop the selling price to $8 to sell the toy.

	Year 1		Year 2	
Sales	$10	100%	$8	100%
COGS	4	40%	4	50%
Gross Profit	$ 6	60%	$4	50%

Notice that the COGS percentage has increased, but the cost to manufacture the toy has not. The decrease in selling price is the cause of the higher COGS percentage and lower gross profit margin.

Always pay attention to the numbers—know the difference between raw dollars and percentages!

---

[2]The Risk Management Association, *Annual Statement Studies*, Philadelphia, PA, 2004.

statement and is a key analytical tool in assessing a firm's operating performance. The gross profit figure indicates how much profit the firm is generating after deducting the cost of products or services sold. Gross profit, expressed as a percentage of net sales, is the gross profit margin.

	2007	2006	2005
$\dfrac{\text{Gross profit}}{\text{Net sales}}$	$\dfrac{86{,}236}{215{,}600} = 40.0\%$	$\dfrac{61{,}121}{153{,}000} = 39.9\%$	$\dfrac{59{,}094}{140{,}700} = 42.0\%$

The gross profit margin and cost of goods sold percentage are complements of each other (the two percentages always add to 100%); therefore, the analysis of these ratios will be the same. Generally, firms want to maintain the relationship between gross profit and sales, or, if possible, increase gross profit margin. In stable industries, such as groceries, one can expect to find the same gross profit margin from year to year because companies will raise prices proportionately as cost of goods sold increases. In volatile industries such as high technology, gross profit margin may increase or decrease significantly from year to year. For example, Target Corporation's gross profit margin for 2002 and 2003 was 32% and 33% for 2004, while Lucent Technologies had a 13%, 31%, and 42% gross profit margin, respectively, in the same three years. In capital intensive industries such as manufacturing, sales volume changes will cause volatility in the gross profit margin because there are fixed costs included in cost of goods sold. Fixed costs do not vary proportionately with volume changes but remain the same within a relevant range of activity.

Companies having more than one revenue source will show each revenue line separately and also show the corresponding cost of goods sold or cost of sales for each revenue source. An illustration of how to calculate and analyze gross profit margin when there are multiple revenue sources is shown in Figure 3.2.

Operating Expense

R.E.C. Inc. discloses four categories of operating expense: selling and administrative, advertising, depreciation and amortization, and repairs and maintenance. In addition, a fifth category, operating lease payments, is disclosed in Note E. These are all areas over which management exercises discretion and that have considerable impact on the firm's current and future profitability. Thus, it is important to track these accounts carefully in terms of trends, absolute amounts, relationship to sales, and relationship to industry competitors.

Selling and administrative expenses are expenses relating to the sale of products or services and to the management of the business. They include salaries, rent, insurance, utilities, supplies, and sometimes depreciation and advertising expense. R.E.C. Inc. provides separate disclosures for advertising and for depreciation and amortization. Note A to the R.E.C. Inc. financial statements indicates that the firm includes the expenses related to the opening of new stores in selling and administrative expense.

Advertising costs are or should be a major expense in the budgets of companies for which marketing is an important element of success. This topic was discussed in Chapter 1. As a retail firm operating in a competitive industry, recreational products,

FIGURE 3.2 **Gross Profit Margin for Multiple Revenue Sources**

ABC Company has two distinct revenue sources, food and tobacco. The following information is from ABC Company's income statement:

	2007	%	2006	%
Food sales	$ 800		$ 750	
Tobacco sales	900		900	
Total sales	$1,700	100.0	$1,650	100.0
Cost of goods sold—food	$ 560		$ 525	
Cost of goods sold—tobacco	450		360	
Total cost of goods sold	$1,010	59.4	$ 885	53.6
Gross profit	$ 690	40.6	$ 765	46.4

To analyze the overall gross profit margin change from 46.4% to 40.6% the gross profit margins of each revenue source should be calculated as follows:

	2007	%	2006	%
Food sales	$800	100.0	$ 750	100.0
Less: Cost of goods sold—food	(560)	70.0	(525)	70.0
Gross profit—food	$240	30.0	$ 225	30.0
Tobacco sales	$900	100.0	$ 900	100.0
Less: Cost of goods sold—tobacco	(450)	50.0	(360)	40.0
Gross profit—tobacco	$450	50.0	$ 540	60.0

The overall decline in gross profit margin has been caused by the tobacco product line, not the food product line. By analyzing each revenue source individually the analyst can better understand which divisions of a company are successful and which may be facing challenges.

R.E.C. Inc. spends 6 to 7 cents of every sales dollar for advertising, as indicated by the ratio of advertising to net sales:

	2007	2006	2005
Advertising Net sales	$\dfrac{14,258}{215,600} = 6.6\%$	$\dfrac{10,792}{153,000} = 7.1\%$	$\dfrac{9,541}{140,700} = 6.8\%$

Lease payments include the costs associated with operating rentals of leased facilities for retail outlets. Note E to the financial statements explains the agreements that apply to the rental arrangements and presents a schedule of minimum annual rental commitments. Observation of the sharp rise in lease payments for R.E.C. Inc. between 2006 and 2007, from $7.1 million to $13.1 million—an increase of 84%—would indicate an expansion of the firm's use of leased space.

Depreciation and Amortization

The cost of assets other than land that will benefit a business enterprise for more than a year is allocated over the asset's service life rather than expensed in the year of purchase. Land is an exception to the rule because land is considered to have an unlimited useful life. The cost allocation procedure is determined by the nature of the long-lived asset. *Depreciation* is used to allocate the cost of tangible fixed assets such as buildings, machinery, equipment, furniture and fixtures, and motor vehicles. *Amortization* is the process applied to capital leases, leasehold improvements, and the cost expiration of intangible assets such as patents, copyrights, trademarks, and franchises. The cost of acquiring and developing natural resources—oil and gas, other minerals, and standing timber—is allocated through *depletion*. The amount of expense recognized in any accounting period will depend on the level of investment in the relevant asset; estimates with regard to the asset's service life and residual value; and for depreciation, the method used.

R.E.C. Inc. recognizes annual depreciation expense for the firm's buildings and equipment and amortization expense for the leasehold improvements on rental property. Note A to the R.E.C. Inc. financial statements explains the company's procedures relating to depreciation and amortization: "Depreciation and Amortization: Property, plant, and equipment is stated at cost. Depreciation expense is calculated principally by the straight-line method based on estimated useful lives for buildings. Estimated useful lives of leasehold improvements represent the remaining term of the lease in effect at the time the improvements are made." Remember that for tax purposes, most firms use the Modified Accelerated Cost Recovery System for depreciation.

With any expense on the income statement, the analyst should evaluate the amount and trend of the expenditure as well as its relationship to the volume of firm activity that is relevant to the expense. For a firm like R.E.C. Inc., one would expect a fairly constant relationship between the investment in buildings, leasehold improvements, and equipment on the balance sheet and the annual expense recorded for depreciation and amortization on the income statement.

	2007	2006
Depreciation and amortization	$\frac{3,998}{39,796} = 10.0\%$	$\frac{2,984}{25,696} = 11.6\%$
Buildings, leasehold improvements, equipment		

The percentage of depreciation and amortization expense has decreased somewhat, possibly due to the fact that new assets were placed in service during 2007 for only a part of the year, rendering less than a full year's depreciation and amortization. To help put these accounts in a broader context, Chapter 5 will include an analysis of long-run trends by using data from earlier years as well as the current year's financial statements.

Repairs and maintenance are the annual costs of repairing and maintaining the firm's property, plant, and equipment. Expenditures in this area should correspond to the level of investment in capital equipment and to the age and condition of the company's fixed assets. Similar to research and development and advertising and marketing expenses, inadequate allowance for repair and maintenance can impair the ongoing success of an organization. This category, like depreciation, should be evaluated in relation to the firm's investments in fixed assets. The percentage decrease in this account for R.E.C. Inc. could be a result of having newer fixed assets needing fewer repairs, or it could be a choice to delay repairs in order to increase operating profit in the short-term.

	2007	2006
Repairs and maintenance / Buildings, leasehold improvements, equipment	$\dfrac{3,015}{39,796} = 7.6\%$	$\dfrac{2,046}{25,696} = 8.0\%$

Firms in industries other than retail will have different expenses that should also be evaluated. For example, the trend of research and development expenses relative to net sales is an important measurement to evaluate for high-technology and pharmaceutical companies. By preparing a common-size income statement, each operating expense can be easily analyzed for any company. When evaluating operating expenses, good judgment must be used to decide if increases or decreases in expenses are warranted. For example, reducing advertising or research and development may be detrimental in the long term if sales decrease; however, unnecessary increases in operating expense accounts could indicate inefficiencies in the company's operations.

Operating Profit

Operating profit (also called *EBIT* or *earnings before interest and taxes*) is the second step of profit determination on the R.E.C. Inc. earnings statement and measures the overall performance of the company's operations: sales revenue less the expenses associated with generating sales. The figure for operating profit provides a basis for assessing the success of a company apart from its financing and investing activities and separate from tax considerations. The *operating profit margin* is calculated as the relationship between operating profit and net sales:

	2007	2006	2005
Operating profit / Net sales	$\dfrac{19,243}{215,600} = 8.9\%$	$\dfrac{11,806}{153,000} = 7.7\%$	$\dfrac{11,256}{140,700} = 8.0\%$

The ratio indicates that R.E.C. Inc. strengthened its return on operations in 2007 after a dip in 2006. Looking at the common-size income statement (Exhibit 3.3) it is easy to see that despite the increase in cost of goods sold over the past two years, R.E.C. Inc. has reduced selling and administrative and advertising expenses enough to increase operating profit.

Other income (Expense)

This category includes revenues and costs other than from operations, such as dividend and interest income, interest expense, gains (losses) from investments, equity earnings (losses), and gains (losses) from the sale of fixed assets. Equity earnings (losses) are discussed in the next section. R.E.C. Inc. recognizes as other income the interest earned on its investments in marketable securities and as other expense the interest paid on its debt. The relative amounts will be dependent on the level of investments and the amount of debt outstanding, as well as the prevailing level of interest rates.

Under the requirements of FASB Statement No. 115, discussed in Chapter 2, firms (primarily financial institutions and insurance companies) that carry debt and equity securities classified as "trading securities" report these investments on the balance sheet at market value with any unrealized gains and losses included in earnings.

In the assessment of earnings quality (discussed in Chapters 1 and 5), it is important that the analyst consider the materiality and the variability of the non operating items of income—for example, gains and losses on the sale of major capital assets, accounting changes, extraordinary items, investment income from temporary investments in cash equivalents, and investment income recognized under the equity method.

Equity Earnings

An additional issue that users sometimes encounter in attempting to evaluate financial statement data is the method—cost or equity—employed to account for investments in the voting stock of other companies. This method is not an issue for R.E.C. Inc. because the parent owns 100% of the voting stock in its subsidiaries; R.E.C. Inc. and its subsidiaries are, in substance, one consolidated entity. Where one firm owns more than 50% of the voting stock of another company, the parent company can obviously control the business operations, financial policies, and dividend declarations of the subsidiary, and consolidated financial statements are prepared with the disclosures relating to consolidation policies provided in the financial statement notes. The accounting rules underlying the preparation of consolidated financial statements, while similar to the equity method, are extremely complicated and beyond the scope of this book.[3] Questions regarding use of cost or equity come into play for stock investments of less than 50%, where consolidated financial statements are not prepared.

Accounting rules permit two different methods to account for stock investments of less than 50%. The equity method allows the investor proportionate recognition of the investee's net income, irrespective of the payment or nonpayment of cash dividends; under the cost method, the investor recognizes investment income only to the extent of any cash dividends received. At issue in the choice of accounting methods is whether the investor exercises control over the investee.

Accounting Principles Board Opinion No. 18 specifies that the equity method of accounting should be used when the investor can exercise significant influence over the investee's operating and financing policies. No problem exists where there is ownership of 50% or more because, clearly, one company can control the other. But at what level below 50% ownership can one firm substantially influence the affairs of another firm? Although there can be exceptions, 20% ownership of voting stock is generally considered to be evidence of substantial influence. There are, however, circumstances in which less than 20% ownership reflects control and cases in which more than 20% does not. Such factors as the extent of representation on the investee's

---

[3]Accounting for consolidated financial statements is fully discussed and explained in advanced accounting textbooks.

board of directors, major intercompany transactions, technological dependence, and other relationships would be considered in the determination.

   Use of the equity method is justified on a theoretical basis because it fits the requirements of the accrual basis of accounting. The investor's share in investee income is recorded by the investor in the period in which it is earned, rather than as cash is received. Analysts, however, should be aware of whether a company uses the cost or the equity method. What difference does it make whether a company uses the cost or equity method? An illustration should help provide the answer.

   Assume that Company A acquires exactly 20% of the voting common stock of Company B for $400,000. Company B reports $100,000 earnings for the year and pays $25,000 in cash dividends. For Company A, the income recognition in the earnings statement and the noncurrent investment account on the balance sheet would be entirely different depending on the accounting method used for the investment.

	Cost	Equity
Income statement: investment income	$ 5,000	$ 20,000
Balance sheet: investment account	$400,000	$415,000

   The cost method allows recognition of investment income only to the extent of any cash dividends actually received ($25,000 × .20), and the investment account is carried at cost.[4] The equity method permits the investor to count as income the percentage interest in the investee's earnings.

Company B's earnings	$100,000
Company A's percent ownership	× .20
Company A's investment income	$ 20,000

   Under the equity method, the investment account is increased by the amount of investment income recognized and is reduced by the amount of cash dividends received.

Investment at cost	$400,000
Investment income	+20,000
Cash dividends received	−5,000
Investment account	$415,000

   Use of the equity method somewhat distorts earnings in the sense that income is recognized even though no cash may ever be received. The theoretical justification for the equity method is that it is presumed that the investor (Company A), through its control of voting shares, could cause Company B to pay dividends. In reality, this may not be true, and Company A is permitted to recognize more income than is received in cash.

   One of the adjustments to net income (illustrated in Chapter 4) to calculate cash flow from operations is to deduct the amount by which income recognized under the equity method of accounting exceeds cash received from dividends. For Company A this amount would be $15,000 (investment income $20,000 less cash dividends $5,000).

---

[4]Or market, depending on the provisions of FASB Statement No. 115; this statement does not apply to investments accounted for under the equity method.

It is also equal to the increase in the balance sheet investment account (ending balance $415,000 less original cost $400,000). For comparative purposes it would be appropriate to eliminate this noncash portion of earnings.

Earnings Before Income Taxes/Effective Tax Rate

Earnings before income taxes is the profit recognized before the deduction of income tax expense. Income taxes are discussed in notes to the financial statements describing the difference between the reported figure for income taxes and the actual amount of income taxes paid (see the discussion of deferred income taxes in Chapter 2). For R.E.C. Inc., refer to Note A, which explains why the differences occur, and Note D, which quantifies the reconciliation between taxes paid and tax expense reported on the income statement. R.E.C. Inc.'s *effective tax rate* would be calculated by dividing income taxes on the income statement by earnings before taxes.

	2007	2006	2005
$\dfrac{\text{Income taxes}}{\text{Earnings before income taxes}}$	$\dfrac{7,686}{17,080} = 45.0\%$	$\dfrac{4,457}{10,367} = 43.0\%$	$\dfrac{4,824}{10,720} = 45.0\%$

In recent years, as revenues have been sluggish or decreasing, some companies have resorted to techniques to reduce taxes in order to increase earnings. Legitimately cutting taxes should always be applauded, however, firms cannot rely on tax-cutting techniques to continually increase earnings. Users of financial statements need to distinguish between earnings increasing due to core operations versus items such as tax rate deductions. (See Chapter 5 for more on this topic.)

Noteworthy items that may affect the effective tax rate are net operating losses (NOLs) and foreign taxes. Companies operating at a loss are allowed to carry back the loss two years and/or carry forward the loss 20 years, offsetting prior or future tax payments. If the NOL is carried back, the company may receive a refund of taxes previously paid.

Companies often have operations in foreign countries and must pay taxes based on that country's tax law. By reading the notes to the financial statements, the user can determine the effect foreign taxes have on the overall effective tax rate. General Electric Company (GE) reported earnings growth from 2003 to 2004 of 10.6%, yet its provision for income taxes declined 18.6%. GE, in 2004, had one of the lowest effective tax rates in the United States at 17.5% (the U.S. federal statutory income tax rate for corporations was 35.0% in 2004). How has GE been able to reduce its tax rate? The key reason is that GE was able to reduce the statutory rate by 12.4% due to lower foreign tax rates, with the remaining 5.1% reduction caused by tax-exempt income, IRS settlements, and miscellaneous items.

Tax legislation signed into law on October 22, 2004, offers new tax breaks to companies. The "American Jobs Creation Act of 2004" cuts the 35% tax rate to 32% for American manufacturers that engage in domestic production. For approximately one year, U.S. multinational corporations can also repatriate profits from abroad at a 5.25% tax rate instead of the statutory rate of 35%.[5]

---

[5]Lingling Wei, "Accounting Body Plans to Clarify Rules for Booking New Tax Break," *Wall Street Journal*, November 10, 2004.

Special Items

If companies are affected by the following three items, they must be disclosed separately on the income statement, net of income tax effects or retrospectively applied to prior periods' financial statements:

- Discontinued operations
- Extraordinary items
- Accounting changes

Special items are often one-time items that will not recur in the future. Because of the special disclosure requirements, it is easier for the analyst to determine if these items should be included when predicting future earnings amounts. R.E.C. Inc. is not affected by any special items, however, each item will be explained in this chapter and examples are discussed further in Chapter 5.

Discontinued operations occur when a firm sells or discontinues a clearly distinguishable portion of its business. The results of continuing operations are shown separately from the operating results of the discontinued portion of the business. Any gain or loss on the disposal is also disclosed separately.

Extraordinary gains and losses are items that meet two criteria: unusual in nature and not expected to recur in the foreseeable future, considering the firm's operating environment. In an interesting decision in 2001, the FASB declared that the terrorist attack on September 11 was not an extraordinary event. While the FASB agreed that in layman's terminology the event was extraordinary, recording revenues or expenses related to September 11 as extraordinary would not improve the financial reporting system. The FASB's task force realized the dilemma as they tried to apply extraordinary treatment to the airline industry. Separating losses caused by the attack from losses already incurred by the economic downturn was an impossible task.[6]

Prior to 2006, the cumulative effect of a change in accounting principle was disclosed when a firm changed an accounting policy. Changes in accounting policy may be voluntary; for example, a company changes inventory methods from FIFO to the average cost method. Other changes are mandated by the FASB or the Securities and Exchange Commission (SEC) when new rules must be implemented. The issuance of FASB Statement No. 154, "Accounting Changes and Error Corrections—a replacement of APB Opinion No. 20 and FASB Statement No. 3," effective for fiscal years beginning after December 15, 2005, has changed the disclosure requirements for accounting changes. This ruling is a result of the FASB's efforts to develop standards that are in agreement with current international accounting standards. Retrospective application to prior periods' financial statements is required for changes in accounting principles.[7] Retrospective application is defined as the application of a different accounting principle to prior accounting periods as if that principle had always been

---

[6]Steve Liesman, "Accountants, in a Reversal, Say Costs from the Attack Aren't 'Extraordinary,' " *Wall Street Journal*, October 1, 2001.

[7]If it is impracticable to determine the period-specific effects of an accounting change on one or more individual prior periods presented, then the new accounting principle should be applied to the balances of assets and liabilities as of the beginning of the earliest period for which retrospective application is practicable and a corresponding adjustment should be made to the opening balance of retained earnings for that period rather than be reported in the income statement.

used or as the adjustment of previously issued financial statements to reflect a change in the reporting entity. The term "restatement" was also redefined in FASB Statement No. 154 as the revising of previously issued financial statements to reflect correction of an error. In addition, the statement specifies that changes to depreciation, amortization, or depletion methods be accounted for as a change in accounting estimate affected by a change in accounting principle.

Net Earnings

Net earnings, or "the bottom line," represents the firm's profit after consideration of all revenue and expense reported during the accounting period. The *net profit margin* shows the percentage of profit earned on every sales dollar.

	2007	2006	2005
$\dfrac{\text{Net earnings}}{\text{Net sales}}$	$\dfrac{9,394}{215,600} = 4.4\%$	$\dfrac{5,910}{153,000} = 3.9\%$	$\dfrac{5,896}{140,700} = 4.2\%$

Earnings Per Common Share

Earnings per common share is the net earnings available to common stockholders for the period divided by the average number of common stock shares outstanding. This figure shows the return to the common stock shareholder for every share owned. R.E.C. Inc. earned $1.96 per share in 2007, compared with $1.29 per share in 2006 and $1.33 per share in 2005.

Companies with complex capital structures—which means existence of convertible securities (such as bonds convertible into common stock), stock options, and warrants—must calculate two amounts for earnings per share: *basic* and *diluted*. If convertible securities were converted into common stock and/or the options and warrants were exercised, there would be more shares outstanding for every dollar earned, and the potential for dilution is accounted for by the dual presentation. R.E.C. Inc. has a complex capital structure and therefore presents both basic and diluted earnings per share. In Note G to the financial statements, R.E.C. Inc. discloses the reconciliation of the basic and diluted earnings per share computations for the three-year period ended December 31, 2007. The diluted earnings per share number is slightly lower each year compared to the basic earnings per share due to the dilutive effect of stock options that employees could exercise in the future.

Another issue that an analyst should consider in assessing earnings quality is any material changes in the number of common stock shares outstanding that will cause a change in the computation of earnings per share. Changes in the number of shares outstanding result from such transactions as treasury stock purchases, the purchase and retirement of a firm's own common stock, stock splits, and reverse stock splits. (Stock splits and reverse stock splits are explained in a later section of this chapter.)

Comprehensive Income

As discussed in Chapter 2 and earlier in this chapter, companies must now report total comprehensive income either on the face of the income statement, in the statement of stockholders' equity, or in a separate financial statement. For example, even though Pfizer, Inc. chooses to report total comprehensive income in the statement of shareholders' equity, if a separate statement had been used, it would appear as illustrated in Exhibit 3.4.

Currently, there are four items that may comprise a company's other comprehensive income: *foreign currency translation effects, unrealized gains and losses, additional pension liabilities*, and *cash flow hedges*. These items are outlined below; however, a detailed discussion of these topics is beyond the scope of this text. A more complete discussion of these four areas can be found in most intermediate or advanced accounting textbooks.

Foreign currency translation effects are the result of disclosures specified in FASB Statement No. 52, "Foreign Currency Translation." When U.S. firms operate abroad, the foreign financial statements must be translated into U.S. dollars at the end of the accounting period. Because the value of the dollar changes in relation to foreign currencies, gains and losses can result from the translation process. These exchange gains and losses, which fluctuate from period to period, are "accumulated" in the stockholders' equity section in most cases.[8]

According to the provisions of FASB Statement No. 115, discussed in Chapter 2, *unrealized gains and losses* on investments in debt and equity securities classified as available-for-sale are reported in comprehensive income. Cumulative net unrealized gains and losses are reported in the accumulated other comprehensive income section of stockholders' equity on the balance sheet.

Additional pension liabilities are reported as other comprehensive income when the accumulated benefit obligation is greater than the fair market value of plan assets less the balance in the accrued pension liability account or plus the balance in the deferred pension asset account. Pension accounting is discussed in Chapter 5.

Companies using *cash flow hedges* (derivatives designated as hedging the exposure to variable cash flows of a forecasted transaction) are required to initially report any gain or loss from a change in the fair market value of the cash flow hedge in other

EXHIBIT 3.4 Pfizer, Inc. Statements of Comprehensive Income for the Years Ended December 31, 2004, 2003, 2002 (in Millions)

	2004	2003	2002
Net income	$11,361	$3,910	$9,126
Other comprehensive income/(expense), net of tax			
Currency translation adjustment	1,961	2,070	85
Net unrealized gain (loss) on available-for-sale securities	128	68	(32)
Minimum pension liability	(6)	(68)	(179)
Total comprehensive income	$13,444	$5,980	$9,000

---

[8]Exceptions are when the U.S. company designates the U.S. dollar as the "functional" currency for the foreign entity—such is the case, for example, when the foreign operations are simply an extension of the parent company's operations. Under this circumstance, the foreign translation gains and losses are included in the calculation of net income on the income statement.

comprehensive income and subsequently reclassify the amount into earnings when the forecasted transaction affects earnings.[9]

The Statement of Stockholders' Equity

The statement of stockholders' equity details the transactions that affect the balance sheet equity accounts during an accounting period. Exhibit 3.5 shows the changes that have occurred in the equity accounts of R.E.C. Inc. Changes to the common stock and additional paid-in capital accounts are due to employees exercising their stock options. The retained earnings account has been increased each year by the net earnings and reduced by the cash dividends that R.E.C. Inc. has paid to their common stockholders. (R.E.C. Inc.'s dividend payment policy is discussed in Chapter 6.)

In 2007, R.E.C. Inc. paid cash dividends of $.33 per share on average shares outstanding (Note G) of 4,792,857 for a total of $1,581,643. The amount of the dividend payment was reduced from $.41 per share in 2006 and 2005.

Some companies have *stock dividends*, *stock splits* or *reverse stock splits* during an accounting period. With stock dividends, the company issues to existing shareholders

EXHIBIT 3.5   R.E.C. Inc. Consolidated Statements of Stockholders' Equity for the Years Ended December 31, 2007, 2006, and 2005 (in Thousands)

	COMMON STOCK		ADDITIONAL	RETAINED	
	SHARES	AMOUNT	PAID-IN CAPITAL	EARNINGS	TOTAL
Balance at December 31, 2004	4,340	$4,340	$857	$24,260	$29,457
Net earnings				5,896	5,896
Proceeds from sale of shares from exercise of stock options	103	103	21		124
Cash dividends				(1,841)	(1,841)
Balance at December 31, 2005	4,443	$4,443	$878	$28,315	$33,636
Net earnings				5,910	5,910
Proceeds from sale of shares from exercise of stock options	151	151	32		183
Cash dividends				(1,862)	(1,862)
Balance at December 31, 2006	4,594	$4,594	$910	$32,363	$37,867
Net earnings				9,394	9,394
Proceeds from sale of shares from exercise of stock options	209	209	47		256
Cash dividends				(1,582)	(1,582)
Balance at December 31, 2007	4,803	$4,803	$957	$40,175	$45,935

---

[9]FASB Statement of Financial Accounting Standards No. 133, "Accounting for Derivative Instruments and Hedging Activities," 1998.

additional shares of stock in proportion to current ownership. Stock dividends reduce the retained earnings account. Unlike a cash dividend, which results in the receipt of cash, a stock dividend represents nothing of value to the stockholder. The stockholder has more shares, but the proportion of ownership is exactly the same, and the company's net assets (assets minus liabilities) are exactly the same. The market value of the stock should drop in proportion to the additional shares issued.

Stock splits also result in the issuance of additional shares in proportion to current ownership and represent nothing of value to the stockholder; they are generally used to lower the market price of a firm's shares to make the common stock more affordable for the average investor. For example, if a company declares a 2–1 stock split, a stockholder with 100 shares ends up with 200 shares and the market price of the stock should fall by 50%. The company makes no accounting entry but does have a memorandum item noting the change in par value of the stock and the change in the number of shares outstanding. A reverse stock split is the opposite of a stock split and occurs when a company decreases, rather than increases, its outstanding shares. A 1–10 reverse stock split would have the effect of reducing 100 shares to 10 shares and the market price should increase 10 times. A reverse stock split usually occurs when a company is struggling financially.

Transactions other than the recognition of net profit/loss and the payment of dividends can cause changes in the retained earnings balance. These include prior period adjustments and certain changes in accounting principles. Prior period adjustments result primarily from the correction of errors made in previous accounting periods; the beginning retained earnings balance is adjusted for the year in which the error is discovered. Some changes in accounting principles, such as a change from LIFO to any other inventory method, also cause an adjustment to retained earnings for the cumulative effect of the change. Retained earnings can also be affected by transactions in a firm's own shares.

Earnings Quality, Cash Flow, Segmental Accounting

Additional topics that are directly related to the income statement are covered in other sections of the book. The assessment of the quality of reported earnings is an essential element of income statement analysis. Many firms now report more than just the generally accepted accounting principles (GAAP) earnings numbers in their annual reports and quarterly press releases. These additional numbers are referred to as pro forma earnings, earnings before interest, taxes, depreciation, and amortization (EBITDA), core earnings, or adjusted earnings and have added not only to the confusion of investors, but have in many cases affected the quality of financial reporting. This important topic is discussed in Chapter 5.

The earnings figure reported on the income statement is rarely the same as the cash generated during an accounting period. Because it is cash that a firm needs to service debt, pay suppliers, invest in new capital assets, and pay cash dividends, cash flow from operations is a key ingredient in analyzing operating performance. The calculation of cash flow from operations, how it differs from reported earnings, and the interpretation of cash flow as a performance measure are discussed in Chapter 4.

The Appendix to Chapter 6 deals with the supplementary information reported by companies that operate in several different business segments. Segmental data include revenue, operating profit or loss, assets, depreciation and amortization, and capital expenditures by industry components. These disclosures facilitate the analysis of operating performance and contribution by each segment of a diversified company.

SELF-TEST

Solutions are provided in Appendix B.

_____ **1.** What does the income statement measure for a firm?
  (a) The changes in assets and liabilities that occurred during the period.
  (b) The financing and investment activities for a period.
  (c) The results of operations for a period.
  (d) The financial position of a firm for a period.

_____ **2.** How are companies required to report total comprehensive income?
  (a) On the face of the income statement.
  (b) In a separate statement of comprehensive income.
  (c) In its statement of stockholders' equity.
  (d) All of the above.

_____ **3.** Which of the following items needs to be disclosed separately in the income statement?
  (a) Discontinued operations.
  (b) Salary expense.
  (c) Warranty expense.
  (d) Bad debt expense.

_____ **4.** What is a common-size income statement?
  (a) An income statement that provides intermediate profit measures.
  (b) An income statement that groups all items of revenue together, then deducts all categories of expense.
  (c) A statement that expresses each item on an income statement as a percentage of net sales.
  (d) An income statement that includes all changes of equity during a period.

_____ **5.** Which of the following statements is incorrect with regard to gross profit or gross profit margin?
  (a) The gross profit margin and cost of goods sold percentage are complements of each other.
  (b) Generally, firms want to maintain the relationship between gross profit and sales, or, if possible, increase gross profit margin.
  (c) The gross profit margin tends to be more stable in industries such as groceries.
  (d) When cost of goods sold increases, most firms do not raise prices.

_____ **6.** Why is it important to evaluate increases and decreases in operating expenses?
  (a) Increases in operating expenses may indicate inefficiencies and decreases in operating expenses may be detrimental to long-term sales growth.
  (b) It is important to determine if companies are spending at least 10 cents of every sales dollar on advertising expenses.
  (c) Increases in operating expenses are always an indication that a firm will increase sales in the future.
  (d) None of the above.

_____ **7.** Which of the following assets will not be depreciated over its service life?
  (a) Buildings.
  (b) Furniture.
  (c) Land.
  (d) Equipment.

_____ **8.** How are costs of assets that benefit a firm for more than one year allocated?
  (a) Depreciation.
  (b) Depletion and amortization.
  (c) Costs are divided by service lives of assets and allocated to repairs and maintenance.
  (d) Both (a) and (b).

_____ **9.** Why should the expenditures for repairs and maintenance correspond to the level of investment in capital equipment and to the age and condition of that equipment?
  (a) Repairs and maintenance expense is calculated in the same manner as depreciation expense.
  (b) Repairs and maintenance are depreciated over the remaining life of the assets involved.
  (c) It is a generally accepted accounting principle that repairs and maintenance expense is generally between 5% and 10% of fixed assets.
  (d) Inadequate repairs of equipment can impair the operating success of a business enterprise.

_____ **10.** Why is the figure for operating profit important?
  (a) This is the figure used for calculating federal income tax expense.
  (b) The figure for operating profit provides a basis for assessing the success of a company apart from its financing and investment activities and separate from its tax status.
  (c) The operating profit figure includes all operating revenues and expenses as well as interest and taxes related to operations.
  (d) The figure for operating profit provides a basis for assessing the wealth of a firm.

_____ **11.** Why can the equity method of accounting for investments in the voting stock of other companies cause distortions in net earnings?
  (a) Significant influence may exist even if the ownership of voting stock is less than 20%.
  (b) Income is recognized where no cash may ever be received.
  (c) Income should be recognized in accordance with the accrual method of accounting.
  (d) Income is recognized only to the extent of cash dividends received.

_____ **12.** Why should the effective tax rate be evaluated when assessing earnings?
  (a) It is important to understand if earnings have increased due to tax techniques as opposed to positive changes in core operations.
  (b) Effective tax rates are irrelevant because they are mandated by law.
  (c) Effective tax rates do not include the effects of foreign taxes.
  (d) Net operating losses allow a firm to change its effective tax rates for each of the five years prior to the loss.

_____ **13.** What causes a firm to record a change in accounting principle?
   (a) Voluntary changes in accounting principles and changes mandated by the FASB or the SEC when new rules are implemented.
   (b) Selling a segment of the business.
   (c) Unusual and infrequent events.
   (d) All of the above.

_____ **14.** What are three profit measures calculated from the income statement?
   (a) Operating profit margin, net profit margin, repairs and maintenance to fixed assets.
   (b) Gross profit margin, cost of goods sold percentage, EBIT.
   (c) Gross profit margin, operating profit margin, net profit margin.
   (d) None of the above.

_____ **15.** When is a dual presentation of basic and diluted earnings per share required?
   (a) When a company has pension liabilities.
   (b) When convertible securities are in fact converted.
   (c) When a company has a simple capital structure.
   (d) When a company has a complex capital structure.

_____ **16.** What is a statement of stockholders' equity?
   (a) It is the same as a retained earnings statement.
   (b) It is a statement that reconciles only the treasury stock account.
   (c) It is a statement that summarizes changes in the entire stockholders' equity section of the balance sheet.
   (d) It is a statement reconciling the difference between stock issued at par value and stock issued at market value.

_____ **17.** What accounts can be found on a statement of stockholders' equity?
   (a) Investments in other companies.
   (b) Treasury stock, accumulated other comprehensive income, and retained earnings.
   (c) Market value of treasury stock.
   (d) Both (a) and (c).

_____ **18.** Which of the following cause(s) a change in the retained earnings account balance?
   (a) Prior period adjustment.
   (b) Payment of dividends.
   (c) Net profit or loss.
   (d) All of the above.

19. Match the following terms with the correct definitions:
   _____ (a) Depreciation.   _____ (h) Cost method.
   _____ (b) Depletion.   _____ (i) Single-step format.
   _____ (c) Amortization.   _____ (j) Multiple-step format.
   _____ (d) Gross profit.   _____ (k) Basic earnings per share.
   _____ (e) Operating profit.   _____ (l) Diluted earnings per share.
   _____ (f) Net profit.   _____ (m) Extraordinary events.
   _____ (g) Equity method.   _____ (n) Discontinued operations.

Definitions

(1) Proportionate recognition of investee's net income for investments in voting stock of other companies.

(2) Presentation of income statement that provides several intermediate profit measures.

(3) Unusual events not expected to recur in the foreseeable future.

(4) Allocation of costs of tangible fixed assets.

(5) Difference between sales revenue and expenses associated with generating sales.

(6) Recognition of income from investments in voting stock of other companies to the extent of cash dividend received.

(7) Operations that will not continue in the future because the firm sold a major portion of its business.

(8) Difference between net sales and cost of goods sold.

(9) Allocation of costs of acquiring and developing natural resources.

(10) Earnings per share figure calculated by dividing the average number of common stock shares outstanding into the net earnings available to common stockholders.

(11) Presentation of income statement that groups all revenue items, then deducts all expenses, to arrive at net income.

(12) Earnings per share figure based on the assumption that all potentially dilutive securities have been converted to common stock.

(13) Allocation of costs of intangible assets.

(14) Difference between all revenues and expenses.

20. The following categories appear on the income statement of Joshua Jeans Company:

(a) Net sales.

(b) Cost of sales.

(c) Operating expenses.

(d) Other revenue/expense.

(e) Income tax expense.

Classify the following items according to income statement category:

_____ (1) Depreciation expense.   _____ (8) Repairs and
_____ (2) Interest revenue.   maintenance.
_____ (3) Sales revenue.   _____ (9) Selling and admin-
_____ (4) Advertising expense.   istrative expenses.
_____ (5) Interest expense.   _____ (10) Cost of products sold.
_____ (6) Sales returns and allowances. _____ (11) Dividend income.
_____ (7) Federal income taxes.   _____ (12) Lease payments.

STUDY QUESTIONS AND PROBLEMS

3.1. What is the difference between a multiple-step and a single-step format of the earnings statement? Which format is the most useful for analysis?

3.2. Discuss the differences among depreciation, amortization, and depletion.

3.3. Explain the importance of assessing the level and trend of operating expenses.

3.4. What is an example of an industry that would need to spend a minimum on advertising to be competitive? On research and development?

3.5. Explain what can be found on a statement of stockholders' equity.

3.6. Why is the bottom line figure, net income, not necessarily a good indicator of a firm's financial success?

3.7. An excerpt from the Sun Company's annual report is presented below. Calculating any profit measures deemed necessary, discuss the implications of the profitability of the company.

Sun Company Income Statements for the Years Ended December 31, 2007, 2006, and 2005

	2007	2006	2005
Net sales	$236,000	$195,000	$120,000
Cost of goods sold	186,000	150,000	85,000
Gross profit	$ 50,000	$ 45,000	$ 35,000
Operating expenses	22,000	18,000	11,000
Operating profit	$ 28,000	$ 27,000	$ 24,000
Income taxes	12,000	11,500	10,500
Net income	$ 16,000	$ 15,500	$ 13,500

3.8. Using the information below for Dean Corporation, calculate the amount of dividends Dean most likely paid to common stockholders in 2007, 2008, and 2009.

Retained earnings balances		Net income	
January 1, 2007	$ 760		
December 31, 2007	1,026	2007	$330
December 31, 2008	1,171	2008	200
December 31, 2009	1,164	2009	48

3.9. Big Company purchased 25% of the voting common stock of Little Company on January 1 and paid $500,000 for the investment. Little Company reported $250,000 of earnings for the year and paid $50,000 in cash dividends. Calculate investment income and the balance sheet investment account for Big Company under the cost method and under the equity method.

3.10. Prepare a multiple-step income statement for Coyote, Inc. from the following single-step statement.

Net sales	$1,833,000
Interest income	13,000
	1,846,000
Costs and expenses:	
Cost of good sold	1,072,000
Selling expenses	279,000
General and admin. expenses	175,000
Depreciation	14,000
Interest expense	16,000
Income tax expense	116,000
Net income	$ 174,000

3.11. Income statements for Yarrick Company for the years ending December 31, 2007, 2006, and 2005 are shown below. Prepare a common-size income statement and analyze the profitability of the company.

Yarrick Company Income Statements for the Years
Ending December 31, 2007, 2006, and 2005

(in millions)	2007	2006	2005
Net sales	$237	$155	$134
Cost of goods sold	138	84	72
Gross profit	$ 99	$ 71	$ 62
Sales, general and administrative expenses	42	31	39
Research and development	38	33	54
Operating profit	$ 19	$ 7	($31)
Income tax expense (benefit)	7	2	(11)
Net profit	$ 12	$ 5	($20)

3.12. Writing Skills Problem

Income statements are presented for the Elf Corporation for the years ending December 31, 2007, 2006, and 2005.

Elf Corporation Income Statements for the Years
Ending December 31, 2007, 2006, and 2005

(in millions)	2007	2006	2005
Sales	$ 700	$ 650	$ 550
Cost of goods sold	350	325	275
Gross profit	$ 350	$ 325	$ 275
Operating expenses:			
Administrative	100	100	100
Advertising and marketing	50	75	75
Operating profit	$ 200	$ 150	$ 100
Interest expense	70	50	30
Earnings before tax	$ 130	$ 100	$ 70
Tax expense (.50)	65	50	35
Net income	$ 65	$ 50	$ 35

Required: Write a one paragraph analysis of Elf Corporation's profit performance for the period.

To the Student: The focus of this exercise is on analyzing financial data rather than simply describing the numbers and trends. Analysis involves breaking the information into parts for study, relating the pieces, making comparisons, drawing conclusions, and evaluating cause and effect.

3.13. Research Problem

Locate the income statement of a company in each of the following industries: pharmaceutical, technology, retailer—groceries, and automobile manufacturer. (See Chapter 1 for help in locating a company's financial statements.) Calculate the gross profit margin, operating profit margin, and net profit margin for all companies. Write a short essay explaining the differences you find between the profit margins calculated and why you think the profit margins differ.

3.14. Internet Problem

Look up the FASB Home Page on the internet at the following address: www.fasb.org/. Find the list of technical projects that are currently on the board's agenda. Choose one of the projects that will impact the income statement. Describe the potential change and how the income statement may be impacted.

3.15. Intel Problem

The 2004 Intel Annual Report can be found at the following Web site: www.prenhall.com/fraser.

(a) Using the consolidated statements of operations, analyze the profitability of Intel by preparing a common-size income statement and by calculating any other ratios deemed necessary for the past three years. Be sure to calculate sales growth and operating expense growth for each two-year period presented.

(b) Using the consolidated statements of stockholders' equity for Intel, explain the key reasons for the changes in the common stock, accumulated other comprehensive income, and retained earnings accounts. Evaluate these changes.

3.16. Eastman Kodak Comprehensive Analysis Problem Using the Financial Statement Analysis Template

Each chapter in the textbook contains a continuation of this problem. The objective is to learn how to do a comprehensive financial statement analysis in steps as the content of each chapter is learned. Using the 2004 Eastman Kodak Annual Report or Form 10-K, which can be found at www.prenhall.com/fraser, complete the following requirements:

(a) Open the financial statement analysis template that you saved from the Chapter 1 Eastman Kodak problem and input the data from the Eastman Kodak income statement. Use the basic earnings per share from continuing operations when inputting the earnings per share amount. When you have finished inputting the data, review the income statement to make sure there are no red blocks indicating that your numbers do not match the cover sheet information you input from the Chapter 1 problem. Make any necessary corrections before printing out both your input and the common-size income statement that the template automatically creates for you.

(b) Analyze the income statement of Eastman Kodak. Write a summary that includes important points that an analyst would use in assessing the profitability of Eastman Kodak.

C A S E S

Case 3.1   Dillard's Inc.

Dillard's Inc. operates in the highly competitive retail merchandise industry. Its department stores are located mainly in the Southwest, Southeast, and Midwest. As of January 29, 2005, there were 329 stores in operation. Selected information from Dillard's 2004 Form 10-K is given on pages 112–114.

Required

1. The Dillard's Inc. income statements should be reformatted before beginning an analysis. Explain what format

Dillard's has used and why the income statements should be redone.
2. Redo the income statements for Dillard's Inc. and prepare common-size income statements for all three years presented.
3. Analyze the profitability of Dillard's Inc. using the common-size income statements you prepared, as well as any other calculations you deem necessary. Be sure to include an explanation of the effective tax rate and any nonrecurring or nonoperating items.

Consolidated Statements of Operations
Dollars in Thousands, Except per Share Data

	Years Ended		
	January 29, 2005	January 31, 2004	February 1, 2003
Net Sales	$7,528,572	$7,598,934	$7,910,996
Service Charges, Interest and Other Income	287,699	264,734	322,943
	7,816,271	7,863,668	8,233,939
Costs and Expenses:			
Cost of sales	5,017,765	5,170,173	5,254,134
Advertising, selling, administrative and general expenses	2,098,791	2,097,947	2,164,033
Depreciation and amortization	301,917	290,661	301,407
Rentals	54,774	64,101	68,101
Interest and debt expense	139,056	181,065	189,779
Asset impairment and store closing charges	19,417	43,727	52,224
Total costs and expenses	7,631,720	7,847,674	8,029,678
Income Before Income Taxes	184,551	15,994	204,261
Income Taxes	66,885	6,650	72,335
Income before cumulative effect of accounting change	117,666	9,344	131,926
Cumulative effect of accounting change, net of tax benefit of $0	—	—	(530,331)
Net Income (Loss)	$ 117,666	$ 9,344	$ (398,405)

Basic Earnings Per Common Share:

Income before cumulative effect of accounting change	$1.41	$0.11	$ 1.56
Cumulative effect of accounting change	—	—	(6.27)
Net Income (Loss)	$1.41	$0.11	$ (4.71)

Diluted Earnings Per Common Share:

Income before cumulative effect of accounting change	$1.41	$0.11	$ 1.55
Cumulative effect of accounting change	—	—	(6.22)
Net Income (Loss)	$1.41	$0.11	$ (4.67)

See notes to consolidated financial statements.

Cumulative Effect of Accounting Change

Effective February 3, 2002, the Company adopted Statement of Financial Accounting Standards ("SFAS") No. 142, "Goodwill and Other Intangible Assets." SFAS No. 142 changes the accounting for goodwill from an amortization method to an "impairment only" approach. Under SFAS No. 142, goodwill is no longer amortized but reviewed for impairment annually or more frequently if certain indicators arise. The Company tested goodwill for impairment as of the adoption date using the two-step process prescribed in SFAS No. 142. The Company identified its reporting units under SFAS No. 142 at the store unit level. The fair value of these reporting units was estimated using the expected discounted future cash flows and market values of related businesses, where appropriate. The cumulative effect of the accounting changes as of February 3, 2002 was to decrease net income for fiscal year 2002 by $530 million or $6.22 per diluted share.

Sales

The percent change by category in the Company's sales for the past two years is as follows:

	Percent Change	
	Fiscal 2004–2003	Fiscal 2003–2002
Cosmetics	1.3	(1.1)
Women's and Juniors' Clothing	(2.4)	(4.8)
Children's Clothing	(2.7)	(8.9)
Men's Clothing and Accessories	(3.2)	(5.8)
Shoes, Accessories and Lingerie	4.0	(0.8)
Home	(2.0)	(4.3)

Cost of Sales

Cost of sales as a percentage of sales decreased to 66.6% during 2004 compared with 68.0% for 2003. The increase of 140 basis points in gross margin during fiscal 2004 was due to the Company's successful efforts to improve its merchandise mix and reduce markdown activity. The lower level of markdown activity decreased cost of sales by 50 basis points of sales. Improved levels of markups were responsible for a decrease in cost of sales of 90 basis points of sales. All product categories had increased gross margins during 2004 except for the home category. Gross margins were notably higher in men's and children's categories with margin improvement well above the average margin improvement for the year.

Cost of sales as a percentage of sales increased to 68.0% during 2003 compared with 66.4% for 2002. The decline of 160 basis points in gross margin during fiscal 2003 was due to competitive pressures in the Company's retail sector and the resulting effort to maintain a competitive position with increased markdown activity. The higher level of markdown activity increased cost of sales by 3.7% of sales. Improved levels of markups partially offset this promotional activity during fiscal 2003. The increased markup percentage was responsible for a decrease in cost of sales of 2.1% of sales. All product categories had decreased gross margins during 2003 except cosmetics, which increased 10 basis points from 2002.

Asset Impairment and Store Closing Charges

A breakdown of the asset impairment and store closing charges for fiscal 2004 is as follows:

(in Thousands of Dollars)	Number of Locations	Impairment Amount
Stores closed during fiscal 2004	3	$ 2, 928
Stores to close during fiscal 2005	4	4,052
Store impaired based on cash flows	1	703
Non-operating facilities	2	4,170
Joint Venture	1	7,564
Total	9	$19,417

A breakdown of the asset impairment and store closing charges for fiscal 2003 is as follows:

(in Thousands of Dollars)	Number of Locations	Impairment Amount
Stores closed during fiscal 2003	3	$ 3,809
Stores to close during fiscal 2004	4	17,115
Store impaired based on cash flows	1	1,293
Non-operating facilities	7	16,030
Joint Venture	1	5,480
Total	16	$43,727

Income Taxes

The Company's actual federal and state income tax rate (exclusive of the effect of nondeductible goodwill write off) was 36% in fiscal 2004, 2003, and 2002.

Case 3.2   Applied Materials

Excerpts from the financial statements, notes to the financial statements, and the management's discussion and analysis of Applied Materials' 2004 Annual Report and Form 10-K are found on pages 115–116.

Required

1. Using the Consolidated Statements of Operations and the excerpts from the notes and management discussion and analysis, analyze the profitability of Applied Materials. Your analysis should include the following calculations for all three years:
   (a) Common-size income statements
   (b) Growth rates of sales and total operating costs
   (c) Effective tax rates
2. Your written interpretation of the income statement and the numbers calculated should offer explanations for why trends have occurred.

Overview

Applied develops, manufactures, markets and services integrated circuit fabrication equipment for the worldwide semiconductor industry. Product development and manufacturing activities occur in North America, the United Kingdom and Israel. Applied's broad range of equipment and service products are highly technical and, as a result, are sold through a direct sales force. Customer demand for spare parts and services is fulfilled through a global spare parts distribution system and trained service engineers located around the world in close proximity to customer sites.

As a supplier to the global semiconductor industry, Applied's results are primarily driven by worldwide demand for integrated circuits, which in turn depends on end-user demand for electronic products. The global semiconductor industry is volatile. The downturn that began in fiscal 2001 and continued into fiscal 2003 constituted what management believes to be the longest and most severe downturn experienced by the semiconductor equipment industry. A recovery began in the fourth fiscal quarter of 2003 and continued throughout fiscal 2004. Applied's results in fiscal 2002 through 2004 reflect this volatility.

Realignment Activities

During fiscal 2003, in response to the continuing difficult business conditions, Applied implemented a series of activities to better align Applied's cost structure with prevailing economic conditions. Realignment activities consisted of consolidation of facilities, reductions in workforce, and refocused product efforts, such as the electron-beam mask pattern product line and implementation of the global spare parts distribution system (which included the closure of a central warehouse). As a result of the realignment activities, Applied vacated approximately two million square feet and reduced approximately 3,800 positions during 2003. Realignment activities resulted in charges across multiple categories, as incurred, including cost of products sold, research, development and engineering (RD&E) expenses, and restructuring and asset impairment charges. During the first fiscal quarter of 2004, realignment activities were completed and reported as restructuring, asset impairments and other charges as discussed below.

Applied Materials, Inc.
Consolidated Statements of Operations

Fiscal year	October 27, 2002	October 26, 2003	October 31, 2004
	(In thousands, except per share amounts)		
Net sales	$5,062,312	$4,477,291	$ 8,013,053
Cost of products sold	3,005,651	2,872,836	4,311,808
Gross margin	2,056,661	1,604,455	3,701,245
Operating expenses:			
Research, development and engineering	1,052,269	920,618	991,873
Marketing and selling	385,693	325,189	394,376
General and administrative	323,262	300,676	357,245
Restructuring, asset impairments and other charges	85,479	371,754	167,459
Litigation settlements, net	—	—	26,627
Income/ (loss) from operations	209,958	(313,782)	1,763,665
Interest expense	49,357	46,875	52,877
Interest income	179,910	149,101	118,462
Income/ (loss) before income taxes	340,511	(211,556)	1,829,250
Provision for/ (benefit from) income taxes	71,507	(62,409)	477,947
Net income/ (loss)	$ 269,004	$ (149, 147)	$1, 351, 303
Earnings/ (loss) per share:			
Basic	$ 0.16	$ (0.09)	$ 0.80
Diluted	$ 0.16	$ (0.09)	$ 0.78
Weighted average number of shares:			
Basic	1,643,612	1,659,557	1,688,121
Diluted	1,701,557	1,659,557	1,721,645

CHAPTER 4

Statement of Cash Flows

"Joan and Joe: A Tale of Woe"
Joe added up profits and went to see Joan,
Assured of obtaining a much-needed loan.
When Joe arrived, he announced with good cheer:
"My firm has had an outstanding year,
And now I need a loan from your bank."
Eyeing the statements, Joan's heart sank
"Your profits are fine," Joan said to Joe
"But where, oh where, is your company's cash flow?
I'm sorry to say: the answer is 'no'."

—L. FRASER

The statement of cash flows, required by Statement of Financial Accounting Standards No. 95, represents a major step forward in accounting measurement and disclosure because of its relevance to financial statement users. Ample evidence has been provided over the years by firms of every conceivable size, structure, and type of business operation that it is possible for a company to post a healthy net income but still not have the cash needed to pay its employees, suppliers, and bankers. The statement of cash flows, which replaced the statement of changes in financial position in 1988, provides information about cash inflows and outflows during an accounting period. On the statement, cash flows are segregated by *operating activities, investing activities,* and *financing activities.*[1] The mandated focus on cash in this statement results in a more useful document than its predecessor. A positive net income figure on the income statement is ultimately insignificant unless a company can translate its earnings into cash, and the only source in financial statements for learning about cash generation is the statement of cash flows.

The objectives of this chapter are twofold: (1) to explain how the statement of cash flows is prepared and (2) to interpret the information presented in the

---

[1]Financing and investing activities not involving cash receipts and payments—such as the exchange of debt for stock or the exchange of property—are reported in a separate schedule on the statement of cash flows.

statement, including a discussion of the significance of cash flow from operations as an analytical tool in assessing financial performance. Readers may legitimately ask at this point why it is necessary to wade through the preparation of this statement in order to understand and use the information it contains. This chapter provides a more extensive treatment of the preparation of the statement—its underpinnings—than the chapters on the balance sheet, income statement, and statement of stockholders' equity. The reason for this approach is its extreme

EXHIBIT 4.1   R.E.C. Inc. Consolidated Statements of Cash Flows for the Years Ended December 31, 2007, 2006, and 2005 (in Thousands)

	2007	2006	2005
Cash Flows from Operating Activities—Indirect Method			
Net income	$ 9,394	$ 5,910	$ 5,896
Adjustments to reconcile net income to cash provided (used) by operating activities			
Depreciation and amortization	3,998	2,984	2,501
Deferred income taxes	208	136	118
Cash provided (used) by current assets and liabilities			
Accounts receivable	(610)	(3,339)	(448)
Inventories	(10,272)	(7,006)	(2,331)
Prepaid expenses	247	295	(82)
Accounts payable	6,703	(1,051)	902
Accrued liabilities	356	(1,696)	(927)
Net cash provided (used) by operating activities	$ 10,024	($ 3,767)	$ 5,629
Cash Flows from Investing Activities			
Additions to property, plant, and equipment	(14,100)	(4,773)	(3,982)
Other investing activities	295	0	0
Net cash provided (used) by investing activities	($ 13,805)	($ 4,773)	($ 3,982)
Cash Flows from Financing Activities			
Sales of common stock	256	183	124
Increase (decrease) in short-term borrowings (includes current maturities of long-term debt)	(30)	1,854	1,326
Additions to long-term borrowings	5,600	7,882	629
Reductions of long-term borrowings	(1,516)	(1,593)	(127)
Dividends paid	(1,582)	(1,862)	(1,841)
Net cash provided (used) by financing activities	$ 2,728	$ 6,464	$ 111
Increase (decrease) in cash and marketable securities	($ 1,053)	($ 2,076)	$ 1,758
Cash and marketable securities, beginning of year	10,386	12,462	10,704
Cash and marketable securities, end of year	$ 9,333	$10,386	$12,462
Supplemental cash flow information:			
Cash paid for interest	$ 2,585	$ 2,277	$ 1,274
Cash paid for taxes	7,478	4,321	4,706

The accompanying notes are an integral part of these statements.

importance as an analytical tool. Understanding the statement is greatly enhanced by understanding how it is developed from the balance sheet and income statement; knowing the nuts and bolts helps the analyst utilize its disclosures to maximum effectiveness.

The Consolidated Statements of Cash Flows for R.E.C. Inc., shown in Exhibit 4.1, will serve as the background for an explanation of how the statement is prepared and a discussion of its usefulness for financial analysis.

Preparing a Statement of Cash Flows

Preparing the statement of cash flows begins with a return to the balance sheet, covered in Chapter 2. The statement of cash flows requires a reordering of the information presented on a balance sheet. The balance sheet shows account balances at the end of an accounting period, and the statement of cash flows shows changes in those same account balances between accounting periods (see Figure 4.1). The statement is called a statement of *flows* because it shows *changes over time rather than the absolute dollar*

FIGURE 4.1   How Cash Flows During an Accounting Period

Operating Activities

Inflows	*Outflows*
Revenue from sales of goods	Payments for purchase of inventory
Revenue from services	Payments for operating expenses (salaries,
Returns on equity securities (dividends)	rent, etc.)
Returns on interest-earning assets	Payments for purchases from suppliers
(interest)	other than inventory
	Payments to lenders (interest)
	Payments for taxes

Investing Activities

Inflows	*Outflows*
Revenue from sales of long-lived assets	Acquisitions of long-lived assets
Returns from loans (principal) to others	Loans (principal) to others
Revenue from sales of debt or equity	Purchases of debt or equity securities of
securities of other entities (except	other entities (except trading securities)
securities traded as cash equivalents)	

Financing Activities

Inflows	*Outflows*
Proceeds from borrowing	Repayments of debt principal
Proceeds from issuing the firm's own	Repurchase of a firm's own shares
equity securities	Payment of dividends

Total Inflows less Total Outflows = Change in cash for the accounting period

amount of the accounts at a point in time. Because a balance sheet balances, the changes in all of the balance sheet accounts balance, and the changes that reflect cash inflows less the changes that result from cash outflows will equal the changes in the cash account.

The statement of cash flows is prepared in exactly that way: by calculating the changes in all of the balance sheet accounts, including *cash;* then listing the changes in all of the accounts except cash as *inflows* or *outflows;* and categorizing the flows by *operating, financing,* or *investing* activities. The *inflows less the outflows balance to and explain the change in cash.*

In order to classify the account changes on the balance sheet, it is first necessary to review the definitions of the four parts of a statement of cash flows:

- Cash
- Operating activities
- Investing activities
- Financing activities

Cash includes cash and highly liquid short-term marketable securities, also called *cash equivalents.* Marketable securities are included as cash for R.E.C. Inc., because they represent, as explained in Chapter 2, short-term highly liquid investments that can be readily converted into cash. They include U.S. Treasury bills, certificates, notes, and bonds; negotiable certificates of deposit at financial institutions; and commercial paper. Some companies will separate marketable securities into two accounts: (1) cash and cash equivalents and (2) short-term investments. When this occurs, the short-term investments are classified as investing activities.

Operating activities include delivering or producing goods for sale and providing services and the cash effects of transactions and other events that enter into the determination of income.

Investing activities include (1) acquiring and selling or otherwise disposing of (a) securities that are not cash equivalents and (b) productive assets that are expected to benefit the firm for long periods of time and (2) lending money and collecting on loans.

Financing activities include borrowing from creditors and repaying the principal and obtaining resources from owners and providing them with a return on the investment.

With these definitions in mind, consider Exhibit 4.2, a worksheet for preparing the statement of cash flows that shows comparative 2007 and 2006 balance sheet accounts for R.E.C. Inc. Included in this exhibit is a column with the account balance changes and the category (or categories) that applies to each account. Explanations of how each account change is used in a statement of cash flow will be provided in subsequent sections of this chapter.

(1)(2) Cash and marketable securities are cash. The changes in these two accounts—a net decrease of $1,053 thousand (decrease in marketable securities of $2,732 thousand less increase in cash of $1,679 thousand)—will be explained by the changes in all of the other accounts. This means that for the year ending 2007, the cash outflows have exceeded the cash inflows by $1,053 thousand.

EXHIBIT 4.2   R.E.C. Inc. Worksheet for Preparing Statement of Cash Flows (in Thousands)

	2007	2006	CHANGE (2007–2006)	CATEGORY
Assets				
(1) Cash	$ 4,061	$ 2,382	$ 1,679	Cash
(2) Marketable securities	5,272	8,004	(2,732)	Cash
(3) Accounts receivable (net)	8,960	8,350	610	Operating
(4) Inventories	47,041	36,769	10,272	Operating
(5) Prepaid expenses	512	759	(247)	Operating
(6) Property, plant, and equipment	40,607	26,507	14,100	Investing
(7) Accumulated depreciation and amortization	(11,528)	(7,530)	(3,998)	Operating
(8) Other assets	373	668	(295)	Investing
Liabilities and Stockholders' Equity				
Liabilities				
(9) Accounts payable	14,294	7,591	6,703	Operating
(10) Notes payable—banks	5,614	6,012	(398)	Financing
(11) Current maturities of long-term debt	1,884	1,516	368	Financing
(12) Accrued liabilities	5,669	5,313	356	Operating
(13) Deferred income taxes	843	635	208	Operating
(14) Long-term borrowings				
Additions to long-term borrowings			5,600	
Reductions of long-term borrowings			(1,516)	
Net change in long-term debt	21,059	16,975	$ 4,084	Financing
Stockholders' Equity				
(15) Common stock	4,803	4,594	209	Financing
(16) Additional paid-in capital	957	910	47	Financing
(17) Retained earnings				
(a) Net income			9,394	Operating
(b) Dividends paid			(1,582)	Financing
Net change in retained earnings	$40,175	$32,363	$ 7,812	

(3)(4)(5) Accounts receivable, inventories, and prepaid expenses are all operating accounts relating to sales of goods, purchases of inventories, and payments for operating expenses.

(6) The net increase in property, plant, and equipment is an investing activity reflecting purchases of long-lived assets.

(7) The change in accumulated depreciation and amortization is classified as operating because it will be used as an adjustment to operating expenses or net income to determine cash flow from operating activities.

(8) Other assets are holdings of land held for resale, representing an investing activity.

(9) Accounts payable is an operating account because it arises from purchases of inventory.

(10) (11) Notes payable and current maturities of long-term debt result from borrowing (debt principal), a financing activity.

(12) Accrued liabilities are operating because they result from the accrual of operating expenses such as wages, rent, salaries, and insurance.

(13) The change in deferred income taxes is categorized as operating because it is part of the adjustment of tax expense to calculate cash flow from operating activities.

(14) The change in long-term debt, principal on borrowings, is a financing activity.

(15)(16) Common stock and paid-in capital are also financing activities because the changes result from sales of the firm's own equity shares.

(17) The change in retained earnings, as explained in Chapter 3, is the product of two activities: (a) net income for the period, which is operating; and (b) the payment of cash dividends, which is a financing activity.

The next step is to transfer the account changes to the appropriate area of a statement of cash flows.[2] In doing so, a determination must also be made of what constitutes an inflow and what constitutes an outflow when analyzing the change in an account balance. The following table should help:

Inflow	Outflow
− Asset account	+ Asset account
+ Liability account	− Liability account
+ Equity account	− Equity account

The table indicates that a decrease in an asset balance and an increase in liability and equity accounts are inflows.[3] Examples from Exhibit 4.2 are the decrease in other assets (cash inflow from the sale of property not used in the business), the increase in long-term debt (cash inflow from borrowing), and the increase in common stock and additional paid-in capital (cash inflow from sales of equity securities). Outflows are represented by the increase in inventories (cash outflow to purchase inventory) and the decrease in notes payable (cash outflow to repay borrowings).

Note that accumulated depreciation appears in the asset section but actually is a contra-asset or credit balance account because it reduces the amount of total assets. Accumulated depreciation is shown in parentheses on the balance sheet and has the same effect as a liability account.

Another complication occurs from the impact of *two transactions in one account.* For example, the net increase in retained earnings has resulted from the combination of net income for the period, which increases the account, and the payment of dividends, which reduces the account. Multiple transactions can also affect other accounts, such as property, plant, and equipment if a firm both acquires and sells capital assets during the period, and debt accounts if the firm both borrows and repays principal.

---

[2]Several alternative formats can be used for presenting the statement of cash flows, provided that the statement is reconciled to the change in cash and shows cash inflows and outflows from operating, financing, and investing activities.

[3]In accounting terminology, an inflow results from the decrease in a debit balance account or an increase in a credit balance account; an outflow results from the increase in a debit balance account or the decrease in a credit balance account.

Calculating Cash Flow From Operating Activities

The R.E.C. Inc. Consolidated Statements of Cash Flows begins with cash flow from operating activities. This represents the cash generated *internally*. In contrast, investing and financing activities provide cash from *external* sources. Firms may use one of two methods prescribed by the Financial Accounting Standards Board (FASB) for calculating and presenting cash flow from operating activities: the direct method and the indirect method. The *direct method* shows cash collections from customers, interest and dividends collected, other operating cash receipts, cash paid to suppliers and employees, interest paid, taxes paid, and other operating cash payments. The *indirect method* starts with net income and adjusts for deferrals; accruals; noncash items, such as depreciation and amortization; and nonoperating items, such as gains and losses on asset sales. The direct and indirect methods yield identical figures for net cash flow from operating activities because the underlying accounting concepts are the same. According to *Accounting Trends and Techniques,* 593 firms out of 600 used the indirect method in 2003.[4] The *indirect method* is illustrated and explained for R.E.C. Inc. in the chapter and the *direct method* is illustrated in the appendix to this chapter.

Indirect Method

Exhibit 4.3 illustrates the steps necessary to convert net income to cash flow from operating activities. The steps shown in Exhibit 4.3 will be used to explain the calculation of cash flow from operating activities for R.E.C. Inc. using the indirect method. Exhibit 4.3 includes some adjustments not present for R.E.C. Inc.

R.E.C. Inc. Indirect Method

Net income	$ 9,394
Adjustments to reconcile net income to cash provided by operating activities:	
+ Depreciation and amortization expense	3,998
+ Increase in deferred tax liability	208
Cash provided (used) by current assets, liabilities	
− Increase in accounts receivables	(610)
− Increase in inventory	(10,272)
+ Decrease in prepaid expenses	247
+ Increase in accounts payable	6,703
+ Increase in accrued liabilities	356
Net cash flow from operating activities	$10,024

Depreciation and amortization are added back to net income because they reflect the recognition of a noncash expense. Remember that depreciation represents a cost allocation, not an outflow of cash. The acquisition of the capital asset was recognized as an investing cash outflow (unless it was exchanged for debt or stock) in

---

[4] *Accounting Trends and Techniques,* American Institute of Certified Public Accountants, 2004.

EXHIBIT 4.3   Net Cash Flow from Operating Activities—Indirect Method

Net income*

Noncash/Nonoperating revenue and expense included in income:

+ Depreciation, amortization, depletion expense for period

+ Increase in deferred tax liability
− Decrease in deferred tax liability
+ Decrease in deferred tax asset
− Increase in deferred tax asset

− Increase in investment account from equity income**
+ Decrease in investment account from equity income***

− Gain on sale of assets
+ Loss on sale of assets

Cash provided (used) by current assets and liabilities
+ Decrease in accounts receivable
− Increase in accounts receivable

+ Decrease in inventory
− Increase in inventory

+ Decrease in prepaid expenses
− Increase in prepaid expenses

+ Decrease in interest receivable
− Increase in interest receivable

+ Increase in accounts payable
− Decrease in accounts payable

+ Increase in accrued liabilities
− Decrease in accrued liabilities

+ Increase in deferred revenue
− Decrease in deferred revenue

Net cash flow from operating activities

*Before extraordinary items, accounting changes, discontinued operations.
**Amount by which equity income exceeds cash dividends received.
***Amount by which cash dividends received exceed equity income recognized.

the statement of cash flows for the period in which the asset was acquired. So depreciation itself does not require any outflow of cash in the year it is recognized. Deducting depreciation expense in the current year's statement of cash flows would be double counting. Amortization is similar to depreciation—an expense that enters into the determination of net income but that does not require an outflow of cash. Depletion would be handled in the same manner as depreciation and amortization. The depreciation and amortization expense for R.E.C. Inc. in 2007 is equal to the change in the balance sheet accumulated depreciation and amortization account.

If the firm had dispositions of capital assets during the accounting period, however, the balance sheet change would not equal the expense recognition for the period because some of the account change would have resulted from the elimination of accumulated depreciation for the asset that was removed. The appropriate figure to subtract would be depreciation and amortization expense from the earnings statement.

The *deferred tax liability* account, as discussed in Chapter 2, reconciles the difference between tax expense recognized in the calculation of net income and the tax expense actually paid. The increase in the liability account for R.E.C. Inc. is added back to net income because more tax expense was recognized in the calculation of net income than was actually paid for taxes.

The increase in *accounts receivable* is deducted because more sales revenue has been included in net income than has been collected in cash from customers.

The increase in *inventory* is subtracted because R.E.C. Inc. has purchased more inventory than has been included in cost of goods sold. Cost of goods sold used in calculating net income includes only the inventory actually sold.

The decrease in *prepaid expenses* is added back because the firm has recognized an expense in the current period for which cash was paid in an earlier period, on a net basis.

The increase in *accounts payable* is added because less has been paid to suppliers for purchases of inventory than was included in cost of goods sold.

The increase in *accrued liabilities* is an addition to net income because it reflects the recognition of expense, on a net basis, prior to the payment of cash.

There are other potential adjustments, not required for R.E.C. Inc., that enter into the net income adjustment for noncash expense and revenues. One such item is the recognition of investment income from unconsolidated subsidiaries by the equity method of accounting, discussed in Chapter 3. When a company uses the equity method, earnings can be recognized in the income statement in excess of cash actually received from dividends, or the reverse can occur, for example, in the case of a loss recorded by an investee. For a firm using the equity method, there would be a deduction from net income for the amount by which investment income recognized exceeded cash received. Other potential adjustment items include changes relating to deferred income, deferred expense, the amortization of bond discounts and premiums, extraordinary items, and gains or losses on sales of long-lived assets.

Although *gains and losses from asset sales* are included in the calculation of net income, they are not considered an operating activity. A gain should be deducted from net income, and a loss should be added to net income to determine cash flow from operating activities. The entire proceeds from sales of long-lived assets are included as cash inflows from investing.

Cash Flow from Investing Activities

Additions to *property, plant, and equipment* represent a net addition to R.E.C. Inc.'s buildings, leasehold improvements, and equipment, a cash outflow of $14.1 million. Other investing activities for R.E.C. Inc. result from a decrease in the *other assets* account on the balance sheet, which represent holdings of investment properties. The sale of these assets has provided a cash inflow of $295 thousand.

Cash Flow from Financing Activities

As a result of the exercise of stock options, R.E.C. Inc. issued new shares of stock during 2007. The total cash generated from stock sales amounted to $256 thousand. Note that two accounts on the balance sheet—*common stock* and *additional paid-in capital*—combine to explain this change:

Common stock	$209	Inflow
Additional paid-in capital	47	Inflow
	$256	Total Inflow

The two accounts—notes payable to banks and current maturities of long-term debt (carried as a current liability since the principal is payable within a year)—jointly explain R.E.C. Inc.'s net reduction in short-term borrowings in 2007 of $30 thousand:

Notes payable—banks	($398)	Outflow
Current maturities of long-term debt	368	Inflow
	($ 30)	Net outflow

In preparing the statement of cash flows, long-term borrowings should be segregated into two components: additions to long-term borrowings and reductions of long-term borrowings. This information is provided in Note C, Long-Term Debt, to the R.E.C. Inc. financial statements, where detail on the various long-term notes is provided. The two figures—additions to long-term debt and reductions of long-term debt—on the R.E.C. Inc. statement of cash flows reconcile the change in the *long-term debt* account on the R.E.C. Inc. balance sheet:

Additions to long-term borrowings	$5,600	Inflow
Reductions of long-term borrowings	(1,516)	Outflow
Increase in long-term debt	$4,084	

The payment of cash dividends by R.E.C. Inc. in 2007 of $1,582 million is the final item in the financing activities section. The change in *retained earnings* results from the combination of net income recognition and the payment of cash dividends; this information is provided in the R.E.C. Inc. Statement of Stockholders' Equity:

Net income	$9,394	Inflow
Dividends paid	(1,582)	Outflow
Change in retained earnings	$7,812	

It should be noted that the *payment* of cash dividends is the financing outflow; the *declaration* of a cash dividend would not affect cash.

Change in Cash

To summarize the cash inflows and outflows for 2007 for R.E.C. Inc., the net cash provided by operating activities, less the net cash used by investing activities, plus the net cash provided by financing activities produced a net decrease in *cash* and *marketable securities* for the period:

FIGURE 4.2   Comparison of Cash Flows

(In thousands of dollars) For the year ended	Argosy Gaming Company December 31, 2004	palmOne, Inc. May 31, 2004
Net cash provided (used) by:		
Operating activities	$ 168,675	$ (13,058)
Investing activities	(69,998)	(45,287)
Financing activities	(85,813)	56,447
Net increase (decrease) in cash and cash equivalents	$ 12,864	$ (1,898)

Argosy Gaming Company, an owner and operator of casinos, generated enough cash from operating activities to cover all investing and financing activities, while also increasing the cash account. palmOne, Inc., a provider of handheld computing and communications devices, generated no cash from operating activities, used cash for investing activities, and therefore had to fund both operating and investing activities with financing activities. In addition, the cash account of palmOne declined overall.

Net cash provided by operating activities	$10,024
Net cash used by investing activities	(13,805)
Net cash provided by financing activities	2,728
Decrease in cash and marketable securities	(1,053)

The statement for 2006 and 2005 would be prepared using the same process that was illustrated for 2007. The cash flows provided (used) by operating, investing, and financing activities vary considerably depending on the company, its performance for the year, its ability to generate cash, its financing and investment strategies, and its success in implementing these strategies. Figure 4.2 illustrates this for two companies in different industries.

Analyzing the Statement of Cash Flows

The statement of cash flows is an important analytical tool for creditors, investors, and other users of financial statement data in order to help determine the following about a business firm:

- Its ability to generate cash flows in the future
- Its capacity to meet obligations for cash
- Its future external financing needs
- Its success in productively managing investing activities
- Its effectiveness in implementing financing and investing strategies

To begin the analysis of a statement of cash flows, it is essential to understand the importance of cash flow from operations, the first category on the statement.

Cash Flow from Operations

It is possible for a firm to be highly profitable and not be able to pay dividends or invest in new equipment. It is possible for a firm to be highly profitable and not be able to service debt. It is also possible for a firm to be highly profitable and go bankrupt.

W. T. Grant is one of the classic examples.[5] How? The problem is cash. Consider the following questions:

1. You are a banker evaluating a loan request from a prospective customer. What is your primary concern when making a decision regarding approval or denial of the loan request?
2. You are a wholesaler of goods and have been asked to sell your products on credit to a potential buyer. What is the major determining factor regarding approval or denial of the credit sale?
3. You are an investor in a firm and rely on the receipt of regular cash dividends as part of your return on investment. What must the firm generate in order to pay dividends?

In each case, the answer is *cash*. The banker must decide whether or not the prospective borrower will have the cash to meet interest and principal payments on the debt. The wholesaler will sell goods on credit only to those customers who can satisfy their accounts. A company can pay cash dividends only by producing cash.

The ongoing operation of any business depends upon its success in generating cash from operations. It is cash that a firm needs to satisfy creditors and investors. Temporary shortfalls of cash can be satisfied by borrowing or other means, such as selling long-lived assets, but ultimately a company must generate cash.

Cash flow from operations has become increasingly important as an analytical tool to determine the financial health of a business enterprise. Periods of high interest rates and inflation contributed to the enhanced attention paid to cash flow by investors and creditors. When interest rates are high, the cost of borrowing to cover short-term cash can be out of reach for many firms seeking to cover temporary cash shortages. Periods of inflation distort the meaningfulness of net income, through the understatement of depreciation and cost of goods sold expenses, making other measures of operating performance and financial success important. Even when interest rates and inflation are low, there are other factors that limit the usefulness of net income as a barometer of financial health. Consider the case of Nocash Corporation.

Nocash Corporation

The Nocash Corporation had sales of $100,000 in its second year of operations, up from $50,000 in the first year. Expenses, including taxes, amounted to $70,000 in year 2, compared with $40,000 in year 1. The comparative income statements for the two years indicate substantial growth, with year 2 earnings greatly improved over those reported in year 1.

Nocash Corporation Income Statement for Year 1 and Year 2

	Year 1	Year 2
Sales	$50,000	$100,000
Expenses	40,000	70,000
Net income	$10,000	$ 30,000

---

[5] J. A. Largay and C. P. Stickney, "Cash Flows, Ratio Analysis, and the W. T. Grant Bankruptcy," *Financial Analysts Journal*, July–August 1980.

So far, so good—a tripling of profit for Nocash. There are some additional facts, however, that are relevant to Nocash's operations but that do not appear on the firm's income statement:

1. In order to improve sales in year 2, Nocash eased its credit policies and attracted customers of a substantially lower quality than in year 1.
2. Nocash purchased a new line of inventory near the end of year 1, and it became apparent during year 2 that the inventory could not be sold, except at substantial reductions below cost.
3. Rumors regarding Nocash's problems with regard to accounts receivable and inventory management prompted some suppliers to refuse the sale of goods on credit to Nocash.

The effect of these additional factors can be found on Nocash's balance sheet.

Nocash Corporation Balance Sheet at December 31

	Year 1	Year 2	$ Change
Cash	$ 2,000	$ 2,000	0
Accounts receivable	10,000	30,000	+20,000[1]
Inventories	10,000	25,000	+15,000[2]
Total assets	$22,000	$57,000	+35,000
Accounts payable	7,000	2,000	−5,000[3]
Notes payable—to banks	0	10,000	+10,000
Equity	15,000	45,000	+30,000
Total liabilities and equity	$22,000	$57,000	+35,000

[1]Accounts receivable increased at a faster pace than sales as a result of deterioration in customer quality.
[2]Ending inventory increased and included items that would ultimately be sold at a loss.
[3]Nocash's inability to purchase goods on credit caused a reduction in accounts payable.

If Nocash's net income is recalculated on a cash basis, the following adjustments would be made, using the account balance changes between year 1 and year 2:

Net income	$30,000
(1) Accounts receivable	(20,000)
(2) Inventories	(15,000)
(3) Accounts payable	(5,000)
Cash income	($10,000)

(1) The increase in accounts receivable is subtracted because more sales revenue was recognized in computing net income than was collected in cash.

Sales recognized in net income		$100,000
Sales collected		
Beginning accounts receivable	$ 10,000	
Plus: sales, year 2	100,000	
Less: ending accounts receivable	(30,000)	80,000
Difference between net income and cash flow		$ 20,000

(2) The increase in inventory is deducted, reflecting the cash outflow for inventory purchases in excess of the expense recognized through cost of goods sold.

Purchases for inventory*	$75,000
Less: cost of goods sold	(60,000)
Difference between net income and cash flow	$15,000

(3) The decrease in accounts payable is deducted because the cash payments to suppliers in year 2 were greater than the amount of expense recorded. (In essence, cash was paid for some year 1 accounts as well as year 2 accounts.)

Payments to suppliers**	$80,000
Less: purchases for inventory*	75,000
Difference between net income and cash flow	$ 5,000
*Ending inventory	$ 25,000
Plus: cost of goods sold	60,000
Less: beginning inventory	(10,000)
Purchases of inventory	$ 75,000
**Beginning accounts payable	$ 7,000
Plus: purchases	75,000
Less: ending accounts payable	(2,000)
Payments to suppliers	$ 80,000

How did Nocash cover its $10,000 cash shortfall? Note the appearance of a $10,000 note payable to banks on the year 2 balance sheet. The borrowing has enabled Nocash to continue to operate, but unless the company can begin to generate cash from operations, its problems will compound. Bankers sometimes refer to this problem as a company's "selling itself out of business." The higher the cost of borrowing, the more costly and difficult it will be for Nocash to continue to operate.

R.E.C. Inc.: Analysis of The Statement of Cash Flows

An analysis of the statement of cash flows should, at a minimum, cover the following areas:

- Analysis of cash flow from operating activities
- Analysis of cash inflows
- Analysis of cash outflows

An example of an analysis of a statement of cash flows is presented for R.E.C. Inc. in the following sections.

R.E.C. Inc. Analysis: Cash Flow from Operating Activities

The statement of cash flows provides the figure "net cash flow from operating activities." An excerpt from the Statement of Cash Flows for R.E.C. Inc. is shown in Exhibit 4.4. The analyst should be concerned with the following in reviewing this information:

- The success or failure of the firm in generating cash from operations
- The underlying causes of the positive or negative operating cash flow
- The magnitude of positive or negative operating cash flow
- Fluctuations in cash flow from operations over time

For R.E.C. Inc. the first point of significance is the negative cash flow from operations in 2006 ($3,767 thousand). It should be noted that the negative cash flow occurred for a year in which the company reported positive net income of $5,910 thousand. The cash flow crunch was apparently caused primarily by a substantial growth in accounts receivable and inventories. Those increases were partly the result of the firm's expansion policies, and it would also be important to evaluate the quality of receivables and inventory—that is, are they collectable and salable? R.E.C. Inc. was able to recover in 2007, returning to strongly positive cash generation of $10,024 thousand, in spite of the continuation of inventory growth to support the expansion. The company obtained good supplier credit in 2007 and controlled the growth in accounts receivable. It will be necessary to monitor R.E.C. Inc.'s cash flow from operations closely and, in particular, the management of inventories. Inventory growth is desirable when supporting an expansion of sales but undesirable when like Nocash Corporation, the inventory is not selling or is selling only at discounted prices.

The calculation of cash flow from operations illustrated for R.E.C. Inc. can be made for any company from its balance sheet and income statement, using the procedures outlined in the examples. Cash flow from operations is especially important for those firms that are heavily invested in inventories and that use trade accounts receivables and payables as a major part of ordinary business operations. Such problems as sales growth that is too rapid, slow-moving or obsolete inventory, price discounting within the industry, a rise in accounts receivable of inferior quality, and the tightening

EXHIBIT 4.4   R.E.C. Inc. Cash Flows from Operating Activities for the Years Ended December 31, 2007, 2006, and 2005 (in Thousands)

	2007	2006	2005
Cash Flow from Operating Activities			
Net income	$ 9,394	$5,910	$ 5,896
Adjustments to reconcile net income to cash provided (used) by operating activities:			
Depreciation and amortization	3,998	2,984	2,501
Deferred income taxes	208	136	118
Cash Provided by (used for) Current Assets and Liabilities			
Accounts receivable	(610)	(3,339)	(448)
Inventories	(10,272)	(7,006)	(2,331)
Prepaid expenses	247	295	(82)
Accounts payable	6,703	(1,051)	902
Accrued liabilities	356	(1,696)	(927)
Net cash provided (used) by operating activities	$ 10,024	($3,767)	$ 5,629

of credit by suppliers can all impair the firm's ability to generate cash from operations and lead to serious financial problems, including bankruptcy.

Summary Analysis of the Statement of Cash Flows

Exhibit 4.5 is an excerpt from R.E.C. Inc.'s Statement of Cash Flows and will be used with Exhibits 4.1 and 4.4 to illustrate how to prepare a summary analysis of the statement of cash flows. The summary analysis is one way to common size the cash flow statement. The purpose of the summary table is to provide an approach to analyzing a statement of cash flows that can be used for any firm that provides comparative cash flow data. The information in the summary table underlines the importance of internal cash generation—from operations—and the implications for investing and financing activities when this does and does not occur.

Exhibit 4.6 presents the summary analysis table to facilitate the analysis of R.E.C. Inc.'s statement of cash flows, including cash flow from operating activities. The columns of the exhibit with dollar amounts show the inflows and outflows over the three-year period from 2005 to 2007 for R.E.C. Inc. The columns of Exhibit 4.6 with percentages show the cash inflows as a percentage of total inflows and the outflows as a percentage of total outflows.

First, consider the dollar amounts. It is apparent that the magnitude of R.E.C. Inc.'s activity has increased sharply over the three-year period, with total cash inflows increasing from $7.7 million to $16.2 million and cash outflows from $6.0 million to $17.2 million. Using the summary analysis, an evaluation of the cash inflows and outflows for R.E.C. Inc. is discussed next.

Analysis of Cash Inflows

In percentage terms, it is noteworthy that operations supplied 62% of needed cash in 2007 and 73 percent in 2005. As a result of negative cash from operations in 2006, the firm had to

EXHIBIT 4.5 R.E.C. Inc. Cash Flows from Investing and Financing Activities for the Years Ended December 31, 2007, 2006, and 2005 (in Thousands)

	2007	2006	2005
Cash Flows from Investing Activities			
Additions to property, plant, and equipment	(14,100)	(4,773)	(3,982)
Other investing activities	295	0	0
Net cash provided (used) by investing activities	($ 13,805)	($ 4,773)	($ 3,982)
Cash Flow from Financing Activities			
Sales of common stock	256	183	124
Increase (decrease) in short-term borrowings (includes current maturities of long-term debt)	(30)	1,854	1,326
Additions to long-term borrowings	5,600	7,882	629
Reductions of long-term borrowings	(1,516)	(1,593)	(127)
Dividends paid	(1,582)	(1,862)	(1,841)
Net cash provided (used) by financing activities	$ 2,728	$ 6,464	$ 111

EXHIBIT 4.6 R.E.C. Inc. Summary Analysis Statement of Cash Flows

	2007	%	2006	%	2005	%
Inflows (dollars in thousands)						
Operations	$10,024	62.0	$ 0	0.0	$5,629	73.0
Sales of other assets	295	1.8	0	0.0	0	0.0
Sales of common stock	256	1.6	183	1.8	124	1.6
Additions to short-term debt	0	0.0	1,854	18.7	1,326	17.2
Additions to long-term debt	5,600	34.6	7,882	79.5	629	8.2
Total	$16,175	100.0	$ 9,919	100.0	$7,708	100.0
Outflows (dollars in thousands)						
Operations	$ 0	0.0	$ 3,767	31.4	$ 0	0.0
Purchase of property, plant, and equipment	14,100	81.8	4,773	40.0	3,982	66.9
Reductions of short-term debt	30	0.2	0	0.0	0	0.0
Reductions of long-term debt	1,516	8.8	1,593	13.2	127	2.1
Dividends paid	$ 1,582	9.2	$ 1,862	15.4	$1,841	31.0
Total	$17,228	100.0	$11,995	100.0	$5,950	100.0
Change in cash and marketable securities	($ 1,053)		($ 2,076)		$1,758	

borrow heavily, with debt (short term and long term) accounting for 98% of 2006 inflows. R.E.C. Inc. also borrowed in 2007 and 2005 to obtain needed cash not supplied by operations. Generating cash from operations is the preferred method for obtaining excess cash to finance capital expenditures and expansion, repay debt, and pay dividends; however, most firms at one time or another will use external sources to generate cash. Using external sources to generate the majority of cash year after year should be investigated further.

Analysis of Cash Outflows

The major increase in cash outflows is capital asset expansion. Although it appears that the purchases of property, plant, and equipment decreased in 2006 (40.0% of cash outflows) compared to 2005 (66.9% of cash outflows), realize that the common denominator in the summary analysis is one particular year's cash outflows. Capital expenditures actually increased in dollars from $3,982 thousand to $4,773 thousand, but the percentages are skewed in 2006 because of the negative cash flow from operations. Also notice that dividends paid increased from 2005 to 2006, decreasing in 2007 (in dollars), yet the percentages decline each year because each year's total cash outflows vary.

When analyzing the cash outflows, the analyst should consider the necessity of the outflow and how the outflow was financed. R.E.C. Inc. was able to cover capital expenditures easily with excess cash generated by operations in 2005. Capital expenditures are usually a good investment for most firms as purchasing new equipment and expansion should result in future revenues and cash flows from operations. Because of the negative cash flow from operations in 2006, R.E.C. Inc. had to borrow to finance capital expenditures, repayment of debt, and dividend payments. In 2007, the company's strong generation of cash from operations supported most of the capital expenditures (82%) with only 35% external financing. It is favorable that R.E.C. Inc. has financed long-term assets (capital expenditures) with either internally generated cash or long-term debt.

Generally, it is best for firms to finance short-term assets with short-term debt and long-term assets with long-term debt or issuance of stock. Financing acquisitions and capital expenditures with short-term debt is risky since the firm may not generate cash flow quickly enough to repay short-term debt.

Repayment of debt is a necessary outflow. If the firm has generated cash from debt in prior years a cash outflow in a subsequent year to repay debt will be required. The notes to the financial statements reveal future debt repayments and are useful in assessing how much cash will be needed in upcoming years to repay outstanding debt.

Dividends are paid at the discretion of the board of directors. In theory, firms should only pay dividends if the company has excess cash, not needed for expansion, property, plant, or equipment, or repayment of debt. It appears that R.E.C. Inc. may have reduced the dividends in 2007 as a result of the lack of cash from operations in 2006.

Are We There Yet?

The journey through the maze of information has taken us through all the financial statements and many other items in the annual report, but no, we are not quite to the end of the maze. Unfortunately, just like the income statement, management has determined ways to manipulate the statement of cash flows. While the cash balances and the overall change in cash can be easily verified, it is possible to manipulate cash amounts through the timing of items such as when cash payments are made, when investments are made or sold, and when loans are taken out or repaid. Some companies have developed creative techniques for manipulating cash flow from operations by how they record certain cash outflows (see discussion in Chapter 5).

SELF-TEST

Solutions are provided in Appendix B.

_____ **1.** The statement of cash flows segregates cash inflows and outflows by:
    (a) Operating and financing activities.
    (b) Financing and investing activities.
    (c) Operating and investing activities.
    (d) Operating, financing, and investing activities.

_____ **2.** Which of the following statements is false?
    (a) Publicly held companies may choose to prepare either a statement of cash flows or a statement of changes in financial position.
    (b) The statement of cash flows was mandated by the FASB in the late 1980s.
    (c) Understanding how to prepare a statement of cash flows helps the analyst to better understand and analyze the cash flow statement.
    (d) The statement of cash flows is prepared by calculating changes in all balance sheet accounts.

_____ **3.** How would revenue from sales of goods and services be classified?
    (a) Operating outflow.
    (b) Operating inflow.
    (c) Investing inflow.
    (d) Financing inflow.

_____ **4.** How would payments for taxes be classified?
   (a) Operating outflow.
   (b) Operating inflow.
   (c) Investing outflow.
   (d) Financing outflow.

_____ **5.** How would the sale of a building be classified?
   (a) Operating outflow.
   (b) Operating inflow.
   (c) Investing inflow.
   (d) Financing inflow.

_____ **6.** How would the repayment of debt principal be classified?
   (a) Operating outflow.
   (b) Operating inflow.
   (c) Investing outflow.
   (d) Financing outflow.

_____ **7.** What type of accounts are accounts receivable and inventory?
   (a) Cash accounts.
   (b) Operating accounts.
   (c) Financing accounts.
   (d) Investing accounts.

_____ **8.** What type of accounts are notes payable and current maturities of long-term debt?
   (a) Cash accounts.
   (b) Operating accounts.
   (c) Financing accounts.
   (d) Investing accounts.

_____ **9.** The change in retained earnings is affected by which of the following?
   (a) Net income and common stock.
   (b) Net income and paid-in capital.
   (c) Net income and payment of dividends.
   (d) Payment of dividends and common stock.

_____ **10.** Which method of calculating cash flow from operations requires the adjustment of net income for deferrals, accruals, noncash, and nonoperating expenses?
   (a) The direct method.
   (b) The indirect method.
   (c) The inflow method.
   (d) The outflow method.

_____ **11.** An inflow of cash would result from which of the following?
   (a) The increase in an asset account other than cash.
   (b) The decrease in an asset account other than cash.
   (c) The decrease in an equity account.
   (d) The decrease in a liability account.

_____ **12.** An outflow of cash would result from which of the following?
   (a) The decrease in an asset account other than cash.
   (b) The increase in a liability account.
   (c) The decrease in a liability account.
   (d) The increase in an equity account.

_____ **13.** What are internal sources of cash?
(a) Cash inflows from operating activities.
(b) Cash inflows from investing activities.
(c) Cash inflows from financing activities.
(d) All of the above.

_____ **14.** What are external sources of cash?
(a) Cash inflows from operating activities.
(b) Cash inflows from investing activities.
(c) Cash inflows from financing activities.
(d) Both (b) and (c).

_____ **15.** Which of the following items is included in the adjustment of net income to obtain cash flow from operating activities?
(a) Depreciation expense for the period.
(b) The change in deferred taxes.
(c) The amount by which equity income recognized exceeds cash received.
(d) All of the above.

_____ **16.** Which statement is true for gains and losses from capital asset sales?
(a) They do not affect cash and are excluded from the statement of cash flows.
(b) They are included in cash flows from operating activities.
(c) They are included in cash flows from investing activities.
(d) They are included in cash flows from financing activities.

_____ **17.** Which of the following current assets is included in the adjustment of net income to obtain cash flow from operating activities?
(a) Accounts receivable.
(b) Inventory.
(c) Prepaid expenses.
(d) All of the above.

_____ **18.** Which of the following current liability accounts is included in the adjustment of expenses to obtain cash flow from operating activities?
(a) Accounts payable.
(b) Notes payable and current maturities of long-term debt.
(c) Accrued liabilities.
(d) Both (a) and (c).

_____ **19.** How is it possible for a firm to be profitable and still go bankrupt?
(a) Earnings have increased more rapidly than sales.
(b) The firm has positive net income but has failed to generate cash from operations.
(c) Net income has been adjusted for inflation.
(d) Sales have not improved even though credit policies have been eased.

_____ **20.** Why has cash flow from operations become increasingly important as an analytical tool?
(a) Inflation has distorted the meaningfulness of net income.
(b) High interest rates can put the cost of borrowing to cover short-term cash needs out of reach for many firms.
(c) Firms may have uncollected accounts receivable and unsalable inventory on the books.
(d) All of the above.

_____ **21.** Which of the following statements is false?
   (a) A negative cash flow can occur in a year in which net income is positive.
   (b) An increase in accounts receivable represents accounts not yet collected in cash.
   (c) An increase in accounts payable represents accounts not yet collected in cash.
   (d) To obtain cash flow from operations, the reported net income must be adjusted.

_____ **22.** Which of the following could lead to cash flow problems?
   (a) Obsolete inventory, accounts receivable of inferior quality, easing of credit by suppliers.
   (b) Slow-moving inventory, accounts receivable of inferior quality, tightening of credit by suppliers.
   (c) Obsolete inventory, increasing notes payable, easing of credit by suppliers.
   (d) Obsolete inventory, improved quality of accounts receivable, easing of credit by suppliers.

The following information is available for Jacqui's Jewelry and Gift Store:

Net income	$ 5,000
Depreciation expense	2,500
Increase in deferred tax liabilities	500
Decrease in accounts receivable	2,000
Increase in inventories	9,000
Decrease in accounts payable	5,000
Increase in accrued liabilities	1,000
Increase in property and equipment	14,000
Increase in short-term notes payable	19,000
Decrease in long-term bonds payable	4,000

Use the indirect method to answer questions 23–26.

_____ **23.** What is net cash flow from operating activities?
   (a) ($3,000)
   (b) ($1,000)
   (c) $5,000
   (d) $13,000

_____ **24.** What is net cash flow from investing activities?
   (a) $14,000
   (b) ($14,000)
   (c) $21,000
   (d) ($16,000)

_____ **25.** What is net cash flow from financing activities?
   (a) $15,000
   (b) ($15,000)
   (c) $17,000
   (d) ($14,000)

_____ **26.** What is the change in cash?
   (a) ($3,000)
   (b) $3,000
   (c) $2,000
   (d) ($2,000)

STUDY QUESTIONS AND PROBLEMS

4.1. Identify the following as financing activities (F) or investing activities (I):
   (a) Purchase of equipment.
   (b) Purchase of treasury stock.
   (c) Reduction of long-term debt.
   (d) Sale of building.
   (e) Resale of treasury stock.
   (f) Increase in short-term debt.
   (g) Issuance of common stock.
   (h) Purchase of land.
   (i) Purchase of common stock of another firm.
   (j) Payment of cash dividends.
   (k) Gain on sale of land.
   (l) Repayment of debt principal.

4.2. Indicate which of the following current assets and current liabilities are operating accounts (O) and thus included in the adjustment of net income to cash flow from operating activities and which are cash (C), investing (I), or financing (F) accounts.
   (a) Accounts payable.
   (b) Accounts receivable.
   (c) Notes payable (to bank).
   (d) Marketable securities.
   (e) Accrued expenses.
   (f) Inventory.
   (g) Notes receivable—officers.
   (h) Current portion of long-term debt.
   (i) Dividends payable.
   (j) Income taxes payable.
   (k) Interest payable.
   (l) Certificates of deposit.

4.3. Condensed financial statements for Luna Enterprises follow.

  (a) Calculate the amount of dividends Luna paid using the information given.

  (b) Prepare a statement of cash flows using the indirect method.

Luna Enterprises
Comparative Balance Sheets
December 31, 2009 and 2008

	2009	2008
Cash	$ 1,200	$ 950
Accounts receivable	1,750	1,200
Inventory	1,150	1,450
Plant and equipment	4,500	3,900
Accumulated depreciation	(1,200)	(1,100)
Long-term investments	900	1,150
Total Assets	8,300	7,550
Accounts payable	1,100	800
Accrued wages payable	250	350
Bonds payable	1,100	1,400
Capital stock	1,000	1,000
Paid-in capital	400	400
Retained earnings	4,450	3,600
Total Liabilities and Equity	$ 8,300	$ 7,550

Income Statement
For Year Ended December 31, 2009

Sales	$ 9,500
Cost of goods sold	6,650
Gross profit	2,850
Other expenses	
Selling	1,200
Depreciation	100
Interest	150
Income tax	350
Net income	$ 1,050

4.4. The following income statement and balance sheet information are available for two firms, Firm A and Firm B.

(a) Calculate the amount of dividends Firm A and Firm B paid using the information given.

(b) Prepare a statement of cash flows for each firm using the indirect method.

(c) Analyze the difference in the two firms.

Income Statement
For Year Ended December 31, 2009

	Firm A	Firm B
Sales	$1,000,000	$1,000,000
Cost of goods sold	700,000	700,000
Gross profit	300,000	300,000
Other expenses		
Selling and administrative	120,000	115,000
Depreciation	10,000	30,000
Interest expense	20,000	5,000
Earnings before taxes	150,000	150,000
Income tax expense	75,000	75,000
Net Income	$ 75,000	$ 75,000

Changes in Balance Sheet Accounts
December 31, 2008, to December 31, 2009

	Firm A	Firm B
Cash and cash equivalents	$ 0	$ +10,000
Accounts receivable	+40,000	+5,000
Inventory	+40,000	−10,000
Property, plant, and equipment	+20,000	+70,000
Less accumulated depreciation	(+10,000)	(+30,000)
Total Assets	$+90,000	$+45,000
Accounts payable	$−20,000	$ −5,000
Notes payable (current)	+17,000	+2,000
Long-term debt	+20,000	−10,000
Deferred taxes (noncurrent)	+3,000	+18,000
Capital, Stock	—	—
Retained earnings	+70,000	+40,000
Total Liabilities and Equity	$+90,000	$+45,000

4.5. The following comparative balance sheets and income statement are available for Little Bit Inc. Prepare a statement of cash flows for 2009 using the indirect method and analyze the statement.

	December 31,	
	2009	2008
Cash	$ 40,000	$ 24,000
Accounts receivable (net)	48,000	41,500
Inventory	43,000	34,500
Prepaid expenses	19,000	15,000
Total Current Assets	$ 150,000	$ 115,000
Plant and equipment	$ 67,000	$ 61,000
Less accumulated depreciation	(41,000)	(23,000)
Plant and equipment (net)	$ 26,000	$ 38,000
Long-term investments	90,000	89,000
Total Assets	$ 266,000	$ 242,000
Accounts payable	$ 13,000	$ 11,000
Accrued liabilities	55,000	71,000
Total Current Liabilities	$ 68,000	$ 82,000
Long-term debt	25,000	8,000
Deferred taxes	4,000	3,500
Total Liabilities	$ 97,000	$ 93,500
Common stock ($1 par) and additional paid-in capital	112,000	97,000
Retained earnings	57,000	51,500
Total Liabilities and Equity	$ 266,000	$ 242,000

Income Statement for 2009		
Sales		$155,000
Cost of goods sold		83,000
Gross profit		$ 72,000
Selling and administrative	$45,700	
Depreciation	18,000	63,700
Operating Profit		$ 8,300
Interest expense		2,000
Earnings before tax		$ 6,300
Tax expense		800
Net income		$ 5,500

4.6. The following cash flows were reported by Techno Inc. in 2008 and 2007.

(In thousands)	2008	2007
Net income	$316,354	$242,329
Noncash charges (credits) to income		
Depreciation and amortization	68,156	62,591
Deferred taxes	15,394	22,814
	$399,904	$327,734
Cash Provided (Used) by Operating Assets and Liabilities:		
Receivables	(288,174)	(49,704)
Inventories	(159,419)	(145,554)
Other current assets	(1,470)	3,832
Accounts payable, accrued liabilities	73,684	41,079
Total Cash Provided by Operations	$ 24,525	$177,387
Investment activities		
Additions to plant and equipment	(94,176)	(93,136)
Other investment activities	14,408	(34,771)
Net investment activities	($79,768)	($127,907)
Financing activities		
Purchases of treasury stock	(45,854)	(39,267)
Dividends paid	(49,290)	(22,523)
Net changes in short-term borrowings	125,248	45,067
Additions to long-term borrowings	135,249	4,610
Repayments of long-term borrowings		(250,564)
Net financing activities	$165,353	($262,677)
Increase (decrease) in cash	$110,110	($213,197)
Beginning cash balance	78,114	291,311
Ending cash balance	$188,224	$ 78,114

(a) Explain the difference between net income and cash flow from operating activities for Techno in 2008.

(b) Analyze Techno Inc.'s cash flows for 2008 and 2007.

4.7. Writing Skills Problem

Write a short article (250 words) for a local business publication in which you explain why cash flow from operations is important information for small business owners.

4.8. Research Problem

Choose five companies from different industries and locate their statements of cash flows for the most recent year.

(a) Create a table to compare the dollars provided or used by operating, investing, and financing activities, as well as the overall increase or decrease in cash.

(b) Create a second table for each company comparing this same information for each of the three years presented in that company's statement of cash flows. Include an additional column that looks at the combined cash flows for all three years.

(c) Write a short analysis of the information gathered. Your discussion should address, among other things, whether cash flow from operating activities is large enough to cover investing and financing activities, and if not, how the company is financing its activities. Discuss differences and similarities between the companies you have chosen.

4.9. Internet Problem

Locate the 2003 Consolidated Statements of Cash Flows for 1-800 Contacts, Inc. Net income for this company is on a downward trend while cash provided by operating activities is on an upward trend. Using any information you can obtain about this company and industry, write a report explaining this abnormal trend between the net income and the cash flow numbers and whether this should be a red flag to investors and creditors.

4.10. Intel Problem

The 2004 Intel Annual Report can be found at the following Web site: *www.prenhall.com/ fraser*.

(a) Prepare a summary analysis of the Statements of Cash Flows for all three years.

(b) Analyze the Consolidated Statements of Cash Flows for Intel for 2004, 2003, and 2002.

4.11. Eastman Kodak Comprehensive Analysis Problem Using the Financial Statement Analysis Template

Each chapter in the textbook contains a continuation of this problem. The objective is to learn how to do a comprehensive financial statement analysis in steps as the content of each chapter is learned. Using the 2004 Eastman Kodak Annual Report or Form 10-K, which can be found at *www.prenhall.com/fraser* complete the following requirements:

(a) Open the financial statement analysis template that you saved from the Chapter 1 Eastman Kodak problem and input the data from the Eastman Kodak cash flow statement. All cash flows from discontinued operations should be combined and input on the line labeled as such toward the bottom of the statement. When you have finished inputting the data, review the cash flow statement to make sure there are no red blocks indicating that your numbers do not match the cover sheet information you input from the Chapter 1 problem. Make any necessary corrections before printing out both your input and the common-size cash flow statement that the template automatically creates for you.

(b) Analyze the cash flow statement of Eastman Kodak. Write a summary that includes important points that an analyst would use in assessing the ability of Eastman Kodak to generate cash flows and the appropriateness of the use of cash flows.

C A S E S

Case 4.1 PetMed Express, Inc.

PetMed Express, Inc. and subsidiaries, d/b/a 1-800-PetMeds, is a leading nationwide pet pharmacy. The company markets prescription and nonprescription pet medications and health and nutritional supplements for dogs and cats direct to the consumer. The company offers consumers an attractive alternative for obtaining pet medications in terms of convenience, price, and speed of delivery.

The company markets its products through national television, online, and direct mail advertising campaigns, which aim to increase the recognition of the "1-800-PetMeds" brand name, increase traffic on its Web site, acquire new customers, and maximize repeat purchases.*

Required

1. Using the Consolidated Statements of Cash Flows on page 145, prepare a summary analysis for the years ended March 31, 2004, 2003, and 2002. Analyze the cash flows for PetMed Express, Inc. for all three years.
2. Evaluate the creditworthiness of PetMed Express, Inc. based on only the cash flow statements.
3. What information from the balance sheet would be useful to a creditor in determining whether to loan PetMed Express, Inc. money?

*Source: PetMed Express, Inc. Form 10-K, March 31, 2004.

PETMED EXPRESS, INC. AND SUBSIDIARIES
CONSOLIDATED STATEMENTS OF CASH FLOWS

	Year Ended March 31,		
	2004	2003	2002
Cash flows from operating activities:			
Net income	$ 5,813,604	$ 3,257,565	$ 825,413
Adjustments to reconcile net income to net cash provided by operating activities:			
Depreciation and amortization	550,392	367,673	376,763
Tax benefit related to stock options exercised	588,872	171,587	—
(Gain) loss on disposal of property and equipment	—	(15,000)	314,332
Deferred income taxes	—	(581,356)	—
Amortization of deferred membership fee revenue	—	—	(140,048)
Bad debt expense	7,432	15,027	6,862
(Increase) decrease in operating assets and liabilities:			
Accounts receivable	(488,850)	(375,397)	(135,907)
Inventories	(6,911,712)	(1,961,526)	(1,675,226)
Prepaid expenses and other current assets	245,890	(329,500)	(126,494)
Other assets	178,333	(150,000)	(42,500)
Accounts payable	702,603	696,535	1,508,542
Income taxes payable	251,693	170,752	—
Accrued expenses and other current liabilities	167,338	(296,059)	(435,713)
Net cash provided by operating activities	1,105,595	970,301	476,024
Cash flows from investing activities:			
Purchases of property and equipment	(741,740)	(744,596)	(555,645)
Purchases of intangible asset	—	(365,000)	—
Net proceeds from the sale of property and equipment	—	15,000	2,016,921
Net cash (used in) provided by investing activities	(741,740)	(1,094,596)	1,461,276
Cash flows from financing activities:			
Proceeds from the exercise of stock options and warrants	1,999,345	580,836	—
Payments on the line of credit	—	(141,214)	—
(Payments) borrowings on loan obligation	(68,443)	(68,442)	205,327
Payments on capital lease obligation	—	—	(247,209)
Payments on mortgage payable	—	—	(1,566,833)
Net cash provided by (used in) financing activities	1,930,902	371,180	(1,608,715)
Net increase in cash and cash equivalents	2,294,757	246,885	328,585
Cash and cash equivalents, at beginning of year	984,169	737,284	408,699
Cash and cash equivalents, at end of year	$ 3,278,926	$ 984,169	$ 737,284
Supplemental disclosure of cash flow information:			
Cash paid for interest	$ 14,302	$ 30,675	$ 29,150
Cash paid for income taxes	$ 2,513,214	$ 508,000	$ —

See accompanying notes to consolidated financial statements.

Case 4.2   Candela Corporation

Excerpts from the Candela Corporation's Form 10-K are on pages 146–147.

Required

1. Using the Consolidated Statements of Cash Flows, prepare a summary analysis for the years ended July 3, 2004, June 28, 2003, and June 29, 2002. Analyze the cash flows for Candela Corporation, Inc. for all three years.
2. Explain what information you gain from the statement of cash flows that cannot be found directly from the balance sheet or income statement.

Item 1. Business.

Candela Corporation is a pioneer in the development and commercialization of advanced aesthetic laser systems that allow physicians and personal care practitioners to treat a wide variety of cosmetic and medical conditions including:

- Vascular lesion treatment of rosacea, facial spider veins, leg veins, scars, stretch marks, warts, port wine stains and hemangiomas
- Hair removal
- Removal of benign pigmented lesions such as age spots, freckles and tattoos
- Skin rejuvenation and wrinkles
- Acne and acne scars
- Psoriasis
- Other skin treatments

Since our founding 34 years ago, we have continuously developed and enhanced applications of laser technology. In the mid-1980s we began developing laser technology for medical applications, and since that time have shipped approximately 7,000 lasers to over 60 countries. Since the early 1990s we have focused our organizational resources on developing laser technology for use solely in the aesthetic and cosmetic laser industry. Our introduction of new dermatology/plastic surgery laser systems during the mid-1990s allowed us to expand rapidly in this area. Candela's current product line offers comprehensive and technologically sophisticated aesthetic and medical laser systems used by dermatologists, plastic surgeons and various other medical and personal care practitioners.

The discretionary income of aging baby boomers continues to rise which creates new opportunities for Candela. This market segment places a premium on good health and personal appearance, and has demonstrated a willingness to pay for health and cosmetic products and services. The growing popularity of laser treatments among the general population is also spurring demand for Candela's products. Last year, Americans spent an estimated $8.3 billion on cosmetic procedures. Increasingly, lasers are proving an attractive alternative for eliminating unwanted hair. The laser hair removal market has experienced significant growth over the last several years.

The Company is dedicated to developing safe and effective products. Our aesthetic laser systems are further distinguished by being among the fastest, smallest and most affordable in their respective markets. We believe that we have increasingly captured significant market share because of these product attributes and we are committed to continual innovation to meet the needs of our markets.

CANDELA CORPORATION AND SUSIDIARIES
CONSOLIDATED STATEMENTS OF CASH FLOWS
For the years ended July 3, 2004, June 28, 2003 and June 29, 2002
(in thousands)

	2004	2003 (Restated)	2002 (Restated)
Cash flows from operating activities:			
Net income (loss)	$ 8,119	$ 6,814	$ (2,154)
Adjustments to reconcile net income (loss) to net cash provided by (used for) operating activities:			
Provision for the disposal of discontinued operations	2,095	—	—
Loss from discontinued operations	298	1,013	743
Depreciation	668	582	355
Accretion of imputed interest on stock warrants	—	475	102
Provision for bad debts	520	(13)	116
Provision for deferred taxes	955	(682)	(115)
Tax benefit from exercised stock options	(1,223)	(505)	(6)
Effect of exchange rate changes on foreign currency denominated assets and liabilities	26	36	(305)
Changes in assets and liabilities:			
Restricted cash	(200)	(57)	—
Accounts receivable	(7,663)	(2,417)	(3,525)
Notes receivable	62	179	(54)
Inventories	(2,134)	1,761	(1,661)
Other current assets	(2,550)	225	175
Other assets	(236)	157	305
Accounts payable	(91)	(1,409)	(3,069)
Accrued payroll and related expenses	707	1,622	1,139
Deferred income	548	574	24
Accrued warranty costs	1,776	(921)	830
Income tax payable	(1,312)	4,168	(784)
Other accrued liabilities	767	53	813
Net cash provided by (used in) operating activities	1,132	11,655	(7,071)
Cash flows from investing activities:			
Purchase of property, plant and equipment	(685)	(1,227)	(1,058)
Net cash used in investing activities	(685)	(1,227)	(1,058)
Cash flows from financing activities:			
Proceeds from issuance of common stock	4,707	4,620	394
Repurchases of treasury stock	—	—	(5,215)
Principal payments of long-term debt	—	(3,330)	(370)
Net borrowings (repayments) on line of credit	—	(1,114)	50
Net cash provided by (used in) financing activities	4,707	176	(5,141)
Effect of exchange rate changes on cash and cash equivalents	172	1,552	890
Net increase (decrease) on cash and cash equivalents	5,326	12,156	(12,380)
Cash and cash equivalents, beginning of year	31,813	19,657	32,037
Cash and cash equivalents, end of year	$ 37,139	$ 31,813	$ 19,657
Cash paid during the year for:			
Interest	$ 15	$ 235	$ 347
Income Taxes	$ 3,265	$ 751	$ (68)

The accompanying notes are an integral part of the financial statements.

A p p e n d i x   4 A

Statement of Cash Flows—Direct Method

Direct Method

Exhibit 4A.1 illustrates the statement of cash flows prepared using the direct method, and Exhibit 4A.2 illustrates the calculation of net cash flow from operating activities by the direct method. This method translates each item on the accrual-based income statement to a cash revenue or expense item. The calculation of cash flow from operating activities in Exhibit 4A.2 represents an approximation of the *actual* receipts and payments of cash required by the direct method.

The steps shown in Exhibit 4A.2 will be used to explain the calculation of net cash flow from operating activities on the R.E.C. Inc. Statement of Cash Flows for 2007.

R.E.C. Inc. Direct Method

Sales	$215,600	
Increase in accounts receivable	(610)	
Cash collections on sales		214,990
Cost of goods sold	129,364	
Increase in inventory	10,272	
Increase in accounts payable	(6,703)	
Cash payments for supplies		−132,933
Selling and administrative expenses		−45,722
Other operating expenses	21,271	
Depreciation and amortization	(3,998)	
Decrease in prepaid expense	(247)	
Increase in accrued liabilities	(356)	
Cash paid for other operating expense		−16,670
Interest revenue		+422
Interest expense		−2,585
Tax expense	7,686	
Increase in deferred tax liability	(208)	
Cash paid for taxes		−7,478
Net cash flow from operating activities		$ 10,024

The increase in accounts receivable is subtracted from sales revenue because more sales revenue was recognized in the income statement than was received in cash.

The increase in inventories is added to cost of goods sold because more cash was paid to purchase inventories than was included in cost of goods sold expense; that is, cash was used to purchase inventory that has not yet been sold.

The increase in accounts payable is subtracted from cost of goods sold because R.E.C. Inc. was able to defer some payments to suppliers for purchases of inventory; more

EXHIBIT 4A.1   R.E.C. Inc. Consolidated Statements of Cash Flows for the Years Ended December 31, 2007, 2006, and 2005 (in Thousands)

	2007	2006	2005
Cash Flow from Operating Activities—Direct Method			
Cash received from customers	$214,990	$149,661	$140,252
Interest received	422	838	738
Cash paid to suppliers for inventory	(132,933)	(99,936)	(83,035)
Cash paid to employees (S&A Expenses)	(45,722)	(26,382)	(25,498)
Cash paid for other operating expenses	(16,670)	(21,350)	(20,848)
Interest paid	(2,585)	(2,277)	(1,274)
Taxes paid	(7,478)	(4,321)	(4,706)
Net cash provided (used) by operating activities	$ 10,024	($ 3,767)	$ 5,629
Cash Flows from Investing Activities			
Additions to property, plant, and equipment	(14,100)	(4,773)	(3,982)
Other investing activities	295	0	0
Net cash provided (used) by investing activities	($ 13,805)	($ 4,773)	($ 3,982)
Cash Flow from Financing Activities			
Sales of common stock	256	183	124
Increase (decrease) in short-term borrowings (includes current maturities of long-term debt)	(30)	1,854	1,326
Additions to long-term borrowings	5,600	7,882	629
Reductions of long-term borrowings	(1,516)	(1,593)	(127)
Dividends paid	(1,582)	(1,862)	(1,841)
Net cash provided (used) by financing activities	$ 2,728	$ 6,464	$ 111
Increase (decrease) in cash and marketable securities	($ 1,053)	($ 2,076)	$ 1,758
Supplementary Schedule			
Cash Flow from Operating Activities—Indirect Method			
Net income	$ 9,394	$ 5,910	$ 5,896
Noncash revenue and expense included in net income			
Depreciation and amortization	3,998	2,984	2,501
Deferred income taxes	208	136	118
Cash provided (used) by current assets and liabilities			
Accounts receivable	(610)	(3,339)	(448)
Inventories	(10,272)	(7,006)	(2,331)
Prepaid expenses	247	295	(82)
Accounts payable	6,703	(1,051)	902
Accrued liabilities	356	(1,696)	(927)
Net cash provided (used) by operations	$ 10,024	($ 3,767)	$ 5,629

cost of goods sold expense was recognized than was actually paid in cash.

Depreciation and amortization expense is subtracted from other operating expenses. Remember that depreciation represents a cost allocation, not an outflow of cash. The acquisition of the capital asset was recognized as an investing cash outflow (unless it was exchanged for debt or stock) in the statement of cash flows for the period in which the asset

EXHIBIT 4A.2 R.E.C. Inc. Net Cash Flow from Operating Activities Direct Method

Sales	− Increase in accounts receivable	
	+ Decrease in accounts receivable	
	+ Increase in deferred revenue	= Cash collections from
	− Decrease in deferred revenue	customers
Cost of Goods Sold	+ Increase in inventory	
	− Decrease in inventory	
	− Increase in accounts payable	= Cash paid to suppliers
	+ Decrease in accounts payable	
Salary Expense	− Increase in accrued salaries payable	
	+ Decrease in accrued salaries payable	= Cash paid to employees
Other Operating Expenses	− Depreciation, amortization, depletion expense for period	
	+ Increase in prepaid expenses	
	− Decrease in prepaid expenses	= Cash paid for other
	− Increase in accrued operating expenses	operating expenses
	+ Decrease in accrued operating expenses	
Interest Revenue	− Increase in interest receivable	
	+ Decrease in interest receivable	= Cash revenue from interest
Interest Expense	− Increase in accrued interest payable	
	+ Decrease in accrued interest payable	= Cash paid for interest
Investment Income	− Increase in investment account from equity income*	
	+ Decrease in investment account from equity income**	= Cash revenue from dividends
Tax Expense	− Increase in deferred tax liability	
	+ Decrease in deferred tax liability	
	− Decrease in deferred tax asset	
	+ Increase in deferred tax asset	
	− Increase in accrued taxes payable	= Cash paid for taxes
	+ Decrease in accrued taxes payable	
	− Decrease in prepaid tax	
	+ Increase in prepaid tax	

Net cash flow from operating activities
_____

*Amount by which equity income recognized exceeds cash dividends received.
**Amount by which cash dividends received exceed equity income recognized.

was acquired. So depreciation itself does not require any outflow of cash in the year it is recognized. Deducting depreciation expense in the current year's statement of cash flows would be double counting. Amortization is similar to depreciation—an expense that enters into the determination of net income but that does not require an outflow of cash. Depletion would be handled in the same manner as depreciation and amortization. The depreciation and amortization expense for R.E.C. Inc. in 2007 is equal to the change in the balance sheet accumulated depreciation and amortization account. If the firm had dispositions of capital assets during the accounting period, however, the balance sheet change would not equal the expense recognition for the period because some of the account change would have resulted from the elimination of accumulated depreciation for the asset that was removed. The appropriate figure to subtract would be depreciation and amortization expense from the earnings statement.

The decrease in prepaid expense is subtracted from other operating expenses because the firm is recognizing as expense in 2007 items for which cash was paid in the previous year; that is, the firm is utilizing on a net basis some of the prior years' prepayments.

The increase in accrued liabilities is subtracted from other operating expenses because R.E.C. Inc. has recognized more in expense on the income statement than has been paid in cash.

Finally, the increase in the deferred tax liability account is subtracted from tax expense to obtain cash payments for taxes. The deferred tax liability, explained in Chapter 2, was created as a reconciliation between the amount of tax expense reported on the income statement and the cash actually paid or payable to the IRS. If a deferred tax liability increases from one year to the next, tax expense deducted on the earnings statement to arrive at net income has exceeded cash actually paid for taxes. Thus, an increase in the deferred tax liability account is subtracted from tax expense to arrive at cash from operations. A decrease in deferred tax liabilities would be added. A change in deferred tax assets would be handled in the opposite way from the deferred tax liability.

Exhibit 4A.2 includes other possible adjustments, not present for R.E.C. Inc., that would be made to calculate net cash flow from operating activities by the direct method.

CHAPTER

A Guide to Earnings and Financial Reporting Quality

Qual-i-ty (n). Synonyms: excellence, superiority, class, eminence, value.

Before delving into the analysis of financial statements in Chapter 6, this chapter considers the *quality* of reported financial information, which is a critical element in evaluating financial statement data. The earnings statement encompasses a number of areas that provide management with opportunities for influencing the outcome of reported earnings in ways that may not best represent economic reality or the future operating potential of a firm. These include:

- Accounting choices, estimates, and judgments.
- Changes in accounting methods and assumptions.
- Discretionary expenditures.
- Nonrecurring transactions.
- Nonoperating gains and losses.
- Revenue and expense recognitions that do not match cash flow.

In evaluating a business firm, it is essential that the financial statement analyst consider the qualitative as well as the quantitative components of earnings for an accounting period. The higher the quality of financial reporting, the more useful is the information for business decision making. The analyst should develop an earnings figure that reflects the future ongoing potential of the firm. This process requires a consideration of qualitative factors and necessitates, in some cases, an actual adjustment of the reported earnings figure.

In addition to earnings quality, the quality of the information on the balance sheet and statement of cash flows is equally important. Because these financial statements are interrelated, quality of financial reporting issues often affects more than one financial statement.

The primary focus of this chapter is to provide the financial statement user with a step-by-step guide that links the items on an earnings statement with the key areas in the financial statement data that affect earnings quality. Exhibit 5.1 is a checklist for earnings quality. Items that affect the quality of information on the balance sheet and statement of cash flows will be covered later in this chapter.

The list does not, by any means, include all of the items that affect earnings quality. Rather, the examples illustrate some of the qualitative issues that are most

EXHIBIT 5.1   A Checklist for Earnings Quality

I. Sales
   1. Premature revenue recognition
   2. Gross vs. net basis
   3. Vendor financing
   4. Allowance for doubtful accounts
   5. Price vs. volume changes
   6. Real vs. nominal growth
II. Cost of Goods Sold
   7. Cost-flow assumption for inventory
   8. Base LIFO layer liquidations
   9. Fulfillment costs
   10. Loss recognitions on write-downs of inventories (also see item 13)
III. Operating Expenses
   11. Discretionary expenses
   12. Depreciation
   13. Asset impairment
   14. "Big bath" or restructuring charges
   15. Reserves
   16. In-process research and development
   17. Pension accounting—interest rate assumptions
IV. Nonoperating Revenue and Expense
   18. Gains (losses) from sales of assets
   19. Interest income
   20. Equity income
   21. Income taxes
   22. Unusual items
   23. Discontinued operations
   24. Accounting changes
   25. Extraordinary items
V. Other Issues
   26. Material changes in number of shares outstanding
   27. Operating earnings, a.k.a. core earnings, pro forma earnings, or EBITDA

commonly encountered in financial statement data. Another purpose of the chapter is to provide the financial statement user with an approach to use in analyzing and interpreting the qualitative factors. The checklist represents an attempt to provide a framework for the analysis of earnings quality rather than a complete list of its components.

Although the examples in this book deal primarily with the financial reporting of wholesale, retail, and manufacturing firms, the concepts and techniques presented can also apply to other types of industries. For instance, there is a discussion in this chapter of the provision for doubtful accounts as it impacts earnings quality. The same principles, on a larger scale, would apply to the provision for loan loss reserves for financial institutions. Almost all of the items on the checklist—other than those directly related to cost of goods sold—would apply to most types of business firms, including service-oriented companies.

Using the Checklist

Each item on the checklist in Exhibit 5.1 will be discussed and illustrated with examples from publicly held corporations.

I. Sales or Revenues
1. Premature Revenue Recognition

According to generally accepted accounting principles (GAAP), revenue should not be recognized until there is evidence that a true sale has taken place; that is, delivery of products has occurred or title to those products has passed to the buyer, or services have been rendered, the price has been determined, and collection is expected. Unfortunately, many firms have violated this accounting principle by recording revenue before these conditions have been met. While users of financial statements usually cannot determine if revenue has been recorded prematurely, clues that something is amiss can be found by analyzing key areas of the financial statements, such as the relationship among sales, accounts receivable, the allowance for doubtful accounts, and inventories.

Sunbeam, in an effort to boost revenues in the years 1995–1997, chose to book sales of backyard grills and related products during the winter months, even though the goods weren't shipped to customers until the spring. Sunbeam permitted customers to defer payment and also to return for full credit any unsold items.[1] What readers of Sunbeam's 1997 annual report could have found as clues to the problems involve the relationship between accounts receivable and sales (discussed in Chapter 2) and the growth in inventories relative to sales. Between 1996 and 1997, sales grew 19%, while receivables grew 38.5%, indicating the company might not be successful in collecting on sales. Inventory increased by 58%, which means the company may not actually be selling the goods produced. Sunbeam ultimately had to restate earnings for 1995–1997 because of its revenue recognition practices and other problems, leading eventually to bankruptcy.

---

[1] Harris Collingwood, "The Earnings Game: Everyone Plays, Nobody Wins," *Harvard Business Review,* June 2001.

Royal Ahold, a Dutch company, corporate parent of U.S. Foodservice, and the world's largest supermarket operator, announced in 2003 that its executives had inflated revenues, requiring a restatement of its earnings by $880 million.[2] With the outlook for bonuses bleak, executives at U.S. Foodservice embarked on a strategy to order huge quantities of food from manufacturers who agreed to pay the distributor hefty rebates. By booking the rebates immediately and prematurely, earnings could be increased. The consequences of this action have resulted in the company's having to cut prices, sometimes below cost, to unload the excess inventory acquired. In addition, the stock price of the firm dropped over 65%, reducing the $33 billion market value as of June, 2001, to about $2.7 billion in March, 2003.[3]

Another scheme used to inflate revenues is to keep the accounting books open longer than the end of the quarter. Computer Associates may have used such a strategy, referred to as the "35-day month practice," to prematurely record more than $1 billion of revenue in fiscal year 2000. The company ended use of this practice in 2001, causing the firm to miss the earnings expectations on Wall Street. A dramatic drop in stock price was the result.[4]

2. Gross Versus Net Basis

Another tactic to boost revenues is to record sales at the gross rather than the net price. Reading the notes to the financial statements to determine how revenue is recorded can enlighten users of financial statements that a firm is recording at gross prices. In the Yahoo! 2004 Annual Report, the company states:

> The Company generates revenue from the display of text based links to the websites of its advertisers which are placed on the websites of third party entities (which the Company refers to as affiliates) who have integrated the Company's sponsored search offerings into their websites. The Company recognizes revenue from these arrangements as "click-throughs" occur. "Click-throughs" are defined as the number of times a user clicks on an advertiser's listing. The Company pays affiliates based on click-throughs on the advertiser's listings that are displayed on the websites of these affiliates. These payments are called traffic acquisition costs. In accordance with EITF Issue No. 99-19, "Reporting Revenue Gross as a Principal Versus Net as an Agent," the revenue derived from these arrangements that involve traffic supplied by affiliates is reported gross of the payments to affiliates. This revenue is reported gross due to the fact that the Company is the primary obligor to the advertisers who are the customers of the advertising service.

Securities and Exchange Commission (SEC) guidelines allow companies such as Yahoo! to record revenues at gross amounts when the company acts as a principal in the transaction.[5] The problem from a financial statement user's perspective is that, in

---

[2]Sarah Ellison and Scott Kilman, "SEC Expands Food-Industry Probe," *Wall Street Journal*, November 6, 2003.

[3]Almar LaTour, "How a Quest for Rebates Sent Ahold on Unusual Buying Spree," *Wall Street Journal*, March 6, 2003.

[4]Charles Forelle, "Improper Booking Wasn't Unusual at CA, Court Told," *Wall Street Journal*, January 23, 2004.

[5]"Revenue Recognition in Financial Statements," *Staff Accounting Bulletin No. 101*, Washington, DC, Securities and Exchange Commission, December 3, 1999.

reality, the company will receive only the net amount when the transaction is complete. Google, on the other hand, records some revenue at gross prices, but other revenue is recorded at net amounts as outlined in notes to its financial statements in the 2004 Google Annual Report:

> In the first quarter of 2000, the Company introduced its first advertising program through which it offered advertisers the ability to place text-based ads on Google web sites targeted to users' search queries. Advertisers paid the Company based on the number of times their ads were displayed on users' search results pages and the Company recognized revenue at the time these ads appeared. In the fourth quarter of 2000, the Company launched Google AdWords, an online self-service program that enables advertisers to place text-based ads on Google web sites. AdWords advertisers originally paid the Company based on the number of times their ads appeared on users' search results pages. In the first quarter of 2000, the Company began offering AdWords exclusively on a cost per click basis, so that an advertiser pays the Company only when a user clicks on one of its ads. The Company recognizes as revenue the fees charged advertisers each time a user clicks on one of the text-based ads that are displayed next to the search results on Google web sites.

Comparability issues occur for the financial statement user trying to compare revenues and profit margins of companies such as Yahoo! and Google. Yahoo!'s revenues appear larger compared to Google, but gross profit margins appear better for Google as a result of the accounting choice to record revenue at the gross or the net amount.

3. Vendor Financing

Sometimes companies will use vendor financing to increase revenues by lending their customers (other companies) money to purchase their products. This increases the risk of the firm since many companies do not have the resources to conduct comprehensive credit analysis. Large, creditworthy customers are unlikely to use vendor financing since they are able to borrow funds at lower rates from alternative sources. Motorola reveals the following information about vendor financing in its 2000 Form 10-K:

> The competitive environment in which Motorola operates requires Motorola and many of its principal competitors to provide significant amounts of medium-term and long-term customer financing. Customer financing arrangements may include all or a portion of the purchase price for Motorola's products and services, as well as working capital.

Motorola disclosed in its first quarter 2001 10-Q filing with the SEC that approximately $2 billion of its $2.7 billion finance receivables related to one customer, Telsim, in Turkey. When $728 million of the note came due in April, Telsim did not pay. This transaction most likely contributed to Motorola's falling stock price from a high of $57.58 in March 2000 when the loan was announced, to as low as $11.50 in April 2001.

In a fraudulent twist on vendor financing, executives at Enterasys Network Systems Inc., a computer-networking company, conspired to boost revenues by secretly purchasing the company's own products. Enterasys funds were invested in companies so financially weak they were unable to pay for products without the Enterasys funds.[6]

4. Allowance for Doubtful Accounts

Most companies sell products on credit. Revenue is recognized on the income statement when the sales are made, and accounts receivable are carried on the balance sheet until the cash is collected. Because some customer accounts are never satisfied, the balance sheet includes an allowance for doubtful accounts. A discussion of sales, accounts receivable, and the allowance for doubtful accounts is provided in Chapters 2 and 3.

The allowance account, which is deducted from the balance sheet accounts receivable account, should reflect the volume of credit sales, the firm's past experience with customers, the customer base, the firm's credit policies, the firm's collection practices, economic conditions, and changes in any of these factors. There should be a consistent relationship, all other things being equal, between the rate of change in sales, accounts receivable, and the allowance for doubtful accounts. If the amounts are changing at different rates or in different directions—for example, if sales and accounts receivable are increasing, but the allowance account is decreasing or is increasing at a much smaller rate—the analyst should be alert to the potential for manipulation through the allowance account. Of course, there could also be a plausible reason for such a change.

As discussed in Chapter 2, the allowance for doubtful accounts is a type of reserve account and can be manipulated by under- or overestimating bad debt expenses. In the 1990s, it appeared that some firms may have been underestimating this account in order to boost net income. An astute analyst could determine this by tracking the patterns and relationships of sales, accounts receivable, and the allowance account, noting that sales and receivables were increasing, but the allowance account was decreasing. On the other hand, by overestimating the allowance account, firms can set themselves up for a later correction that will ultimately boost net income. During the early 2000s when the economy was in a downturn, it appeared that firms might have been using this approach since investors were already anticipating poor earnings numbers anyway.

The relevant items needed to relate sales growth with accounts receivable and the allowance for doubtful accounts are found on the income statement (sales) and balance sheet (accounts receivable and allowance for doubtful accounts).[7]

The following information is from the 2001 Cisco Form 10-K:

(In millions)	2001	2000	Percentage Change
Sales	$22,293	$18,298	21.8
Receivables	1,754	2,342	(25.1)
Less allowance for doubtful accounts	(288)	(43)	569.8
Receivables (net)	1,466	2,299	

Despite the sales increase, Cisco had fewer accounts receivable in 2001, and this should mean they are doing a better job collecting receivables. Generally, if receivables decline, the allowance for doubtful accounts would decline as well, but Cisco's allowance account

---

[6]Mark Maremont, "Former Enterasys CEO Pleads Guilty," *Wall Street Journal*, September 16, 2004.
[7]The underlying liquidity of accounts receivable is also extremely important in assessing earnings quality. This topic is covered in Chapters 4 and 6.

increased 569.8%. Cisco's actual write-offs in 2000 and 2001 were $24 and $23 million, respectively. If Cisco has reason to believe that a major customer could default, this should be revealed in the notes or the management discussion and analysis, yet no mention is made to explain this extraordinary increase. Whether this charge is reasonable or not, the quality of the company's earnings is brought into question. Manipulation would be unethical, but if this charge is legitimate, the analyst would question the credit policy strategies of the firm. The valuation schedule for the allowance for doubtful accounts for Cisco in 2004 reveals the following charges and write-offs:

(In Millions)	2002	2003	2004
Beginning balance	288	335	183
Charges (credits)	91	(59)	19
Write-offs	(44)	(93)	(23)
Ending balance	335	183	179

Cisco continued to overestimate the allowance account in 2002 and then reversed charges in 2003, thus giving a boost to earnings in 2003. Without a legitimate explanation offered by Cisco in its Form 10-K the analyst should be concerned that Cisco is intentionally manipulating the earnings numbers or is not very proficient at estimating bad debt expense.

5. Price Versus Volume Changes

If a company's sales are increasing (or decreasing), it is important to determine whether the change is a result of price, volume, or a combination of both factors. Are sales growing because the firm is increasing prices or because more units are being sold, or both? It would seem that, in general, higher-quality earnings would be the product of both volume and price increases (during inflation). The firm would want to sell more units and keep prices increasing at least in line with the growth rate of general inflation.

Information regarding the reasons for sales growth (or decline) is one of the areas covered in a firm's management discussion and analysis section of the annual or 10-K report, discussed in Chapter 1. To relate sales growth to reasons for sales growth, use sales data from the income statement and the volume/price discussion from the management discussion and analysis section.

Micron Technology, Inc.'s Consolidated Statements of Operations include the following:

	2004	2003
Net sales (in millions)	$4,404.2	$3,091.3

The following is an excerpt from the Micron Technology Management Discussion and Analysis of Financial Condition and Results of Operations:

Net sales for 2004 increased by 42% as compared to 2003 primarily due to a 20% increase in megabits sold and a 16% increase in average per megabit selling prices for the Company's memory products as a result of generally improved market conditions.

A determination can be made from this information that the sales growth in 2004 was the result of both volume increases and price increases.

6. Real Versus Nominal Growth

A related issue is whether sales are growing in "real" (inflation-adjusted) as well as "nominal" (as reported) terms. The change in sales in nominal terms can be readily calculated from the figures reported on the income statement. An adjustment of the reported sales figure with the Consumer Price Index (CPI) (or some other measure of general inflation) will enable the analyst to make a comparison of the changes in real and nominal terms. To make the calculation to compare real with nominal sales, begin with the sales figures reported in the income statement, and adjust years prior to the current year with the CPI or some other price index. An example using information from the 2004 Annual Report of General Motors Corporation Automotive Division is shown here:

Sales (in millions)	2004	2003	Percentage Change
As reported (nominal)	$161,545	$155,831	3.67
Adjusted (real)	161,545	$158,760	1.75
Using base period CPI (1982–1984 = 100)			
(2004 CPI/2003 CPI) × 2003 Sales = Adjusted sales			
(184.3/180.9) × $155,831 = $158,760			

Sales, when adjusted for general inflation, did not increase as much. An alternative approach would be to compare the growth in nominal sales—an increase of 3.67%—with the change in the CPI—an increase from 180.9 to 184.3 of 1.88%. Either way, it is apparent that General Motors Automotive sales growth did not keep pace with the rate of general inflation.

II. Cost of Goods Sold

7. Cost-Flow Assumption for Inventory

During periods of inflation, the last-in, first-out (LIFO) cost-flow assumption for inventory accounting, described in Chapter 2, produces lower earnings than first-in, first-out (FIFO) or average cost. Just the reverse occurs if the firm operates in an industry with volatile or falling prices. But LIFO results in the matching of current costs with current revenues and therefore produces higher quality earnings than either FIFO or average cost. The inventory accounting system used by the company is described in the note to the financial statements that details accounting policies or the note discussing inventory. The following excerpt from the 2000 annual report of Varian, Inc., a manufacturer of scientific instruments, illustrates an interesting example of inventory method choices:

> The Company has accounted for all inventories using the average cost method beginning July 1, 2000, whereas in all prior years, certain inventories maintained in the U.S. were valued using the last-in, first-out (LIFO) method. The new method of accounting for inventory was adopted because the Company believes

the average cost method of accounting for inventory will result in more consistent matching of product costs with revenues due to expected ongoing decreases in product costs and ongoing significant technological improvements in components. The financial statements of prior years have been restated to apply the new method retroactively, and accordingly, retained earnings as of September 26, 1997 have been increased by $9.3 million to reflect the restatement.

Of concern is that management believes average cost will more consistently match current costs to current revenues — an untrue statement. FIFO would be a better choice for the firm since they believe product costs will be decreasing. FIFO lowers taxes for firms operating in deflationary environments and many high technology firms use FIFO for this reason.

8. Base LIFO Layer Liquidations

A base LIFO layer liquidation occurs with the use of LIFO in a situation in which the firm sells more goods than purchased during an accounting period. During inflation, this situation results in the lowest cost of goods sold expense from using LIFO because the older, less expensive items were sold. Usually, companies maintain a base layer of LIFO inventory that remains fairly constant. Goods are bought during the year and sales are made from the more recent purchases (for purposes of cost allocation). It is only when stocks of inventory are substantially reduced that the base layer is affected and LIFO earnings are higher. Base LIFO layer liquidations occur when companies are shrinking rather than increasing inventories. There is an actual reduction of inventory levels, but the earnings boost stems from the cost flow assumption: that the older and lower-priced products are those being sold. The effects of LIFO reductions, which are disclosed in notes to the financial statements, can be substantial. A base LIFO layer liquidation reduces the quality of earnings in the sense that there is an improvement in operating profit from what would generally be considered a negative occurrence: inventory reductions. In considering the future, ongoing potential of the company, it would be appropriate to exclude from earnings the effect of LIFO liquidations because a firm would not want to continue benefiting from inventory shrinkages. An example of a base LIFO layer liquidation occurred at Amcast Industrial Corporation in 2003. The following excerpt is from the notes to the financial statements of Amcast Industrial Corporation's 2003 annual report:

> During 2003, inventory balances declined which resulted in liquidation of LIFO inventory layers carried at lower costs prevailing in prior years compared with the cost of current-year inventory additions. The effect of the inventory reduction decreased cost of sales by $1,461 and decreased the net loss by approximately $935, or $0.10 per share.

9. Fulfillment Costs

In recent years, some companies have added an expense category to operating expenses called *fulfillment costs*. Sometimes costs that are typically classified as cost of goods sold are being recorded in this account. The effect of this classification, different from the norm, is that the gross profit margin is affected leading to comparability issues between firms, and hence, lower quality of earnings. According to the 2004 Amazon.com Annual

Report, the company records fulfillment costs that include ". . . costs attributable to buying, receiving, inspecting and warehousing inventories . . ." These costs are typically cost of goods sold. The problem, however, is that the analyst cannot determine the dollar amounts that are misclassified since Amazon.com does include some items that are properly placed in this account such as credit card fees, bad debt expenses, and customer service costs. The analyst, in this case, would probably rely on operating profit more than gross profit when comparing Amazon.com to other firms.

10. Loss Recognitions on Write-Downs of Inventories

The principle of conservatism in accounting requires that firms carry inventory in the accounting records at the lower of cost (as determined by the cost flow assumption such as LIFO, FIFO, average cost) or market. If the value of inventory falls below its original cost, the inventory is written down to market value. Market generally is determined by the cost to replace or reproduce the inventory but should not exceed the net realizable amount (selling price less completion and disposal costs) the company could generate from selling the item. The amount of the write-down will affect comparability, thus quality, of the profit margins from period to period.

When the write-down of inventory is included in cost of goods sold, the gross profit margin is affected in the year of the write-down. Significant write-downs of inventory are relatively infrequent; however, an example of an inventory write-down was announced by Ford Motor Company in January 2002. Due to the large drop in value of the metal palladium, used in auto manufacturing, the company announced they would record a $1 billion write-off. Ford had purchased this metal, once priced at less than $100 per ounce, for amounts over $1,000 per ounce. When prices fell, Ford revalued their palladium inventory to $440 per ounce.[8] In comparing the gross profit margin between periods, the analyst should be aware of the impact on the margin that occurs from such write-downs.

III. Operating Expenses
11. Discretionary Expenses

A company can increase earnings by reducing variable operating expenses in a number of areas such as the repair and maintenance of capital assets, research and development, and advertising and marketing. If such discretionary expenses are reduced primarily to benefit the current year's reported earnings, the long-run impact on the firm's operating profit may be detrimental and thus the quality lowered. The analyst should review the trends of these discretionary expenses and compare them with the firm's volume of activity and level of capital investment. Amounts of discretionary expenditures are disclosed in the financial statements and notes, such as the following for palmOne:

(In Millions)	2004	2003	2002
Advertising	$63.0	$66.9	$100.6
Research and development	69.4	70.2	91.1

---

[8]Gregory L. White, "How Ford's Big Batch of Rare Metal Led to $1 Billion Write-Off," *Wall Street Journal,* February 6, 2002.

PalmOne has decreased expenditures in all years for advertising and research and development. In 2003 sales and profits declined significantly. In addition the company was reducing its capital expenditures as can be seen in the following table:

(In Millions)	2004	2003	2002
Revenues	$950	$838	$1,004
Operating loss	(4)	(198)	(93)
Property, plant, equipment purchases	6	8	15

According to the Management Discussion and Analysis in palmOne's 2004 annual report, the revenue increase in 2004 is a result of price increases as the volume of sales declined in both 2003 and 2004. The analyst would want to research further the reasons for such reductions in discretionary expenses and assess the long-run effect of these policies on profitability.

12. Depreciation

The amount of annual depreciation expense recognized for an accounting period, as discussed in Chapter 1, depends on the choice of depreciation method and estimates regarding the useful life and salvage value of the asset being depreciated. Most companies use the straight-line method rather than an accelerated method for reporting purposes because it produces a smoother earnings stream and higher earnings in the early years of the depreciation period. The straight-line method, however, is lower in quality in most cases because it does not reflect the economic reality of product usefulness in that most machinery and equipment do not wear evenly over the depreciation period.

There are additional issues that affect earnings quality with regard to the depreciation expense figure. Companies that misclassify operating expenses as capital expenditures have created poor quality of financial reporting not only on the income statement, but on all financial statements. Recording an amount that should be deducted in its entirety in one year as a capital expenditure results in the expense being depreciated over several years. This is exactly what WorldCom did in 2001 and 2002. The firm was able to increase profits by $11 billion. The cash flow effects of this are discussed later in this chapter. While it is nearly impossible to determine that a company has misclassified expenses by reading the annual report or Form 10-K, a thorough financial statement analysis would most likely raise red flags that something was amiss.[9]

Another issue affecting the area of depreciation is that comparing companies is difficult when each firm chooses not only different depreciation methods, but also different lives for their long-lived assets. Depreciation policy is explained in the notes to the financial statements, such as the two following excerpts from 2004 annual reports from competitors Mattel, Inc. and Hasbro, Inc.:

> Mattel, Inc.—Depreciation is computed using the straight-line method over estimated useful lives of 10 to 40 years for buildings, 3 to 10 years for machinery and equipment, and 10 to 20 years, not to exceed the lease term, for leasehold

---

[9]For additional reading about this issue, see Lyn Fraser and Aileen Ormiston, *Understanding the Corporate Annual Report: Nuts, Bolts and a Few Loose Screws*, Upper Saddle River, NJ: Prentice Hall 2003.

improvements. Tools, dies and molds are amortized using the straight-line method over 3 years.

Hasbro, Inc.—Depreciation and amortization are computed using accelerated and straight-line methods to amortize the cost of property, plant and equipment over their estimated useful lives. The principal lives, in years, used in determining depreciation rates of various assets are: land improvements 15 to 19, buildings and improvements 15 to 25, and machinery and equipment 3 to 12.

Tools, dies and molds are amortized over a three year period or their useful lives, whichever is less, using an accelerated method.

13. Asset Impairment

As was discussed in item 10, the write-down of asset values, following the principle of carrying assets at the lower of cost or market value, affects the comparability and thus the quality of financial data. The reasons for the write-downs would also be important in assessing the quality of the financial data. Information on asset write-downs is presented in notes to the financial statements. Firms also write down the carrying cost of property, plant, and equipment when there is a permanent impairment in value and certain investments in marketable equity securities (according to the provisions of FASB Statement No. 115 discussed in Chapter 2) are carried at market value. Emulex, a storage networking systems supplier, reported the following asset impairment charges in its 2004 annual report:

> *Impairment of Goodwill.* The impairment of goodwill expense of $583.5 million in 2004 is a full impairment of our goodwill, which originally resulted from our acquisition of Vixel in November 2004 and Giganet in March 2001. Our annual impairment test occurred in the fourth quarter of fiscal 2004, and the initial test indicated that no impairment existed. However, tepid demand experienced in the fourth fiscal quarter of 2004 from two of our customers, resulted in lower than expected revenue, earnings and cash flows in the fourth fiscal quarter of 2004 and is expected to result in lower sequential revenue, earnings and cash flows in the first fiscal quarter of 2005. These events and circumstances resulted in a subsequent drop in the Company's stock price, which indicated a potential impairment might have occurred. As a result, the Company conducted a FAS 144, "Accounting for the Impairment or Disposal of Long-Lived Assets," analysis, as well as a FAS 142, "Goodwill and Other Intangible Assets," analysis, including a second step goodwill impairment test. The results of the FAS 144 analysis indicated that the Company's long-lived assets were not impaired. However, the FAS 142 analysis indicated that goodwill was impaired. This determination is made at the reporting unit level and consists of two steps. First, the fair value of Emulex's only reporting unit was determined, based on a market approach, and compared to its carrying amount. Next, as the carrying amount exceeded the fair value, the second step of FAS 142 was performed. The implied fair value of goodwill was determined by allocating the fair value in a manner similar to a purchase price allocation, in accordance with FAS 141, "Business Combinations." As a result of this FAS 142 analysis, on September 9, 2004, the Company concluded that a

$583.5 million charge for goodwill impairment should be recorded as of June 27, 2004. After recording this impairment charge, there was no goodwill remaining on the Company's balance sheet as of June 27, 2004. The Company does not believe that such impairment charges will result in any future cash expenditures.

Several additional and interesting pieces of information can be gained from the 2004 Emulex Annual Report. The impairment charge of $583.5 million was larger than Emulex's net revenues of $364.4 million for the year ended June 27, 2004 resulting in a net loss of $532.3 million. The acquisition of Vixel occurred in November 2003 (the date is a typographical error in the 2004 Emulex annual report) and less than a year later the goodwill attached to this investment was deemed worthless. A concern is whether the impairment was in fact 100 percent or if Emulex is using the charge to make future earnings appear much better compared to the reported net loss in 2004. If the goodwill is truly worthless, one has to wonder about management's ability to make good strategic investment decisions.

The FASB has to a certain extent eliminated an earnings management opportunity resulting from asset impairment charges. If it is later deemed that too much was written off, FASB Statement No. 144, "Accounting for the Impairment or Disposal of Long-Lived Assets," does not allow a firm to write back up the value of the asset.

14. "Big Bath" or Restructuring Charges

Large charges classified as restructuring charges are sometimes used by companies to clean up their balance sheet. These charges are often referred to as "Big Bath" charges. The analyst should review the footnote disclosures carefully to assess whether the restructuring charges are associated with a significant reorganization of the company rather than ordinary business expenses. Companies that erroneously classify ordinary business expenses as restructuring charges hope that analysts will ignore what appears to be a one-time charge. Ongoing restructuring of a company can also be a signal of underlying problems. This topic was discussed in Chapter 2 and an example of restructuring charges for Eastman Kodak was discussed.

15. Reserves

Companies often create reserve accounts to set aside funds today to cover some known future cost. In the 1990s, the SEC, under the leadership of Arthur Levitt, sent a message to Corporate America that continued abuse of reserve accounts would not be tolerated. The abuse, or cookie-jar accounting, occurs when companies create reserve accounts for the purpose of setting aside funds in good years (i.e., reducing net income) and then shifting the reserve amounts to the income statement in poor years. The net effect is to smooth out earnings from year to year. Despite the SEC's message, abuses continue to occur in this area. An example of a reserve account is the allowance for doubtful accounts and Cisco's allowance account was analyzed earlier in this chapter. One of Cisco's competitors in the telecom industry, Nortel Networks Corporation, emptied the "cookie jar" in order to pump up earnings in 2003. Red flags existed in Nortel's annual reports for those willing to thoroughly read and analyze the information. For example, despite declining revenues, Nortel reported income from continuing operations in 2003 of $387 million, up from a $3.29 billion loss in 2002. The company had charged over $17 billion in special charges in 2001, which probably should have been recorded in later years.[10]

Other interesting examples of abuse of reserve accounts have been in the news with regard to Royal Dutch/Shell Group, the oil firm, and American International Group (AIG), the world's largest business insurance company.

16. In-Process Research and Development

In-process research and development charges are one-time charges taken at the time of an acquisition. The charged amounts are part of the acquisition price that the acquiring company determines are not yet viable research and development because they are still in process. These charges can be written off immediately under current accounting rules. Any revenue gains from the research in the future will cause higher earnings that have not been matched to the expenses that created them.

Estimating the value of the research and development that is to be written off is difficult, and, as a result, users of financial statements are unlikely to be able to determine if these charges are appropriate. From a user's perspective, this is a problematic area, since companies can write off significant amounts of research and development the year of an acquisition in order to boost earnings in later years. In 2003, Johnson & Johnson made acquisitions for $3.1 billion and immediately wrote off just under $1 billion of in-process research and development. While these amounts may be accurate, investors and creditors have no way to know for sure.

17. Pension Accounting—Interest Rate Assumptions

Although a detailed explanation of pension accounting is beyond the scope of this book, it is important to be aware of some basic pension accounting principles as they impact earnings quality. The reader is referred to the discussion of disclosure requirements for postretirement benefits other than pensions in Chapter 2.

Pension accounting is based on expectations regarding the benefits that will be paid when employees retire and on the interest that pension assets will earn over time. The provisions for pension accounting are specified in Statement of Financial Accounting Standards (SFAS) No. 87, "Employers' Accounting for Pensions."[11]

If a company changes, based on actuarial estimates, the interest rate assumptions used in pension accounting, this change affects the amount of annual pension expense and the present value of the pension benefits. If the assumed rate of interest is increased, pension cost is reduced and earnings increased. For example, if you need $5,000 in 20 years, the amount you would have to invest today would be different if your investment earned 6% or 8%. At 6% you would have to invest $1,560 to accumulate to $5,000 at annual compound interest in 20 years; if the interest rate were increased to 8%, you would have to contribute only $1,075.[12] Also, the present value of the benefits to be paid in the future is affected by increasing the interest rate. The present value of $5,000 to be paid in 20 years is $1,560 at a 6% discount rate and $1,075 at an 8% rate.

---

[10]Jonathan Weil, "At Nortel, Warning Signs Existed Months Ago," *Wall Street Journal*, May 18, 2004.

[11]For a detailed discussion of FASB Statement 87, see L. Revsine, "Understanding Financial Accounting Standard 87," *Financial Analysts Journal*, January–February 1989.

[12](5,000 × .312 = $1,560; $5,000 × .215 = $1,075) (factors for present value of single sum for 20 periods, 6% and 8%).

To summarize the effects of a change in the pension interest rate assumption, if the assumed interest rate is lowered, the annual pension cost will increase and the present value of the benefits will also increase; if the assumed interest rate is increased, pension cost and the present value of the benefits are reduced.

FASB Statement No. 87 requires companies with a defined benefit pension plan—a plan that states the benefits to be received by employees after retirement or the method of determining such benefits—to disclose the following:

1. A description of the plan, including employee groups covered, type of benefit formula, funding policy, and types of assets held.
2. The amount of pension expense showing separately the service cost component, the interest cost component, the actual return on assets for the period, and the net total of other components.[13]
3. A schedule reconciling the funded status of the plan with amounts reported in the company's balance sheet.
4. The weighted average discount rate and rate of compensation increase used to measure the projected benefit obligation and the weighted average expected long-term rate of return on plan assets.
5. The amounts and types of securities included in plan assets.

A liability is recognized if the pension expense recognized to date is greater than the amount funded; an asset is reported if the pension expense to date is less than the amount funded. An additional liability is recognized if the accumulated benefit obligation is greater than the fair market value of plan assets less the balance in the accrued pension liability account or plus the balance in the deferred pension asset account.

Tables from the footnote disclosures relating to employees' defined benefit plans from the 2004 Kennametal, Inc. Annual Report are provided below:

(In Thousands)	2004	2003	2002
Service cost	$13,707	$13,098	$11,195
Interest cost	31,305	30,103	27,328
Expected return on plan assets	(38,157)	(43,166)	(45,367)
Amortization of transition obligation	141	(1,355)	(1,998)
Amortization of prior service cost	702	772	757
Effect of curtailment	1,299	–	–
Recognition of actuarial losses (gains)	1,606	(495)	(2,317)
Net cost (benefit)	$10,603	$(1,043)	$(10,402)
Rates of return on plan assets:			
U.S. plans	8.5%	9.5%	10.0%
International plans	6.5–7.3%	6.5–7.3%	6.5–8.0%

---

[13] The service cost represents the increase during the year in the discounted present value of payable benefits, resulting from employees' working an additional year; interest cost arises from the passage of time and increases interest expense; return on plan assets reduces pension expense; other components include net amortization and deferrals and are related to the choice of discount and interest rates. The same rate must be used to compute service cost and interest cost, but a different rate can be used to compute the expected rate of return on pension plan assets.

There are three noteworthy items from this information. First, Kennametal included $1,043 and $10,402 thousand in 2003 and 2002 net income respectively as a result of the calculation of net pension cost, which in this case is a benefit. Second, the firm recorded income from their pension plans in these years as a result of the $43,166 and $45,367 thousand of "expected" return on plan assets. Third, the expected returns were based on the expected rates of return on plan assets, which Kennametal estimated to be 9.5% and 10.0% in the U.S. in 2003 and 2002. Kennametal decreased their interest rate assumption from 10.0% in 2002 to 8.5% in 2004. Given the large decline in interest rates and the economic downturn, it is surprising that Kennametal had not lowered the interest rate earlier than 2003.[14] An analyst may wish to adjust net income downward if he or she believes the assumed interest rate is too high and that the firm merely kept the rate high to inflate net income. The next table allows the user to compare the expected return to the actual return on the plan assets:

(In Thousands)	2004	2003
Fair value of plan assets, beginning of year	$ 405,430	$403,388
Actual return on plan assets	64,586	5,591
Company contributions	6,716	5,021
Participant contributions	787	729
Benefits paid	(27,378)	(19,288)
Other	–	(435)
Effect of acquired businesses	–	6,625
Foreign currency translation adjustments	3,953	3,799
Fair value of plan assets, end of year	$ 454,094	$405,430

The fair value of the plan assets has increased from 2003 to 2004. In 2003 the actual return on assets was significantly less ($5,591 thousand) than the expected return on plan assets shown in the first table. In 2004, the actual return is much higher than the expected return. The trend the company has estimated is backwards from the actual trend.

The funded status of Kennametal's pension plans is calculated as follows:

	2004	2003
Fair value of plan assets, end of year	$454,094	$405,430
Less: Benefit obligation, end of year	557,829	562,568
Funded status of plans	($103,734)*	($157,138)

*Numbers are rounded.

---

[14]An interesting article on the effect of interest rate assumptions is Susan Pulliam, "Hopeful Assumptions Let Firms Minimize Pension Contributions," *Wall Street Journal*, September 2, 1993.

The following table reveals whether the pension plan is over- or underfunded:

(In Thousands)	2004	2003
Funded status of plans	$(103,734)	$(157,138)
Unrecognized transition obligation	2,622	2,483
Unrecognized prior service cost	3,883	5,283
Unrecognized actuarial losses	73,952	134,058
Net accrued liability	$ (23,277)	$ (15,314)
Amounts recognized in the balance sheet consist of:		
Prepaid benefit	$ 58,389	$ 1,589
Intangible assets	4,520	8,382
Accumulated other comprehensive income	20,614	86,405
Accrued benefit obligation	(106,800)	(111,690)
Net accrued liability	$ (23,277)	$ (15,314)

Kennametal has an underfunded plan and, therefore, records an overall pension liability on the balance sheet. The reconciliation of the funded status of the plan with the amounts shown on the balance sheet is a result of a combination of items. The FASB has included smoothing mechanisms that serve to reduce the volatility to the net income number when recording pension costs. In addition, the many estimates and assumptions used to calculate pension costs cause this amount to be different than the actual amount, and the firm must incorporate the correction of these errors in the amounts shown in the above table.

IV. Nonoperating Revenue and Expense
18. Gains (Losses) from Sales of Assets

When a company sells a capital asset, such as property or equipment, the gain or loss is included in net income for the period. The sale of a major asset is sometimes made to increase earnings and/or to generate needed cash during a period when the firm is performing poorly. Such transactions are not part of the normal operations of the firm and should be excluded from net income when considering the future operating potential of the company.

The following table found in the Goodyear Tire & Rubber Company's 2004 Annual Report illustrates nonoperating revenues and expenses:

Note 4. Other (Income) and Expense

		Restated	
(In Millions)	2004	2003	2002
Asset sales	$ 4.2	$ 25.1	$(28.0)
Interest income	(34.4)	(25.9)	(18.8)
Financing fees and financial instruments	116.5	99.4	48.4
General and product liability—discontinued products	52.7	138.1	33.8
Insurance fire loss deductible	11.7	—	—
Environmental insurance settlement	(156.6)	—	—
Miscellaneous	14.1	26.7	21.4
	$ 8.2	$263.4	$ 56.8

The asset sales, insurance fire loss deductible, and environmental insurance settlement would most likely be excluded when projecting future earnings.

19. Interest Income

Interest income is also nonoperating in nature except for certain types of firms such as financial institutions. Interest income results primarily from short-term temporary investments in marketable securities to earn a return on cash not immediately needed in the business. These security investments were explained in Chapter 2. In the assessment of earnings quality, the analyst should be alert to the materiality and variability in the amount of interest income because it is not part of operating income. Interest income is disclosed on the face of the income statement or in notes to the financial statements.

Using the information given on interest income for Goodyear Tire & Rubber Company in the previous item (number 18) one can see that more interest income has been earned each year. Further investigation reveals that the increase of interest income in 2003 and 2004 was a result of higher levels of cash deposits in the United States. This information is important in analyzing earnings quality because the 2004 interest income may not be sustainable. Projecting future cash balances is important to determining future amounts of interest income.

20. Equity Income

Use of the equity method to account for investments in unconsolidated subsidiaries, discussed and illustrated in Chapter 3, permits the investor to recognize as investment income the investor's percentage ownership share of the investee's reported income rather than recognizing income only to the extent of cash dividends actually received. The net effect is that the investor, in most cases, records more income than is received in cash. Insituform Technologies, Inc. reported the following equity earnings in its 2004 income statement:

(In Thousands)	2004	2003	2002
Equity in earnings (losses) of affiliated companies	($216)	($434)	$834

Cash flow from operations, discussed in Chapter 4, excludes the amount by which investment income recognized exceeds or is less than cash received. Since Insituform Technologies, Inc. received no dividends from these affiliated companies it would be appropriate to eliminate this non-cash portion of earnings for comparative purposes, by adding back equity losses or deducting equity earnings.

21. Income Taxes

The provision for income tax expense on the income statement differs from the tax actually paid, as was discussed in Chapters 2 and 3. When assessing the net earnings number, it is important to differentiate between increases and decreases to net earnings caused by tax events. A significant change in the effective tax rate may be a one-time nonrecurring item. Included in the income tax notes to the financial statements is a reconciliation of the United States federal statutory tax rate to the company's effective tax rate, such as the following from the 2004 Reader's Digest Association, Inc. Annual Report:

	2004	2003	2002
U.S. statutory tax rate	35.0%	35.0%	35.0%
International operations	(11.6)	1.9	(2.5)
State taxes, net	3.6	1.3	3.3
Nontaxable gain from disposition of assets	(3.2)	—	—
Favorable settlement with the Internal Revenue Service	(8.0)	—	—
Changes in valuation allowance	7.9	0.1	—
Other operating items, net	0.2	2.5	0.3
Other, net	1.2	(1.9)	(1.0)
Effective Tax Rate	25.1%	38.9%	35.1%

In 2004, Reader's Digest Association's effective tax rate of 25.1% is significantly lower than the statutory rate as well as the company's effective tax rate the prior two years. The reasons are that Reader's Digest was taxed at lower rates in foreign markets and the company received a favorable settlement with the Internal Revenue Service. Had this settlement not occurred, Reader's Digest's effective tax rate would have been 33.1%. The analyst should take this into consideration when projecting future net earnings.

In addition, the income tax notes to the financial statements reveal year to year changes in deferred tax accounts.

22. Unusual Items

Some companies will create a line item on the income statement for unusual items or special charges. The company wants the user of the financial statements to realize that these items are not recurring operating expenses. The analyst should always investigate these items by reading the notes and the management discussion and analysis to determine if these items are nonoperating and/or nonrecurring. The second quarter earnings release of Waste Management in 2001 revealed that the company included $1 million for the painting of trash trucks and $30 million in consulting fees as "unusual expenses."[15] When adjusting operating and net profit figures for comparison purposes, it would be appropriate to include these items as ordinary operating expenses.

An example of items that would be properly classified as unusual are shown as operating expenses in the 2004 income statements of Pilgrim's Pride Corporation and labeled as "non-recurring recoveries." Pilgrim's Pride explains this line item as follows:

> Non-recurring recoveries in fiscal year 2004 consisted mainly of a $23.8 million gain from insurance proceeds related to our 2002 product recall. In fiscal 2003, we had Non-recurring recoveries of $46.5 million consisting of $26.6 million in payments from the federal government to compensate turkey producers for avian influenza losses and $19.9 million related to the anti-trust lawsuits involving vitamins and methionine.

---

[15] Aaron Elstein, " 'Unusual Expenses' Raise Concerns," *Wall Street Journal*, August 23, 2001.

23. Discontinued Operations

Discontinued operations should be excluded in considering future earnings. Two items are recorded if the discontinued operations have been sold: the gain or loss from operations of the division up to the time of sale, and the gain or loss as a result of the sale, both net of tax. The footnote disclosure for Verizon Communications, from its 2004 Annual Report is as follows:

Summarized results of operations for Verizon Information Services Canada are as follows:

Years Ended December 31,	(Dollars in Millions)		
	2004	2003	2002
Income from operations of Verizon Information Services Canada before income taxes	$ 99	$88	$127
Gain on sale of investment	1,017	—	—
Income tax provision	(546)	(39)	(57)
Income on discontinued operations, net of tax	$ 570	$49	$ 70

Summarized results of operations for Iusacell, which was part of our International segment, follows:

Years Ended December 31,	(Dollars in Millions)	
	2003	2002
Loss from operations of Iusacell before income taxes	$ —	$(74)
Investment loss	(957)	—
Income tax benefit (provision)	22	(12)
Loss on discontinued operations, net of tax	$ (935)	$(86)

It would be appropriate to deduct the income on discontinued operations each year from earnings for comparative purposes.

24. Accounting Changes

Accounting changes are explained and quantified in financial statement notes. Verizon Communications reported a net $503 million gain in 2003 as a result of the cumulative effects of two changes in accounting principle, net of taxes. The footnote disclosures explained the accounting changes as follows:

Directory Accounting

As discussed in Note 1, effective January 1, 2003, we changed our method for recognizing revenues and expenses in our directory business from the publication-date method to the amortization method. The cumulative effect of this accounting change resulted in a charge of $2,697 million ($1,647 million after-tax), recorded as of January 1, 2003.

Asset Retirement Obligations

We adopted the provisions of SFAS No. 143 on January 1, 2003. SFAS No. 143 requires that companies recognize the fair value of a liability for asset retirement obligations in the period in which the obligations are incurred and capitalize that amount as part of the book value of the long-lived asset. We determined that Verizon does not have a material legal obligation to remove long-lived assets as described by this statement. However, prior to the adoption of SFAS No. 143, we included estimated removal costs in our group depreciation models. Consequently, in connection with the initial adoption of SFAS No. 143 we reversed accrued costs of removal in excess of salvage from our accumulated depreciation accounts for these assets. The adjustment was recorded as a cumulative effect of an accounting change, resulting in the recognition of a gain of $3,499 million ($2,150 million after-tax).

For Verizon the cumulative effect of the changes, net of tax, is shown separately on the income statement and should be eliminated in making comparisons with future and prior years' earnings because prior years' earnings were computed using a different accounting method. Once companies have implemented FASB Statement No. 154 (discussed in Chapter 3) elimination from the income statement will be unnecessary since all years presented will have been restated as if the accounting change had always been in place. While the new FASB requirements make comparability and consistency better, users of financial statements should still read carefully any footnote disclosures regarding accounting changes. A quality of earnings issue still exists if a firm is changing accounting methods for the purpose of boosting earnings in the short term. In fact, the new requirements may even encourage this behavior since the disclosure for accounting changes is no longer prominently displayed on the income statement.

25. Extraordinary Items

Extraordinary items are gains and losses that are both unusual and infrequent in nature. They are shown separately, net of tax, on the income statement. Because very few transactions meet the definition of extraordinary, it is rare to see such items on an earnings statement. For many years the FASB required gains and losses on debt extinguishments to be reported as extraordinary items; however, the issuance of FASB Statement No. 145, "Rescission of FASB Statements No. 4, 44, 64, Amendment of FASB Statement No. 13, and Technical Corrections," only allows this treatment if the gain or loss meets the criteria for an extraordinary item.

United States Steel Corporation reported an extraordinary loss in 2003. The item is explained as follows in the notes to the financial statements:

Divestiture

On June 30, 2003, U. S. Steel completed the sale of the coal mines and related assets of U. S. Steel Mining Company, LLC (Mining Sale) to PinnOak Resources, LLC (PinnOak), which is not affiliated with U. S. Steel, thereby ending U. S. Steel's participation in coal mining operations. PinnOak acquired the Pinnacle No. 50 mine complex located near Pineville, West Virginia and the Oak Grove mine complex located near Birmingham, Alabama. In conjunction with the sale, U. S. Steel and PinnOak entered into a long-term coal supply agreement, which runs through December 31, 2006.

The gross proceeds from the sale were $55 million and resulted in a pretax gain on disposal of assets of $13 million in the second quarter of 2003. In addition, EITF 92-13, "Accounting for Estimated Payments in Connection with the Coal Industry Retiree Health Benefit Act of 1992" requires that enterprises no longer having operations in the coal industry must account for their entire obligation related to the multiemployer health care benefit plans created by the Act as a loss in accordance with FAS No. 5, "Accounting for Contingencies." Accordingly, U. S. Steel recognized the present value of these obligations in the amount of $85 million, resulting in the recognition of an extraordinary loss of $52 million, net of tax of $33 million.

The loss should be eliminated from earnings when evaluating a firm's future earnings potential.

V. Other Issues
26. Material Changes in Number of Shares Outstanding
The number of common stock shares outstanding and thus the computation of earnings per share can change materially from one accounting period to the next. These changes result from such transactions as treasury stock purchases and the purchase and retirement of a firm's own common stock. The reasons for the repurchase of common stock should be determined if possible. Some firms use repurchase programs to obtain shares of stock to be used in employee stock option programs. In its 2004 annual report, Microsoft explains its repurchase program as follows:

> Our board of directors has approved a program to repurchase shares of our common stock to reduce the dilutive effect of our stock option and stock purchase plans.

In 2004, Microsoft repurchased 124 million shares of stock, but issued 215 million shares, causing an overall increase in common stock outstanding of 91 million shares. The financial statement user should look at the Statement of Stockholders' Equity to determine if a firm is repurchasing more shares than are needed for issuance. In addition, how these repurchases are financed is important. If companies have to borrow to repurchase stock, the analyst would want to determine if this was a wise choice.

Some firms offer no reason for their repurchase program. It is important to consider whether a firm is spending scarce resources to merely increase earnings per share (EPS). The effects of reducing outstanding shares of common stock result in an increase to EPS. Consider the repurchase program of Autozone, Inc. In 2004, the board of directors approved an amendment to the firm's repurchase program to allow the repurchase of stock to increase from $3.6 to $3.9 billion of outstanding stock. From 2002 to 2004, Autozone, Inc. repurchased $2.4 billion of outstanding stock while only generating $2.1 billion of cash flow from operations during the same time frame. Since cash flow from operations was not enough to cover all other investing and financing activities in addition to repurchasing stock, Autozone took on new debt of over $1.1 billion from 2002 to 2004.

Other firms, like The Walt Disney Company, repurchase their own shares as an investment, as illustrated in its 2001 Annual Report:

> Disney also seeks to increase returns through the repurchase of its own stock. In 2001, the company invested a total of $1.1 billion to purchase 63.9 million shares of Disney common stock at an average price of $16.62 per share. Since 1983, the company has repurchased nearly 549 million shares at a cost of just

under $4.4 billion. At the November 30 stock price, these shares represent a market value of more than $11 billion.

27. Operating Earnings, a.k.a. Core Earnings, Pro Forma Earnings, or EBITDA

Operating earnings or profit (discussed in Chapter 3) is an important figure for assessing the ongoing potential of a firm. Some companies have created their own operating profit numbers and tried to convince users that these figures are the ones to focus on instead of the GAAP-based amounts. These "company created" numbers go by a variety of names such as core earnings, pro forma earnings, or EBITDA. EBITDA, for example, refers to operating earnings before interest, tax, depreciation, and amortization expenses are deducted. Those who support focusing on EBITDA argue that depreciation and amortization charges are not cash items and should be ignored. In essence, they are asking that users ignore the fact that companies make long-term investments. Depreciation and amortization expenses are the allocation of an original cash amount spent for items such as equipment. In January 2003, the SEC adopted a new rule requiring companies that report pro forma financial information to present this information in a manner that is not misleading and also to reconcile the pro forma financial information with GAAP.

What Are the Real Earnings?

Each individual user of financial statements should adjust the earnings figure to reflect what that particular user believes is relevant to the decision at hand. Based on the checklist, Exhibit 5.2 shows the items that should be considered as adjustments to earnings.

EXHIBIT 5.2 Adjustments to Earnings

Start with net income, then consider the following adjustments:

a. add or deduct amounts for questionable items charged to bad debt expense (item 4)

b. deduct base LIFO layer liquidations (item 8)

c. add back loss recognized on write-downs of assets (items 10 and 13)

d. deduct amounts for discretionary expenses that firm may have delayed (item 11)

e. add or deduct amounts recorded as charges or credits for restructuring costs (item 14)

f. add back charges for in-process research and development (item 16)

g. add or deduct losses and gains from sales of assets (item 18)

h. deduct nonrecurring amounts of interest income (item 19)

i. add or deduct equity losses or income (item 20)

j. add or deduct nonrecurring amounts of income tax expense (item 21)

k. add back unusual expenses that are nonrecurring (item 22)

l. add or deduct losses or gains attributable to discontinued operations and extraordinary items (items 23 and 25)

Quality of Financial Reporting—The Balance Sheet

Many items discussed in the earnings quality section also impact balance sheet quality, such as the value attached to accounts receivable, inventory, and long-term assets. When evaluating balance sheet information, several items should also be assessed. The type of debt used to finance assets should generally be matched; that is, short-term debt should be used to finance current assets, and long-term debt (or equity) should be used to finance long-term assets. A mismatching of debt to assets could be an indication that the firm may be having trouble finding financing sources. The accounting fraud that led to the bankruptcy of Parmalat, the Italian dairy company, revolved around debt issues at the firm. Despite supposedly large cash balances (later found to be nonexistent) Parmalat went to the markets continuously and issued bonds to raise more funding. This inconsistency should have raised red flags well before the scandal unfolded.

As discussed in Chapter 2, the "Commitments and Contingencies" disclosures in the notes to the financial statements should be evaluated carefully. These disclosures are often presented in the section where information on off-balance-sheet financing and other complex financing arrangements can be found. Despite the seeming surprise of Enron's downfall, many clues could have been found by tracking the complexities of the references to commitments and contingencies for several years preceding its bankruptcy.

The six pages of notes to the financial statements related to the commitments and contingencies of Pfizer Inc. in 2004 may help explain why the firm's stock price has fallen from a high of $38.89 per share in the first quarter of 2004 to a low of $21.99 per share in the fourth quarter of 2004 despite a 17% growth in sales and 190% growth in net income in the same year. Besides operating lease commitments, environmental matters, and guarantees, Pfizer is involved in many legal proceedings. Some of the lawsuits Pfizer is party to involve patents, product liability, commercial matters, violations of securities laws, false advertising, and antitrust violations. While most of the information in the notes cannot be quantified on a financial statement the notes allow readers to determine for themselves the significance of the lawsuits.

Also included in the commitments note is information on capital and operating leases. While capital leases are included on the balance sheet, the financial statement user should consider the effects on certain leverage ratios (discussed in Chapter 6) if operating leases are extensive. The firm is committed to make lease payments, and if these leases had been negotiated as capital leases, there would be a higher amount of debt on the balance sheet. For example, Walgreen Company, a drug retailer, has no short-term or long-term debt according to its 2004 balance sheet. Reading the note on leases the analyst can see that the firm is committed to pay a minimum of $21,876.7 million for leases in the future. This amount is greater than Walgreen's total assets in 2004 of $13,342.1 million.

Quality of Financial Reporting—The Statement of Cash Flows

Since the requirement of the statement of cash flows in the 1980s, many investors and creditors have focused on cash flow from operations (CFO) more heavily than the earnings numbers. Readers should be aware that the cash flow from operations figure, while highly useful, can also be manipulated. The demise of WorldCom in 2002 brought to the forefront one issue of manipulating CFO.

WorldCom recorded as capital expenditures billions of dollars that should have been recorded as operating expenses. For the cash flow statement, these outflows appear as investing activities rather than as a direct reduction of cash flow from operations. (The expense portion of a capital expense is depreciation, which is added back to net income in determining cash flow from operating activities.) The effects of recording operating expenses as capital expenditures are illustrated by the following example:

> A company records $100 million in operating expenses as a capital expenditure to be depreciated over 10 years with no salvage value.
> —Net income is overstated by $90 million. (Only the $10 million in depreciation expense has been included as an expense.)
> —Cash flow from operations is overstated by $100 million. On the statement of cash flows, depreciation expense of $10 million is added back to net income in determining cash flow from operations.
> —Investing activity outflows are overstated by $100 million.

Other techniques exist for companies to inflate the CFO figure. Through the management of current asset and liability accounts, companies can cause increases to CFO. For example, by selling accounts receivable, a firm receives cash immediately, and this is recorded as a decrease in accounts receivable and an increase to CFO. Delaying cash payment on accounts payable also has the effect of increasing CFO. Significant changes in current asset and current liability accounts should be scrutinized in the assessment of CFO.

The SEC's concerns about how companies accounted for vendor financing transactions in their cash flow statements led to restatements in 2004 of prior cash flow numbers at companies such as General Motors, Ford Motor Company, General Electric, and Caterpillar. The SEC has made it clear that vendor financing is a result of operating activities and as such, should be included as part of CFO, not cash from investing activities as the above-mentioned companies were reporting these amounts. Caterpillar's CFO, positive before the restatement, declined $6.3 billion in 2002 and $7.7 billion in 2003 after the restatement, causing CFO to be negative both years.[16]

Nonfinancial companies that invest in trading securities (discussed in Chapter 2) record purchases and sales of these securities in the operating activities section of the cash flow statement. While this treatment is within GAAP guidelines, these items are investing, not operating activities and should be eliminated if the financial statement user wants a more accurate operating figure for cash flow. CFO should also be adjusted for any other items that are deemed nonrecurring or nonoperating. In addition to the elimination of cash flows from investments in trading securities, cash flows from items such as discontinued operations or nonrecurring expenses or income should be removed for analytical purposes.

---

[16]Michael Rapoport, "'Cash Flow' Isn't What It Used to Be," *Wall Street Journal*, March 24, 2005.

SELF-TEST

Solutions are provided in Appendix B.

_____ 1. When should revenue be recognized, assuming generally accepted accounting principles are followed?
   (a) Revenue should be recognized when cash is collected from the customer.
   (b) Revenue should be recognized based on the company's individual policy.
   (c) Revenue should be recognized when delivery of products or title to those products has passed to the buyer or services have been rendered and the price has been determined with the expectation of collection.
   (d) Revenue should be recognized when a contract has been signed that details the date and time that the product will be delivered or the services rendered and the price has been determined.

_____ 2. Which of the following is a technique for boosting revenues?
   (a) Follow the "35-day month practice" in which the books are kept open longer than the month end in order to record extra sales.
   (b) Record transactions at the net amount.
   (c) Delay shipment of goods.
   (d) Increase the allowance for doubtful accounts.

_____ 3. Why is it important to analyze the relationship among sales, accounts receivable, and the allowance for doubtful accounts?
   (a) Comparing the three accounts' growth rates is the only way to determine if the firm is using vendor financing.
   (b) The allowance for doubtful accounts is a reserve account that can be used to manipulate the earnings number.
   (c) Price and volume changes will cause the relationship among the three accounts to be volatile.
   (d) It is important to determine if the three accounts are changing with the inflation rate.

_____ 4. Where can information about sales price and volume changes be found?
   (a) On the face of the income statement.
   (b) In the notes to the financial statements.
   (c) On the balance sheet.
   (d) In the management's discussion and analysis.

_____ 5. Which method of inventory is generally thought to produce the highest quality of earnings?
   (a) FIFO.
   (b) LIFO.
   (c) Average cost.
   (d) All of the above.

_____ 6. When does a base LIFO layer liquidation occur?
   (a) A base LIFO layer liquidation occurs during a deflationary environment.
   (b) A base LIFO layer liquidation occurs when companies are shrinking rather than increasing inventories after a period of inflation.

(c) A base LIFO layer liquidation occurs when a company switches from the FIFO to the LIFO method of inventory valuation.

(d) A base LIFO layer liquidation occurs when a firm increases inventories after a period of inflation.

_____ 7. How does the recording of fulfillment costs cause a quality of financial reporting issue?

(a) Many companies record fulfillment costs as operating expenses when they should be recorded as miscellaneous expenses.

(b) Bad debt expenses are recorded as fulfillment costs.

(c) Fulfillment costs can include items that are properly classified as cost of goods sold, as well as other operating costs, therefore causing a comparability issue when comparing firms' gross profit and operating profit margins.

(d) Fulfillment costs cause the operating profit margin to be wrong.

_____ 8. If a firm has written down the value of their inventory, what should be of concern to the analyst?

(a) The analyst should consider removing the effects of the write-down from the profit margins in order to better compare changes from one period to the next.

(b) The analyst should deduct the loss from the write-down from the net earnings amount.

(c) The analyst does not need to do anything since write-downs of inventory are so frequent.

(d) The analyst cannot determine the effect of the write-down and, therefore, is unable to make any adjustments.

_____ 9. Which of the following expenses is (are) usually considered to be discretionary?

(a) Research and development.

(b) Advertising.

(c) Depreciation.

(d) Both (a) and (b).

_____ 10. Which of the following statements is false?

(a) The straight-line method of depreciation is lower in quality than other methods, in most cases, because it does not reflect the economic reality of product usefulness.

(b) Poor quality of financial reporting results when firms misclassify operating expenses as capital expenditures.

(c) Firms must follow the schedule prescribed by the FASB for determining the lives of long-lived assets.

(d) Analysts can learn about the depreciation policy of a firm by reading the notes to the financial statements.

_____ 11. What is meant by the term "cookie-jar accounting"?

(a) The abuse that occurs when companies create reserve accounts for the purpose of setting aside funds in good years and then shifting the reserve amounts to the income statement in poor years.

(b) The abuse that occurs when companies use operational funds for non-operational items such as parties, doughnuts, cookies, and personal travel expenses.

(c) The abuse that occurs when firms acquire another company and then write down the cost of in-process research and development.

(d) The abuse that occurs when firms charge ordinary business expenses as restructuring charges.

_____ 12. Which of the following statements is true?

(a) The quality issues of pension accounting have been largely eliminated by the issuance of FASB Statement No. 87.

(b) If the assumed pension interest rate assumption is lowered, the annual pension cost will increase.

(c) If the assumed pension interest rate assumption is increased, the annual pension cost will increase.

(d) Due to the accounting rules for pension plans, most companies have underfunded pension plans.

_____ 13. Which of the following is not classified as a nonoperating revenue or expense?

(a) Interest income.

(b) Equity income or loss.

(c) Gains or losses on the sales of assets.

(d) Salaries expense.

_____ 14. What information cannot be found in the notes to the financial statements regarding income taxes?

(a) A reconciliation of the United States federal statutory tax rate to the company's effective tax rate.

(b) Year to year changes in deferred tax accounts.

(c) A reconciliation of any foreign statutory tax rate to the company's effective tax rate.

(d) None of the above.

_____ 15. If discontinued operations have been sold, what must be recorded on the income statement?

(a) The gain or loss from operations of the division up to the time of sale, net of tax.

(b) The amount that the buyer paid for the discontinued operations.

(c) The gain or loss from the sale of the discontinued operations, net of tax.

(d) Both (a) and (c).

_____ 16. What must be true for an item to be classified as an extraordinary item?

(a) The item must be both unusual and infrequent in nature.

(b) The item must be either unusual or infrequent in nature.

(c) The item must be registered as extraordinary with the FASB.

(d) The item must be approved as extraordinary by the SEC.

_____ 17. Why would a firm repurchase its own common stock?

(a) The firm believes their stock is undervalued and purchases it as an investment.

(b) The firm purchases stock to be used in employee stock option programs.

(c) The firm is trying to reduce the number of shares outstanding in order to boost the earnings per share amount.

(d) All of the above.

_____ **18.** Which of the following statements is false?

(a) If a firm uses operating leases extensively, the analyst should investigate the impact of those leases on leverage ratios.

(b) The analyst should read the "Commitments and Contingencies" disclosures to learn of any off-balance-sheet financing or other complex financing arrangements.

(c) The analyst should assess whether the right type of debt is used to finance assets, i.e., short-term debt is used to finance long-term assets and long-term debt is used to finance current assets.

(d) The analyst should determine the significance of any legal proceedings.

_____ **19.** How have companies been able to manipulate the information on the statement of cash flows?

(a) Companies cannot manipulate cash flow information.

(b) Some companies recorded vendor financing transactions as investing, rather than operating activities.

(c) Some companies recorded increases to accounts receivable as decreases to cash flow from operations.

(d) Some companies borrowed money to increase the cash flow from financing activities.

_____ **20.** Which earnings number is the most relevant for decision-making purposes?

(a) An earnings number adjusted for items that are not relevant for the decision at hand.

(b) Pro forma earnings.

(c) EBITDA.

(d) Core earnings.

STUDY QUESTIONS AND PROBLEMS

5.1. Discuss the qualitative issues related to reported revenue.

5.2. Explain the importance of understanding inventory valuation methods in determining the quality of the profit numbers.

5.3. How is it possible for a firm to benefit from the write-down of an asset?

5.4. Should restructuring charges be classified as an operating expense or as a nonoperating expense?

5.5. When is it appropriate for a firm to repurchase its own common stock? When would it be considered a poor decision?

5.6. From 1998 until the third quarter of fiscal 2000, WorldCom, Inc. did not write off numerous accounts of customers who were in default and unlikely to pay their bills. In the third quarter of 2000, WorldCom management, who had earlier refused to approve any write-offs, told the accounting area to write off $405 million of accounts receivable. Wall Street analysts viewed this write-off as a one-time nonrecurring event. Explain the significance of this transaction to an analyst.

5.7. The following calculations have been made using Metro Tech's income statement:

Sales growth, current year	20%
Gross profit margin, current year	64%
Gross profit margin, last year	52%

Discuss all the reasons you can think of to explain the 12% change in gross profit margin. Which reasons would be considered a quality issue by an analyst?

5.8. The following information from a *Business Week* article, "The Costco Way," in the April 12, 2004 issue, reveals key differences between Costco's and Wal-Mart's wage strategies. Explain how this information relates to the discussion in this chapter of discretionary expenses.

	Costco	Wal-Mart's Sam's Club
Average hourly wage	$15.97	$11.52*
Annual health costs per worker	$5,735	$3,500
Covered by health plan	82%	47%
Annual retirement costs per worker	$1,330	$747
Covered by retirement plans	91%**	64%
Employee turnover	6% a year	21% a year
Labor and overhead costs	9.8% of sales	17% of sales***
Sales per square foot	$795	$516
Profits per employee	$13,647	$11,039
Yearly operating-income growth****	10.1%	9.8%

*Excludes 25% of workforce that is lower-paid part-timers.
**Those on the job for less than a year aren't covered.
***For all of Wal-Mart.
****Over the past five years in the U.S.

5.9. Writing Skills Problem

Even though firms follow the accounting rules (GAAP) when presenting their financial statements it is still possible for conflicts of interest to exist between what management wants investors and creditors to see and the economic reality of transactions. Write a short essay explaining how this can occur.

5.10. Research Problem

Locate a firm that has been involved in an investigation of its accounting practices by the SEC. Discuss the quality issues in the case and how they relate to the material learned in this chapter.

5.11. Internet Problem

Look up the SEC homepage on the Internet at the following address: www.sec.gov/. Research and locate links related to accounting issues. Write a short summary of the types of items related to accounting that can be found on the SEC's Web site.

5.12. Intel Problem

The 2004 Intel report can be found at the following Web site: www.prenhall.com/fraser. Review the quality of financial reporting for Intel. Write a summary explaining whether the quality is good or poor.

5.13. Eastman Kodak Comprehensive Analysis Problem Using the Financial Statement Analysis Template

The 2004 Eastman Kodak Annual Report and Form 10-K can be found at the following Web site: www.prenhall.com/fraser.

(a) Using the checklist and the quality of financial reporting sections of Chapter 5, discuss the quality of Eastman Kodak's annual report and Form 10-K.

(b) Adjust the 2004 net earnings figure for Eastman Kodak, for purposes of comparing this amount to future earnings.

Note: The CPI for 2004 is 184.3 and for 2003 is 180.9.

C A S E S

Case 5.1 Nortel Networks Corporation

Nortel Networks Corporation is a global communications company that designs, develops, manufactures, installs and supports networking solutions. Nortel's customers include wireless service providers, large and small businesses, government agencies, educational institutions, utility organizations, and telephone companies. Competitors include Nokia, Motorola, Siemens, Cisco, Lucent, and many others.

The liabilities and stockholders' equity section of Nortel's balance sheet, as well as excerpts from the notes regarding guarantees and commitments, are given on pages 182–187.

Required

1. Assess the capital structure of Nortel Networks Corporation.
2. Read the notes related to guarantees and commitments for Nortel Networks Corporation and discuss what is learned by reading these notes. Make connections to the ways this information impacts Nortel's capital structure.
3. Discuss the quality of the disclosures for guarantees and commitments. Could these disclosures be improved?

12. Guarantees

Nortel has entered into agreements that contain features which meet the definition of a guarantee under FIN 45. FIN 45 defines a guarantee as a contract that contingently requires Nortel to make payments (either in cash, financial instruments, other assets, common shares of Nortel Networks Corporation or through the provision of services) to a third party based on changes in an underlying economic characteristic (such as interest rates or market value) that is related to an asset, a liability or an equity security of the guaranteed party or a third party's failure to perform under a specified agreement. A description of the major types of Nortel's outstanding guarantees as of December 31, 2004 is provided below:

(a) Business sale and business combination agreements

In connection with agreements for the sale of portions of its business, including certain discontinued operations, Nortel has typically retained the liabilities of a business which relate to events occurring prior to its sale, such as tax, environmental, litigation and employment matters. Nortel generally indemnifies the purchaser of a Nortel business in the event that a third party asserts a claim against the purchaser that relates to a liability retained by Nortel. Some of these types of guarantees have indefinite terms while others have specific terms extending to June 2008.

Nortel also entered into guarantees related to the escrow of shares in business combinations in prior periods. These types of agreements generally include indemnities that require Nortel to indemnify counterparties

Excerpts From Nortel Networks Corporation
Consolidated Balance Sheets as of December 31

(Millions of U.S. Dollars, Except for Share Amounts)	2004	2003
Liabilities and Shareholders' Equity		
Current liabilities		
Trade and other accounts payable	$ 996	$ 878
Payroll and benefit-related liabilities	515	764
Contractual liabilities	569	530
Restructuring liabilities	254	206
Other accrued liabilities	2,823	2,505
Long-term debt due within one year	15	119
Total current liabilities	5,172	5,002
Long-term debt	3,862	3,891
Deferred income taxes – net	144	191
Other liabilities	3,189	2,945
Total liabilities	12,367	12,029
Minority interests in subsidiary companies	630	617
Guarantees, commitments and contingencies (notes 12, 13, and 21)		
Shareholders' Equity		
Common shares without par value—Authorized shares unlimited;		
Issued and outstanding shares: 4,272,671,213 for 2004 and 4,166.714,475 for 2003	33,840	33,674
Additional paid in capital	3,282	3,341
Accumulated deficit	(32,583)	(32,532)
Accumulated other comprehensive loss	(552)	(538)
Total shareholders' equity	3,987	3,945
Total liabilities and shareholders' equity	$16,984	$16,591

The accompanying notes are an integral part of these consolidated financial statements.

for loss incurred from litigation that may be suffered by counterparties arising under such agreements. These types of indemnities apply over a specified period of time from the date of the business combinations and do not provide for any limit on the maximum potential amount.

Nortel is unable to estimate the maximum potential liability for these types of indemnification guarantees as the business sale agreements generally do not specify a maximum amount and the amounts are dependent upon the outcome of future contingent events, the nature and likelihood of which cannot be determined.

Historically, Nortel has not made any significant indemnification payments under such agreements and no significant liability has been accrued in the consolidated financial statements with respect to the obligations associated with these guarantees.

In conjunction with the sale of a subsidiary to a third party, Nortel guaranteed to the purchaser that specified annual volume levels would be achieved by the business sold over a ten year period ending December 31, 2007. The maximum amount that Nortel may be required to pay under the volume guarantee as of December 31, 2004 is $9. A liability of $9 has been accrued in the consolidated financial statements with respect to the obligation associated with this guarantee as of December 31, 2004.

(b) Intellectual property indemnification obligations

Nortel has periodically entered into agreements with customers and suppliers that include limited intellectual property indemnification obligations that are customary in the industry. These types of guarantees typically have indefinite terms and generally require Nortel to compensate the other party for certain damages and costs incurred as a result of third party intellectual property claims arising from these transactions.

The nature of the intellectual property indemnification obligations generally prevents Nortel from making a reasonable estimate of the maximum potential amount it could be required to pay to its customers and suppliers. Historically, Nortel has not made any significant indemnification payments under such agreements. A liability of $6 has been accrued in the consolidated financial statements with respect to the obligations associated with these guarantees as of December 31, 2004.

(c) Lease agreements

Nortel has entered into agreements with certain of its lessors that guarantee the lease payments of certain assignees of its facilities to lessors. Generally, these lease agreements relate to facilities Nortel vacated prior to the end of the term of its lease. These lease agreements require Nortel to make lease payments throughout the lease term if the assignee fails to make scheduled payments. Most of these lease agreements also require Nortel to pay for facility restoration costs at the end of the lease term if the assignee fails to do so. These lease agreements have expiration dates through June 2015. The maximum amount that Nortel may be required to pay under these types of agreements is $48 as of December 31, 2004. Nortel generally

has the ability to attempt to recover such lease payments from the defaulting party through rights of subrogation.

Historically, Nortel has not made any significant payments under these types of guarantees and no significant liability has been accrued in the consolidated financial statements with respect to the obligations associated with these guarantees.

(d) Third party debt agreements

Nortel has guaranteed the debt of certain customers. These third party debt agreements require Nortel to make debt payments throughout the term of the related debt instrument if the customer fails to make scheduled debt payments. These third party debt agreements have expiration dates extending to May 2012. The maximum amount that Nortel may be required to pay under these types of debt agreements is $7 as of December 31, 2004. Under most such arrangements, the Nortel guarantee is secured, usually by the assets being purchased or financed. No liability has been accrued in the consolidated financial statements with respect to the obligations associated with these financial guarantees as of December 31, 2004.

(e) Indemnification of banks and agents under credit facilities, EDC Support Facility and security agreements

As of December 31, 2004, Nortel had agreed to indemnify the banks and agents under its credit facilities against costs or losses resulting from changes in laws and regulations which would increase the banks' costs or reduce their return and from any legal action brought against the banks or agents related to the use of loan proceeds. Nortel has also agreed to indemnify EDC under the EDC Support Facility against any legal action brought against EDC that relates to the provision of support under the EDC Support Facility. Nortel has also agreed to indemnify the collateral agent under the security agreements against any legal action brought against the collateral agent in connection with the collateral pledged under the security agreements. These indemnifications generally apply to issues that arise during the term of the credit and support facilities, or for as long as the security agreements remain in effect (see notes 10 and 22).

Nortel is unable to estimate the maximum potential liability for these types of indemnification guarantees as the agreements typically do not specify a maximum amount and the amounts are dependent upon the outcome of future contingent events, the nature and likelihood of which cannot be determined at this time.

Historically, Nortel has not made any significant indemnification payments under such agreements and no significant liability has been accrued in the consolidated financial statements with respect to the obligations associated with these indemnification guarantees.

Nortel has agreed to indemnify certain of its counterparties in certain receivables securitization transactions. The indemnifications provided to counterparties in these types of transactions may require Nortel to compensate counterparties for costs incurred as a result of changes in laws and regulations (including tax legislation) or in the interpretations of such laws and regulations, or as a result of regulatory penalties that may be suffered by the counterparty as a consequence of the transaction. Certain receivables securitization transactions include indemnifications requiring the repurchase of the receivables if the particular transaction becomes invalid. As of December 31, 2004, Nortel had approximately $266 of securitized receivables which were subject to repurchase under this provision, in which case Nortel would assume all rights to collect such receivables. The indemnification provisions generally expire upon expiration of the securitization agreements, which extend through 2005, or collection of the receivable amounts by the counterparty.

Nortel is generally unable to estimate the maximum potential liability for all of these types of indemnification guarantees as certain agreements do not specify a maximum amount and the amounts are dependent upon the outcome of future contingent events, the nature and likelihood of which cannot be determined at this time.

Historically, Nortel has not made any significant indemnification payments or receivable repurchases under such agreements and no significant liability has been accrued in the consolidated financial statements with respect to the obligations associated with these guarantees.

(f) Other indemnification agreements

Nortel has also entered into other agreements that provide indemnifications to counterparties in certain transactions including investment banking agreements, guarantees related to the administration of capital trust accounts, guarantees related to the administration of employee benefit plans, indentures for its outstanding public debt and asset sale agreements (other than the business sale agreements noted above). These indemnification agreements generally require Nortel to indemnify the counterparties for costs incurred as a result of changes in laws and regulations (including tax legislation) or in the interpretations of such laws and regulations and/or as a result of losses from litigation that may be suffered by the counterparties arising from the transactions. These types of indemnification agreements normally extend over an unspecified period of time from the date of the transaction and do not typically provide for any limit on the maximum potential payment amount.

The nature of such agreements prevents Nortel from making a reasonable estimate of the maximum potential amount it could be required to pay to its counterparties. The difficulties in assessing the amount of liability result primarily from the unpredictability of future changes in laws, the inability to determine how laws apply to counterparties and the lack of limitations on the potential liability.

Historically, Nortel has not made any significant indemnification payments under such agreements and no significant liability has been accrued in the consolidated financial statements with respect to the obligations associated with these guarantees.

Product warranties

The following summarizes the accrual for product warranties that was recorded as part of other accrued liabilities in the consolidated balance sheets as of December 31:

	2004	2003
Balance at the beginning of the year	$387	$408
Payments	(349)	(347)
Warranties issued	229	337
Revisions	8	(11)
Balance at the end of the year	$275	$387

13. Commitments

Bid, performance related and other bonds

Nortel has entered into bid, performance related and other bonds associated with various contracts. Bid bonds generally have a term of less than twelve months, depending on the length of the bid period for the applicable contract. Other bonds primarily relate to warranty, rental, real estate and customs contracts. Performance related and other bonds generally have a term of twelve months and are typically renewed, as required, over the term of the applicable contract. The various contracts to which these bonds apply generally have terms ranging from two to five years. Any potential payments which might become due under these bonds would be related to Nortel's nonperformance under the applicable contract. Historically, Nortel has not had to make material payments under these

types of bonds and does not anticipate that any material payments will be required in the future. The following table sets forth the maximum potential amount of future payments under bid, performance related and other bonds, net of the corresponding restricted cash and cash equivalents, as of December 31:

	2004	2003
Bid and performance related bonds[a]	$362	$427
Other bonds[b]	68	53
Total bid performance related and other bonds	$430	$480

[a]Net of restricted cash and cash equivalent amounts of $36 and $14 as of December 31, 2004 and 2003, respectively.
[b]Net of restricted cash and cash equivalent amounts of $28 and $31 as of December 31, 2004 and 2003, respectively.

Venture capital financing

Nortel has entered into agreements with selected venture capital firms where the venture capital firms make and manage investments in start-ups and emerging enterprises. The agreements require Nortel to fund requests for additional capital up to its commitments when and if requests for additional capital are solicited by the venture capital firm. Nortel had remaining commitments, if requested, of $16 as of December 31, 2004. These commitments expire at various dates through to 2012.

Purchase commitments

Nortel has entered into purchase commitments with certain suppliers under which it commits to buy a minimum amount or percentage of designated products in exchange for price guarantees or similar concessions. In certain of these agreements, Nortel may be required to acquire and pay for such products up to the prescribed minimum or forecasted purchases. As of December 31, 2004, Nortel had aggregate purchase commitments of $1,254.

Operating leases and other commitments

As of December 31, 2004, the future minimum payments under operating leases, outsourcing contracts, special charges related to lease commitments accrued for as part of restructuring contract settlement and lease costs and related sublease recoveries under contractual agreements consisted of:

	Operating leases	Outsourcing contracts	Special charges	Sublease income
2005	$ 96	$ 96	$118	$ (28)
2006	108	94	63	(26)
2007	95	92	53	(19)
2008	74	91	45	(17)
2009	59	90	35	(15)
Thereafter	389	–	185	(48)
Total future minimum payments	$821	$463	$499	$(153)

Rental expense on operating leases for the years ended December 31, 2004, 2003 and 2002, net of applicable sublease income, amounted to $179, $260, and $469, respectively.

Case 5.2 FindWhat.com, Inc.

FindWhat.com, Inc. has been providing e-commerce solutions since 1998. The types of services offered by FindWhat.com include Internet advertising services, primarily in North America and Europe; the opportunity for large companies to brand and sell their own performance-based, keyword-targeted advertising; services such as toolbars, screensavers, and other interactive products; and systems that allow a merchant to create a complete online store within an existing Web site. During 2004, FindWhat.com acquired Miva Corporation and Comet Systems, Inc., as well as certain assets of B&B Enterprises, Inc. A subsidiary of the firm also merged with Espotting Media, Inc., a European company.*

Required

Using the excerpts given on pages 188–191 from FindWhat.com's 2004 Annual Report, assess the quality of sales using the first five items included in Part I of the Checklist for Earnings Quality (Exhibit 5.1).

Excerpt From Report of Independent Registered Certified Public Accountants on Internal Controls

A material weakness is a control deficiency, or combination of control deficiencies, that results in more than a remote likelihood that a material misstatement of the annual or interim financial statements will not be prevented or detected. The following material weaknesses have been identified and included in management's assessment: (i) insufficient controls over the determination and application of generally accepted accounting principles with respect to purchase accounting for certain

2004 acquisitions, (ii) insufficient controls over the determination and application of generally accepted accounting principles with respect to evaluating and measuring impairment of goodwill, (iii) insufficient controls over the determination and application of generally accepted accounting principles with respect to revenue recognition for private label agreements and other revenue agreements, excluding those related to FindWhat.com Network revenue, (iv) insufficient personnel resources and technical accounting expertise within the accounting function to resolve non-routine or complex accounting matters, (v) insufficient controls over and review of the quarterly and year-end financial statement close and review process, and (vi) insufficient segregation of duties whereby financial accounting personnel had access to financial accounting IT applications and data and also performed incompatible duties with respect to the authorization, recording, and control activities. The first five of these material weaknesses affected several financial statement accounts, including accounts receivable and allowance for doubtful accounts, goodwill, deferred revenue, accrued expenses, stockholders' equity, revenues and various expense accounts. As a result of the first five identified material weaknesses, the Company recorded various adjustments to the consolidated financial statements as of December 31, 2004 and for the year then ended. The sixth material weakness affects all financial statement accounts, however we did not identify any adjustments to our financial statements as a result of this control weakness. These material weaknesses were considered in determining the nature, timing, and extent of audit tests applied in

*Source: Find What.com, Inc. Annual Report 2004.

our audit of the December 31, 2004 consolidated financial statements, and this report does not affect our report dated March 16, 2005 on those financial statements.

Results of Operations

Revenue

Revenue was $169.5 million in 2004, compared to $72.2 million in 2003, an increase of $97.2 million or 135%. The increase in revenue is primarily the result of the inclusion of results from businesses acquired during 2004 (approximately $73.4 million). In addition, revenue increased in our FindWhat.com Network and Private Label divisions as a result of adding new distribution partners, expanding our relationships with our existing distribution partners, adding private label partners and increasing the amount advertisers spent with us for traffic from our distribution and private label partners.

Uses of Estimates and Critical Accounting Policies

Revenue

Revenue is generated primarily through click-throughs on our managed advertisers' paid listings. Certain advertisers make deposits in advance and these deposits are recorded as deferred revenue. When an Internet user clicks on a keyword advertisement, revenue is recognized in the amount of the advertiser's bid price. Revenue is also generated from our private label service and is recognized in accordance with the contractual payment agreements as the services are rendered and the click-

throughs performed. In accordance with the guidance of Emerging Issue Task Force No. 99-19, "Reporting Revenue Gross as a Principal Versus Net as an Agent," we record FindWhat.com and Espotting Network click-through revenue gross, and private label revenue net.

Revenue for network set-up fees are deferred and recognized over the expected life of the advertiser's relationship. Revenue for software licenses is recognized when persuasive evidence of an arrangement exists, delivery has occurred, the fee is fixed or determinable, and collectibility is probable. Revenue from support arrangements is recognized ratably over the contract period of the invoice. When a Comet user clicks on a sponsored advertisement on a partner's network, revenues are recognized in the amount of the partner's fee due to Comet. Non-click-through-related revenue from Comet is recognized when earned under the terms of the contractual arrangement with the advertiser or advertising agency, provided that collection is probable.

Allowance for Doubtful Accounts

We maintain allowances for doubtful accounts for estimated losses resulting from non-payments by our billable advertisers for services rendered. Most of our advertisers prepay for services. The allowance for doubtful accounts was approximately $3.1 million and $0.2 million as of as of December 31, 2004 and 2003, respectively. The following table illustrates the related bad debt expense as a percentage of revenues for 2004, 2003, and 2002 (in thousands, except percentages):

	2004	2003	2002
Revenues	$169,470	$72,221	$42,805
Bad debt expense	$ 658	$ 262	$ 126
Bad debt expense as a percent of revenue	0.4%	0.4%	0.3%

The allowance for doubtful accounts, which increased significantly in 2004 due to the merger with Espotting (which has higher portion of billable advertisers than the FindWhat Network), is an estimate calculated based on an analysis of current business and economic risks, customer credit-worthiness, specific identifiable risks such as bankruptcies, terminations or discontinued customers, or other factors that may indicate a potential loss. The allowance is reviewed on a periodic basis to provide for all reasonably expected losses in the receivable balances. An account may be determined to be uncollectible if all collection efforts have been exhausted, the customer has filed for bankruptcy and all recourse against the account is exhausted, or disputes are unresolved and negotiations to settle are exhausted. This uncollectible amount is written off against the allowance. If our billable advertisers' ability to pay our invoices were to suffer, resulting in the likelihood that we would not be paid for services rendered, additional allowances may be necessary which would result in an additional general and administrative expense in the period such determination was made.

Historically, our actual losses have been consistent with these allowances. However, future changes in trends could result on a material impact to future consolidated statement of income and cash flows. Based on our results for the year ended December 31, 2004, a 25 point basis deviation from our estimates would have resulted in an increase or decrease in operating income of approximately $0.4 million. The following demonstrates, for illustrative purposes only, the potential effect such a change would have upon our consolidated financial statements and is not intended to provide a range of exposure or expected deviation (in thousands, except share data):

	−25 Basis Points	2004	+25 Basis Points
Bad debt expense	$ 234	$ 658	$ 1,082
Income from operations	27,327	26,903	26,479
Net income	17,452	17,028	16,604
Diluted earnings per share	$ 0.61	$ 0.60	$ 0.58

The following table lists the accounts receivable and allowance for doubtful accounts information from the FindWhat.com, Inc. balance sheet at December 31, 2004:

	December 31, 2004	December 31, 2003
Accounts receivable, less allowance for doubtful accounts of $3,095 and $223 at December 31, 2004 and 2003, respectively	$26,117	$5,051

FindWhat.com, Inc.
Valuation and Qualifying Accounts
(in Thousands)

Description	Balance at the Beginning of Period	Charges to Earning	Charges to Other Accounts	Acquisitions	Deductions	Balance at End of Period
Allowance for doubtful accounts:						
Year Ended December 31, 2004	$223	$658	$235 (1)	$2,194 (2)	$(215) (3)	$3,095
Year Ended December 31, 2003	$ 95	$262	$ —	$ —	$(134) (3)	$ 223
Year Ended December 31, 2002	$ 22	$126	$ —	$ —	$ (53) (3)	$ 95

(1) Change due to foreign currency translation, which is included in other comprehensive income
(2) Includes amount from merger with Espotting completed in 2004
(3) Write-off fully reserved accounts receivable

CHAPTER

The Analysis of
Financial Statements

*Ratios are tools, and their value is limited when used alone. The more tools used, the
better the analysis. For example, you can't use the same golf club for every shot and
expect to be a good golfer. The more you practice with each club, however, the better
able you will be to gauge which club to use on one shot. So too, we need to be skilled
with the financial tools we use.*

—DIANNE MORRISON
Chief Executive Officer, R.E.C. Inc.

The preceding chapters have covered in detail the form and content of the four basic
financial statements found in the annual reports of U.S. firms: the balance sheet, the
income statement, the statement of stockholders' equity, and the statement of cash
flows; and Chapter 5 presented an in-depth approach to evaluating the quality of
reported financial statement information. This chapter will develop tools and techniques for the interpretation of financial statement information.

Objectives of Analysis

Before beginning the analysis of any firm's financial statements, it is necessary to specify the objectives of the analysis. The objectives will vary depending on the perspective
of the financial statement user and the specific questions that are addressed by the
analysis of the financial statement data.

A *creditor* is ultimately concerned with the ability of an existing or prospective
borrower to make interest and principal payments on borrowed funds. The questions
raised in a credit analysis should include:

- What is the *borrowing cause*? What do the financial statements reveal about the
  reason a firm has requested a loan or the purchase of goods on credit?
- What is the firm's *capital structure*? How much debt is currently outstanding?
  How well has debt been serviced in the past?

- What will be the *source of debt repayment*? How well does the company manage working capital? Is the firm generating cash from operations?

The credit analyst will use the historical record of the company, as presented in the financial statements, to such questions and to predict the potential of the firm to satisfy future demands for cash, including debt service.

The *investor* attempts to arrive at an estimation of a company's future earnings stream in order to attach a value to the securities being considered for purchase or liquidation. The investment analyst poses such questions as:

- What is the company's *performance record*, and what are the *future expectations*? What is its record with regard to growth and stability of earnings? Of cash flow from operations?
- How much *risk* is inherent in the firm's existing capital structure? What are the *expected returns*, given the firm's current condition and future outlook?
- How successfully does the firm compete in its industry, and how well positioned is the company to hold or improve its *competitive position*?

The investment analyst also uses historical financial statement data to forecast the future. In the case of the investor, the ultimate objective is to determine whether the investment is sound.

Financial statement analysis from the standpoint of management relates to all of the questions raised by creditors and investors because these user groups must be satisfied in order for the firm to obtain capital as needed. Management must also consider its employees, the general public, regulators, and the financial press. Management looks to financial statement data to determine:

- How *well* has the firm performed and *why*? What *operating areas* have contributed to success and which have not?
- What are the *strengths and weaknesses* of the company's financial position?
- What *changes* should be implemented in order to improve future performance?

Financial statements provide insight into the company's current status and lead to the development of policies and strategies for the future. It should be pointed out, however, that management also has responsibility for preparing the financial statements. The analyst should be alert to the potential for management to influence the outcome of financial statement reporting in order to appeal to creditors, investors, and other users. It is important that any analysis of financial statements include a careful reading of the notes to the financial statements, and it may be helpful to supplement the analysis with other material in the annual report and with other sources of information apart from the annual report.

Sources of Information

The financial statement user has access to a wide range of data sources in the analysis of financial statements. The objective of the analysis will dictate to a considerable degree not only the approach taken in the analysis but also the particular resources that should be consulted in a given circumstance. The beginning point, however, should always be the financial statements themselves and the notes to the financial statements. In addition, the analyst will want to consider the following resources.

Proxy Statement

The proxy statement, discussed in Chapter 1, contains useful information about the board of directors, director and executive compensation, option grants, audit-related matters, related party transactions, and proposals to be voted on by shareholders.

Auditor's Report

The report of the independent auditor contains the expression of opinion as to the fairness of the financial statement presentation. Most auditor's reports are *unqualified*, which means that in the opinion of the auditor the financial statements present fairly the financial position, the results of operations, and the cash flows for the periods covered by the financial statements. A *qualified* report, an adverse opinion, or a disclaimer of opinion, is rare and therefore suggests that a careful evaluation of the firm be made. An unqualified opinion with explanatory language should be reviewed carefully by the analyst. In addition, the analyst should read the report and certification regarding the effectiveness of the internal controls over financial reporting.

Management Discussion and Analysis

The Management Discussion and Analysis of the Financial Condition and Results of Operations, discussed in Chapter 1, is a section of the annual report that is required and monitored by the Securities and Exchange Commission (SEC). In this section, management presents a detailed coverage of the firm's liquidity, capital resources, and operations. The material can be especially helpful to the financial analyst because it includes facts and estimates not found elsewhere in the annual report. For example, this report is expected to cover forward-looking information such as projections of capital expenditures and how such investments will be financed. There is detail about the mix of price relative to volume increases for products sold. Management must disclose any favorable or unfavorable trends and any significant events or uncertainties that relate to the firm's historical or prospective financial condition and operations.

Supplementary Schedules

Certain supplementary schedules are required for inclusion in an annual report and are frequently helpful to the analysis. For example, companies that operate in several unrelated lines of business provide a breakdown of key financial figures by operating segment. (The analysis of segmental data is covered in the appendix to this chapter.)

Form 10-K and Form 10-Q

Form 10-K is an annual document filed with the SEC by companies that sell securities to the public and contains much of the same information as the annual report issued to shareholders. It also shows additional detail that may be of interest to the financial analyst, such as schedules listing information about management, a description of material litigation and governmental actions, and elaborations of some financial statement disclosures. Form 10-Q, a less extensive document, provides quarterly financial information.

Both reports, as well as other SEC forms filed by companies, are available through the SEC Electronic Data Gathering, Analysis, and Retrieval (EDGAR) database.

Other Sources

There is a considerable body of material outside of the corporate annual report that can contribute to an analysis of financial statements. Most academic libraries and many public libraries have available computerized search systems and computerized databases that can greatly facilitate financial analysis.[1] Although not a replacement for the techniques that are discussed in this chapter, these research materials supplement and enhance the analytical process as well as provide time-saving features. Computerized financial statement analysis packages are also available that perform some of the ratio calculations and other analytical tools described in this chapter. (See the financial statement analysis template available at *www.prenhall.com/fraser.*)

Other general resources useful as aids in the analysis of financial statements can be found in the general reference section of public and university libraries. The following sources provide comparative statistical ratios to help determine a company's relative position within its industry:

1. Dun & Bradstreet Information Services, *Industry Norms and Key Business Ratios.* Murray Hill, NJ.
2. The Risk Management Association, *Annual Statement Studies.* Philadelphia, PA.
3. Standard & Poor's Corporation, *Ratings Handbook and Industry Surveys.* New York, NY.
4. Gale Research Inc., *Manufacturing U.S.A. Industry Analyses.* Detroit, MI.

When analyzing a company it is also important to review the annual reports of suppliers, customers, and competitors of that company. The bankruptcy of a supplier could affect the firm's supply of raw materials, while the bankruptcy of a customer could negatively impact the collection of accounts receivable and future sales. Knowing how one company compares financially to its competitors, and understanding other factors such as innovation and customer service provided by the competition allows for a better analysis to predict the future prospects of the firm.

Additional resources for comparative and other information about companies can be found on the following free Internet sites:[2]

1. Yahoo!, http://finance.yahoo.com/
2. Market Watch, www.marketwatch.com
3. Reuters, www.investor.reuters.com

Many other Internet sites charge subscription fees to access information, but public and university libraries often subscribe, making this information free to the public. Libraries are currently in the process of converting information from hard

---

[1]One resource that is commonly available in both public and academic libraries is the Infotrak—General Business Index. This CD-ROM database provides indexing to approximately 800 business, trade, and management journals; it has company profiles, investment analyst reports, and a wide range of business news. To learn about the availability and use of this system or other search systems and databases, consult the library's reference librarian or the business reference librarian.

[2]Internet sites are constantly changing; therefore, the content and Web addresses may change after publication of this book.

copy format to online databases; the following useful references may be available at a local library:

1. Moody's Investor Service, *Mergent Manuals* and *Mergent Handbook*. New York, NY. (Formerly *Moody's Manuals and Handbook*. The online version is *Mergent FIS Online and Mergent Industry Surveys Disc.*)
2. Standard & Poor's Corporation, *Corporation Records, The Outlook, Stock Reports*, and *Stock Guide*. New York, NY. (The online version is *Standard and Poor's Net Advantage*.)
3. Value Line, Inc., *The Value Line Investment Survey*. New York, NY (www.valueline.com).
4. Zack's Investment Research Inc., *Earnings Forecaster*. Chicago, IL (www.zacks.com).
5. Gale Research Inc., *Market Share Reporter*. Detroit, MI.
6. Dow Jones-Irwin, *The Financial Analyst's Handbook*. Homewood, IL.
7. For mutual funds: Morningstar, *Morningstar Mutual Funds*. Chicago, IL. (www.morningstar.com).

The following Web sites contain useful investment and financial information including company profile and stock prices; some sites charge fees for certain information:

1. SEC EDGAR Database, www.sec.gov/edgarhp.htm
2. Hoover's Corporate Directory, www.hoovers.com/
3. Dun & Bradstreet, www.dnb.com/
4. Standard & Poor's Ratings Services, www.standardpoor.com/ratings/
5. CNN Financial Network, www.money.cnn/

Articles from current periodicals such as *BusinessWeek, Forbes, Fortune*, and the *Wall Street Journal* can add insight into the management and operations of individual firms as well as provide perspective on general economic and industry trends. The financial analysis described in this chapter should be used in the context of the economic and political environment in which the company operates. Reading about the economy regularly in business publications allows the analyst to assess the impact of unemployment, inflation, interest rates, gross domestic product, productivity, and other economic indicators on the future potential of particular firms and industries.

Tools and Techniques

Various tools and techniques are used by the financial statement analyst in order to convert financial statement data into formats that facilitate the evaluation of a firm's financial condition and performance, both over time and in comparison with industry competitors. These include common-size financial statements, which express each account on the balance sheet as a percentage of total assets and each account on the income statement as a percentage of net sales; financial ratios, which standardize financial data in terms of mathematical relationships expressed in the form of percentages or times; trend analysis, which requires the evaluation of financial data over several accounting periods; structural analysis, which looks at the internal structure of a business enterprise; industry comparisons, which relate one firm with averages compiled for the industry in which it operates; and most important of all, common sense and judgment. These tools and techniques will be illustrated by walking through a financial statement analysis of R.E.C. Inc. This first part will cover number crunching—the calculation of key financial ratios. The second part will provide the integration of these numbers with other information—such as the statement of cash flows from Chapter 4 and background on the economy and the environment in which the firm operates—in order to perform an analysis of R.E.C. Inc. over a five-year period and to assess the firm's strengths, weaknesses, and future prospects.

Common-Size Financial Statements

Common-size financial statements were covered in Chapters 2 and 3. Exhibits 2.2 (p. 47) and 3.3 (p. 90) present the common-size balance sheet and common-size income statement, respectively, for R.E.C. Inc. The information from these statements presented in prior chapters is summarized again, and will be used in the comprehensive analysis illustrated in this chapter.

From the common-size balance sheet in Exhibit 2.2, it can be seen that inventories have become more dominant over the five-year period in the firm's total asset structure and in 2007 comprised almost half (49.4%) of total assets. Holdings of cash and marketable securities have decreased from a 20% combined level in 2003 and 2004 to about 10% in 2007. The company has elected to make this shift in order to accommodate the inventory requirements of new store openings. The firm has opened 43 new stores in the past two years, and the effect of this market strategy is also reflected in the overall asset structure. Buildings, leasehold improvements, equipment, and accumulated depreciation and amortization have increased as a percentage of total assets. On the liability side, the proportion of debt required to finance investments in assets has risen, primarily from long-term borrowing.

The common-size income statement shown in Exhibit 3.3 reveals the trends of expenses and profit margins. Cost of goods sold has increased slightly in percentage terms, resulting in a small decline in the gross profit percentage. To improve this margin, the firm will either have to raise its own retail prices, change the product mix, or figure ways to reduce costs on goods purchased for resale. In the area of operating expenses, depreciation and amortization have increased relative to sales, again reflecting costs associated with new store openings. Selling and administrative expenses rose in 2005, but the company controlled these costs more effectively in 2006 and 2007 relative to overall sales. Operating and net profit percentages will be discussed more extensively in connection with the five-year trends of financial ratios later in the chapter. It can be seen from the common-size income statements that both profit percentages deteriorated through 2006 and rebounded in the most recent year as R.E.C. Inc. enjoyed the benefits of an economic recovery and profits from expansion.

Key Financial Ratios

The R.E.C. Inc. financial statements will be used to compute a set of key financial ratios for the years 2007 and 2006. Later in the chapter, these ratios will be evaluated in the context of R.E.C. Inc.'s five-year historical record and in comparison with industry competitors. The four categories of ratios to be covered are (1) liquidity ratios, which measure a firm's ability to meet cash needs as they arise; (2) activity ratios, which measure the liquidity of specific assets and the efficiency of managing assets; (3) leverage ratios, which measure the extent of a firm's financing with debt relative to equity and its ability to cover interest and other fixed charges; and (4) profitability ratios, which measure the overall performance of a firm and its efficiency in managing assets, liabilities, and equity.

Before delving into the R.E.C. Inc. financial ratios, it is important to introduce a word of caution in the use of financial ratios generally. Although extremely valuable as analytical tools, financial ratios also have limitations. They can serve as screening devices, indicate areas of potential strength or weakness, and reveal matters that need further investigation. But financial ratios do not provide answers in and of themselves, and they are not predictive. Financial ratios should be used with caution and common sense, and they should be used in combination with other elements of financial analysis. It should also be noted that there is no one definitive set of key financial ratios, there is no uniform definition for all ratios, and there is no standard that should be met for each ratio. Finally, there are no "rules of thumb" that apply to the interpretation of financial ratios. Each situation should be evaluated within the context of the particular firm, industry, and economic environment.[3]

Figures from the R.E.C. Inc. Consolidated Balance Sheets, Statements of Earnings, and Statements of Cash Flows, Exhibits 6.1 (pp. 199–200) and 6.2 (p. 217), are used to illustrate the calculation of financial ratios for 2007 and 2006, and these financial ratios will subsequently be incorporated into a five-year analysis of the firm.

Liquidity Ratios: Short-Term Solvency

Current Ratio

	2007	2006
$\dfrac{\text{Current assets}}{\text{Current liabilities}}$	$\dfrac{65,846}{27,461} = 2.40 \text{ times}$	$\dfrac{56,264}{20,432} = 2.75 \text{ times}$

The current ratio is a commonly used measure of short-run solvency, the ability of a firm to meet its debt requirements as they come due. Current liabilities are used as the denominator of the ratio because they are considered to represent the most urgent debts, requiring retirement within one year or one operating cycle. The available cash resources to satisfy these obligations must come primarily from cash or the conversion to cash of other current assets. Some analysts eliminate prepaid expenses from the numerator because they are not a potential source of cash but, rather, represent future obligations that have already been satisfied. The current ratio for R.E.C. Inc. indicates that at year-end 2007 current assets covered current liabilities 2.4 times, down from 2006. In order to interpret the significance of this ratio it will be necessary to evaluate the trend of liquidity over a longer period and to compare R.E.C. Inc.'s coverage with industry competitors. It is also essential to assess the composition of the components that comprise the ratio.

As a barometer of short-term liquidity, the current ratio is limited by the nature of its components. Remember that the balance sheet is prepared as of a particular date, and the actual amount of liquid assets may vary considerably from the date on which the balance sheet is prepared. Further, accounts receivable and inventory may not be truly liquid. A firm could have a relatively high current ratio but not be able to

---

[3]Analysts sometimes use an average number in the denominator of ratios that have a balance sheet account in the denominator. This is preferable when the company's balance sheet accounts vary significantly from one year to the next. The illustrations in this chapter do not use an average number in the denominator.

EXHIBIT 6.1   R.E.C. Inc. Consolidated Balance Sheets at December 31, 2007 and 2006 (in Thousands)

	2007	2006
Assets		
Current Assets		
Cash	$ 4,061	$ 2,382
Marketable securities (Note A)	5,272	8,004
Accounts receivable, less allowance for doubtful accounts of $448 in 2007 and $417 in 2006	8,960	8,350
Inventories (Note A)	47,041	36,769
Prepaid expenses	512	759
Total current assets	65,846	56,264
Property, Plant, and Equipment (Notes A, C, and E)		
Land	811	811
Buildings and leasehold improvements	18,273	11,928
Equipment	21,523	13,768
	40,607	26,507
Less accumulated depreciation and amortization	11,528	7,530
Net property, plant, and equipment	29,079	18,977
Other Assets (Note A)	373	668
Total Assets	$95,298	$75,909
Liabilities and Stockholders' Equity		
Current Liabilities		
Accounts Payable	$14,294	$ 7,591
Notes payable—banks (Note B)	5,614	6,012
Current maturities of long-term debt (Note C)	1,884	1,516
Accrued liabilities	5,669	5,313
Total current liabilities	27,461	20,432
Deferred Federal Income Taxes (Notes A and D)	843	635
Long-Term Debt (Note C)	21,059	16,975
Commitments (Note E)		
Total liabilities	49,363	38,042
Stockholders' Equity		
Common stock, par value $1, authorized, 10,000,000 shares; issued, 4,803,000 shares in 2007 and 4,594,000 shares in 2006 (Note F)	4,803	4,594
Additional paid-in capital	957	910
Retained Earnings	40,175	32,363
Total stockholders' equity	45,935	37,867
Total Liabilities and Stockholders' Equity	$95,298	$75,909

The accompanying notes are an integral part of these statements.

EXHIBIT 6.1 (Continued) R.E.C. Inc. Consolidated Statements of Earnings for the Years Ended December 31, 2007, 2006, and 2005 (in Thousands Except per Share Amounts)

	2007	2006	2005
Net sales	$215,600	$153,000	$140,700
Cost of goods sold (Note A)	129,364	91,879	81,606
Gross profit	86,236	61,121	59,094
Selling and administrative expenses (Notes A and E)	45,722	33,493	32,765
Advertising	14,258	10,792	9,541
Depreciation and amortization (Note A)	3,998	2,984	2,501
Repairs and maintenance	3,015	2,046	3,031
Operating profit	19,243	11,806	11,256
Other income (expense)			
Interest income	422	838	738
Interest expense	(2,585)	(2,277)	(1,274)
Earnings before income taxes	17,080	10,367	10,720
Income taxes (Notes A and D)	7,686	4,457	4,824
Net earnings	$ 9,394	$ 5,910	$ 5,896
Basic earnings per common share (Note G)	$ 1.96	$ 1.29	$ 1.33
Diluted earnings per common share (Note G)	$ 1.92	$ 1.26	$ 1.31

meet demands for cash because the accounts receivable are of inferior quality or the inventory is salable only at discounted prices. It is necessary to use other measures of liquidity, including cash flow from operations and other financial ratios that rate the liquidity of specific assets, to supplement the current ratio.

Quick or Acid-Test Ratio

	2007	2006
$\dfrac{\text{Current assets} - \text{Inventory}}{\text{Current liabilities}}$	$\dfrac{65,846 - 47,041}{27,461} = .68$ times	$\dfrac{56,264 - 36,769}{20,432} = .95$ times

The quick or acid-test ratio is a more rigorous test of short-run solvency than the current ratio because the numerator eliminates inventory, considered the least liquid current asset and the most likely source of losses. Like the current ratio and other ratios, there are alternative ways to calculate the quick ratio. Some analysts eliminate prepaid expenses and supplies (if carried as a separate item) from the numerator. The quick ratio for R.E.C. Inc. indicates some deterioration between 2006 and 2007; this ratio must also be examined in relation to the firm's own trends and to other firms operating in the same industry.

Cash Flow Liquidity Ratio

	2007	2006
$\dfrac{\text{Cash} + \text{Marketable securities} + \text{CFO*}}{\text{Current liabilities}}$	$\dfrac{4,061 + 5,272 + 10,024}{27,461} = .70$ times	$\dfrac{2,382 + 8,004 + (3,767)}{20,432} = .32$ times

*Cash flow from operating activities.

Another approach to measuring short-term solvency is the cash flow liquidity ratio,[4] which considers cash flow from operating activities (from the statement of cash flows). The cash flow liquidity ratio uses in the numerator, as an approximation of cash resources, cash and marketable securities, which are truly liquid current assets, and cash flow from operating activities, which represents the amount of cash generated from the firm's operations, such as the ability to sell inventory and collect the cash.

Note that both the current ratio and the quick ratio decreased between 2006 and 2007, which could be interpreted as a deterioration of liquidity. But the cash flow ratio increased, indicating an improvement in short-run solvency. Which is the correct assessment? With any ratio, the analyst must explore the underlying components. One major reason for the decreases in the current and quick ratios was the 88% growth in accounts payable in 2007, which could actually be a plus if it means that R.E.C. Inc. strengthened its ability to obtain supplier credit. Also, the firm turned around from negative to positive its generation of cash from operations in 2007, explaining the improvement in the cash flow liquidity ratio and indicating stronger short-term solvency.

Average Collection Period

	2007		2006	
Net accounts receivable	8,960	= 15 days	8,350	= 20 days
Average daily sales	215,600/365		153,000/365	

The average collection period of accounts receivable is the average number of days required to convert receivables into cash. The ratio is calculated as the relationship between net accounts receivable (net of the allowance for doubtful accounts) and average daily sales (sales/365 days). Where available, the figure for credit sales can be substituted for net sales because credit sales produce the receivables. The ratio for R.E.C. Inc. indicates that during 2007 the firm collected its accounts in 15 days on average, which is an improvement over the 20-day collection period in 2006.

The average collection period helps gauge the liquidity of accounts receivable, the ability of the firm to collect from customers. It may also provide information about a company's credit policies. For example, if the average collection period is increasing over time or is higher than the industry average, the firm's credit policies could be too lenient and accounts receivables not sufficiently liquid. The loosening of credit could be necessary at times to boost sales, but at an increasing cost to the firm. On the other hand, if credit policies are too restrictive, as reflected in an average collection period that is shortening and less than industry competitors, the firm may be losing qualified customers.

The average collection period should be compared with the firm's stated credit policies. If the policy calls for collection within 30 days and the average collection period is 60 days, the implication is that the company is not stringent in collection

---

[4]For additional reading about this ratio and its applications, see Lyn Fraser, "Cash Flow from Operations and Liquidity Analysis, A New Financial Ratio for Commercial Lending Decisions," *Cash Flow*, Robert Morris Associates, Philadelphia, PA. For other cash flow ratios, see C. Carslaw and J. Mills, "Developing Ratios for Effective Cash Flow Statement Analysis," *Journal of Accountancy*, November 1991; D.E. Giacomino and D. E. Mielke, "Cash Flows: Another Approach to Ratio Analysis," *Journal of Accountancy*, March 1993; and John R. Mills and Jeanne H. Yamamura, "The Power of Cash Flow Ratios," *Journal of Accountancy*, October 1998.

efforts. There could be other explanations, however, such as temporary problems due to a depressed economy. The analyst should attempt to determine the cause of a ratio that is too long or too short.

Another factor for consideration is the strength of the firm within its industry. There are circumstances that would enable a company in a relatively strong financial position within its industry to extend credit for longer periods than weaker competitors.

Days Inventory Held

	2007	2006
$\dfrac{\text{Inventory}}{\text{Average daily cost of sales}}$	$\dfrac{47,041}{129,364/365} = 133 \text{ days}$	$\dfrac{36,769}{91,879/365} = 146 \text{ days}$

The days inventory held is the average number of days it takes to sell inventory to customers. This ratio measures the efficiency of the firm in managing its inventory. Generally, a low number of days inventory held is a sign of efficient management; the faster inventory sells, the fewer funds tied up in inventory. On the other hand, too low a number could indicate understocking and lost orders, a decrease in prices, a shortage of materials, or more sales than planned. A high number of days inventory held could be the result of carrying too much inventory or stocking inventory that is obsolete, slow-moving, or inferior; however, there may be legitimate reasons to stockpile inventory, such as increased demand, expansion and opening of new retail stores, or an expected strike. R.E.C. Inc.'s days inventory held has decreased from 2006, an improvement over 2007.

The type of industry is important in assessing days inventory held. It is expected that florists and produce retailers would have a relatively low days inventory held because they deal in perishable products, whereas retailers of jewelry or farm equipment would have higher days inventory held, but higher profit margins. When making comparisons among firms, it is essential to check the cost flow assumption, discussed in Chapter 2, used to value inventory and cost of goods sold.

Days Payable Outstanding

	2007	2006
$\dfrac{\text{Accounts payable}}{\text{Average daily cost of sales}}$	$\dfrac{14,294}{129,364/365} = 41 \text{ days}$	$\dfrac{7,591}{91,879/365} = 31 \text{ days}$

The days payable outstanding is the average number of days it takes to pay payables in cash. This ratio offers insight into a firm's pattern of payments to suppliers. Delaying payment of payables as long as possible, but still making payment by the due date, is desirable. R.E.C. Inc. is taking longer to pay suppliers in 2007 compared to 2006.

Cash Conversion Cycle or Net Trade Cycle

The cash conversion cycle or net trade cycle is the normal operating cycle of a firm that consists of buying or manufacturing inventory, with some purchases on credit and the creation of accounts payable; selling inventory, with some sales on credit and the creation of accounts receivable; and collecting the cash. The cash conversion cycle measures this process in number of days and is calculated as follows for R.E.C. Inc.:

	2007	2006
Average collection period	15 days	20 days
plus		
Days inventory held	133 days	146 days
minus		
Days payable outstanding	(41 days)	(33 days)
equals		
Cash conversion or net trade cycle	107 days	133 days

The cash conversion cycle helps the analyst understand why cash flow generation has improved or deteriorated by analyzing the key balance sheet accounts—accounts receivable, inventory, and accounts payable—that affect cash flow from operating activities. R.E.C. Inc. has improved its cash conversion cycle by improving collection of accounts receivable, moving inventory faster, and taking longer to pay accounts payable. Despite this improvement, the firm has a mismatching of cash inflows and outflows since it takes 148 days to sell inventory and collect the cash, yet R.E.C. Inc.'s suppliers are being paid in 41 days. As mentioned previously, the company opened 43 new stores, and that is most likely the cause of the high level of inventory. In the future, R.E.C. Inc. should be able to improve further the days inventory held and the cash conversion cycle.

Activity Ratios: Asset Liquidity, Asset Management Efficiency

Accounts Receivable Turnover

	2007	2006
$\dfrac{\text{Net Sales}}{\text{Net accounts receivable}}$	$\dfrac{215,600}{8,960} = 24.06$ times	$\dfrac{153,000}{8,350} = 18.32$ times

Inventory Turnover

	2007	2006
$\dfrac{\text{Cost of goods sold}}{\text{Inventory}}$	$\dfrac{129,364}{47,041} = 2.75$ times	$\dfrac{91,879}{36,769} = 2.50$ times

Accounts Payable Turnover

	2007	2006
$\dfrac{\text{Cost of goods sold}}{\text{Accounts payable}}$	$\dfrac{129,364}{14,294} = 9.05$ times	$\dfrac{91,879}{7,591} = 12.10$ times

The accounts receivable, inventory, and payables turnover ratios measure how many times, on average, accounts receivable are collected in cash, inventory is sold, and payables are paid during the year. These three measures are mathematical complements to the ratios that make up the cash conversion cycle, and therefore, measure exactly what the average collection period, days inventory held, and days payable outstanding measure for a firm; they are merely an alternative way to look at the same information.

R.E.C. Inc. converted accounts receivable into cash 24 times in 2007, up from 18 times in 2006. Inventory turned over 2.75 times in 2007 compared to 2.5 times in 2006, meaning that inventory was selling slightly faster. The lower payables turnover indicates that the firm is taking longer to repay payables.

Fixed Asset Turnover

	2007		2006	
$\dfrac{\text{Net sales}}{\text{Net property, plant, equipment}}$	$\dfrac{215,600}{29,079}$	$= 7.41$ times	$\dfrac{153,000}{18,977}$	$= 8.06$ times

Total Asset Turnover

	2007		2006	
$\dfrac{\text{Net sales}}{\text{Total assets}}$	$\dfrac{215,600}{95,298}$	$= 2.26$ times	$\dfrac{153,000}{75,909}$	$= 2.02$ times

The fixed asset turnover and total asset turnover ratios are two approaches to assessing management's effectiveness in generating sales from investments in assets. The fixed asset turnover considers only the firm's investment in property, plant, and equipment and is extremely important for a capital-intensive firm, such as a manufacturer with heavy investments in long-lived assets. The total asset turnover measures the efficiency of managing all of a firm's assets. Generally, the higher these ratios, the smaller is the investment required to generate sales and thus the more profitable is the firm. When the asset turnover ratios are low relative to the industry or the firm's historical record, either the investment in assets is too heavy and/or sales are sluggish. There may, however, be plausible explanations; for example, the firm may have undertaken an extensive plant modernization or placed assets in service at year-end, which will generate positive results in the long-term.

For R.E.C. Inc., the fixed asset turnover has slipped slightly, but the total asset turnover has improved. The firm's investment in fixed assets has grown at a faster rate (53%) than sales (41%), and this occurrence should be examined within the framework of the overall analysis of R.E.C. Inc. The increase in total asset turnover is the result of improvements in inventory and accounts receivable turnover.

Leverage Ratios: Debt Financing and Coverage

Debt Ratio

	2007		2006	
$\dfrac{\text{Total liabilities}}{\text{Total assets}}$	$\dfrac{49,363}{95,298}$	$= 51.8\%$	$\dfrac{38,042}{75,909}$	$= 50.1\%$

Long-Term Debt to Total Capitalization

	2007	2006
$\dfrac{\text{Long-term debt}}{\text{Long-term debt} + \text{Stockholders' equity}}$	$\dfrac{21{,}059}{21{,}059 + 45{,}935} = 31.4\%$	$\dfrac{16{,}975}{16{,}975 + 37{,}867} = 31.0\%$

Debt to Equity

	2007	2006
$\dfrac{\text{Total liabilities}}{\text{Stockholders' equity}}$	$\dfrac{49{,}363}{45{,}935} = 1.07 \text{ times}$	$\dfrac{38{,}042}{37{,}867} = 1.00 \text{ times}$

Each of the three debt ratios measures the extent of the firm's financing with debt. The amount and proportion of debt in a company's capital structure is extremely important to the financial analyst because of the trade-off between risk and return. Use of debt involves risk because debt carries a fixed commitment in the form of interest charges and principal repayment. Failure to satisfy the fixed charges associated with debt will ultimately result in bankruptcy. A lesser risk is that a firm with too much debt has difficulty obtaining additional debt financing when needed or finds that credit is available only at extremely high rates of interest. Although debt implies risk, it also introduces the potential for increased benefits to the firm's owners. When debt is used successfully—if operating earnings are more than sufficient to cover the fixed charges associated with debt—the returns to shareholders are magnified through financial leverage, a concept that is explained and illustrated later in this chapter.

The debt ratio considers the proportion of all assets that are financed with debt. The ratio of long-term debt to total capitalization reveals the extent to which long-term debt is used for the firm's permanent financing (both long-term debt and equity). The debt-to-equity ratio measures the riskiness of the firm's capital structure in terms of the relationship between the funds supplied by creditors (debt) and investors (equity). The higher the proportion of debt, the greater is the degree of risk because creditors must be satisfied before owners in the event of bankruptcy. The equity base provides, in effect, a cushion of protection for the suppliers of debt. Each of the three ratios has increased somewhat for R.E.C. Inc. between 2007 and 2006, implying a slightly riskier capital structure.

The analyst should be aware that the debt ratios do not present the whole picture with regard to risk. There are fixed commitments, such as lease payments, that are similar to debt but are not included in debt. The fixed charge coverage ratio, illustrated later, considers such obligations. Off-balance-sheet financing arrangements, discussed in Chapter 1, also have the characteristics of debt and must be disclosed in notes to the financial statements according to the provisions of FASB Statement No. 105. These arrangements should be included in an evaluation of a firm's overall capital structure.

Times Interest Earned

	2007	2006
$\dfrac{\text{Operating profit}}{\text{Interest expense}}$	$\dfrac{19{,}243}{2{,}585} = 7.4$ times	$\dfrac{11{,}806}{2{,}277} = 5.2$ times

Cash Interest Coverage

	2007	2006
$\dfrac{\text{CFO + interest paid + taxes paid}^5}{\text{Interest paid}}$	$\dfrac{10{,}024 + 2{,}585 + 7{,}478}{2{,}585} = 7.77$ times	$\dfrac{(3{,}767)+2{,}277+4{,}321}{2{,}277} = 1.24$ times

In order for a firm to benefit from debt financing, the fixed interest payments that accompany debt must be more than satisfied from operating earnings.[6] The higher the times interest earned ratio the better; however, if a company is generating high profits, but no cash flow from operations, this ratio is misleading. It takes cash to make interest payments! The cash interest coverage ratio measures how many times interest payments can be covered by cash flow from operations before interest and taxes. Although R.E.C. Inc. increased its use of debt in 2007, the company also improved its ability to cover interest payments from operating profits and cash from operations. Note that in 2006, the firm could cover interest payments only 1.24 times due to the poor cash generated from operations before interest and taxes. The times interest earned ratio in 2006 is somewhat misleading in this instance.

Fixed Charge Coverage

	2007	2006
$\dfrac{\text{Operating profit + Rent expense*}}{\text{Interest expense + Rent expense*}}$	$\dfrac{19{,}243 + 13{,}058}{2{,}585 + 13{,}058} = 2.1$ times	$\dfrac{11{,}806 + 7{,}111}{2{,}277 + 7{,}111} = 2.0$ times

*Rent expense = operating lease payments

The fixed charge coverage ratio is a broader measure of coverage capability than the times interest earned ratio because it includes the fixed payments associated with leasing. Operating lease payments, generally referred to as rent expense in annual reports, are added back in the numerator because they were deducted as an operating expense to calculate operating profit. Operating lease payments are similar in nature to interest expense in that they both represent obligations that must be met on an annual basis. The fixed charge coverage ratio is important for firms that operate extensively with operating leases. R.E.C. Inc. experienced a significant increase in the amount of annual lease payments in 2007 but was still able to improve its fixed charge coverage slightly.

---

[5]The amounts for interest and taxes paid are found in the supplemental disclosures on the statement of cash flows.
[6]The operating return, operating profit divided by assets, must exceed the cost of debt, interest expense divided by liabilities.

Cash Flow Adequacy

	2007	2006
Cash flow from operating activities	10,024	(3,767)
Capital expenditures + debt repayments + dividends paid	14,100 + 30 +1,516 + 1,582 = 0.58 times	4,773 + 1,593 + 1,862 = (0.46) times

Credit rating agencies often use cash flow adequacy ratios to evaluate how well a company can cover annual payments of items such as debt, capital expenditures, and dividends from operating cash flow. Cash flow adequacy is generally defined differently by analysts; therefore, it is important to understand what is actually being measured. Cash flow adequacy is being used here to measure a firm's ability to cover capital expenditures, debt maturities, and dividend payments each year. Companies over the long run should generate enough cash flow from operations to cover investing and financing activities of the firm. If purchases of fixed assets are financed with debt, the company should be capable of covering the principal payments with cash generated by the company. A larger ratio would be expected if the company pays dividends annually because cash used for dividends should be generated internally by the company, rather than by borrowing. As indicated in Chapter 4, companies must generate cash to be successful. Borrowing each year to pay dividends and repay debt is a questionable cycle for a company to be in over the long run.

In 2007, R.E.C. Inc. had a cash flow adequacy ratio of .58 times, an improvement over 2006 when the firm failed to generate cash from operations.

Profitability Ratios: Overall Efficiency and Performance

Gross Profit Margin

	2007	2006
$\dfrac{\text{Gross profit}}{\text{Net sales}}$	$\dfrac{86,236}{215,600} = 40.0\%$	$\dfrac{61,121}{153,000} = 39.9\%$

Operating Profit Margin

	2007	2006
$\dfrac{\text{Operating profit}}{\text{Net sales}}$	$\dfrac{19,243}{215,600} = 8.9\%$	$\dfrac{11,806}{153,000} = 7.7\%$

Net Profit Margin

	2007	2006
$\dfrac{\text{Net earnings}}{\text{Net sales}}$	$\dfrac{9,394}{215,600} = 4.4\%$	$\dfrac{5,910}{153,000} = 3.9\%$

Gross profit margin, operating profit margin, and net profit margin represent the firm's ability to translate sales dollars into profits at different stages of measurement.

The gross profit margin, which shows the relationship between sales and the cost of products sold, measures the ability of a company both to control costs of inventories or manufacturing of products and to pass along price increases through sales to customers. The operating profit margin, a measure of overall operating efficiency, incorporates all of the expenses associated with ordinary business activities. The net profit margin measures profitability after consideration of all revenue and expense, including interest, taxes, and nonoperating items.

There was little change in the R.E.C. Inc. gross profit margin, but the company improved its operating margin. Apparently, the firm was able to control the growth of operating expenses while sharply increasing sales. There was also a slight increase in net profit margin, a flow-through from operating margin, but it will be necessary to look at these ratios over a longer term and in conjunction with other parts of the analysis to explain the changes.

Cash Flow Margin

	2007	2006
$\dfrac{\text{Cash flow from operating activities}}{\text{Net sales}}$	$\dfrac{10,024}{215,600} = 4.6\%$	$\dfrac{(3,767)}{153,000} = (2.5\%)$

Another important perspective on operating performance is the relationship between cash generated from operations and sales. As pointed out in Chapter 4, it is cash, not accrual-measured earnings, that a firm needs to service debt, pay dividends, and invest in new capital assets. The cash flow margin measures the ability of the firm to translate sales into cash.

In 2007, R.E.C. Inc. had a cash flow margin that was greater than its net profit margin, the result of a strongly positive generation of cash. The performance in 2007 represents a solid improvement over 2006 when the firm failed to generate cash from operations and had a negative cash flow margin.

Return on Total Assets (ROA) or Return on Investment (ROI)

	2007	2006
$\dfrac{\text{Net earnings}}{\text{Total assets}}$	$\dfrac{9,394}{95,298} = 9.9\%$	$\dfrac{5,910}{75,909} = 7.8\%$

Return on Equity (ROE)

	2007	2006
$\dfrac{\text{Net earnings}}{\text{Stockholders' equity}}$	$\dfrac{9,394}{45,935} = 20.5\%$	$\dfrac{5,910}{37,867} = 15.6\%$

Return on investment and return on equity are two ratios that measure the overall efficiency of the firm in managing its total investment in assets and in generating return to shareholders. Return on investment or return on assets indicates the amount of profit earned relative to the level of investment in total assets. Return on equity measures the return to common shareholders; this ratio is also calculated as return on common equity if a firm has preferred stock outstanding. R.E.C. Inc. registered a solid improvement in 2004 of both return ratios.

Cash Return on Assets

	2007	2006
$\dfrac{\text{Cash flow from operating activities}}{\text{Total assets}}$	$\dfrac{10,024}{95,298} = 10.5\%$	$\dfrac{(3,767)}{75,909} = (5.0\%)$

The cash return on assets offers a useful comparison to return on investment. Again, the relationship between cash generated from operations and an accrual-based number allows the analyst to measure the firm's cash generating ability of assets. Cash will be required for future investments.

Market Ratios

Four market ratios of particular interest to the investor are earnings per common share, the price-to-earnings ratio, the dividend payout ratio, and dividend yield. Despite the accounting scandals, including Enron and WorldCom, that illustrated the flaws in the earnings numbers presented to the public, investors continue to accept and rely on the earnings per share and price-to-earnings ratios. A discussion of these ratios is included since the reporting of these numbers does, in fact, have a significant impact on stock price changes in the marketplace. The authors hope, however, that readers of this book understand that a thorough analysis of the company, its environment, and its financial information offers a much better gauge to the future prospects of the company than looking exclusively at earnings per share and price-to-earnings ratios. These two ratios are based on an earnings number that can be misleading at times due to the many accounting choices and techniques used to calculate it.

Earnings per common share is net income for the period divided by the weighted average number of common shares outstanding. One million dollars in earnings will look different to the investor if there are 1 million shares of stock outstanding or 100,000 shares. The earnings per share ratio provides the investor with a common denominator to gauge investment returns.

The basic earnings per share computations for R.E.C. Inc. are made as follows:

	2007	2006	2005
$\dfrac{\text{Net earnings}}{\text{Average shares outstanding}}$	$\dfrac{9,394,000}{4,792,857} = 1.96$	$\dfrac{5,910,000}{4,581,395} = 1.29$	$\dfrac{5,896,000}{4,433,083} = 1.33$

Earnings per share figures must be disclosed on the face of the income statement for publicly held companies.

The price-to-earnings ratio (P/E ratio) relates earnings per common share to the market price at which the stock trades, expressing the "multiple" that the stock market

FIGURE 6.1 Summary of Financial Ratios

Summary of Financial Statement Analysis
How to Use Financial Ratios

Liquidity	Leverage	Operating Efficiency	Profitability	Market Measures
Short Run Solvency / Liquidity of Current Assets	Amount of Debt / Coverage of Debt	Asset Management	Margins / Returns	Earnings per Share
Current Ratio / Average Collection Period	Debt/Assets / Times Interest Earned	Accounts Receivable Turnover	Gross Profit Margin / Return on Total Assets	Price/Earnings
Quick Ratio / Days Inventory Held	Debt/Equity / Cash Interest Coverage	Inventory Turnover	Operating Profit Margin / Return on Equity	Dividend Payout
Cash Flow Liquidity Ratio / Days Payable Outstanding	Fixed Charge Coverage	Accounts Payable Turnover	Net Profit Margin / Cash Return on Assets	Dividend Yield
Cash Conversion Cycle	Long-Term Debt / Total Capitalization · Cash Flow Adequacy	Fixed Asset Turnover	Cash Flow Margin	
	Financial Leverage Index	Total Asset Turnover		
		Return on Total Assets		

places on a firm's earnings. For instance, if two competing firms had annual earnings of $2.00 per share, and Company 1 shares sold for $10.00 each and Company 2 shares were selling at $20.00 each, the market is placing a different value on the same $2.00 earnings: a multiple of 5 for Company 1 and 10 for Company 2. The P/E ratio is the function of a myriad of factors, which include the quality of earnings, future earnings potential, and the performance history of the company.[7]

---

[7]Using diluted earnings per share in market ratios offers a worst-case scenario figure that analysts may find useful.

The price-to-earnings ratio for R.E.C. Inc. would be determined as follows:

	2007	2006	2005
$\dfrac{\text{Market price of common stock}}{\text{Earnings per share}}$	$\dfrac{30.00}{1.96} = 15.3$	$\dfrac{17.00}{1.29} = 13.2$	$\dfrac{25.00}{1.33} = 18.8$

The P/E ratio is higher in 2007 than 2006 but below the 2005 level. This could be due to developments in the market generally and/or because the market is reacting cautiously to the firm's good year. Another factor could be the reduction of cash dividend payments.

The dividend payout ratio is determined by the formula cash dividends per share divided by earnings per share:

	2007	2006	2005
$\dfrac{\text{Dividends per share}}{\text{Earnings per share}}$	$\dfrac{.33}{1.96} = 16.8\%$	$\dfrac{.41}{1.29} = 31.8\%$	$\dfrac{.41}{1.33} = 30.8\%$

R.E.C. Inc. reduced its cash dividend payment in 2007. It is unusual for a company to reduce cash dividends because this decision can be read as a negative signal regarding the future outlook. It is particularly uncommon for a firm to reduce dividends during a good year. The explanation provided by management is that the firm has adopted a new policy that will result in lower dividend payments in order to increase the availability of internal funds for expansion; management expects the overall long-term impact to be extremely favorable to shareholders and has committed to maintaining the $.33 per share annual cash dividend.

The dividend yield shows the relationship between cash dividends and market price:

	2007	2006	2005
$\dfrac{\text{Dividends per share}}{\text{Market price of common stock}}$	$\dfrac{.33}{30.00} = 1.1\%$	$\dfrac{.41}{17.00} = 2.4\%$	$\dfrac{.41}{25.00} = 1.6\%$

The R.E.C. Inc. shares are yielding a 1.1% return based on the market price at year-end 2007; an investor would likely choose R.E.C. Inc. as an investment more for its long-term capital appreciation than for its dividend yield.

Figure 6.1 shows in summary form the use of key financial ratios discussed in the chapter.

Analyzing the Data

Would you as a bank loan officer extend $1.5 million in new credit to R.E.C. Inc.? Would you as an investor purchase R.E.C. Inc. common shares at the current market price of $30 per share? Would you as a wholesaler of running shoes sell your products on credit to R.E.C. Inc.? Would you as a recent college graduate accept a position as manager-trainee with R.E.C. Inc.? Would you as the chief financial officer of R.E.C. Inc. authorize the opening of 25 new retail stores during the next two years?

In order to answer such questions, it is necessary to complete the analysis of R.E.C. Inc.'s financial statements, utilizing the common-size financial statements and key financial ratios as well as other information presented throughout the book. Ordinarily, the analysis would deal with only one of the above questions, and the perspective of the

FIGURE 6.2 Steps of a Financial Statement Analysis

1. Establish objectives of the analysis.
2. Study the industry in which firm operates and relate industry climate to current and projected economic developments.
3. Develop knowledge of the firm and the quality of management.
4. Evaluate financial statements.
   - Tools: Common size financial statements, key financial ratios, trend analysis, structural analysis, and comparison with industry competitors.
   - Major Areas: Short-term liquidity, operating efficiency, capital structure and long-term solvency, profitability, market ratios, segmental analysis (when relevant), and quality of financial reporting.
5. Summarize findings based on analysis and reach conclusions about firm relevant to the established objectives.

financial statement user would determine the focus of the analysis. Because the purpose of this chapter is to present a general approach to financial statement analysis, however, the evaluation will cover each of five broad areas that would typically constitute a fundamental analysis of financial statements: (1) background on firm, industry, economy, and outlook; (2) short-term liquidity; (3) operating efficiency; (4) capital structure and long-term solvency; and (5) profitability. From this general approach, each analytical situation can be tailored to meet specific user objectives.

Figure 6.2 shows the steps of a financial statement analysis.

Background: Economy, Industry, and Firm

An individual company does not operate in a vacuum. Economic developments and the actions of competitors affect the ability of any business enterprise to perform successfully. It is therefore necessary to preface the analysis of a firm's financial statements with an evaluation of the environment in which the firm conducts business. This process involves blending hard facts with guesses and estimates. Reference to the section entitled "Other Sources" in this chapter may be beneficial for this part of the analysis. A brief section discussing the business climate of R.E.C. Inc. follows.[8]

Recreational Equipment and Clothing Incorporated (R.E.C. Inc.) is the third largest retailer of recreational products in the United States. The firm offers a broad line of sporting goods and equipment and active sports apparel in medium to higher price ranges. R.E.C. Inc. sells equipment used in running, aerobics, walking, basketball, golf, tennis, skiing, football, scuba diving, and other sports; merchandise for camping, hiking, fishing, and hunting; men's and women's sporting apparel; gift items; games; and consumer electronic products. The firm also sells sporting goods on a direct basis to institutional customers such as schools and athletic teams.

The general and executive offices of the company are located in Dime Box, Texas, and these facilities were expanded in 2007. Most of the retail stores occupy leased

---

[8]The background section of R.E.C. Inc. is based on an unpublished paper by Kimberly Ann Davis, "A Financial Analysis of Oshman's Sporting Goods, Inc."

spaces and are located in major regional or suburban shopping districts throughout the southwestern United States. Eighteen new retail outlets were added in late 2006, and 25 new stores were opened in 2007. The firm owns distribution center warehouses located in Arizona, California, Colorado, Utah, and Texas.

The recreational products industry is affected by current trends in consumer preferences, a cyclical sales demand, and weather conditions. The running boom has shifted to walking and aerobics; golf, once on the downswing, is increasing in popularity; with multiple wins in the Tour de France, American Lance Armstrong invigorated the cycling industry in the United States. Recreational product retailers also rely heavily on sales of sportswear for their profits, because the markup on sportswear is generally higher than on sports equipment, and these products are also affected by consumer preference shifts. With regard to seasonality, most retail sales occur in November, December, May, and June. Sales to institutions are highest in August and September. Weather conditions also influence sales volume, especially of winter sports equipment—come on, Rocky Mountain snow!

Competition within the recreational products industry is based on price, quality, and variety of goods offered as well as the location of outlets and the quality of services offered. R.E.C. Inc.'s two major competitors are also full-line sporting goods companies. One operates in the northwest and the other primarily in the eastern and southeastern United States, reducing direct competition among the three firms.

The current outlook for the sporting goods industry is promising, following a recessionary year in 2006.[9] Americans have become increasingly aware of the importance of physical fitness and have become more actively involved in recreational activities. The 25-to-44 age group is the most athletically active and is projected to be the largest age group in the United States during the next decade. The southwestern United States is expected to provide a rapidly expanding market because of its population growth and excellent weather conditions for year-round recreational participation.

Short-Term Liquidity

Short-term liquidity analysis is especially important to creditors, suppliers, management, and others who are concerned with the ability of a firm to meet near-term demands for cash. The evaluation of R.E.C. Inc.'s short-term liquidity position began with the preparation and interpretation of the firm's common-size balance sheet earlier in the chapter. From that assessment, it was evident that inventories have increased relative to cash and marketable securities in the current asset section, and there has been an increase in the proportion of debt, both short and long term. These developments were traced primarily to policies and financing needs related to new store openings. Additional evidence useful to short-term liquidity analysis is provided by a five-year trend of selected financial ratios and a comparison with industry averages. Sources of comparative industry ratios include Dun & Bradstreet, *Industry Norms and Key Business Ratios,* New York, NY; The Risk Management Association, *Annual Statement Studies,* Philadelphia, PA; and Standard & Poor's Corporation, *Industry Surveys,* New York, NY. As a source of industry comparative ratios, the analyst may prefer to develop a set of financial ratios for one or more major competitors.

---

[9]The recession is assumed for purposes of writing this book and does not represent the authors' forecast.

R.E.C. Inc.	2007	2006	2005	2004	2003	Industry Average 2007
Current ratio	2.40	2.75	2.26	2.18	2.83	2.53
Quick ratio	.68	.95	.87	1.22	1.20	.97
Cash flow liquidity	.70	.32	.85	.78	.68	*
Average collection period	15 days	20 days	13 days	11 days	10 days	17 days
Days inventory held	133 days	146 days	134 days	122 days	114 days	117 days
Days payable outstanding	41 days	33 days	37 days	34 days	35 days	32 days
Cash conversion cycle	107 days	133 days	110 days	99 days	89 days	102 days
Cash flow from operating activities ($ thousands)	10,024	(3,767)	5,629	4,925	3,430	*

*Not available

Liquidity analysis involves the prediction of the future ability of the firm to meet prospective needs for cash. This prediction is made from the historical record of the firm, and no one financial ratio or set of financial ratios or other financial data can serve as a proxy for future developments. For R.E.C. Inc., the financial ratios are somewhat contradictory.

The current and quick ratios have trended downward over the five-year period, indicating a deterioration of short-term liquidity. On the other hand, the cash flow liquidity ratio improved strongly in 2007 after a year of negative cash generation in 2006. The average collection period for accounts receivable and the days inventory held ratio—after worsening between 2003 and 2006—also improved in 2007. These ratios measure the quality or liquidity of accounts receivable and inventory. The average collection period increased to a high of 20 days in 2006, which was a recessionary year in the economy, then decreased to a more acceptable 15-day level in 2007. Days payable outstanding has varied each year, but has increased overall from 2003 to 2007. As long as the company is not late paying bills, this should not be a significant problem. The net trade cycle worsened from 2003 to 2006 due to an increasing collection period and longer number of days inventory was held. In 2007, a significant improvement in management of current assets and liabilities has caused the cash conversion cycle to drop by 26 days from the high of 133 days in 2006. It is now much closer to the industry average.

The common-size balance sheet for R.E.C. Inc. revealed that inventories now comprise about half of the firm's total assets. The growth in inventories has been necessary to satisfy the requirements associated with the opening of new retail outlets but has been accomplished by reducing holdings of cash and cash equivalents. This represents a trade-off of highly liquid assets for potentially less liquid assets. The efficient management of inventories is a critical ingredient for the firm's ongoing liquidity. In 2007, days inventory held improved in spite of the buildups necessary to stock new stores. Sales demand in 2007 was more than adequate to absorb the 28% increase in inventories recorded for the year.

The major question in the outlook for liquidity is the ability of the firm to produce cash from operations. Problems in 2006 resulted partly from the depressed state of the economy and poor ski conditions, which reduced sales growth. The easing of sales demand hit the company in a year that marked the beginning of a major market expansion. Inventories and receivables increased too fast for the limited sales growth of a recessionary year, and R.E.C. also experienced some reduction of credit availability from suppliers that felt the economic pinch. The consequence was a cash crunch and negative cash flow from operations.

In 2007, R.E.C. Inc. enjoyed considerable improvement, generating more than $10 million in cash from operations and progress in managing inventories and receivables. There appears to be no major problem with the firm's short-term liquidity position at the present time. Another poor year, however, might well cause problems similar to those experienced in 2006. The timing of further expansion of retail outlets will be of critical importance to the ongoing success of the firm.

Operating Efficiency

R.E.C. Inc.	2007	2006	2005	2004	2003	Industry Average 2007
Accounts receivable turnover	24.06	18.32	28.08	33.18	36.50	21.47
Inventory turnover	2.75	2.50	2.74	2.99	3.20	3.12
Accounts payable turnover	9.05	12.10	9.90	10.74	10.43	11.40
Fixed asset turnover	7.41	8.06	8.19	10.01	10.11	8.72
Total asset turnover	2.26	2.02	2.13	2.87	2.95	2.43

The turnover ratios measure the operating efficiency of the firm. The efficiency in managing the company's accounts receivable, inventory, and accounts payable was discussed in the short-term liquidity analysis. R.E.C. Inc.'s fixed asset turnover has decreased over the past five years and is now below the industry average. As noted earlier, R.E.C. Inc. has increased its investment in fixed assets as a result of home office and store expansion. The asset turnover ratios reveal a downward trend in the efficiency with which the firm is generating sales from investments in fixed and total assets. The total asset turnover rose in 2007, progress traceable to improved management of inventories and receivables. The fixed asset turnover ratio is still declining, a result of expanding offices and retail outlets, but should improve if the expansion is successful.

Capital Structure and Long-Term Solvency

The analytical process includes an evaluation of the amount and proportion of debt in a firm's capital structure as well as the ability to service debt. Debt implies risk because debt involves the satisfaction of fixed financial obligations. The disadvantage of debt financing is that the fixed commitments must be met in order for the firm to continue operations. The major advantage of debt financing is that, when used successfully, shareholder returns are magnified through financial leverage. The concept of financial leverage can best be illustrated with an example (Figure 6.3).

R.E.C. Inc.	2007	2006	2005	2004	2003	Industry Average 2007
Debt to total assets	51.8%	50.1%	49.2%	40.8%	39.7%	48.7%
Long-term debt to total capitalization	31.4%	31.0%	24.1%	19.6%	19.8%	30.4%
Debt to equity	1.07	1.00	.96	.68	.66	.98

FIGURE 6.3 Example of Financial Leverage

Sockee Sock Company has $100,000 in total assets, and the firm's capital structure consists of 50% debt and 50% equity:

Debt	$ 50.000
Equity	50.000
Total assets	$100.000

Cost of debt = 10%
Average tax rate = 40%

If Sockee has $20,000 in operating earnings, the return to shareholders as measured by the return on equity ratio would be 18%:

Operating earnings	$20.000
Interest expense	5.000
Earnings before tax	15.000
Tax expense	6.000
Net earnings	$ 9.000

Return on equity: 9,000/50,000 = 18%

If Sockee is able to double operating earnings from $20,000 to $40,000, the return on equity will more than double, increasing from 18% to 42%:

Operating earnings	$40.000
Interest expense	5.000
Earnings before tax	35.000
Tax expense	14.000
Net earnings	$21.000

Return on equity: 21.000/50.000 = 42%

The magnified return on equity results from financial leverage. Unfortunately, leverage has a double edge. If operating earnings are cut in half from $20,000 to $10,000, the return on equity is more than halved, declining from 18% to 6%:

Operating earnings	$10.000
Interest expense	5.000
Earnings before tax	5.000
Tax expense	2.000
Net earnings	$ 3.000

Return on equity: 3.000/50.000 = 6%

The amount of interest expense is fixed, regardless of the level of operating earnings. When operating earnings rise or fall, financial leverage produces positive or negative effects on shareholder returns. In evaluating a firm's capital structure and solvency, the analyst must constantly weigh the potential benefits of debt against the risks inherent in its use.

The debt ratios for R.E.C. Inc. reveal a steady increase in the use of borrowed funds. Total debt has risen relative to total assets, long-term debt has increased as a proportion of the firm's permanent financing, and external or debt financing has increased relative to internal financing. Given the greater degree of risk implied by borrowing, it is important to determine (1) why debt has increased; (2) whether the firm is employing debt successfully; and (3) how well the firm is covering its fixed charges.

Why has debt increased? The Summary Statement of Cash Flows, discussed in Chapter 4 and repeated here as Exhibit 6.2, provides an explanation of borrowing cause. Exhibit 6.2 shows the inflows and outflows of cash both in dollar amounts and percentages.

Exhibit 6.2 shows that R.E.C. Inc. has substantially increased its investment in capital assets, particularly in 2007 when additions to property, plant, and equipment accounted for 82% of the total cash outflows. These investments have been financed largely by borrowing, especially in 2006 when the firm had a sluggish operating performance and no internal cash generation. Operations supplied 73% of R.E.C. Inc.'s cash in 2005 and 62% in 2007, but the firm had to borrow heavily in 2006 (98% of cash inflows). The impact of this borrowing is seen in the firm's debt ratios.

How effectively is R.E.C. Inc. using financial leverage? The answer is determined by calculating the financial leverage index (FLI), as follows:

$$\frac{\text{Return on equity}}{\text{Adjusted return on assets}} = \text{Finanacial leverage index}$$

EXHIBIT 6.2   R.E.C. Inc. Summary Analysis Statement of Cash Flows (in Thousands)

	2007	%	2006	%	2005	%
Inflows (thousands)						
Operations	$10,024	62.0	$ 0	0.0	$5,629	73.0
Sales of other assets	295	1.8	0	0.0	0	0.0
Sales of common stock	256	1.6	183	1.8	124	1.6
Additions of short-term debt	0	0.0	1,854	18.7	1,326	17.2
Additions of long-term debt	5,600	34.6	7,882	79.5	629	8.2
Total	$16,175	100.0	$ 9,919	100.0	$7,708	100.0
Outflows (thousands)						
Operations	$ 0	0.0	$ 3,767	31.4	$ 0	0.0
Purchase of property, plant, and equipment	14,100	81.8	4,773	40.0	3,982	66.9
Reductions of short-term debt	30	0.2	0	0.0	0	0.0
Reductions of long-term debt	1,516	8.8	1,593	13.2	127	2.1
Dividends paid	1,582	9.2	1,862	15.4	1,841	31.0
Total	$17,228	100.0	$11,995	100.0	$5,950	100.0
Change in cash and marketable securities	($1,053)		($2,076)		$1,758	

The adjusted return on assets in the denominator of this ratio is calculated as follows:

$$\frac{\text{Net earnings} + \text{interest expense} (1 - \text{tax rate})^{10}}{\text{Total assets}}$$

When the FLI is greater than 1, which indicates that return on equity exceeds return on assets, the firm is employing debt beneficially. An FLI of less than 1 means the firm is not using debt successfully. For R.E.C. Inc., the adjusted return on assets and FLI are calculated as follows:

	2007	2006	2005
Net earnings + interest expense (1 − tax rate)	$\dfrac{9{,}394 + 2{,}585(1 - .45)}{95{,}298}$	$\dfrac{5{,}910 + 2{,}277(1 - .43)}{75{,}909}$	$\dfrac{5{,}896 + 1{,}274(1 - .45)}{66{,}146}$
Total assets			

	2007	2006	2005
$\dfrac{\text{Return on equity}}{\text{Adjusted return on assets}}$	$\dfrac{20.45}{11.35} = 1.8$	$\dfrac{15.61}{9.50} = 1.6$	$\dfrac{17.53}{9.97} = 1.8$

The FLI for R.E.C. Inc. of 1.8 in 2007, 1.6 in 2006, and 1.8 in 2005 indicates a successful use of financial leverage for the three-year period when borrowing has increased. The firm has generated sufficient operating returns to more than cover the interest payments on borrowed funds.

How well is R.E.C. Inc. covering fixed charges? The answer requires a review of the coverage ratios.

R.E.C. Inc.	2007	2006	2005	2004	2003	Industry Average 2007
Times interest earned	7.44	5.18	8.84	13.34	12.60	7.2
Cash interest coverage	7.77	1.24	9.11	11.21	11.90	*
Fixed charge coverage	2.09	2.01	2.27	2.98	3.07	2.5
Cash flow adequacy	0.58	(0.46)	0.95	1.03	1.24	*

* Not available

Given the increased level of borrowing, the times interest earned and cash interest coverage ratios have declined over the five-year period but times interest earned remains above the industry average. Cash interest coverage indicates that R.E.C. Inc. is generating enough cash to actually make the cash payments. R.E.C. Inc. leases the majority of its retail outlets so the fixed charge coverage ratio, which considers lease payments as well as interest expense, is a more relevant ratio than times interest earned. This ratio has also decreased, as a result of store expansion and higher payments for leases and interest. Although below the industry average, the firm is still

---

[10]The effective tax rate to be used in this ratio was calculated in Chapter 3.

covering all fixed charges by more than two times out of operating earnings, and coverage does not at this point appear to be a problem. The fixed charge coverage ratio is a ratio to be monitored closely in the future, however, particularly if R.E.C. Inc. continues to expand. The cash flow adequacy ratio has dropped below 1.0 in 2005, 2006, and 2007 indicating the company does not generate enough cash from operations to cover capital expenditures, debt repayments, and cash dividends. To improve this ratio, the firm needs to begin reducing accounts receivables and inventories, thereby increasing cash from operations. Once the expansion is complete this should occur, however, if the expansion continues, cash flow adequacy will likely remain below 1.0.

Profitability

The analysis now turns to a consideration of how well the firm has performed in terms of profitability, beginning with the evaluation of several key ratios.

R.E.C. Inc.	2007	2006	2005	2004	2003	Industry Average 2007
Gross profit margin	40.00%	39.95%	42.00%	41.80%	41.76%	37.25%
Operating profit margin	8.93%	7.72%	8.00%	10.98%	11.63%	7.07%
Net profit margin	4.36%	3.86%	4.19%	5.00%	5.20%	3.74%
Cash flow margin	4.65%	(2.46)%	4.00%	4.39%	3.92%	*

* Not available

Profitability—after a relatively poor year in 2006 due to economic recession, adverse ski conditions, and the costs of new store openings—now looks more promising. Management adopted a growth strategy reflected in aggressive marketing and the opening of 18 new stores in 2006 and 25 in 2007. With the exception of the cash flow margin, the profit margins are all below their 2003 and 2004 levels but have improved in 2007 and are above industry averages. The cash flow margin, as a result of strong cash generation from operations in 2007, was at its highest level of the five-year period.

The gross profit margin was stable, a positive sign in light of new store openings featuring many "sale" and discounted items to attract customers, and the firm managed to improve its operating profit margin in 2007. The increase in operating profit margin is especially noteworthy because it occurred during an expansionary period with sizable increases in operating expenses, especially lease payments required for new stores. The net profit margin also improved in spite of increased interest and tax expenses and a reduction in interest revenue from marketable security investments.

R.E.C. Inc.	2007	2006	2005	2004	2003	Average 2007
Return on assets	9.86%	7.79%	8.91%	14.35%	15.34%	9.09%
Return on equity	20.45%	15.61%	17.53%	24.25%	25.46%	17.72%
Cash return on assets	10.52%	(4.96)%	8.64%	15.01%	15.98%	*

* Not available

After declining steadily through 2006, return on assets, return on equity, and cash return on assets rebounded strongly in 2007. The return on assets and return on equity ratios measure the overall success of the firm in generating profits, whereas the cash return on assets measures the firm's ability to generate cash from its investment and management strategies. It would appear that R.E.C. Inc. is well positioned for future growth. As discussed earlier, it will be important to monitor the firm's management of inventories, which account for half of total assets and have been problematic in the past. The expansion will necessitate a continuation of expenditures for advertising, at least at the current level, in order to attract customers to both new and old areas. R.E.C. Inc. has financed much of its expansion with debt, and thus far its shareholders have benefited from the use of debt through financial leverage.

R.E.C. Inc. experienced a negative cash flow from operations in 2006, another problem that bears watching in the future. The negative cash flow occurred in a year of only modest sales and earnings growth:

R.E.C. Inc.	2007	2006	2005	2004	2003
Sales growth	40.9%	8.7%	25.5%	21.6%	27.5%
Earnings growth	59.0%	.2%	5.2%	16.9%	19.2%

Sales expanded rapidly in 2007 as the economy recovered and the expansion of retail outlets began to pay off. The outlook is for continued economic recovery.

Relating the Ratios—The Du Pont System

Having looked at individual financial ratios as well as groups of financial ratios measuring short-term liquidity, operating efficiency, capital structure and long-term solvency, and profitability, it is helpful to complete the evaluation of a firm by considering the interrelationship among the individual ratios. That is, how do the various pieces of financial measurement work together to produce an overall return? The Du Pont System helps the analyst see how the firm's decisions and activities over the course of an accounting period—which is what financial ratios are measuring—interact to produce an overall return to the firm's shareholders, the return on equity. The summary ratios used are the following:

$$\underset{\textbf{Net profit margin}}{\underset{\dfrac{\text{Net income}}{\text{Net sales}}}{(1)}} \times \underset{\textbf{Total asset turnover}}{\underset{\dfrac{\text{Net sales}}{\text{Total assets}}}{(2)}} = \underset{\textbf{Return on investment}}{\underset{\dfrac{\text{Net income}}{\text{Total assets}}}{(3)}}$$

$$\underset{\textbf{Return on investment}}{\underset{\dfrac{\text{Net income}}{\text{Total assets}}}{(3)}} \times \underset{\textbf{Financial leverage}}{\underset{\dfrac{\text{Total assets}}{\text{Stockholders' equity}}}{(4)}} = \underset{\textbf{Return on equity}}{\underset{\dfrac{\text{Net income}}{\text{Stockholders' equity}}}{(5)}}$$

By reviewing this series of relationships, the analyst can identify strengths and weaknesses as well as trace potential causes of any problems in the overall financial condition and performance of the firm.

The first three ratios reveal that the (3) return on investment (profit generated from the overall investment in assets) is a product of the (1) net profit margin (profit generated from sales) and the (2) total asset turnover (the firm's ability to produce sales from its assets). Extending the analysis, the remaining three ratios show how the (5) return on equity (overall return to shareholders, the firm's owners) is derived from the product of (3) return on investment and (4) financial leverage (proportion of debt in the capital structure). Using this system, the analyst can evaluate changes in the firm's condition and performance, whether they are indicative of improvement or deterioration or some combination. The evaluation can then focus on specific areas contributing to the changes.

Evaluating R.E.C. Inc. using the Du Pont System over the five-year period 2003 to 2007 would show the following relationships:

Du Pont System applied to R.E.C. Inc.

	(1)		(2)		(3)		(4)		(5)
	NPM	×	TAT	=	ROI	×	FL	=	ROE
2003	5.20	×	2.95	=	15.34	×	1.66	=	25.46
2004	5.00	×	2.87	=	14.35	×	1.69	=	24.25
2005	4.19	×	2.13	=	8.92	×	1.97	=	17.57
2006	3.86	×	2.02	=	7.80	×	2.00	=	15.60
2007	4.36	×	2.26	=	9.85	×	2.07	=	20.39

As discussed earlier in the chapter, return on equity is below earlier year levels but has improved since its low point in 2006. The Du Pont System helps provide clues as to why these changes have occurred. Both the profit margin and the asset turnover are lower in 2007 than in 2003 and 2004. The combination of increased debt (financial leverage) and the improvement in profitability and asset utilization has produced an improved overall return in 2007 relative to the two previous years. Specifically, the firm has added debt to finance capital asset expansion and has used its debt effectively. Although debt carries risk and added cost in the form of interest expense, debt has the positive benefit of financial leverage when debt is employed successfully, which is the case for R.E.C. Inc. The 2007 improvement in inventory management has impacted the firm favorably, showing up in the improved total asset turnover ratio. The firm's ability to control operating costs while increasing sales during expansion has improved the net profit margin. The overall return on investment is now improving as a result of these combined factors.

Projections and Pro Forma Statements

Some additional analytical tools and financial ratios are relevant to financial statement analysis, particularly for investment decisions and long-range planning. Although an in-depth discussion of these tools is beyond the scope of this chapter, we provide an introductory treatment of projections, pro forma financial statements, and several investment-related financial ratios.

The investment analyst, in valuing securities for investment decisions, must project the future earnings stream of a business enterprise. References that provide earnings forecasts are found in the "Other Sources" section earlier in the chapter.

Pro forma financial statements are projections of financial statements based on a set of assumptions regarding future revenues, expenses, level of investment in assets, financing methods and costs, and working capital management. Pro forma financial statements are utilized primarily for long-range planning and long-term credit decisions. A bank considering the extension of $1.5 million in new credit to R.E.C. Inc. would want to look at the firm's pro forma statements, assuming the loan is granted, and determine—using different scenarios regarding the firm's performance—whether cash flow from operations would be sufficient to service the debt. R.E.C. Inc.'s CEO, who is making a decision about new store expansion, would develop pro forma statements based on varying estimates of performance outcomes and financing alternatives.

It is important that the above described pro forma financial statements not be confused with "pro forma" earnings or "pro forma" financial statements that many firms now report in their annual reports and financial press releases. Many companies in recent years have made up their own definition of pro forma in order to present more favorable financial information than the generally accepted accounting principles (GAAP)-based number required to be reported. By eliminating items such as depreciation, amortization, interest, and tax expense from earnings, for example, some firms have tried to convince users of their annual reports to focus on the "pro forma" amount that is usually a profit, instead of the GAAP-based amount that is usually a loss. (This topic was discussed in Chapter 5.)

Summary of Analysis

The analysis of any firm's financial statements consists of a mixture of steps and pieces that interrelate and affect each other. No one part of the analysis should be interpreted in isolation. Short-term liquidity impacts profitability; profitability begins with sales, which relate to the liquidity of assets. The efficiency of asset management influences the cost and availability of credit, which shapes the capital structure. Every aspect of a firm's financial condition, performance, and outlook affects the share price. The last step of financial statement analysis is to integrate the separate pieces into a whole, leading to conclusions about the business enterprise. The specific conclusions drawn will be affected by the original objectives established at the initiation of the analytical process.

The major findings from the analysis of R.E.C. Inc.'s financial statements can be summarized by the following strengths and weaknesses.

Strengths

1. Favorable economic and industry outlook; firm well-positioned geographically to benefit from expected economic and industry growth
2. Aggressive marketing and expansion strategies
3. Recent improvement in management of accounts receivable and inventory
4. Successful use of financial leverage and solid coverage of debt service requirements
5. Effective control of operating costs
6. Substantial sales growth, partially resulting from market expansion and reflective of future performance potential
7. Increased profitability in 2007 and strong, positive generation of cash flow from operations

Weaknesses

1. Highly sensitive to economic fluctuations and weather conditions
2. Negative cash flow from operating activities in 2006
3. Historical problems with inventory management and some weakness in overall asset management efficiency
4. Increased risk associated with debt financing

The answers to specific questions regarding R.E.C. Inc. are determined by the values placed on each of the strengths and weaknesses. In general, the outlook for the firm is promising. R.E.C. Inc. appears to be a sound credit risk with attractive investment potential. The management of inventories, a continuation of effective cost controls, and careful timing of further expansion will be critically important to the firm's future success.

This book began with the notion that financial statements should serve as a map to successful business decision making, even though the user of financial statement data would confront mazelike challenges in seeking to find and interpret the necessary information. The chapters have covered the enormous volume of material found in corporate financial reporting, the complexities and confusions created by accounting rules and choices, the potential for management manipulations of financial statement results, and the difficulty in finding necessary information. The exploration of financial statements has required a close examination of the form and content of each financial statement presented in corporate annual reporting as well as the development of tools and techniques for analyzing the data. It is the hope of the authors that readers of this book will find that financial statements are a map, leading to sound and profitable business decisions.

FIGURE 6.4 The Maze Becomes a Map

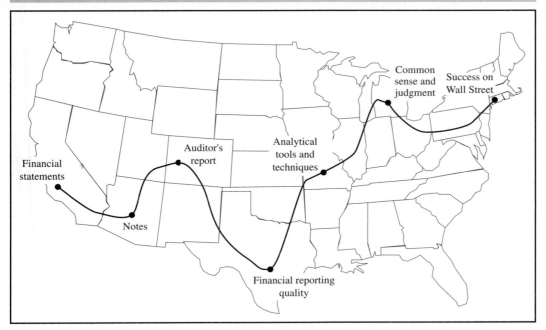

SELF-TEST

Solutions are provided in Appendix B.

_____ 1. What is the first step in an analysis of financial statements?
(a) Check the auditor's report.
(b) Check references containing financial information.
(c) Specify the objectives of the analysis.
(d) Do a common size analysis.

_____ 2. What is a creditor's objective in performing an analysis of financial statements?
(a) To decide whether the borrower has the ability to repay interest and principal on borrowed funds.
(b) To determine the firm's capital structure.
(c) To determine the company's future earnings stream.
(d) To decide whether the firm has operated profitably in the past.

_____ 3. What is an investor's objective in financial statement analysis?
(a) To determine if the firm is risky.
(b) To determine the stability of earnings.
(c) To determine changes necessary to improve future performance.
(d) To determine whether an investment is warranted by estimating a company's future earnings stream.

_____ 4. What information does the auditor's report contain?
(a) The results of operations.
(b) An unqualified opinion.
(c) An opinion as to the fairness of the financial statements.
(d) A detailed coverage of the firm's liquidity, capital resources, and operations.

_____ 5. Which of the following would be helpful to an analyst evaluating the performance of a firm?
(a) Understanding the economic and political environment in which the company operates.
(b) Reviewing the annual reports of a company's suppliers, customers, and competitors.
(c) Preparing common-size financial statements and calculating key financial ratios for the company being evaluated.
(d) All of the above.

_____ 6. Which of the following is not required to be discussed in the Management Discussion and Analysis of the Financial Condition and Results of Operations?
(a) Liquidity.
(b) Capital resources.
(c) Operations.
(d) Earnings projections.

_____ 7. What type of information found in supplementary schedules is required for inclusion in an annual report?
(a) Segmental data.
(b) Inflation data.

      (c) Material litigation and management photographs.

      (d) Management remuneration and segmental data.

_____ **8.** What is Form 10-K?

      (a) A document filed with the American Institute of Certified Public Accountants (AICPA) containing supplementary schedules showing management remuneration and elaborations of financial statement disclosures.

      (b) A document filed with the SEC by companies selling securities to the public, containing much of the same information as the annual report as well as additional detail.

      (c) A document filed with the SEC containing key business ratios and forecasts of earnings.

      (d) A document filed with the SEC containing nonpublic information.

_____ **9.** What information can be gained from sources such as Industry Norms and Key Business Ratios, Annual Statement Studies, Analyst's Handbook, and Industry Surveys?

      (a) The general economic condition.

      (b) Forecasts of earnings.

      (c) Elaborations of financial statement disclosures.

      (d) A company's relative position within its industry.

_____ **10.** Which of the following is not a tool or technique used by a financial statement analyst?

      (a) Common-size financial statements.

      (b) Trend analysis.

      (c) Random sampling analysis.

      (d) Industry comparisons.

_____ **11.** What do liquidity ratios measure?

      (a) A firm's ability to meet cash needs as they arise.

      (b) The liquidity of fixed assets.

      (c) The overall performance of a firm.

      (d) The extent of a firm's financing with debt relative to equity.

_____ **12.** Which category of ratios is useful in assessing the capital structure and long-term solvency of a firm?

      (a) Liquidity ratios.

      (b) Activity ratios.

      (c) Leverage ratios.

      (d) Profitability ratios.

_____ **13.** What is a serious limitation of financial ratios?

      (a) Ratios are screening devices.

      (b) Ratios can be used only by themselves.

      (c) Ratios indicate weaknesses only.

      (d) Ratios are not predictive.

_____ **14.** What is the most widely used liquidity ratio?

      (a) Quick ratio.

      (b) Current ratio.

      (c) Inventory turnover.

      (d) Debt ratio.

_____ **15.** What is a limitation common to both the current and the quick ratio?
  (a) Accounts receivable may not be truly liquid.
  (b) Inventories may not be truly liquid.
  (c) Marketable securities are not liquid.
  (d) Prepaid expenses are potential sources of cash.

_____ **16.** Why is the quick ratio a more rigorous test of short-run solvency than the current ratio?
  (a) The quick ratio considers only cash and marketable securities as current assets.
  (b) The quick ratio eliminates prepaid expenses for the numerator.
  (c) The quick ratio eliminates prepaid expenses for the denominator.
  (d) The quick ratio eliminates inventories from the numerator.

_____ **17.** What does an increasing collection period for accounts receivable suggest about a firm's credit policy?
  (a) The credit policy is too restrictive.
  (b) The firm is probably losing qualified customers.
  (c) The credit policy may be too lenient.
  (d) The collection period has no relationship to a firm's credit policy.

_____ **18.** Which of the following statements about inventory turnover is false?
  (a) Inventory turnover measures the efficiency of the firm in managing and selling inventory.
  (b) Inventory turnover is a gauge of the liquidity of a firm's inventory.
  (c) Inventory turnover is calculated with cost of goods sold in the numerator.
  (d) A low inventory turnover is generally a sign of efficient inventory management.

_____ **19.** Which of the following items would cause the cash conversion cycle to decrease?
  (a) Increasing days payable outstanding.
  (b) Increasing the average collection period.
  (c) Increasing the days inventory held.
  (d) None of the above.

_____ **20.** What do the asset turnover ratios measure?
  (a) The liquidity of the firm's current assets.
  (b) Management's effectiveness in generating sales from investments in assets.
  (c) The overall efficiency and profitability of the firm.
  (d) The distribution of assets in which funds are invested.

_____ **21.** Which of the following ratios would not be used to measure the extent of a firm's debt financing?
  (a) Debt ratio.
  (b) Debt to equity.
  (c) Times interest earned.
  (d) Long-term debt to total capitalization.

_____ **22.** Why is the amount of debt in a company's capital structure important to the financial analyst?
  (a) Debt implies risk.

(b) Debt is less costly than equity.

(c) Equity is riskier than debt.

(d) Debt is equal to total assets.

_____ 23. Why is the fixed charge coverage ratio a broader measure of a firm's coverage capabilities than the times interest earned ratio?

(a) The fixed charge ratio indicates how many times the firm can cover interest payments.

(b) The times interest earned ratio does not consider the possibility of higher interest rates.

(c) The fixed charge ratio includes lease payments as well as interest payments.

(d) The fixed charge ratio includes both operating and capital leases while the times interest earned ratio includes only operating leases.

_____ 24. Which profit margin measures the overall operating efficiency of the firm?

(a) Gross profit margin.

(b) Operating profit margin.

(c) Net profit margin.

(d) Return on equity.

_____ 25. Which ratio or ratios measure the overall efficiency of the firm in managing its investment in assets and in generating return to shareholders?

(a) Gross profit margin and net profit margin.

(b) Return on investment.

(c) Total asset turnover and operating profit margin.

(d) Return on investment and return on equity.

_____ 26. What does a financial leverage index greater than one indicate about a firm?

(a) The unsuccessful use of financial leverage.

(b) Operating returns more than sufficient to cover interest payments on borrowed funds.

(c) More debt financing than equity financing.

(d) An increased level of borrowing.

_____ 27. What does the price to earnings ratio measure?

(a) The "multiple" that the stock market places on a firm's earnings.

(b) The relationship between dividends and market prices.

(c) The earnings for one common share of stock.

(d) The percentage of dividends paid to net earnings of the firm.

Use the following data to answer questions 28 through 31:

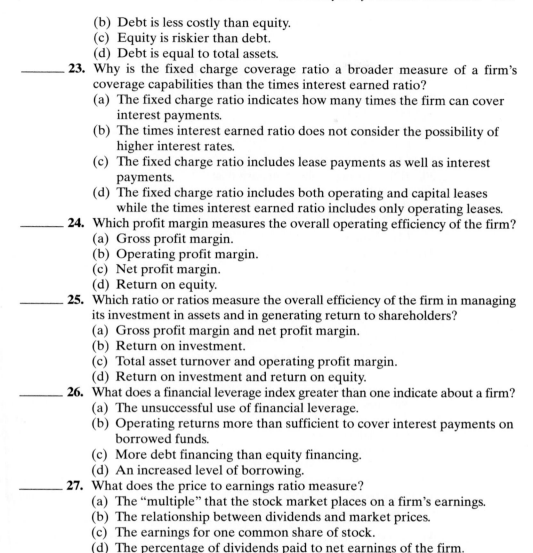

JDL Corporation Selected Financial Data
December 31, 2009

Current assets	$150,000
Current liabilities	100,000
Inventories	50,000
Accounts receivable	40,000
Net sales	900,000
Cost of goods sold	675,000

_____ **28.** JDL's current ratio is:
    (a) 1.0 to 1.
    (b) 0.7 to 1.
    (c) 1.5 to 1.
    (d) 2.4 to 1.
_____ **29.** JDL's quick ratio is:
    (a) 1.0 to 1.
    (b) 0.7 to 1.
    (c) 1.5 to 1.
    (d) 2.4 to 1.
_____ **30.** JDL's average collection period is:
    (a) 6 days.
    (b) 11 days.
    (c) 16 days.
    (d) 22 days.
_____ **31.** JDL's inventory turnover is:
    (a) 1.25 times.
    (b) 13.5 times.
    (c) 3.0 times.
    (d) 37.5 times.

Use the following data to answer questions 32 through 35:

RQM Corporation Selected Financial Data
December 31, 2009

Net sales	$1,800,000
Cost of goods sold	1,080,000
Operating expenses	315,000
Net operating income	405,000
Net income	195,000
Total stockholders' equity	750,000
Total assets	1,000,000
Cash flow from operating activities	25,000

_____ **32.** RQM's gross profit margin, operating profit margin, and net profit margin, respectively, are:
    (a) 40.00%, 22.50%, 19.50%
    (b) 60.00%, 19.50%, 10.83%
    (c) 60.00%, 22.50%, 19.50%
    (d) 40.00%, 22.50%, 10.83%
_____ **33.** RQM's return on equity is:
    (a) 26%
    (b) 54%
    (c) 42%
    (d) 19%
_____ **34.** RQM's return on investment is:
    (a) 22.5%
    (b) 26.5%

    (c) 19.5%
    (d) 40.5%

_____ **35.** RQM's cash flow margin is:
    (a) 1.4%
    (b) 2.5%
    (c) 10.8%
    (d) 12.8%

STUDY QUESTIONS AND PROBLEMS

6.1. Eleanor's Computers is a retailer of computer products. Using the financial data provided, complete the financial ratio calculations for 2007. Advise management of any ratios that indicate potential problems and provide an explanation of possible causes of the problems.

Financial Ratios	2005	2006	2007	Industry Averages 2007
Current ratio	1.71X	1.65X		1.70X
Quick ratio	.92X	.89X		.95X
Average collection period	60 days	60 days		65 days
Inventory turnover	4.20X	3.90X		4.50X
Fixed asset turnover	3.20X	3.33X		3.00X
Total asset turnover	1.40X	1.35X		1.37X
Debt ratio	59.20%	61.00%		60.00%
Times interest earned	4.20X	3.70X		4.75X
Gross profit margin	25.00%	23.00%		22.50%
Operating profit margin	12.50%	12.70%		12.50%
Net profit margin	6.10%	6.00%		6.50%
Return on total assets	8.54%	8.10%		8.91%
Return on equity	20.93%	20.74%		22.28%

Income Statement for Year Ended 12/31/07		Balance Sheet at 12/31/07	
Sales	$1,500,000	Cash	$ 125,000
Cost of goods sold	1,200,000	Accounts receivable	275,000
Gross profit	$ 300,000	Inventory	325,000
Operating expenses	100,000	Current assets	$ 725,000
Operating profit	$ 200,000	Fixed assets (net)	$ 420,000
Interest expense	72,000	Total Assets	$1,145,000
Earnings before tax	128,000	Accounts payable	$ 150,000
Income tax (0.4)	51,200	Notes payable	225,000
Net Income	$ 76,800	Accrued liabilities	100,000
		Current liabilities	475,000
		Long-term debt	400,000
		Total liabilities	$ 875,000
		Equity	270,000
		Total liabilities and equity	$1,145,000

6.2. Luna Lighting, a retail firm, has experienced modest sales growth over the past three years but has had difficulty translating the expansion of sales into improved profitability. Using three years' financial statements, you have developed the following ratio calculations and industry comparisons. Based on this information, suggest possible reasons for Luna's profitability problems.

	2009	2008	2007	Industry 2009
Current	2.3X	2.3X	2.2X	2.1X
Average collection period	45 days	46 days	47 days	50 days
Inventory turnover	8.3X	8.2X	8.1X	8.3X
Fixed asset turnover	2.7X	3.0X	3.3X	3.5X
Total asset turnover	1.1X	1.2X	1.3X	1.5X
Debt ratio	50%	50%	50%	54%
Times interest earned	8.1X	8.2X	8.1X	7.2X
Fixed charge coverage	4.0X	4.5X	5.5X	5.1X
Gross profit margin	43%	43%	43%	40%
Operating profit margin	6.3%	7.2%	8.0%	7.5%
Net profit margin	3.5%	4.0%	4.3%	4.2%
Return on assets	3.7%	5.0%	5.7%	6.4%
Return on equity	7.4%	9.9%	11.4%	11.8%

6.3. RareMetals, Inc. sells a rare metal found only in underdeveloped countries overseas. As a result of unstable governments in these countries and the rarity of the metal, the price fluctuates significantly. Financial information is given assuming the use of the first-in, first-out (FIFO) method of inventory valuation and also the last-in, first-out (LIFO) method of inventory valuation. Current assets other than inventory total $1,230 and current liabilities total $1,600. The ending inventory balances are $1,350 for FIFO and $525 for LIFO.

Raremetals, Inc. Income Statements (in Thousands)

	FIFO	LIFO
Net sales	$3,000	$3,000
Cost of goods sold	1,400	2,225
Gross profit	1,600	775
Selling, general and administrative	600	600
Operating profit	1,000	175
Interest expense	80	80
Earnings before taxes	920	95
Provision for income taxes	322	33
Net earnings	$ 598	$ 62

Required

    a. Calculate the following ratios assuming RareMetals, Inc. uses the FIFO method of inventory valuation: gross profit margin, operating profit margin, net profit margin, current ratio, and quick ratio.

b. Calculate the ratios listed in (a) assuming RareMetals, Inc. uses the LIFO method of inventory valuation.

c. Evaluate and explain the differences in the ratios calculated in (a) and (b).

d. Will cash flow from operating activities differ depending on the inventory valuation method used? If so, estimate the difference and explain your answer.

6.4. Eastman Kodak Company and Canon, Inc. are competitors in the camera manufacturing industry. The following ratios and financial information have been compiled for these two companies:

Financial ratios (2000)	Kodak	Canon
Liquidity		
Current (times)	.88	1.71
Quick (times)	.61	1.21
Cash flow liquidity (times)	.20	.87
Cash flow from operations (millions of $)	982	2,610
Activity		
Accounts receivable turnover (times)	5.27	5.80
Inventory turnover (times)	4.67	3.21
Payables turnover (times)	2.45	3.55
Fixed asset turnover (times)	2.36	3.60
Total asset turnover (times)	.98	.98
Leverage		
Debt ratio (%)	75.88	54.13
Times interest earned (times)	12.44	16.39
Cash interest coverage (times)	9.84	30.39
Cash flow adequacy (times)	.40	1.29
Profitability		
Gross profit margin (%)	42.70	43.28
Operating profit margin (%)	15.82	8.84
Net profit margin (%)	10.05	4.82
Cash flow margin (%)	7.02	12.46
Return on assets (%)	9.90	4.73
Return on equity (%)	41.04	10.33
Cash return on assets (%)	6.91	12.24
Earnings per share	4.62	1.16
Closing stock price	$39 per share	$34 per share

Required

a. Compare and evaluate the strengths and weaknesses of Eastman Kodak and Canon.

b. Calculate the price-to-earnings (PE) ratios for both firms. Explain what a PE ratio tells an analyst. What could be the cause of the difference between Eastman Kodak's and Canon's PE ratios?

6.5. Determine the effect on the current ratio, the quick ratio, net working capital (current assets less current liabilities), and the debt ratio (total liabilities to total assets) of each of the following transactions. Consider each transaction separately and assume that prior to each transaction the current ratio is 2X, the quick ratio is 1X, and the debt ratio is 50%. The company uses an allowance for doubtful accounts.

Use I for increase, D for decrease, and N for no change.

	Current Ratio	Quick Ratio	Net Working Capital	Debt Ratio
(a) Borrows $10,000 from bank on short-term note				
(b) Writes off a $5,000 customer account				
(c) Issues $25,000 in new common stock for cash				
(d) Purchases for cash $7,000 of new equipment				
(e) $5,000 inventory is destroyed by fire				
(f) Invests $3,000 in short-term marketable securities				
(g) Issues $10,000 long-term bonds				
(h) Sells equipment with book value of $6,000 for $7,000				
(i) Issues $10,000 stock in exchange for land				
(j) Purchases $3,000 inventory for cash				
(k) Purchases $5,000 inventory on credit				
(l) Pays $2,000 to supplier to reduce account payable				

6.6. Laurel Street, president of Uvalde Manufacturing Inc. is preparing a proposal to present to her board of directors regarding a planned plant expansion that will cost $10 million. At issue is whether the expansion should be financed with debt (a long-term note at First National Bank of Uvalde with an interest rate of 15%) or through the issuance of common stock (200,000 shares at $50 per share).

Uvalde Manufacturing currently has a capital structure of:

Debt (12% interest)	40,000,000
Equity	50,000,000

The firm's most recent income statement is presented next:

Sales	$100,000,000
Cost of goods sold	65,000,000
Gross profit	35,000,000
Operating expenses	20,000,000
Operating profit	15,000,000
Interest expense	4,800,000
Earnings before tax	10,200,000
Income tax expense (40%)	4,080,000
Net income	$ 6,120,000
Earnings per share (800,000 shares)	$ 7.65

Laurel Street is aware that financing the expansion with debt will increase risk but could also benefit shareholders through financial leverage. Estimates are that the plant expansion will increase operating profit by 20%. The tax rate is expected to stay at 40%. Assume a 100% dividend payout ratio.

Required

a. Calculate the debt ratio, time interest earned, earnings per share, and the financial leverage index under each alternative, assuming the expected increase in operating profit is realized.

b. Discuss the factors the board should consider in making a decision.

6.7. Using the ratios and information given for Amazon.com, an Internet retailer, analyze the short-term liquidity and operating efficiency of the firm as of 2004.

Financial ratios	2004	2003
Liquidity		
Current (times)	1.57	1.45
Quick (times)	1.27	1.22
Cash flow liquidity (times)	1.45	1.43
Average collection period	11 days	9 days
Days inventory held	33 days	27 days
Days payable outstanding	79 days	75 days
Cash conversion cycle	(35 days)	(39 days)
Activity		
Accounts receivable turnover (times)	34.76	40.04
Inventory turnover (times)	11.09	13.63
Payables turnover (times)	4.66	4.89
Fixed asset turnover (times)	28.12	23.47
Total asset turnover (times)	2.13	2.43
Other information		
Cash flow from operations (millions of $)	567	392
Revenues (millions of $)	6,921	5,264

6.8. The following ratios have been calculated for AMC Entertainment Inc., owner and operator of movie theaters. Analyze the capital structure, long-term solvency, and profitability of AMC.

Financial ratios	2004	2003
Leverage		
Debt ratio (%)	81.4	81.1
Long-term debt to total capital (%)	72.6	72.2
Debt to equity (times)	4.4	4.3
Times interest earned (times)	1.2	0.7
Cash interest coverage (times)	3.4	2.5
Fixed charge coverage (times)	1.0	0.9
Cash flow adequacy (times)	0.5	1.2
Profitability		
Gross profit margin (%)	34.5	32.4
Operating profit margin (%)	5.2	3.1
Net profit margin (%)	(0.6)	(1.7)
Cash flow margin (%)	10.3	7.2
Return on assets (%)	(0.7)	(2.0)
Return on equity (%)	(3.8)	(10.6)
Cash return on assets (%)	12.2	8.7

6.9. Writing Skills Problem

R.E.C. Inc.'s staff of accountants finished preparing the financial statements for 2007 and will meet next week with the company's CEO as well as the Director of Investor Relations and representatives from the marketing and art departments to design the current year's annual report.

Required

Write a paragraph in which you present the main idea(s) you think the company should present to shareholders in the annual report.

6.10. Research Problem

Using the articles referenced in footnote 4 in this chapter regarding cash flow ratios, create a list of cash flow ratios that you believe would be a good set of ratios to assess the cash flows of a firm. Choose an industry and locate four companies in that industry. Calculate the cash flow ratios for each company and then create an industry average of all four companies. Comment on how well you think your industry average would work as a guide when analyzing other firms in this industry.

6.11. Internet Problem

Choose an industry and find four companies in that industry. Using a financial Internet database such as www.marketwatch.com, calculate or locate the four market ratios discussed in the chapter for each of the four companies. Write an analysis comparing the market ratios of the four companies.

6.12. Intel Problem

The 2004 Intel Annual Report can be found at the following Web site: www.prenhall.com/fraser.

(a) Using the Intel Annual Report, calculate key financial ratios for all years presented.

(b) Using the library, find industry averages to compare to the calculations in (a).

(c) Write a report to the management of Intel. Your report should include an evaluation of short-term liquidity, operating efficiency, capital structure and long-term solvency, profitability, market measures, and a discussion of any quality of financial reporting issues. In addition, strengths and weaknesses should be identified, and your opinion of the investment potential and the creditworthiness of the firm should be conveyed to management.

Hint: Use the information from the Intel Problems at the end of Chapters 1 through 5 to complete this problem.

6.13. Eastman Kodak Comprehensive Analysis Problem Using the Financial Statement Analysis Template

Each chapter in the textbook contains a continuation of this problem. The objective is to learn how to do a comprehensive financial statement analysis in steps as the content of each chapter is learned. Using the 2004 Eastman Kodak Annual Report or Form 10-K, which can be found at www.prenhall.com/fraser, complete the following requirements:

(a) Open the financial statement analysis template that you have been using in the prior chapters. Link to the "Ratios" by clicking on the tab at the bottom of the template. All of the ratios should be automatically calculated for you, assuming you have input all required data from prior chapters. Print this page.

(b) Using all of your data and calculations for Eastman Kodak from prior chapters, write a comprehensive analysis of the company. Use Figure 6.2 as a guide.

CASES

Case 6.1   Action Performance Companies, Inc.

Action Performance Companies, Inc. designs and sells licensed motorsports collectible and consumer products. In the United States the company is a licensee of among others, NASCAR, Indy Racing League, World of Outlaws, and National Hot Rod Association. In Germany, the firm merchandises Formula One and high-end auto manufacturer die-cast replica vehicles. The company outsources most of the production, but retains ownership of the designs and tooling. Products are marketed through distributors, trackside stores, mass-merchant retailers and collectors' catalog club, television programming, and Internet sites managed by QVC.

In September 2003, Funline Merchandise Co., Inc. (Funline) was acquired by Action Performance Companies, Inc. Funline distributes non-NASCAR die-cast vehicles. Selected information from the 2004 Form 10-K of

Action Performance Companies, Inc. is on pages 236–241.*

Required

1. Analyze the firm's financial statements and supplementary information. Your analysis should include the preparation of common-size financial statements, key financial ratios, and an evaluation of short-term liquidity, operating efficiency, capital structure and long-term solvency, profitability, and market measures. (The financial statement analysis template can be accessed and used at www.prenhall.com/fraser.)
2. Identify the strengths and weaknesses of the company.
3. What is your opinion of the investment potential and the creditworthiness of Action Performance Companies, Inc.?

*Source: Action Performance Companies, Inc. 2004 Form 10-K.

ACTION PERFORMANCE COMPANIES, INC.
CONSOLIDATED BALANCE SHEETS
September 30, 2004, and 2003
(in Thousands, Except per Share Data)

	2004	2003
Assets		
Current Assets:		
Cash and cash equivalents	$ 12,580	$ 49,462
Accounts receivable, net of allowance of $9,367 and $3,634	51,769	69,890
Inventories	56,947	43,232
Prepaid royalties	2,834	4,470
Taxes receivable	2,126	–
Deferred income taxes	8,766	5,291
Prepaid expenses and other	5,920	3,161
Total current assets	140,942	175,506
Long-Term Assets:		
Property and equipment, net	64,878	62,951
Goodwill	88,653	87,448
Licenses and other intangibles, net	56,614	44,426
Other	3,196	2,357
Total long-term assets	213,341	197,182
	$ 354,283	$372,688
Liabilities and Shareholders' Equity		
Current Liabilities:		
Accounts payable	$ 28,778	$ 36,734
Accrued royalties	10,702	9,692
Accrued expenses	8,757	11,764
Taxes payable	1,742	3,156
Current portion of long-term debt	4,009	567
Total current liabilities	53,988	61,913
Long-Term Liabilities:		
Deferred income taxes	24,979	10,890
$4\frac{3}{4}$% convertible subordinated notes	–	29,935
Other long-term debt	11,882	4,490
Other	298	926
Total long-term liabilities	37,159	46,241
Minority Interests	2,509	2,941
Commitments and Contingencies		
Shareholders' Equity:		
Preferred stock, no par value, 5,000 shares authorized, no shares issued and outstanding	–	–
Common stock, $.01 par value, 62,500 shares authorized; 18,560 and 18,464 shares issued	186	185
Additional paid-in capital	158,429	157,301
Treasury stock, at cost, 190 and 190 shares	(3,999)	(3,999)
Accumulated other comprehensive loss	(1,456)	(2,488)
Retained earnings	107,467	110,594
Total shareholders' equity	260,627	261,593
	$ 354,283	$372,688

The accompanying notes are an integral part of these consolidated financial statements.

ACTION PERFORMANCE COMPANIES, INC.
CONSOLIDATED STATEMENTS OF OPERATIONS AND COMPREHENSIVE INCOME
Years Ended September 30, 2004, 2003, and 2002
(in Thousands, Except per Share Data)

	2004	2003	2002
Net sales	$ 344,330	$ 369,458	$ 406,558
Cost of sales	247,959	245,879	250,810
Gross profit	96,371	123,579	155,748
Operating expenses:			
Selling, general, and administrative	90,713	82,598	76,870
Amortization of licenses and other intangibles	3,802	3,416	2,797
Total operating expenses	94,515	86,014	79,667
Income from operations	1,856	37,565	76,081
Interest expense	(1,832)	(2,085)	(3,029)
Gain (loss) on extinguishment of debt	(322)	34	(1,361)
Foreign exchange gains	1,545	3,574	1,500
Earnings from joint venture	1,370	62	–
Other income	204	485	773
Other expense	(1,215)	(1,909)	(1,411)
Income before income taxes	1,606	37,726	72,553
Income taxes	1,066	13,499	27,606
Net income	540	24,227	44,947
Currency translation	1,032	2,118	1,019
Comprehensive income	$ 1,572	$ 26,345	$ 45,966
Earnings Per Common Share:			
Basic	$ 0.03	$ 1.36	$ 2.56
Diluted	$ 0.03	$ 1.33	$ 2.41

The accompanying notes are an integral part of these consolidated financial statements.

Debt and Financing

Other long-term debt consists of the following at September 30 (in thousands):

	2004	2003
Term Loan A due June 30, 2008, variable rate	$ 1,644	$ –
Term Loan B due June 30, 2007, variable rate	9,444	–
Notes payable, secured by property and equipment, 6.0% to 8.4%	4,803	5,057
Less current portion	(4,009)	(567)
	$ 11,882	$ 4,490

On August 2, 2004, we redeemed $29.9 million of 4¾% convertible subordinated notes at a price of 100.68% for cash of $30.1 million. We funded the redemption with cash on hand, revolving credit facility borrowings, and the term loans under the loan and security agreement. The subordinated notes were convertible, at the option of the holders, into shares of common stock at the initial conversion price of $48.20 per share, subject to adjustments in certain events and would have matured on April 1, 2005.

ACTION PERFORMANCE COMPANIES, INC.
CONSOLIDATED STATEMENTS OF CASH FLOWS
Years Ended September 30, 2004, 2003, and 2002
(in Thousands)

	2004	2003	2002
Cash Flows From Operating Activities:			
Net income	$ 540	$ 24,227	$ 44,947
Adjustments to reconcile net income to net cash provided by operating activities-			
Deferred income taxes	(885)	3,354	(133)
Depreciation and amortization	30,184	26,153	23,722
(Gain) loss on extinguishment of debt	322	(34)	1,361
Stock option tax benefits	142	623	2,864
Undistributed earnings from joint venture	(1,370)	(62)	–
Other	1,149	982	1,976
Change in assets and liabilities, net of businesses acquired and disposed:			
Accounts receivable, net of allowance	18,456	(1,865)	(18,518)
Inventories	(13,077)	(363)	(4,522)
Prepaid royalties	3,706	15	3,285
Other assets	(2,785)	2,890	(2,116)
Accounts payable and accrued expenses	(9,469)	(6,117)	5,869
Accrued royalties	(1,167)	(4,241)	(1,655)
Taxes payable and receivable, net	(3,660)	(1,851)	(3,366)
Other liabilities	(2,273)	(4,285)	(989)
Net cash provided by operating activities	19,813	39,426	52,725
Cash Flows From Investing Activities:			
Property and equipment purchases	(24,940)	(33,366)	(25,800)
Property and equipment sales proceeds	84	245	261
Acquisitions of businesses and intangibles, net of costs	(8,142)	(15,733)	(19,006)
Other	615	–	(238)
Net cash used in investing activities	(32,383)	(48,854)	(44,783)
Cash Flow From Finanving Activities:			
Long-term debt borrowings	11,700	3,001	–
Long-term debt repayments	(31,303)	(9,429)	(6,397)
Stock option and other exercise proceeds	330	871	6,618
Common stock purchases for treasury	–	(2,024)	(1,975)
Dividends paid - common shareholders	(3,663)	(2,497)	–
Dividends paid - minority interest shareholders	(1,609)	(1,256)	(1,353)
Net cash used in financing activities	(24,545)	(11,334)	(3,107)
Effect of exchange rate changes on cash and cash equivalents	233	639	236
Net change in cash and cash equivalents	(36,882)	(20,123)	5,071
Cash and cash equivalents, beginning of year	49,462	69,585	64,514
Cash and cash equivalents, end of year	$ 12,580	$ 49,462	$ 69,585

The accompanying notes are an integral part of these consolidated financial statements.

Income Taxes

A reconciliation of the federal income tax rate to the Company's effective rate follows:

	2004	2003	2002
Statutory federal rate	34%	35%	35%
State taxes, net of federal benefit	(2)	2	2
Foreign incremental rate	28	2	1
Valuation allowances and other	6	(3)	–
	66%	36%	38%

Supplemental Cash Flow Information

The supplemental cash flow disclosures follow (in thousands):

	2004	2003	2002
Supplemental disclosures:			
Interest paid	$ 2,252	$ 2,199	$ 2,705
Income taxes paid	5,070	11,420	27,815

Commitments and Contingencies

Rent expense recognized for noncancellable operating leases, net of sublease income, totaled $3.9 million, $4.1 million, and $2.1 million for 2004, 2003 and 2002.

Contractual Obligations and Commercial Commitments

Aggregate future minimum payments due contractually under royalty agreement guarantees, personal service agreements, long-term debt, noncancellable operating leases, commercial letters of credit, and other unconditional purchase obligations are as follows as of September 30, 2004 (in thousands):

Year	Royalty Agreement Guarantees	Personal Service Agreements	Long-term Debt	Interest Payments	Lease Payments	Unconditional Purchase Obligations	Total
2005	$ 19,145	$ 1,514	$ 4,009	$ 260	$ 5,681	$ 12,600	$ 43,209
2006	17,938	843	4,036	238	5,189	–	28,244
2007	15,996	379	3,504	213	4,923	–	25,015
2008	14,514	135	1,036	188	4,092	–	19,965
2009	14,491	135	254	163	3,650	–	18,693
Thereafter	39,695	68	3,052	1,084	10,004	–	53,903
Total	$ 121,779	$ 3,074	$ 15,891	$ 2,146	$ 33,539	$ 12,600	$189,029

Year Ended September 30, 2004 Compared with Year Ended September 30, 2003

Net sales decreased to $344.3 million for 2004, compared to $369.5 million in 2003, a decline of $25.1 million, or 6.8%, from the 2003 fiscal year. Revenues for the year included $42.1 million from Funline, which was acquired in 2003 and contributed $0.5 million in that year. Excluding the impact of the Funline acquisition, revenues were down $66.8 million, or 18.1% from 2003.

Domestic die-cast sales decreased $6.2 million, or 4.2%, from the prior year while foreign die-cast sales increased $2.3 million, or 6.6%. The domestic die-cast segment sales decrease of $6.2 million is comprised of a $38.3 million decrease in our wholesale distribution and promotion revenues, a $4.9 million decrease in our die-cast retail collectors' catalog club revenues, and an offsetting $37.0 million increase in domestic die-cast wholesale sales to mass-merchant retailers. Domestic die-cast wholesale distribution and promotion revenues and collector's catalog club revenues were down as a result of problems in our wholesale distribution network and from a weak NASCAR collector die-cast market. In 2004, approximately one-third of our distributors experienced financial hardships of varying degrees, which impacted both their ordering patterns as well as their ability to pay our invoices on a timely basis. The NASCAR collector die-cast market in 2004 suffered from over production of both the number of units in a given production run and the varieties of product offerings. The increase in the variety of production runs made our approval and production process difficult to manage, resulting in a failure to ship product into the market on a timely basis thereby negatively impacting sales. We expect comparable sales from our domestic die-cast wholesale distribution and promotion revenues and collectors' catalog club revenues in 2005 as we continue to work to improve our die-cast distribution model and focus our product offerings. Domestic die-cast wholesale sales to mass-merchant retailers increased $37.0 million as a result of the $41.7 million impact of increased revenues from Funline, acquired in September 2003, offset by the $4.7 million decrease in

NASCAR die-cast sales to mass-merchant retailers. NASCAR die-cast sales to mass-merchant retailers have been trending up year-over-year in the last two quarters of 2004. We expect double-digit growth in Funline sales in 2005 and single digit growth in NASCAR die-cast sales to mass-merchant retailers, based on merchant feedback.

Year Ended September 30, 2003 Compared with Year Ended September 30, 2002

Net sales decreased 9.1% to $369.5 million for 2003, from $406.6 million in 2002. Domestic die-cast sales decreased $60.6 million, or 29.0%, from the prior year while foreign die-cast sales increased $5.2 million, or 17.7%. Domestic wholesale distribution and promotion die-cast revenues were down in part due to the four-month delay in producing Monte Carlo and Pontiac products arising from the retooling of those products, and in part due to reduced "special paint scheme" product volumes resulting from the lack of high-impact specials and the economic environment. Mass-merchant retail domestic die-cast revenues were down because our largest customer ordered virtually no product for delivery in the second half of 2003. The 17.7% increase in foreign die-cast sales approximated the change in the average euro-to-U.S. dollar exchange rate between 2003 and 2002. The increase in domestic apparel and memorabilia segment sales, exclusive of trackside was $23.3 million, or 21.7% from the prior year, and included a $22.5 million increase from businesses acquired in 2002. Trackside sales decreased 8.4% to $52.5 million from revenues of $57.3 million in the prior year. Trackside revenues were impacted by adverse weather conditions and a weak economy.

ACTION PERFORMANCE COMPANIES, INC.
VALUATION AND QUALIFYING ACCOUNTS
Years Ended September 30, 2004, 2003, and 2002
(in Thousands)

Description	Balance at beginning of year	Additions— Charged to costs and expenses	(Charged to) or credited from other accounts	Deductions (A)	Balance at end of year
Allowance for doubtful accounts:					
2004	$ 3,634	$ 6,768	$ 2,440 (B)	$ (3,475)	$ 9,367
2003	2,127	3,121	(1,009) (C)	(605)	3,634
2002	2,141	1,589	(548) (D)	(1,055)	2,127

(A) Amounts indicated as deductions are for amounts charged against these reserves in the ordinary course of business.

(B) Amounts indicated as charged to other accounts represent recoveries of $0.5 million and a reclassification of $1.9 million from allowance for doubtful accounts, long term (Other Assets).

(C) Amounts indicated as charged to other accounts represent a reclassification of ($0.9) million to allowance for doubtful accounts, long term (Other Assets), and ($0.1) million to other liabilities.

(D) Amounts indicated as charged to other accounts represent recoveries of $0.4 million, a reclassification of $(1.0) million to allowance for doubtful accounts, long term (Other Assets), and $0.1 million acquired in the acquisition of Jeff Hamilton Collection, Inc.

ITEM 5. MARKET FOR THE REGISTRANT'S COMMON EQUITY, RELATED STOCKHOLDER MATTERS, AND ISSUER PURCHASES OF EQUITY SECURITIES

	Common Stock		Fiscal Year
	High	Low	Closing Price
2004:			
First Quarter	$ 19.89	$ 12.58	
Second Quarter	18.13	13.57	
Third Quarter	15.49	9.74	
Fourth Quarter (through December 10, 2004)	11.20	8.37	$ 10.13
2003:			
First Quarter	$ 21.60	$ 14.65	
Second Quarter	24.56	16.50	
Third Quarter	26.99	18.15	
Fourth Quarter	27.71	16.74	$ 24.44
2002:			
First Quarter	$ 50.27	$ 30.03	
Second Quarter	51.99	27.75	
Third Quarter	34.30	20.68	
Fourth Quarter	26.71	15.80	$ 25.70

Case 6.2 Taser International, Inc.

Taser International, Inc. began operations in 1993, and completed an initial public offering in 2001. The firm is the developer and manufacturer of less-lethal self-defense devices sold to law enforcement agencies, commercial airlines, the military, security firms and individuals.

Required

1. Analyze the firm's financial statements and supplementary information on pages 242–248. Your analysis should include the preparation of common-size financial

statements, key financial ratios, and an evaluation of short-term solvency, operating efficiency, capital structure and long-term solvency, profitability, and market measures. (The financial statement analysis template can be accessed and used at *www.prenhall.com/fraser.*)

2. Using your analysis list reasons for and against investment in Taser International, Inc.'s common stock.

3. Using your analysis list reasons for and against loaning Taser International, Inc. additional funds.

TASER INTERNATIONAL, INC.
STATEMENTS OF INCOME

	For the Year Ended December 31,	
	2004	2003
	(As restated see Note 11)	
Net Sales	$ 67,639,879	$ 24,455,506
Cost of Products Sold:		
Direct manufacturing expense	16,898,559	6,973,757
Indirect manufacturing expense	5,556,937	2,428,859
Total Cost of Products Sold	22,455,496	9,402,616
Gross Margin	45,184,383	15,052,890
Sales, general and administrative expenses	13,880,322	6,973,721
Research and development expenses	823,593	498,470
Income from Operations	30,480,468	7,580,699
Interest income	439,450	50,375
Interest expense	(1,485)	(9,307)
Other income (expense), net	2,309	(254,476)
Income before income taxes	30,920,742	7,367,291
Provision for income tax	12,039,000	2,913,601
Net Income	$ 18,881,742	$ 4,453,690
Income per common and common equivalent shares		
Basic	$ 0.33	$ 0.12
Diluted	$ 0.30	$ 0.10
Weighted average number of common and common equivalent shares outstanding		
Basic	57,232,329	37,889,640
Diluted	62,319,590	46,598,312

The accompanying notes are an integral part of these financial statements.

TASER INTERNATIONAL, INC.
BALANCE SHEETS

	December 31,	
	2004	2003
	(As restated see Note 11)	
Assets		
Current Assets		
Cash and cash equivalents	$ 14,757,159	$ 15,878,326
Short-term investments	17,201,477	—
Accounts receivable, net	8,460,112	5,404,333
Inventory	6,840,051	3,125,974
Prepaids and other assets	1,639,734	536,815
Income tax receivable	52,973	292,321
Deferred income tax asset	11,083,422	1,137,196
Total Current Assets	60,034,928	26,374,965
Long-term investments	18,071,815	—
Property and Equipment, net	14,756,512	3,946,881
Deferred Income Tax Asset	15,310,207	—
Intangible Assets, net	1,279,116	1,122,844
Total Assets	$109,452,578	$31,444,690
Liabilities and Stockholders' Equity		
Current Liabilities		
Notes payable	$ —	$ 250,000
Current portion of capital lease obligations	4,642	15,223
Accounts payable and accrued liabilities	8,827,132	3,444,346
Customer deposits	102,165	185,802
Total Current Liabilities	8,933,939	3,895,371
Capital Lease Obligations	—	3,655
Deferred Revenue	607,856	78,093
Deferred Income Tax Liability	—	40,121
Total Liabilities	9,541,795	4,017,240
Commitments and Contingencies		
Stockholders' Equity		
Preferred Stock, $0.00001 par value per share; 25 million shares authorized; 0 shares issued and outstanding at December 31, 2004 and 2003	—	—
Common Stock, $0.00001 par value per share; 200 million shares authorized; 60,992,156 and 50,698,824 shares issued and outstanding at December 31, 2004 and 2003	609	507
Additional Paid-in Capital	75,850,810	22,249,321
Retained Earnings	24,059,364	5,177,622
Total Stockholders' Equity	99,910,783	27,427,450
Total Liabilities and Stockholders' Equity	$ 109,452,578	$ 31,444,690

The accompanying notes are an integral part of these financial statements.

TASER INTERNATIONAL, INC.
STATEMENTS OF CASH FLOWS

	For the Year Ended December 31,	
	2004	2003
	(As restated see Note 11)	
Cash Flows from Operating Activities:		
Net income	$ 18,881,742	$ 4,453,690
Adjustments to reconcile net income to net cash provided by operating activities:		
Loss on disposal of assets	—	15,873
Depreciation and amortization	551,793	393,568
Provision for doubtful accounts	90,000	12,908
Provision for warranty	361,058	302,165
Compensatory stock options	625,714	177,142
Deferred income taxes	727,892	(369,627)*
Stock option tax benefit	11,321,554	3,315,339*
Change in assets and liabilities:		
Accounts receivable	(3,145,779)	(4,529,099)
Inventory	(3,714,077)	(791,165)
Prepaids and other assets	(1,102,919)	(423,066)
Income tax receivable	239,348	(217,369)
Accounts payable and accrued liabilities	5,551,491	1,853,114
Customer deposits	(83,637)	171,074
Net cash provided by operating activities	30,304,180	4,366,546
Cash Flows from Investing Activities:		
Purchases of investments	(35,273,292)	—
Purchases of property and equipment	(11,322,299)	(3,651,110)
Purchases of intangible assets	(195,397)	(565,110)
Net cash used in investing activities	(46,790,988)	(4,216,220)
Cash Flows from Financing Activities:		
Payments under capital leases	(14,236)	(34,026)
Payments on notes payable	(250,000)	(250,000)
Payments on revolving line of credit	—	(385,000)
Proceeds from warrants exercised	2,545,065	11,000,519
Proceeds from options exercised	13,084,812	1,819,570
Net cash provided by financing activities	15,365,641	12,151,063
Net (Decrease) Increase In Cash and Cash Equivalents	(1,121,167)	12,301,389
Cash and Cash Equivalents, beginning of period	15,878,326	3,576,937
Cash and Cash Equivalents, end of period	$ 14,757,159	$ 15,878,326
Supplemental Disclosure:		
Cash paid for interest	$ 1,364	$ 9,922
Cash (refunded) paid for income taxes—net	$ (264,026)	$ 202,410

Non Cash Transactions

Increase to deferred tax asset related to tax benefits realized from the exercise of stock options (with a related increase to additional paid in capital of $37,346,000 and 3,961,928)	$ 26,024,446	$ 646,589
Note Payable issued for purchase of intangible assets	$ —	$ 500,000

The accompanying notes are an integral part of these financial statements.

*Due to the 2004 restatement, Taser International filed this statement with the SEC, but these two numbers were restated from the 2003 Annual Report. As a result the column for 2003 does not add correctly. For mathematical purposes it is suggested that the numbers originally filed in 2003 be used, which are as follows: Deferred income taxes, (1,014,217) and Stock option tax benefit 3,961,928.

Results of Operations

Sales and marketing expenses were also reduced by 31%, to 11% of sales for 2004 compared to 16% for 2003 due to better leverage of the fixed expenses. In total, the Company spent $7.2 million in promoting new sales and servicing existing customers in 2004, compared to $3.8 million for 2003. The most significant increases were in the areas of public relations activities, law enforcement training programs, and travel and salaries expenses. The increase in public relations activities is associated with the Company's continuing efforts to educate the public in regard to the safety and efficacy of its products. In addition, the training programs presented cost the Company $1.1 million for 2004 compared to $482,000 for 2003.

n. Concentration of Credit Risk and Major Customers

Financial instruments that potentially subject the Company to concentrations of credit risk consist of accounts receivable. Sales are typically made on credit and the Company generally does not require collateral. The Company performs ongoing credit evaluations of its customers' financial condition and maintains an allowance for estimated potential losses. Accounts receivable are presented net of an allowance for doubtful accounts. The allowance for bad debts totaled $120,000 and $30,000 as of December 31, 2004 and 2003, respectively.

The Company sells primarily through a network of unaffiliated distributors. The Company also reserves the right to sell directly to the end user to secure its credit interests. In 2004, the Company had three distributors that met or exceeded 10% of total sales; one of which represented 14% of sales, and two of which individually represented 10% of sales. No other customer exceeded 10% of product sales in 2004. Sales to one U.S. customer represented 15% of total product sales for 2003. No other customer exceeded 10% of total product sales in 2003.

At December 31, 2004, the Company had receivables from two customers comprising 21% and 16% of the aggregate accounts receivable balance. These customers are unaffiliated distributors of the Company's products. At December 31, 2003, the Company had a receivable from one customer comprising 19% of the aggregate accounts receivable balance. This customer was one of the ten largest U.S. police forces.

The Company currently purchases finished circuit boards and injection-molded plastic components from suppliers located in the Phoenix area. Although the Company currently obtains these components from single source suppliers, the Company owns the injection molded component tooling used in their production. As a result, the Company believes it could obtain alternative suppliers in most cases without incurring significant production delays. The

Company also purchases small, machined parts from a vendor in Taiwan, custom cartridge assemblies from a proprietary vendor in Arizona, and electronic components from a variety of foreign and domestic distributors. The Company believes that there are readily available alternative suppliers in most cases who can consistently meet our needs for these components. The Company acquires most of its components on a purchase order basis and does not have long-term contracts with suppliers.

3. Property and Equipment

Property and equipment consist of the following at December 31, 2004 and 2003:

	Estimated Useful Life	2004	2003
Leasehold Improvements	Lease Term	$ 90,658	$ 56,198
Land		2,899,962	2,899,962
Building/Construction in Progress		8,689,046	131,980
Production Equipment	5 Years	1,555,988	1,159,886
Telephone Equipment	5 Years	35,555	35,555
Computer Equipment	3–5 Years	2,501,928	812,869
Furniture and Office Equipment	5–7 Years	834,728	189,117
Total Cost		16,607,865	5,285,567
Less: Accumulated Depreciation		1,851,353	1,338,686
Net Property and Equipment		$ 14,756,512	$ 3,946,881

Depreciation expense for the years ended December 31, 2004 and 2003 was $512,668 and $363,899, respectively.

5. Commitments and Contingencies

a. Operating Leases

The Company has entered into operating leases for office space and equipment. Rent expense under these leases for the years ended December 31, 2004 and 2003, was $339,524 and $162,743, respectively.

Future Minimum lease payments under operating leases as of December 31, 2004, are as follows for the years ending December 31:

2005	$ 197,400
2006	19,788
2007	4,113
2008	—
2009	—
Thereafter	—
	$ 221,301

b. Purchase Commitments

The Company has approximately $3,344,000 remaining on the contract to construct its new manufacturing and headquarters facility. The amount due is expected to be paid during 2005.

c. Litigation

Securities Litigation On January 10, 2005, a securities class action lawsuit was filed in the United States District Court for the District of Arizona against the Company and certain of its officers and directors, captioned *Malasky v. TASER International, Inc., et al.*, Case No. 2:05 CV 115. Since then, numerous other securities class action lawsuits were filed against the Company and certain of its officers and directors. The majority of these lawsuits were filed in the District of Arizona.

Shareholder Derivative Litigation

On January 11, 2005, a shareholder derivative lawsuit was filed in the United States District Court for the District of Arizona purportedly on behalf of the Company and against certain of its officers and directors, captioned *Goldfine v. Culver, et al.*, Case No. 2:05 CV 123. Since then, five other shareholder derivative lawsuits were filed in the District of Arizona, two shareholder derivative lawsuits were filed in the Arizona Superior Court, Maricopa County, and one shareholder derivative lawsuit was filed in the Delaware Chancery Court. On February 9, 2005, the shareholder derivative actions pending in federal court were consolidated into a single action under the caption, *In re TASER International Shareholder Derivative Litigation*, Case No. 2:05 CV 123. Pursuant to the consolidating order, defendants will not respond to any of the complaints originally in these actions. Instead, defendants will respond to plaintiffs' consolidated amended complaint. Defendants have not responded to the cases filed in the Arizona Superior Court or in Delaware Chancery Court.

The complaints in the shareholder derivative lawsuits generally allege that the defendants breached the fiduciary duties owed to the Company and its shareholders by reason of their positions as officers and/or directors of the Company. The complaints claim that such duties were breached by defendants' disclosure of allegedly false or misleading statements about the safety and effectiveness of Company products and the Company's financial prospects. The complaints also claim that fiduciary duties were breached by defendants' alleged use of non-public information regarding the safety of Company products and the Company's financial condition and future business prospects for personal gain through the sale of the Company's stock. The Company is named solely as a nominal defendant against which no recovery is sought.

Securities and Exchange Commission Informal Inquiry

The Securities and Exchange Commission has initiated an informal inquiry into Taser with respect to the basis for the Company's public statements concerning the safety and performance of the Company's products, disclosure issues and the accounting for certain transactions. The inquiry is ongoing.

Product Liability Litigation

From April 2003 to March 2005, the Company was named as a defendant in 18 lawsuits in which the plaintiffs alleged either wrongful death or personal injury in situations in which the TASER device was used by law enforcement officers or during training exercises. One case has been dismissed with prejudice, another case has been dismissed without prejudice and the balance of the cases are pending. We have submitted the defense of each of these lawsuits to our insurance carriers as we maintained during these periods and continue to maintain product liability insurance coverage with varying limits and deductibles. The Company's product liability insurance coverage during these periods ranged from $5,000,000 to $10,000,000 in coverage limits and from $10,000 to $250,000 in deductibles. The Company is defending each of these lawsuits vigorously.

11. Restatement

In April 2005, subsequent to the issuance of our financial statements for the year ended December 31, 2004, we discovered an error in that certain stock option grants were treated as incentive stock options when the grants should have been classified as non-statutory stock options because of the annual limitation on incentive stock options under applicable tax regulations. For employees who exercised stock option grants and held the underlying stock, to the extent such option grants should have been classified as non-statutory stock options (as opposed to incentive stock options), the employee's taxable compensation was understated and we were entitled to a deduction from our taxable income equal to the amount of additional compensation attributable to the exercise of non-statutory stock options. This resulted in an increase in our previously reported deferred tax assets at December 31, 2004 by approximately $3.0 million, with a corresponding increase to our additional paid in capital. In addition, while incentive stock options are not subject to payroll tax withholding, non-statutory stock options that result in ordinary income when exercised are subject to payroll tax withholding for the employee and an equal amount to be paid by the employer. The impact to us in the year ended December 31, 2004 of the additional payroll tax withholding was approximately $395,000, which was recorded as an increase to our selling, general and administrative expenses over amounts previously reported. As a result, our provision for income tax decreased by approximately $152,000, which resulted in a corresponding increase in our deferred tax assets. This adjustment impacted our previously reported net income for the year ended December 31, 2004 by approximately $243,000 which reduced our diluted earnings per share for such period by $0.01 to $0.30. The change in net income was not significant enough to affect basic earnings per share for the year ended December 31, 2004.

Closing Stock Price (adjusted for stock splits)

12-31-04	$31.65
12-31-03	$ 6.86

A p p e n d i x   6 A

The Analysis of Segmental Data

Beginning in calendar year 1998, companies were required by the provisions of FASB Statement No. 131, "Disclosures about Segments of an Enterprise and Related Information," to disclose supplementary financial data for each reportable segment. FASB Statement No. 131 also covers reporting requirements for foreign operations, sales to major customers, and disclosures required for enterprises that have only one reportable segment. Segmental disclosures are valuable to the financial analyst in identifying areas of strength and weakness within a company, proportionate contribution to revenue and profit by each division, the relationship between capital expenditures and rates of return for operating areas, and segments that should be deemphasized or eliminated. The information on segments is presented as a supplementary section in the notes to the financial statements, as part of the basic financial statements, or in a separate schedule that is referenced and incorporated into the financial statements.

An operating segment is defined by FASB Statement No. 131 as a component of a business enterprise:

1. That engages in business activities from which it may earn revenues and incur expenses,
2. Whose operating results are regularly reviewed by the company's chief operating decision maker to make decisions about resources allocated to the segment and assesses its performance, and

3. For which discrete financial information is available.

A segment is considered to be reportable if any one of three criteria is met:

1. Revenue is 10% or more of combined revenue, including intersegment revenue.
2. Operating profit or loss is 10% or more of the greater of combined profit of all segments with profit or combined loss of all segments with loss.
3. Segment assets exceed 10% or more of combined assets of all segments.

The following information must be disclosed according to FASB Statement No. 131:

1. *General Information.* The "management approach" is used to identify operating segments in the enterprise. The management approach is based on the way that management organizes the segments within the company for making operating decisions and assessing performance. A company must identify how it is organized and what factors were used to identify operating segments and describe the types of products and services from which each operating segment derives its revenues.
2. *Information About Profit or Loss.* A company must report a measure of profit or loss for each reportable segment. In addition, certain amounts must be disclosed if the specified amounts are included in information reviewed by the chief operating decision maker. For companies basing profit or loss on pretax income from

continuing operations, the following amounts must be disclosed[1]:

- Revenues (separated into sales to external customers and intersegment sales)
- Interest revenue
- Interest expense
- Depreciation, depletion, and amortization expense

3. *Information About Assets.* A company must report a measure of the total operating segments' assets. Only assets included in reports to the chief operating decision maker should be included. The total capital expenditures that have been added to long-lived assets must also be reported for each operating segment.

The total of the operating segments' revenues, profit or loss, assets, and any other items reported shall be reconciled to the company's total consolidated amounts for each of these items.

The following analysis of Motorola's segment disclosures provides an illustration of how to interpret segmental data.

Exhibit 6A.1 illustrates an excerpt from the general information and the geographic area information disclosed by Motorola, Inc. in the Company's 2004 annual report. Exhibit 6A.2 illustrates the revenue, profit (loss), assets, capital expenditures, and depreciation expense for Motorola's six reportable segments: Personal Communications; Global Telecom Solutions; Commercial, Government, and Industrial Solutions; Integrated Electronic Systems; Broadband Communications; and Other Products. Segmental reporting does not include complete financial statements,

but it is feasible to perform an analysis of the key financial data presented.

Refer first to Exhibit 6A.1. The majority of Motorola's sales are from the United States. With the exception of China, sales have increased each year in all geographic regions.

Referring to Exhibit 6A.2, notice that total revenue for Motorola declined in 2003, but rebounded in 2004. The company is now generating overall operating profits in 2004 compared to operating losses in 2002. In order to analyze the performance for each segment, six tables have been prepared from computations based on the figures provided in Exhibit 6A.2.

Table 6A.1 shows the percentage of contribution to total revenue by segment. Note the change in trends over the three-year period. Personal Communications not only continues to be the largest revenue producer, but also is contributing more in 2004 to total revenues. All other segments are contributing less to revenue in 2004 compared to 2002.

Table 6A.2 reveals the contribution by segment to operating profit or loss and provides a basis for assessing the ability of a segment to translate revenue into profit. Personal Communications was the leading contributor to operating profit in 2004. Global Telecom Solutions contributed positively to operating profits in 2004 and has improved significantly since operating at a loss in 2002. Commercial, Government, and Industrial Solutions and Integrated Electronic Systems have continued to generate operating profits but have declined significantly from 2002 to 2004 in the percentage of profit generated overall. Broadband Communications and Other Products generated operating losses in 2002 and 2003, but Broadband Communications is now generating a profit in 2004 and Other Products has generated less of a loss compared to 2002.

---

[1]If more complex profit measures are used, the company must also disclose any unusual items, equity income, income tax expense, extraordinary items, and other significant noncash items.

EXHIBIT 6A.1   Information by Segment and Geographic Region, Motorola Inc.

The Company's reportable segments have been determined based on the nature of the products offered to customers and are comprised of the following:

- The Personal Communications segment ("PCS") designs, manufactures, sells and services wireless handsets with integrated software and accessory products.
- The Global Telecom Solutions segment ("GTSS") designs, manufactures, sells, installs, and services wireless infrastructure communication systems, including hardware and software. GTSS provides end-to-end wireless networks, including radio base stations, base site controllers, associated software and services, mobility soft switching, application platforms and third-party switching for CDMA 2000, GSM, iDEN® and UMTS technologies.
- The Commercial, Government and Industrial Solutions segment ("CGISS") designs, manufactures, sells, installs, and services analog and digital two-way radio, voice and data communications products and systems to a wide range of public-safety, government, utility, courier, transportation and other worldwide markets. The segment continues to invest in the market for broadband data, including infrastructure, devices, service and applications. In addition, the segment participates in the expanding market for integrated information management, mobile and biometric applications and services.
- The Integrated Electronic Systems segment ("IESS") designs, manufactures and sells: (i) automotive and industrial electronics systems, (ii) telematics systems that enable automated roadside assistance, navigation and advanced safety features for automobiles, (iii) portable energy storage products and systems, and (iv) embedded computing systems.
- The Broadband Communications segment ("BCS") designs, manufactures and sells a wide variety of broadband products, including: (i) digital systems and set-top terminals for cable television and broadcast networks, (ii) high speed data products, including cable modems and cable modem termination systems, as well as Internet Protocol-based telephony products, (iii) access network technology, including hybrid fiber coaxial network transmission systems and fiber-to-the-premise transmission systems, used by cable television operators, (iv) digital satellite television systems; (v) direct-to-home satellite networks and private networks for business communications, and (vi) high-speed data, video and voice broadband systems over existing phone lines.
- Other is comprised of the Other Products segment and general corporate items. The Other Products segment includes: (i) various corporate programs representing developmental businesses and research and development projects, which are not included in any major segment, and (ii) Motorola Credit Corporation, the Company's wholly-owned finance subsidiary.

Geographic Area Information (Dollars in Millions)

Years Ended December 31	Net Sales*			Assets**			Property, Plant, and Equipment		
	2004	2003	2002	2004	2003	2002	2004	2003	2002
United States	$18,693	$15,570	$14,400	$19,580	$19,190	$18,910	$1,304	$1,406	$1,599
China	4,639	3,679	4,431	3,565	2,450	2,654	218	242	294
Germany	2,824	1,796	1,591	975	581	441	141	137	140
Other nations	16,915	10,217	9,869	11,480	8,734	6,913	699	707	852
Adjustments and Eliminations	(11,748)	(8,107)	(6,869)	(4,711)	(4,153)	(3,874)	(30)	(19)	(22)
	$31,323	$23,155	$23,422	$30,889	$26,802	$25,044	$2,332	$2,473	$2,863

* As measured by the location of the revenue-producing operations.

** Excludes assets from discontinued operations of $5.2 billion and $6.2 billion, at December 31, 2003 and 2002, respectively.

EXHIBIT 6A.2 **Motorola Inc. and Subsidiaries Segment Information (Dollars in Millions)**

Years Ended December 31	Net Sales			Operating Earnings (Loss)		
	2004	2003	2002	2004	2003	2002
Personal Communications Segment	$16,823	$10,978	$11,174	$1,708	$479	$503
Global Telecom Solutions Segment	5,457	4,417	4,611	759	247	(621)
Commercial, Government and Industrial Solutions Segment	4,588	4,131	3,749	753	562	313
Integrated Electronic Systems Segment	2,696	2,265	2,189	142	161	52
Broadband Communications Segment	2,335	1,857	2,143	116	(38)	(216)
Other Products Segment	387	323	430	(229)	(44)	(214)
Adjustments and Eliminations	(963)	(816)	(874)	47	3	13
	$31,323	$23,155	$23,422	3,296	1,370	(170)
General Corporate				(164)	(97)	(273)
Operating earnings (loss)				3,132	1,273	(443)
Total other income (expense)				120	103	(1,628)
Earnings (loss) from continuing operations before income taxes				$3,252	$1,376	$(2,071)

General Corporate Operating Earnings (Loss) consists of expenses which are not identifiable with segment activity. Such items primarily consist of legal expenses, restructuring costs related to corporate employees and facilities, Iridium-related costs (recoveries), and corporate costs that were not allocated to Freescale Semiconductor in accordance with the discontinued operations presentation.

Years Ended December 31	Assets			Capital Expenditures			Depreciation Expense		
	2004	2003	2002	2004	2003	2002	2004	2003	2002
Personal Communications Segment	$ 5,292	$ 3,783	$ 3,733	$ 91	$ 74	$ 101	$ 128	$ 159	$ 203
Global Telecom Solutions Segment	2,616	2,746	3,630	91	67	84	129	155	218
Commercial, Government and Industrial Solutions Segment	2,215	1,938	1,961	149	76	83	90	96	115
Integrated Electronic Systems Segment	1,368	1,102	1,032	99	44	55	77	74	75
Broadband Communications Segment	2,314	2,354	2,480	27	23	20	59	66	77
Other Products Segment	391	611	444	—	—	—	11	9	21
Adjustments and Eliminations	(66)	(124)	(138)	—	—	—	2	—	—
	14,130	12,410	13,142	457	284	343	496	559	709
General Corporate	16,759	14,392	11,902	37	60	44	65	104	194
Discontinued Operations	—	5,244	6,189						
	$ 30,889	$ 32,046	$ 31,233	$ 494	$ 344	$ 387	$ 561	$ 663	$ 903

General corporate assets include primarily cash and cash equivalents, marketable securities, property, plant and equipment, cost-based investments, deferred income taxes and the administrative headquarters of the Company.

TABLE 6A.1   Contribution by Segment to Revenue (Percentages)

	2004	*2003*	*2002*
Personal Communications	53.71	47.41	47.71
Global Telecom Solutions	17.42	19.08	19.69
Commercial, Government, and Industrial Solutions	14.65	17.84	16.01
Integrated Electronic Systems	8.61	9.78	9.34
Broadband Communications	7.45	8.02	9.14
Other Products	1.23	1.39	1.84
Adjustments and Eliminations	(3.07)	(3.52)	(3.73)
Total revenue	100.00	100.00	100.00

TABLE 6A.2   Contribution by Segment to Operating Profit (Loss) (Percentages)

	2004	*2003*	*2002*
Personal Communications	51.82	34.96	295.88
Global Telecom Solutions	23.03	18.03	(365.29)
Commercial, Government, and Industrial Solutions	22.84	41.02	184.12
Integrated Electronic Systems	4.31	11.75	30.59
Broadband Communications	3.52	(2.77)	(127.06)
Other Products	(6.95)	(3.21)	(125.88)
Adjustments and Eliminations	1.43	0.22	7.64
Total revenue	100.00	100.00	(100.00)

Operating profit margin (operating profit divided by revenue) is presented for each segment in Table 6A.3. The operating profit margin shows the percent of every sales dollar that is converted to (before-tax) profit. The profit margin is highest and increasing in all three years for the Commercial, Government, and Industrial Solutions segment. All other segments, except Other Products, have improved operating profit margins from 2002 to 2004. Global Telecom Solutions and Broadband Communications now generate operating profits after having losses in prior years.

Table 6A.4 is a percentage breakdown of capital expenditures by segment. Motorola has chosen to invest the most in

TABLE 6A.3   Operating Profit Margin by Segment (Percentages)

	2004	*2003*	*2002*
Personal Communications	10.15	4.36	4.50
Global Telecom Solutions	13.91	5.59	(13.47)
Commercial, Government, and Industrial Solutions	16.41	13.60	8.35
Integrated Electronic Systems	5.27	7.11	2.38
Broadband Communications	4.97	(2.05)	(10.08)
Other Products	(59.17)	(13.62)	(49.77)

TABLE 6A.4 Capital Expenditures by Segment (Percentages)

	2004	*2003*	*2002*
Personal Communications	19.91	26.06	29.45
Global Telecom Solutions	19.91	23.59	24.49
Commercial, Government, and Industrial Solutions	32.61	26.76	24.20
Integrated Electronic Systems	21.66	15.49	16.03
Broadband Communications	5.91	8.10	5.83
Other Products	0.00	0.00	0.00
Total capital expenditures	100.00	100.00	100.00

Commercial, Government, and Industrial Solutions in 2004. This investment has resulted in higher sales and better profit margins. Motorola has continued to invest in Personal Communications and Global Telecom Solutions but at a smaller rate. This has not negatively impacted these segments so it is possible that greater dollar amounts are not necessary in these divisions. Despite spending more in the Integrated Electronic Systems segment in 2004, Motorola has not realized better profits in this segment. Broadband Communications receives the least in capital expenditures but is steadily improving despite the low investment.

It is important to examine the relationship between investment and return, and this information is provided in Table 6A.5, which shows return on investment by segment (operating profit divided by identifiable assets). All segments except Integrated Electronic Systems (and Other Products) have increasing returns on investments from 2002 to 2004. Given the fact that the major U.S. automobile manufacturers were not doing well in 2004, it is possible that this could be the cause of the lower returns and profits in this segment.

Table 6A.6 compares a ranking of segments in 2004 by segment assets with percentage contribution to operating profit, operating profit margin, and return on investment. Commercial, Government, and Industrial Solutions is the largest segment when considering total investment in assets. Overall Motorola appears to be moving in the right direction in most segments. The two segments that should be monitored closely are Integrated Electronic Systems and Broadband Communications.

TABLE 6A.5 Return on Investment by Segment (Percentages)

	2004	*2003*	*2002*
Personal Communications	32.28	12.66	13.47
Global Telecom Solutions	29.01	8.99	(17.11)
Commercial, Government, and Industrial Solutions	34.00	29.00	15.96
Integrated Electronic Systems	10.38	14.61	5.04
Broadband Communications	5.01	(1.61)	(8.71)
Other Products	(58.57)	(7.20)	(48.20)

TABLE 6A.6   Ranking of Segments in 2004

Segment	Percentage of Total Segment Assets	Percent Contribution to Operating Profit	Operating Profit Margin	Return on Investment
Commercial, Government, and Industrial Solutions	32.61	22.84	16.41	34.00
Integrated Electronic Systems	21.66	4.31	5.27	10.38
Personal Communications	19.91	51.82	10.15	32.28
Global Telecom Solutions	19.91	23.03	13.91	29.01
Broadband Communications	5.91	3.52	4.97	5.01
Other Products	0.00	(6.95)	(59.17)	(58.57)

STUDY PROBLEM

6A.1. The 2004 Eastman Kodak segment information from the annual report can be found at the following Web site: www.prenhall.com/fraser. Using the segment information from the 2004 Eastman Kodak annual report, analyze all segments. Be sure to prepare tables comparable to Tables 6A.1 through 6A.6 illustrated in the appendix to the chapter.

Appendix A: Summary of Financial Ratios

Ratio	Method of Computation	Significance
Liquidity:		
Current	$$\frac{\text{Current assets}}{\text{Current liabilities}}$$	Measures short-term liquidity, the ability of a firm to meet needs for cash as they arise.
Quick or acid-test	$$\frac{\text{Current assets} - \text{inventory}}{\text{Current liabilities}}$$	Measures short-term liquidity more rigorously than the current ratio by eliminating inventory, usually the least liquid current asset.
Cash flow liquidity	$$\frac{\text{Cash} + \text{marketable securities} + \text{cash flow from operating activities}}{\text{Current liabilities}}$$	Measures short-term liquidity by considering as cash resources (numerator) cash plus cash equivalents plus cash flow from operating activities.
Average collection period	$$\frac{\text{Net accounts receivable}}{\text{Net sales/365}}$$	Indicates days required to convert receivables into cash.
Days inventory held	$$\frac{\text{Inventory}}{\text{Average daily cost of sales}}$$	Indicates days required to sell inventory.
Days payable outstanding	$$\frac{\text{Accounts payable}}{\text{Average daily cost of sales}}$$	Indicates days required to pay suppliers.
Cash conversion or net trade cycle	Average collection period + days inventory held − days payable outstanding	Indicates the days in the normal operating cycle or cash conversion cycle of a firm.

Activity:

Accounts receivable turnover	$$\frac{\text{Net sales}}{\text{Net accounts receivable}}$$	Indicates how many times receivables are collected during a year, on average.
Inventory turnover	$$\frac{\text{Cost of goods sold}}{\text{Inventories}}$$	Measures efficiency of the firm in managing and selling inventory.
Payables turnover	$$\frac{\text{Cost of goods sold}}{\text{Accounts payable}}$$	Measures efficiency of the firm in paying suppliers.
Fixed asset turnover	$$\frac{\text{Net sales}}{\text{Net property, plant, and equipment}}$$	Measures efficiency of the firm in managing fixed assets.
Total asset turnover	$$\frac{\text{Net sales}}{\text{Total assets}}$$	Measures efficiency of the firm in managing all assets.

Leverage:

Debt ratio	$$\frac{\text{Total liabilities}}{\text{Total assets}}$$	Shows proportion of all assets that are financed with debt.
Long-term debt to total capitalization	$$\frac{\text{Long-term debt}}{\text{Long-term debt} + \text{stockholders' equity}}$$	Measures the extent to which long-term debt is used for permanent financing.
Debt to equity	$$\frac{\text{Total liabilities}}{\text{Stockholders' equity}}$$	Measures debt relative to equity base.
Financial leverage index	$$\frac{\text{Return on equity}}{\text{Adjusted return on assets}}$$	Indicates if a firm is employing debt successfully.
Times interest earned	$$\frac{\text{Operating profit}}{\text{Interest expense}}$$	Measures how many times interest expense is covered by operating earnings.
Cash interest coverage	$$\frac{\text{Cash flow from operating activities} + \text{interest paid} + \text{taxes paid}}{\text{Interest paid}}$$	Measures how many times interest payments are covered by cash flow from operating activities.
Fixed charge coverage	$$\frac{\text{Operating profit} + \text{lease payments}}{\text{Interest expense} + \text{lease payments}}$$	Measures coverage capability more broadly than times interest earned by including operating lease payments as a fixed expense.
Cash flow adequacy	$$\frac{\text{Cash flow from operating activities}}{\text{Capital expenditures} + \text{debt repayments} + \text{dividends paid}}$$	Measures how many times capital expenditures, debt repayments, and cash dividends are covered by operating cash flow.

Profitability:

Gross profit margin	$\dfrac{\text{Gross profit}}{\text{Net sales}}$	Measures profit generated after consideration of cost of products sold.
Operating profit margin	$\dfrac{\text{Operating profit}}{\text{Net sales}}$	Measures profit generated after consideration of operating expenses.
Effective tax rate	$\dfrac{\text{Income taxes}}{\text{Earnings before income taxes}}$	Measures the percentage the company recognizes as tax expense relative to income before taxes.
Net profit margin	$\dfrac{\text{Net profit}}{\text{Net sales}}$	Measures profit generated after consideration of all expenses and revenues.
Cash flow margin	$\dfrac{\text{Cash flow from operating activities}}{\text{Net sales}}$	Measures the ability of the firm to generate cash from sales.
Return on total assets	$\dfrac{\text{Net earnings}}{\text{Total assets}}$	Measures overall efficiency of firm in managing assets and generating profits.
Return on equity	$\dfrac{\text{Net earnings}}{\text{Stockholders' equity}}$	Measures rate of return on stockholders' (owners') investment.
Cash return on assets	$\dfrac{\text{Cash flow from operating activities}}{\text{Total assets}}$	Measures the return on assets on a cash basis.

Market:

Earnings per common share	$\dfrac{\text{Net earnings}}{\text{Average common shares outstanding}}$	Shows return to common stock shareholders for each share owned.
Price to earnings	$\dfrac{\text{Market price of common stock}}{\text{Earnings per share}}$	Expresses a multiple that the stock market places on a firm's earnings.
Dividend payout	$\dfrac{\text{Dividends per share}}{\text{Earnings per share}}$	Shows percentage of earnings paid to shareholders.
Dividend yield	$\dfrac{\text{Dividends per share}}{\text{Market price of common stock}}$	Shows the rate earned by shareholders from dividends relative to current price of stock.

Appendix B: Solutions to Self-Tests

Chapter 1

1. (d)	8. (d)	15. (c)	(6) a
2. (d)	9. (c)	16. (d)	(7) d
3. (d)	10. (d)	17. (1) c	(8) b
4. (b)	11. (c)	(2) b	(9) d
5. (a)	12. (b)	(3) a	(10) a or b
6. (d)	13. (c)	(4) c	
7. (b)	14. (d)	(5) b	

Chapter 2

1. (b)	16. (a)	(i) NC	(n) 6
2. (a)	17. (c)	(j) NC	(o) 8
3. (c)	18. (b)	24. (a) 4	25. (a) 7
4. (b)	19. (b)	(b) 5	(b) 1
5. (b)	20. (d)	(c) 8	(c) 5
6. (a)	21. (d)	(d) 7	(d) 9
7. (d)	22. (c)	(e) 1	(e) 4
8. (c)	23. (a) NC	(f) 2	(f) 6
9. (b)	(b) C	(g) 2	(g) 10
10. (c)	(c) C	(h) 5	(h) 2
11. (d)	(d) C or NC	(i) 8	(i) 3
12. (a)	(e) NC	(j) 5	(j) 8
13. (c)	(f) C	(k) 3	
14. (b)	(g) C	(l) 2	
15. (d)	(h) C	(m) 1	

Chapter 3

1. (c)	9. (d)	17. (b)	(g) 1
2. (d)	10. (b)	18. (d)	(h) 6
3. (a)	11. (b)	19. (a) 4	(i) 11
4. (c)	12. (a)	(b) 9	(j) 2
5. (d)	13. (a)	(c) 13	(k) 10
6. (a)	14. (c)	(d) 8	(l) 12
7. (c)	15. (d)	(e) 5	(m) 3
8. (d)	16. (c)	(f) 14	(n) 7

20. (1) c   (4) c   (7) e   (10) b
    (2) d   (5) d   (8) c   (11) d
    (3) a   (6) a   (9) c   (12) c

Chapter 4

1. (d)	8. (c)	15. (d)	22. (b)
2. (a)	9. (c)	16. (c)	23. (a)
3. (b)	10. (b)	17. (d)	24. (b)
4. (a)	11. (b)	18. (d)	25. (a)
5. (c)	12. (c)	19. (b)	26. (d)
6. (d)	13. (a)	20. (d)	
7. (b)	14. (d)	21. (c)	

Chapter 5

1. (c)	6. (b)	11. (a)	16. (a)
2. (a)	7. (c)	12. (b)	17. (d)
3. (b)	8. (a)	13. (d)	18. (c)
4. (d)	9. (d)	14. (c)	19. (b)
5. (b)	10. (c)	15. (d)	20. (a)

Chapter 6

1. (c)	10. (c)	19. (a)	28. (c)
2. (a)	11. (a)	20. (b)	29. (a)
3. (d)	12. (c)	21. (c)	30. (c)
4. (c)	13. (d)	22. (a)	31. (b)
5. (d)	14. (b)	23. (c)	32. (d)
6. (d)	15. (a)	24. (b)	33. (a)
7. (a)	16. (d)	25. (d)	34. (c)
8. (b)	17. (c)	26. (b)	35. (a)
9. (d)	18. (d)	27. (a)	

Appendix C: Glossary

Accelerated Cost Recovery System The system established by the Economic Recovery Tax Act of 1981 to simplify depreciation methods for tax purposes and to encourage investment in capital by allowing rapid write-off of asset costs over predetermined periods, generally shorter than the estimated useful lives of the assets. The system remains in effect for assets placed in service between 1981 and 1986 but was modified by the Tax Reform Act of 1986 for assets placed in service after 1986. *See* Modified Accelerated Cost Recovery System.

Accelerated depreciation An accounting procedure under which larger amounts of expense are apportioned to the earlier years of an asset's depreciable life and lesser amounts to the later years.

Accounting period The length of time covered for reporting accounting information.

Accounting principles The methods and procedures used in preparing financial statements.

Accounts payable Amounts owed to creditors for items or services purchased from them.

Accounts receivable Amounts owed to an entity, primarily by its trade customers.

Accounts receivable turnover *See* Summary of financial ratios, Appendix A.

Accrual basis of accounting A method of earnings determination under which revenues are recognized in the accounting period when earned, regardless of when cash is received, and expenses are recognized in the period incurred, regardless of when cash is paid.

Accrued liabilities Obligations resulting from the recognition of an expense prior to the payment of cash.

Accumulated depreciation A balance sheet account indicating the amount of depreciation expense taken on plant and equipment up to the balance sheet date.

Accumulated other comprehensive income or loss An account that includes unrealized gains or losses in the market value of investments of marketable securities classified as available for sale, specific types of pension liability adjustments, certain gains and losses on derivative financial instruments, and foreign currency translation adjustments resulting when financial statements from a foreign currency are converted into U.S. dollars.

Acid-test ratio *See* Summary of financial ratios, Appendix A.

Activity ratio A ratio that measures the liquidity of specific assets and the efficiency of the firm in managing assets.

Additional paid-in-capital The amount by which the original sales price of stock shares sold exceeds the par value of the stock.

Adverse opinion Opinion rendered by an independent auditor stating that the financial statements have not been presented fairly in accordance with generally accepted accounting principles.

Allowance for doubtful accounts The balance sheet account that measures the amount of outstanding accounts receivable expected to be uncollectable.

Amortization The process of expense allocation applied to the cost expiration of intangible assets.

Annual report The report to shareholders published by a firm; contains information required by generally accepted accounting principles and/or by specific Securities and Exchange Commission requirements.

Asset impairment The decline in value of assets.

Assets Items possessing service or use potential to owner.

Auditor's report Report by independent auditor attesting to the fairness of the financial statements of a company.

Average collection period *See* Summary of financial ratios, Appendix A.

Average cost method A method of valuing inventory and cost of products sold; all costs, including those in beginning inventory, are added together and divided by the total number of units to arrive at a cost per unit.

Balance sheet The financial statement that shows the financial condition of a company on a particular date.

Balancing equation Assets = Liabilities + Stockholders' equity.

Basic earnings per share The earnings per share figure calculated by dividing net earnings available to common shareholders by the average number of common shares outstanding.

Book value *See* Net book value.

Calendar year The year starting January 1 and ending December 31.

Capital assets *See* Fixed assets.

Capital in excess of par value *See* Additional paid-in-capital.

Capital lease A leasing arrangement that is, in substance, a purchase by the lessee, who accounts for the lease as an acquisition of an asset and the incurrence of a liability.

Capital structure The permanent long-term financing of a firm represented by long-term debt, preferred stock, common stock, and retained earnings.

Capitalize The process whereby initial expenditures are included in the cost of assets and allocated over the period of service.

Cash basis of accounting A method of accounting under which revenues are recorded when cash is received and expenses are recognized when cash is paid.

Cash conversion cycle The amount of time (expressed in number of days) required to sell inventory and collect accounts receivable, less the number of days credit extended by suppliers.

Cash equivalents Security investments that are readily converted to cash.

Cash flow adequacy *See* Summary of financial ratios, Appendix A.

Cash flow from financing activities On the statement of cash flows, cash generated from/used by financing activities.

Cash flow from investing activities On the statement of cash flows, cash generated from/used by investing activities.

Cash flow from operating activities On the statement of cash flows, cash generated from/used by operating activities.

Cash flow from operations The amount of cash generated from/used by a business enterprise's normal, ongoing operations during an accounting period.

Cash flow liquidity ratio *See* Summary of financial ratios, Appendix A.

Cash flow margin *See* Summary of financial ratios, Appendix A.

Cash flow return on assets *See* Summary of financial ratios, Appendix A.

Cash interest coverage *See* Summary of financial ratios, Appendix A.

Commercial paper Unsecured promissory notes of large companies.

Commitments Contractual agreements that will have a significant impact on the company in the future.

Common-size financial statements A form of financial ratio analysis that allows the comparison of firms with different levels of sales or total assets by introducing a common denominator. A common-size balance sheet expresses each item on the balance sheet as a percentage of total assets, and a common-size income statement expresses each item as a percentage of net sales.

Common stock Shares of stock representing ownership in a company.

Complex capital structure Capital structures including convertible securities, stock options, and warrants.

Comprehensive income The concept that income should include all revenues, expenses, gains, and losses recognized during an accounting period, regardless of whether they are the results of operations.

Conservatism The accounting concept holding that in selecting among accounting methods the choice should be the one with the least favorable effect on the firm.

Consolidation The combination of financial statements for two or more separate legal entities when one company, the parent, owns more than 50% of the voting stock of the other company or companies.

Contingencies Potential liabilities of a company.

Contra-asset account An account shown as a deduction from the asset to which it relates in the balance sheet.

Convertible securities Securities that can be converted or exchanged for another type of security, typically common stock.

Core earnings *See* Pro forma earnings.

Cost flow assumption An assumption regarding the order in which inventory is sold; used to value cost of goods sold and ending inventory.

Cost method A procedure to account for investments in the voting stock of other companies under which the investor recognizes investment income only to the extent of any cash dividends received.

Cost of goods sold The cost to the seller of products sold to customers.

Cost of goods sold percentage The percentage of cost of goods sold to net sales.

Cost of sales *See* Cost of goods sold.

Cumulative effect of change in accounting principle The difference in the actual amount of retained earnings at the beginning of the period in which a change in accounting principle is instituted and the amount of retained earnings that would have been reported at that date if the new accounting principle had been applied retroactively for all prior periods.

Current (assets/liabilities) Items expected to be converted into cash or paid out in cash in one year or one operating cycle, whichever is longer.

Current maturities of long-term debt The portion of long-term debt that will be repaid during the upcoming year.

Current ratio *See* Summary of financial ratios, Appendix A.

Days inventory held *See* Summary of financial ratios, Appendix A.

Days payable outstanding *See* Summary of financial ratios, Appendix A.

Debt ratio *See* Summary of financial ratios, Appendix A.

Debt to equity ratio *See* Summary of financial ratios, Appendix A.

Deferred credits *See* Unearned revenue.

Deferred taxes The balance sheet account that results from temporary differences in the recognition of revenue and expense for taxable income and reported income.

Depletion The accounting procedure used to allocate the cost of acquiring and developing natural resources.

Depreciation The accounting procedure used to allocate the cost of an asset, which will benefit a business enterprise for more than a year, over the asset's service life.

Derivatives Financial instruments that derive their value from an underlying asset or index.

Diluted earnings per share The earnings per share figure calculated using all potentially dilutive securities in the number of shares outstanding.

Direct method On the statement of cash flows, a method of calculating cash flow from operating activities that shows cash collections from customers; interest and dividends collected; other operating cash receipts; cash paid to suppliers and employees; interest paid; taxes paid; and other operating cash payments.

Disclaimer of opinion Independent auditor could not evaluate the fairness of the financial statements and, as a result, expresses no opinion on them.

Discontinued operations The financial results of selling a major business segment.

Discretionary items Revenues and expenses under the control of management with respect to budget levels and timing.

Dividend payout ratio *See* Summary of financial ratios, Appendix A.

Dividend yield *See* Summary of financial ratios, Appendix A.

Double-declining balance method An accounting procedure for depreciation under which the straight-line rate of depreciation is doubled and applied to the net book value of the asset.

Du Pont System An analytical technique used to evaluate the profitability and return on equity for a firm.

EBITDA Earnings before interest, taxes, depreciation and amortization. *See* Pro forma earnings.

Earnings before income taxes The profit recognized before the deduction of income taxes.

Earnings before interest and taxes The operating profit of a firm.

Earnings per common share *See* summary of financial ratios, Appendix A.

Earnings statement *See* Income statement.

Effective tax rate *See* Summary of financial ratios, Appendix A.

Equity *See* Stockholders' equity.

Equity method The procedure used for an investment in common stock when the investor company can exercise significant influence over the investee company; the investor recognizes investment income of the investee's net income in proportion to the percent of stock owned.

Expenses Cost incurred to produce revenue.

Extraordinary transactions Items that are unusual in nature and not expected to recur in the foreseeable future.

Financial Accounting Standards Board (FASB) The private sector organization primarily responsible for establishing generally accepted accounting principles.

Financial leverage The extent to which a firm finances with debt, measured by the relationship between total debt and total assets.

Financial leverage index *See* Summary of financial ratios, Appendix A.

Financial ratios Calculations made to standardize, analyze, and compare financial data; expressed in terms of mathematical relationships in the form of percentages or times.

Financial statements Accounting information regarding the financial position of a firm, the results of operations, and the cash flows. Four statements comprise the basic set of financial statements: the balance sheet, the income statement, the statement of stockholder's equity, and the statement of cash flows.

Financing activities On the statement of cash flows, transactions that include borrowing from creditors and repaying the principal; obtaining resources from owners and providing them with a return on the investment.

Finished goods Products for which the manufacturing process is complete.

First-in, first-out (FIFO) A method of valuing inventory and cost of goods sold under which the items purchased first are assumed to be sold first.

Fiscal year A 12-month period starting on a date other than January 1 and ending 12 months later.

Fixed assets Tangible, long-lived assets that are expected to provide service benefit for more than one year.

Fixed asset turnover *See* Summary of financial ratios, Appendix A.

Fixed charge coverage *See* Summary of financial ratios, Appendix A.

Foreign currency translation effects Adjustment to the equity section of the balance sheet resulting from the translation of foreign financial statements.

Form 10-K An annual document filed with the Securities and Exchange Commission by companies that sell securities to the public.

Form 10-Q A quarterly report filed with the Securities and Exchange Commission by companies that sell securities to the public.

Fulfillment costs Expenses associated with completing an order.

Generally accepted accounting principles The accounting methods and procedures used to prepare financial statements.

Goodwill An intangible asset representing the unrecorded assets of a firm; appears in the accounting records only if the firm is acquired for a price in excess of the fair market value of its net assets.

Gross margin *See* Gross profit.

Gross profit The difference between net sales and cost of goods sold.

Gross profit margin *See* Summary of financial ratios, Appendix A.

Historical cost The amount of cash or value of other resources used to acquire an asset; for some assets, historical cost is subject to depreciation, amortization, or depletion.

Income statement The financial statement presenting the revenues and expenses of a business enterprise for an accounting period.

Indirect method On the statement of cash flows, a method of calculating cash flow from operating activities that adjusts net income for deferrals, accruals, and noncash and nonoperating items.

Industry comparisons Average financial ratios compiled for industry groups.

Industry segment *See* segment.

In-process research and development One-time charges taken at the time of an acquisition to write-off amounts of research and development that are not considered viable.

Intangible assets Assets such as goodwill that possess no physical characteristics but have value for the company.

Integrated disclosure system A common body of information required by the Securities and Exchange Commission for both the 10-K Report filed with the Securities and Exchange Commission and the annual report provided to shareholders.

Interim statements Financial statements issued for periods shorter than one year.

Inventories Items held for sale or used in the manufacture of products that will be sold.

Inventory turnover *See* Summary of financial ratios, Appendix A.

Investing activities On the statement of cash flows, transactions that include acquiring and selling or otherwise disposing of (1) securities that are not cash equivalents and (2) productive assets that are expected to benefit the firm for long periods of time; lending money and collecting on loans.

Last-in, first-out (LIFO) A method of valuing inventory and cost of goods sold under which the items purchased last are assumed to be sold first.

Leasehold improvement An addition or improvement made to a leased structure.

Leverage ratio A ratio that measures the extent of a firm's financing with debt relative to equity and its ability to cover interest and other fixed charges.

Liabilities Claims against assets.

Line of credit A prearranged loan allowing borrowing up to a certain maximum amount.

Liquidity The ability of a firm to generate sufficient cash to meet cash needs.

Liquidity ratio A ratio that measures a firm's ability to meet needs for cash as they arise.

Long-term debt Obligations with maturities longer than one year.

Long-term debt to total capitalization *See* Summary of financial ratios, Appendix A.

Lower of cost or market method A method of valuing inventory under which cost or market, whichever is lower, is selected for each item, each group, or for the entire inventory.

Management Discussion and Analysis (MD&A) of the Financial Condition and Results of Operation A section of the annual and 10-K report that is required and monitored by the Securities and Exchange Commission in which management presents a detailed coverage of the firm's liquidity, capital resources, and operations.

Mandatorily redeemable preferred stock Securities that have characteristics of both debt and equity.

Marketable securities Cash not needed immediately in the business and temporarily invested to earn a return; also referred to as short-term investments.

Matching principle The accounting principle holding that expenses are to be matched with the generation of revenues in order to determine net income for an accounting period.

Merchandise inventories Goods purchased for resale to the public.

Minority interest Claims of shareholders other than the parent company against the net assets and net income of a subsidiary company.

Modified accelerated cost recovery system (MACRS) A modification of the accelerated tax recovery system (ACRS) in the Tax Reform Act of 1986 for assets placed in service after 1986.

Multiple-step format A format for presenting the income statement under which several intermediate profit measures are shown.

Net assets   Total assets less total liabilities.

Net book value of capital assets   The difference between original cost of property, plant, and equipment and any accumulated depreciation to date.

Net earnings   The firm's profit or loss after consideration of all revenue and expense reported during the accounting period.

Net income   *See* Net earnings.

Net profit margin   *See* Summary of financial ratios, Appendix A.

Net sales   Total sales revenue less sales returns and sales allowances.

Net trade cycle   *See* Cash conversion cycle and Summary of financial ratios, Appendix A.

Noncurrent assets/liabilities   Items expected to benefit the firm for/with maturities of more than one year.

Notes payable   A short-term obligation in the form of a promissory note to suppliers or financial institutions.

Notes to the financial statements   Supplementary information to financial statements that explain the firm's accounting policies and provide detail about particular accounts and other information such as pension plans.

Off–balance-sheet financing   Financial techniques for raising funds that do not have to be recorded as liabilities on the balance sheet.

Operating activities   On the statement of cash flows, transactions that include delivering or producing goods for sale and providing services; the cash effects of transactions and other events that enter into the determination of income.

Operating cycle   The time required to purchase or manufacture inventory, sell the product, and collect the cash.

Operating efficiency   The efficiency of a firm in managing its assets.

Operating expenses   Costs related to the normal functions of a business.

Operating lease   A rental agreement wherein no ownership rights are transferred to the lessee at the termination of the rental contract.

Operating profit   Sales revenue less the expenses associated with generating sales. Operating profit measures the overall performance of a company on its normal, ongoing operations.

Operating profit margin   *See* Summary of financial ratios, Appendix A.

Options   *See* Stock options.

Par value   The floor price below which stock cannot be sold initially.

Payables turnover   *See* Summary of financial ratios, Appendix A.

Plant and equipment   *See* Fixed assets.

Preferred stock   Capital stock of a company that carries certain privileges or rights not carried by all outstanding shares of stock.

Premature revenue recognition   Recording revenue before it should be recorded in order to increase earnings.

Prepaid expenses   Expenditures made in the current or prior period that will benefit the firm at some future time.

Price-earnings ratio   *See* Summary of financial ratios, Appendix A.

Principal   The original amount of a liability.

Prior period adjustment   A change in the retained earnings balance primarily resulting from the correction of errors made in previous accounting periods.

Pro forma earnings   Alternative earnings numbers that adjust net income in some way for items not expected to be part of ongoing business operations.

Pro forma financial statements   Projections of future financial statements based on a set of assumptions regarding future revenues, expenses, level of investment in assets, financing methods and costs, and working capital management.

Profitability ratio   A ratio that measures the overall performance of a firm and its efficiency in managing assets, liabilities, and equity.

Property, plant, and equipment   *See* Fixed assets.

Prospectus   A formal written description of a mutual fund required by the SEC.

Proxy statement   A document required by the SEC that companies use to solicit shareholders' votes and that contains information about directors, director and executive compensation plans, and the audit committee report.

Public Company Accounting Oversight Board (PCAOB) A private, nonprofit organization with the authority to register, inspect, and discipline auditors of all publicly owned companies.

Publicly held companies Companies that operate to earn a profit and issue shares of stock to the public.

Qualified opinion An opinion rendered by an independent auditor when the overall financial statements are fairly presented "except for" certain items (which the auditor discloses).

Quality of financial reporting A subjective evaluation of the extent to which financial reporting is free of manipulation and accurately reflects the financial condition and operating success of a business enterprise.

Quick ratio *See* Summary of financial ratios, Appendix A.

Raw materials Basic commodities or natural resources that will be used in the production of goods.

Replacement cost The estimated cost of acquiring new and substantially equivalent property at current prices.

Reported income The net income published in financial statements.

Reserve accounts Accounts used to estimate obligations, recorded as accrued liabilities; also to record declines in asset values, recorded as contra-asset accounts.

Restructuring charges Costs to reorganize a company.

Retained earnings The sum of every dollar a company has earned since its inception, less any payments made to shareholders in the form of cash or stock dividends.

Return on equity *See* Summary of financial ratios, Appendix A.

Return on investment *See* Return on total assets.

Return on total assets *See* Summary of financial ratios, Appendix A.

Revenue The inflow of assets resulting from the sale of goods or services.

Reverse stock split Decreasing the number of shares of outstanding stock to existing stockholders in proportion to current ownership, usually to increase the market price of a firm's stock.

Sales allowance A deduction from the original sales invoice price.

Sales return A cancellation of a sale.

Salvage value The amount of an asset estimated to be recoverable at the conclusion of the asset's service life.

Sarbanes-Oxley Act of 2002 Legislation passed by the United States Congress in hopes of ending future accounting scandals and renewing investor confidence in the marketplace.

Securities and Exchange Commission (SEC) The public-sector organization primarily responsible for establishing generally accepted accounting principles.

Segment A component of a business enterprise that sells primarily to outside markets and for which information about revenue and profit is accumulated.

Segment operating expenses Expenses relating to unaffiliated customers and segment revenue; expenses not directly traceable to segments are allocated to segments on a reasonable basis.

Segment operating profit/loss Segment revenue less all operating expenses.

Segment revenue Sales of products and services to unaffiliated customers and intersegment sales, with company transfer prices used to determine sales between segments.

Selling and administrative expenses Costs relating to the sale of products or services and to the management function of the firm.

Short-term Generally indicates maturity of less than a year.

Single-step format A format for presenting the income statement under which all items of revenue are grouped together and then all items of expense are deducted to arrive at net income.

Stated value The floor price below which stock cannot be sold initially; *see also* par value.

Statement of cash flows The financial statement that provides information about the cash inflows and outflows from operating, financing, and investing activities during an accounting period.

Statement of retained earnings The financial statement that presents the details of the transactions affecting the retained earnings account during an accounting period.

Statement of stockholders' equity A financial statement that summarizes changes in the shareholders' equity section of the balance sheet during an accounting period.

Stock dividends The issuance of additional shares of stock to existing shareholders in proportion to current ownership.

Stock options A contract that conveys the right to purchase shares of stock at a specified price within a specified time period.

Stock splits The issuance of additional shares of stock to existing shareholders in proportion to current ownership, usually to lower the market price of a firm's stock.

Stockholders' equity Claims against assets by the owners of the business; represents the amount owners have invested including income retained in the business since inception.

Straight-line depreciation An accounting procedure under which equal amounts of expense are apportioned to each year of an asset's life.

Structural analysis Analysis looking at the internal structure of a business enterprise.

Summary of financial ratios *See* Appendix A.

Tangible Having physical substance.

Taxable income The net income figure used to determine taxes payable to governments.

Temporary differences Differences between pretax accounting income and taxable income caused by reporting items of revenue or expense in one period for accounting purposes and in an earlier or later period for income tax purposes.

Times interest earned *See* Summary of financial ratios, Appendix A.

Total asset turnover *See* Summary of financial ratios, Appendix A.

Treasury stock Shares of a company's stock that are repurchased by the company and not retired.

Trend analysis Evaluation of financial data over several accounting periods.

Unearned revenue A liability caused by receipt of cash in advance of earning revenue.

Units-of-production method An accounting method under which depreciation expense is based on actual usage.

Unqualified opinion An opinion rendered by an independent auditor of financial statements stating that the financial statements have been presented fairly in accordance with generally accepted accounting principles.

Unqualified opinion with explanatory language An opinion rendered by an independent auditor of financial statements stating that the financial statements have been presented fairly in accordance with generally accepted accounting principles, but there are items which the auditor wishes to explain to the user.

Unrealized gains (losses) on marketable equity securities The gains (losses) disclosed in the equity section resulting from the accounting rule that requires investments in marketable equity securities to be carried at the lower of cost or market value.

Vendor financing Lending money to customers so they can purchase the lender's products or services.

Warrant A certificate issued by a corporation that conveys the right to buy a stated number of shares of stock at a specified price on or before a predetermined date.

Work-in-process Products for which the manufacturing process is only partially completed.

Working capital The amount by which current assets exceed current liabilities.

Index